INSIGHT GUIDES

NORWAY

APA PUBLICATIONS

Part of the Langenscheidt Publishing Group

INSIGHT GUIDE
NORWAY

ABOUT THIS BOOK

Editorial
Project Editor
Simon Ryder
Managing Editor
Cameron Duffy
Editorial Director
Brian Bell

Distribution

UK & Ireland
GeoCenter International Ltd
The Viables Centre , Harrow Way
Basingstoke, Hants RG22 4BJ
Fax: (44) 1256 817988

United States
Langenscheidt Publishers, Inc.
46–35 54th Road, Maspeth, NY 11378
Fax: (1) 718 784 0640

Canada
Thomas Allen & Son Ltd
390 Steelcase Road East
Markham, Ontario L3R 1G2
Fax: (1) 905 475 6747

Australia
Universal Publishers
1 Waterloo Road
Macquarie Park, NSW 2113
Fax: (61) 2 9888 9074

New Zealand
Hema Maps New Zealand Ltd (HNZ)
Unit D, 24 Ra ORA Drive
East Tamaki, Auckland
Fax: (64) 9 273 6479

Worldwide
Apa Publications GmbH & Co.
Verlag KG (Singapore branch)
38 Joo Koon Road, Singapore 628990
Tel: (65) 6865 1600. Fax: (65) 6861 6438

Printing

Insight Print Services (Pte) Ltd
38 Joo Koon Road, Singapore 628990
Tel: (65) 6865 1600. Fax: (65) 6861 6438

© 2004 Apa Publications GmbH & Co.
Verlag KG (Singapore branch)
All Rights Reserved
First Edition 1991; Third Edition 1999
Updated and Reprinted 2004

CONTACTING THE EDITORS
We would appreciate it if readers
would alert us to errors or out-
dated information by writing to:
**Insight Guides, P.O. Box 7910,
London SE1 1WE, England.
Fax: (44 20) 7403 0290.
insight@apaguide.co.uk**

This guidebook combines the interests and enthusiasms of two of the world's best-known information providers: Insight Guides, whose titles have set the standard for visual travel guides since 1970, and Discovery Channel, the world's premier source of nonfiction television programming.

The editors of Insight Guides provide practical advice and general understanding about a destination's history, culture, institutions and people. Discovery Channel and its website, www.discovery.com, help millions of viewers explore their world from the comfort of their own home and also encourage them to explore it first-hand.

Fjords, midnight sun and Vikings are the aspects most often identified with Norway – apart, that is, from the high cost of beer. But to see what else Norway has to offer there is no better place to start than Snorri Sturluson's chronicle of the lives of the Vikings.

How to use this book

This book is carefully struc-
tured to convey an under-
standing of the country
and its culture, and to
guide readers through its
sights and activities:

◆ To understand Norway today, you need to know something of its past. The first section, headed by a yellow colour bar, covers the country's history and culture in lively **features** written by specialists.

◆ The main **Places** section, with a blue bar, provides a complete run-down of all the attractions worth seeing.

◆ The **Travel Tips** section is a convenient point of reference for practical information on travel, hotels, restaurants, shops and festivals. Information may be located quickly on the index printed on the back cover flap – and the flaps are designed to serve as bookmarks.

The contributors

Originally edited by **Simon Ryder**, this fully updated guide builds on earlier editions produced by the late **Doreen Taylor-Wilkie**, a Scottish broadcaster and travel writer, who was first inspired to write about travel by Norway. Taylor-Wilkie also wrote the chapters on the fjord country.

The history section was the work of **Rowlinson Carter**, who became obsessed during his researches with the tales recounted by Snorri Sturlusson. **Michael Brady** arrived in Norway in 1958 from the United States. As an outdoor man and specialist on skiing and fitness, he was well suited to writing about customs, sport and the outdoor life.

Other contributors included one of Sweden's most eminent journalists, **Inga Wallerius**, who has a deep interest in ethnic cultures and wrote on the Sami people. **Bobby Tulloch's** chapter on Svalbard was the result of an expedition there, while **Jim Hardy** contributed his knowledge on Scandinavian arts. **Karen Fossli** wrote on the oil industry, film and Norway's neighbours, and **Anita Peltonen** provided chapters on Oslo and its environs. **Robert Spark** contributed the Places chapters outside of Oslo and the fjord country.

Previously updated by the Oslo-based writer **John Harley**, who described Norway as "one of God's best-kept secrets", the book was revised in 2003 by **Lance Price** with help from **Lars Bevanger**. This version was updated by **Daniel Cash** and edited in-house by **Jason Mitchell**.

Map Legend

——··—	International Boundary
————	County Boundary
⊖	Border Crossing
—·—·—	National Park/Reserve
————	Ferry Route
Ⓣ	Metro
✈ ✈	Airport: International/Regional
🚌	Bus Station
Ⓟ	Parking
❶	Tourist Information
✉	Post Office
✝ ✝ ✝	Church / Ruins
✝	Monastery
☾	Mosque
✡	Synagogue
🏰	Castle / Ruins
∴	Archaeological Site
∩	Cave
👤	Statue/Monument
★	Place of Interest

The main places of interest in the Places section are co-ordinated by number with a full-colour map (e.g. ❶), and a symbol at the top of every right-hand page tells you where to find the map.

INSIGHT GUIDE
NORWAY

CONTENTS

Maps

A map of the whole country showing the extent of the area maps listed above is in the inside front cover.

A map of Oslo is in the inside back cover.

Introduction

History

Features

Norwegian
patriotism
runs strong

Travel Tips

Information panels

Insight on ...

Places

NORTHERN CONTRASTS

Norway offers the visitor a beguiling mix of tradition and modern convenience, spectacular nature and city delights

The most accurate observation made about Norway is that it is a land of contrasts: the landscape is both beautiful and brutal, hospitable and hostile; barren rock submits to soft fertile plains, majestic mountains tower above mysterious fjords; harsh winters are relieved by glorious summers; and long polar nights give way to the radiant midnight sun. One of the oldest civilisations in Europe has become one of its youngest nations. The Norwegians themselves have adapted rather quickly. The rapacious Vikings have turned into global peacemakers. It is a country where Grieg and Ibsen compete with Aqua and Disney; where environmental concern challenges over-consumption. Norway has urban excitement and rural tranquillity; shopping malls and Mercedes rub shoulders with compass and rucksack; high-technology parallels steadfast tradition.

A thriving offshore oil industry has brought prosperity, and as a consequence, social habits are changing rapidly, though, in a society where the divorce rate is high and co-habitation the norm, the home and family still remain important. Politically, democracy and debate pervade all levels of society, and a blend of national pride and an engaged electorate continue to ensure political independence. Murray's *Handbook for Travellers in Norway* described the Norwegians in 1874 thus: "Great patriotism and hospitality are two of the leading characteristics of the Norwegians; they are often cold and reserved, and combine great simplicity of manner with firmness and kindness. 'Deeds, not words' is their motto." – 125 years later, little has changed.

But where does all this place the visitor?

Most people are pleasantly surprised when they visit Norway. For a start, the people are friendlier and far more open than the stereotypical Scandinavian image would have us believe, and secondly, the scenery is even more breathtaking in reality than any guidebook can ever hope to inspire. Although the country is vast – stick a pin in Kristiansand and rotate the country through 180° and the people in Kirkenes would be eating pasta. – the main town centres are more than manageable with good public transport and everywhere within walking distance anyway. Add to this the fact that things work, communications and services are efficient, and that it is safe to go out at night, and you have all the ingredients for a pleasant stay.

As for prices, it all depends on the reason for your visit and how you spend your money. Surveys persistently place Oslo among the top ten most expensive cities in the world, but the statistics tend rather to reflect the spending habits of businessmen with expense accounts than those of the selective tourist. ❑

PRECEDING PAGES: winter on the fjord; snow on the fishing fleet; wooden houses in the old copper-mining town of Røros; waiting for confirmation in Kautokeino.
LEFT: Norwegian fjords provide breathtaking views.

Decisive Dates

ICE AGE TO BRONZE AGE

10,000 years ago The first people appear in the territory of what is now Norway, following the retreat of the great inland ice sheets. They hunt reindeer and other prey as they gradually spread northwards.

5,000 to 6,000 years ago First agricultural settlements appear around Oslofjord.

1500–500 BC Agricultural settlements develop in southern Norway, while people in the north continue hunting.

ROMAN AGE

AD 0–400 Burial sites indicate links with the civilised countries to the south – utensils of bronze and glass have been discovered. Latin-based runic letters appear for the first time.

(The migrations of AD 400–550, including to coastal areas in the west, herald a restless period. Farmers are pushed into marginal areas. Forts have been found on Lake Mjøsa.)

AD 793 Norwegian Vikings loot the English monastery of Lindisfarne. They raid (or trade with) and colonise parts of west and south-west Europe. Vikings settle in the Orkneys, the Shetlands, the Hebrides, and on the Isle of Man (remaining there until 1405).

VIKING AGE

AD 800–1030 Our knowledge of this period is largely based on archaeological remains. Although written down some time later, the Norse sagas reveal that the Viking Age was the richest of all the early periods in Norway.

840 Vikings found Dublin, which remains under Nordic rule until 1171.

844 Dublin's Norwegian king exchanges envoys with Emir Abderrhaman II, the Moorish king in Spain.

861 Vikings sack Paris.

866 Vikings control most of England.

872 Battle at Hafrsfjord near Stavanger. King Harald Fairhair strengthens his position as ruler of large areas of the country.

1001 The sagas relate that it was Leiv Eiriksson who discovered Vinland (America).

1028 King Canute of Denmark invades Norway. King Olav flees, but later regains control.

1030 Battle of Stiklestad. Christianity arrives through trading contacts with the rest of Europe. This culminates with three missionary kings, Håkon the Good, Olaf Trygvasson and Olaf the Stout, who becomes St Olav following his death at the Battle of Stiklestad.

1050 Harald Hardråde founds Oslo.

1066 King Harald Hardråde is defeated at the Battle of Stamford Bridge, in England, bringing the Viking Age to an end.

MIDDLE AGES

1100 The first bishoprics appear, among them the see of Nidaros (Trondheim) in 1152.

1130 Start of civil wars which last until 1227. This period was also the start of the High Middle Ages. It was a period of population growth, consolidation within the Church and the development of towns. The monarchy dominates both Church and nobility. Farmers change from being freeholders to tenants.

1241 Saga writer Snorri Sturluson is put to death by the King of Norway's men.

1299–1319 Oslo becomes the capital during the reign of King Håkon V.

1319–43 Inter-Scandinavian royal marriages produce joint Norwegian-Swedish monarchy, later to include Denmark.

1349 Onslaught of the Black Death. Population (Oslo: 3,000; Bergen: 7,000; Trondheim: 4,000) reduced by 50 percent. Towards the end of the Middle Ages state revenues are inadequate to finance the desired expansion of the Crown and state. The king and the nobility seek revenues from neighbouring lands, leading to the growth of political unions.

1380 Olav, son of Håkon VI (1340–80) becomes King of Denmark and Norway.
Trinity Sunday 1397 The union of the three crowns is formalised in the Swedish town of Kalmar.
1450 Union with Denmark set up by treaty.

UNION WITH DENMARK

1536 Norway ceases to be an independent kingdom. Norway's Council of the Realm is disbanded. Danish noblemen start to take over control of the running of Norway.
1537 The Reformation of the Norwegian church is enforced by royal (Danish) decree. From the early 1600s the Lutheranism is the sole creed of Norway.
1624 Oslo burns to the ground.
1645 The Danish king surrenders Jemtland and Herjedalen to Sweden. The fief of Trondheim is surrendered in 1658 (but is then regained in 1660).
1660 Frederik III is acclaimed heir to the throne by an assembly of the States General in Copenhagen and assigned the task of giving the kingdoms a new constitution. (In this way the two kingdoms were subject to an absolute monarchy. However, the real power lay in the hands of the state officials and Denmark and Norway were treated as one.)
1662 Town privileges are introduced to concentrate wealth from the timber trade in the hands of urban, middle-class merchants.
1807–14 Napoleonic Wars. Denmark/Norway ally with France, and the resulting blockade isolates Norway both from Denmark and from the market. Shipping and timber exports collapse, and famine and hunger spread.

INDEPENDENCE AND NEW UNION

January 1814 Secession from Denmark.
17 May 1814 The new Norwegian constitution is formally adopted at Eidsvoll.
10 October 1814 Norway unites with Sweden.
1825 The great exodus to the USA begins.
1854 The first railway line is laid.
1872 The first trade union is formed.
1884 Norway's first political parties are set up.
August 1905 National referendum leads to the end of the union with Sweden.

NORWEGIAN INDEPENDENCE

18 November 1905 The Storting (Parliament) voted

PRECEDING PAGES: Viking gold.
LEFT: the Stiklestad open-air play.
RIGHT: 1905, Danish Prince Carl arrives in Norway, carrying his son, who became King Håkon VII.

unanimously for Prince Carl of Denmark to become elected as King (Håkon VII) of Norway.
1913 Universal suffrage is granted to women.
1920 Norway joins the League of Nations. Following WWI, Norway retains its claim on Spitsbergen.
1939 Norway proclaims neutrality in WWII.
9 April 1940 German forces attack Norway.
7 June 1945 King Håkon returns from exile.
1957 King Håkon VII dies. Olav V is crowned.
1960s Oil exploration in the North Sea begins.
1972 Norway votes against EU membership.
1991 King Olav V dies. King Harald V is crowned.
1993 Norway brokers Israeli/Palestinian peace.
1994 Norway declines again to join the EU. The

Winter Olympics are held in Lillehammer.
1997 Socialist rule ends. Kjell Magne Bondevika, a Christian Democrat, is elected as Prime Minister to head a centre-right coalition.
2000 Oslo celebrates its 1000 years. Bergen is named as European City of Culture 2000.
2001 Norway is elected to serve on the United Nations Security Council. Crown Prince Haakon controversially marries a divorced commoner with a child. First centre-right government for over 65 years takes office. Explorer Thor Heyerdal dies.
2002 Princess Martha Louise marries writer Ari Behn in May in Trondheim.
2003 Princess Martha Louise gives birth to a daughter, Maud Angelica Behn, in April. ❑

BEGINNINGS

For two centuries the Vikings terrorised large parts of Europe, travelling far and wide in search of land, wealth and, when it suited them, trade

Life in Norway has been influenced to an extraordinary degree by the terrain and the weather. The original inhabitants hugged the coastal areas which, warmed by the Gulf Stream, made life more bearable. With the gradual recession of the last Ice Age about 12,000 years ago, the hunters and fishers inched northwards but again only along the coast because the interior remained inhospitable.

The thaw was followed by mild weather, unknown before or since. Around 500 BC, however, just as iron was beginning to replace bronze and the Athenians were getting ready to build the Parthenon, the climate inexplicably deteriorated. The impact of suddenly colder, wetter weather was dramatic.

Taking a step back

During the preceding Bronze Age considerable progress had been made in weapons, ornaments and utensils made out of metal imported from Britain and Continental Europe. Contemporary rock drawings show boats that were capable of carrying 30 men (although not yet with sails), warriors on horseback and either two- or four-wheeled carts drawn by horses or oxen. These developments were thrown into reverse by the climate change and a large part of the population perished.

Survival in the new Ice Age demanded cultural adjustments. Men, who until then had usually worn a kind of belted cloak, pulled on underwear and trousers. Instead of a semi-nomadic existence, all had to settle on farms in order to secure winter fodder and shelter livestock, which had previously grazed outside all year round. People and animals occupied either end of the same house, an unhygienic but necessary form of early central heating.

In common with most of Europe, Norway was again struck by the weather in the 14th century. The economic decline that followed

was exacerbated terribly by the Black Death. The resulting acute shortage of labour led to the collapse of the aristocratic estates, demoting the owners to peasantry. The number of knights in Norway dropped from 270 to 60.

But who were these people? The recorded history of Norway begins remarkably late, only

in about AD 800, and the archaeological pointers towards specific events in earlier times are comparatively scanty. The ancient world had curious opinions about the ancient northerners: one, advanced by Pomponius Mela, was that, living on birds' eggs, the people had hoofed feet, and ears so large that they covered their bodies, thereby dispensing with the need for any clothing.

Another, Greek in origin and containing an element of truth, had the territory populated by Hyperboreans, a jolly race who lived in forests and sang and danced their way to incredible longevity. When eventually tired of life, they feasted, bedecked themselves with flowers and

---

LEFT: discovered in 1880, the Gokstad ship is now in the *Vikingskipshuset* (Viking Ship Museum), Oslo.
RIGHT: Odin, king of the Norse gods.

threw themselves off cliffs. Norwegians continue to live longer than practically anyone else in Europe. Furthermore, they remain energetic to the end. It is one thing for a foreigner struggling on skis to be overtaken by a blasé six-year-old, quite another if the speed demon turns out to be a venerable grandmother.

Lieutenant W.H. Breton, a 19th-century tourist, was amazed by reports of a man who married at 113 and lasted until he was 146. Another visitor commented on four peasants who were the principal dancers at an entertainment laid on for King Christian VI: all of them were well over 100. One Derwent Conway, in

about 1820, asked a fit 74-year-old in Telemark for the secret of his robust health. Pouring himself a fifth glass of home-made corn brandy, he replied that it was due to this excellent drink.

New blood

That the original inhabitants of Norway received infusions of new blood, probably from the east, is indicated by artefacts which have given their name to their respective cultures: Funnel-Beaker, Battle-Axe and Boat-Axe peoples. Changing burial practices are another reliable sign of influential immigration.

It was once thought that the Sami (Lapps of Finnmark) were the original inhabitants. Being Mongoloid and short of stature, they are very different from the familiar Scandinavian stereotype. However, it seems theirs was a relatively recent migration from Siberia, long after European types had moved in. The great majority of Norwegians are directly descended from the people who were occupying their territory long before 3000 BC, the date customarily taken as the beginning of Western civilisation.

Like a Nordic Rip van Winkle, Norway slept through the millennium in which Greece and then Rome flourished, although the runic alphabet did appear around the 3rd century AD. It was Latin in origin but dispensed with the curved Latin letters because, perhaps, straight lines were easier to cut into wood, stone and metal, as runic inscriptions invariably were.

Norway was ignored by the civilised world until the late 8th century, by which time the Muslim tide had been turned back and Charlemagne was building his empire. Nowhere in Pliny the Elder, Tacitus, Ptolemy or any of the celebrated descriptions of the then known world are the Norwegian people mentioned by name. Even the term "Scandinavia" is a misreading of a text by Pliny, who referred to the unknown land beyond Jutland as *Scatinavia*.

Development in secret

Foreign ignorance, however, did not mean that nothing was happening locally. The evolution of ship design was the most potent of these hidden developments. Although the Phoenicians had undertaken stupendous voyages very much earlier, they routinely stayed within sight of land. The Norwegians were working on vessels capable of crossing oceans.

The Gokstad ship, found in a burial mound near Sandefjord in 1880, was a masterpiece. Made out of oak planks, it was 25 metres (82 ft) long and 5 metres (16 ft) wide. It had a mast and 16 pairs of oars. The crew handled one oar each which left enough room for an equal number of marines. The *styrbord* or rudder, which hung on the right (hence, starboard) side, could be raised for fast beaching. A modern replica crossed the Atlantic in just four weeks. These ships represented a menacing mobility, and once the Norwegians had cause to take their unsuspecting neighbours to the south by surprise, they were able to do so with stunning efficiency.

The Norwegians introduced themselves to

the rest of the world with deceptive tranquillity. The *Anglo-Saxon Chronicle* of 787 contains the laconic entry: "In this year King Breohtric married King Offa's daughter Eadburge. And in his days came the first three ships of the Northmen from Hereoalande" (known today as Hordaland, on Norway's west coast).

The Vikings appear

In 793 the Vikings opened their account in earnest by plundering the monastery of Lindisfarne off the north east coast of England near the

BAD NEIGHBOURS

In Arthurian romances the Vikings were described as being "wild and savage and had not in them the love of God nor their neighbours."

among their victims in the 9th and 10th centuries that it was synonymous with the term "pirate" or "sea robber". This is further confused by the tendency in English chronicles to call all Vikings "Danes", while many were actually "Northmen", "Norsemen" or, in present terminology, Norwegians. In contrast, in Continental records Norwegians take all the credit (or blame) for what was usually the work of Danes. Swedish Vikings were busy too, but they tended to direct their attentions overland via Russia.

Scottish border, one of the great sanctuaries of the Western Christian church. The next year they attacked the monastery of Jarrow in modern-day Tyne and Wear further down the coast. Northumbria, and the year after that they arrived in South Wales with more than 100 ships. They were driven off by King Maredudd and that, together with the resistance they had encountered in England, persuaded them, for a period of 40 years, to turn their attention to softer targets in Ireland.

Various opinions prevail about the origin of the name "Viking", but there was no doubt

LEFT: early sailing equipment.
ABOVE: a set of Viking keys.

Proper outside investigation into the geography and demography of Norway began with King Alfred the Great of England, who had every reason to wonder about people who had become painful tormentors. He was enlightened by Ottar, a Norwegian chieftain from Hålogaland, at the same time as Alfred was waging war with other Viking chieftains. Ottar told the king that Norway was a very long and narrow country, full of rocks and mountains. The only places that could be pastured or ploughed were those close to the sea; the inhabitants kept sheep and swine and bred tame deer, which they called reindeer.

In reality, the Vikings were land-hungry

adventurers for whom rich and undefended coastal abbeys were irresistible business opportunities. They had no scruples about violating their supposed sacrosanctity; on the contrary, they saw Christianity as a heretical threat to their own heathen beliefs.

Truculent population

While Christians put their faith in the sign of the cross, the Vikings trusted the hammer of Thor the Thunderer, defender of heaven against giants, men against monsters, and themselves from the "Followers of the White Cross", as they called Christians. Small Viking raiding

parties faced with a large and truculent population found that a reputation for uncompromising destruction and cruelty served their purposes well, encouraging the enemy to flee rather than put up a fight. Viking victory celebrations – "[a] wild outburst of triumphant rejoicing" – included the proven intimidatory tactic of transfixing captured children with spears and drinking out of the skulls of fallen enemies.

The Vikings also have apologists who prefer to concentrate on their apparent managerial talents in occupied territory and an artistic streak manifested in the finely worked ornaments recovered from excavated ships. In the early

18th century, Baron de Montesquieu praised them as an army of free men in an age when armies were usually press-ganged.

The historian Snorri Sturluson is disarmingly indifferent to matters which others might consider to be grave flaws in their heroes. The royal pretender Harald Gille is summarised as "friendly, jovial, playful, unassuming, generous, accommodating and easily led". All this glosses over the fact, which Sturluson himself recounts, that he blinded and castrated a rival, hanged a bishop and died drunk in the arms of his mistress with his wife standing by.

The reason sometimes given for the sudden explosion of Viking activity abroad is that it was the result of another explosion, that of population because of uniform polygamy. Overpopulation was certainly the case in Western Norway where agricultural land was so scarce, but the problem was less acute elsewhere.

Nevertheless, all sons, legitimate and otherwise, were entitled to equal shares of their father's inheritance, and as political power and social standing were invested in property, the aristocracy especially were reluctant to carve land up into smaller and smaller parcels. The surfeit of sons was thus encouraged to seek a fortune abroad.

The profits of piracy

Women and children often accompanied the men but they were usually parked in fortified camps while the men "harried". Occasionally they did join in and one of them – an Amazon who rose to command her own army in Ireland – was acclaimed as the fearsome Red Maiden.

When the Vikings came across unoccupied land or, as in the Orkneys, rendered it so by annihilating the natives, they were keen to settle it. If that proved to be impractical, a raid might at least produce some slaves who could either be sold or, increasingly, put to good use at home. When piracy could not be made to pay, however, the Vikings were willing to engage in conventional trade.

Profits from piracy and trade generated in Norway the nucleus of a merchant class which complemented the traditional structure of aristocratic earls, free men and thralls (or slaves). The pecking order was reflected in Western Norway by *wergild*, a system which stipulated the compensation due in the event of murder. A slave was worth half the value of an ordinary peasant and a quarter of that of a land owner, who in turn was worth only a quarter of a chieftain and one-eighth of a king.

Slaves must have been worked hard because there was a provision in law which absolved owners of guilt if a slave died through exhaustion or ill-treatment. Owners were permitted, when slaves died, to throw their children into an open grave to die from exposure. They were obliged, however, to step in and rescue the last one left alive.

Some slaves, such as captured craftsmen,

VIKINGS ABROAD

The Viking kingdom on the Isle of Man lasted until 1263, when it was sold to Alexander III of Scotland along with the Western Isles.

exchanged envoys with Emir Abderrhaman II, the Moorish leader in Spain. Alghazal, a poet, was appointed to the court of the King of the Pagans and became enchanted by the queen. While keen to further their acquaintance, he was alarmed at the prospect of the king finding out.

The queen reassured him that "it is not customary with us to be jealous. Our women stay with their husbands only as long as they please, and leave them whenever they choose." She seems not to have added that Viking husbands reciprocated in kind.

were prized, as were young women with whom masters could replenish or increase the labour pool. Unlike the custom in nearby Sweden, the child of the union between a Norwegian master and slave woman remained a slave.

Viking women made an impression abroad in a way that hints at the emancipated attitudes ascribed to them in the 20th century, albeit a reputation bestowed less frequently on Norwegian women than on the other Scandinavians. In 844 a Norwegian king ruling in Dublin

LEFT: a confrontation from the *Frithiof Saga* by E. Tégnér, illustrated by Knut Ekwall.
ABOVE: runic script at Skjeberg, south of Oslo.

Viking men traded wives, or even gave them away to friends, if they bored or displeased them.

Protection money

The renewed Viking campaigns were launched from the west coast of Norway, from strongholds on the Scottish islands or from the Norwegian kingdom in Ireland, centred on a castle built in Dublin in 841 by Torgisl. The Vikings were overlords rather than settlers in Ireland, although some intermarried. Norway might still have overseas territories today if a Danish king, as we shall see, had not mortgaged the Orkney and Shetland Isles to raise money for his daughter's dowry.

The Viking raids into Europe were conducted like annual summer holidays, and year after year the fleets grew larger. An alarmed Charlemagne threw up military posts along his northern borders to guard against them. The defence of Paris against the Vikings was led by another King Charles, known as Charles the Bald. The city was attacked in 857 and sacked in 861. Charles offered one lot of Vikings 1,360 kg (3,000 lb) of silver to go and fight some of their compatriots instead of him. In 885, however, both were back and it cost a further 318 kg (700 lb) of silver to get rid of them.

The most enduring Viking presence in France was in Normandy which, of course, was named after them. Over the years the Viking armies on the continent grew to massive proportions and were not finally driven off until 891, by the German emperor Arnulf.

Although geographical proximity recommended the British Isles, Vikings were active wherever the pickings looked good. At one point they laid siege to Lisbon and they penetrated the Mediterranean as far as Constantinople. Nor did they restrict their territorial ambitions to Continental Europe. Vikings sailed west to Iceland, Greenland and eventually to the American continent. As many as 20,000

THE VIKINGS IN BRITAIN

The Vikings attacked the British Isles in earnest from 834. The most spectacular effort was in 851 when they took 350 ships up the Thames, stopping off to capture Canterbury before storming London, only to be finally turned back by Ethelwulf at the battle of Aclea. By 866 most of England was under their control with only Wessex, ruled by Alfred the Great, staying independent. After the initial success of a winter campaign in 878, they were defeated by Alfred, but continued to rule large parts of England and a kingdom based in York. All further territorial ambitions were curtailed with the arrival of William the Conqueror in 1066.

Norwegians emigrated to Iceland; by the latter half of the 10th century there were no fewer than 39 petty kingdoms established there.

This surging mixture of colonialism, plunder, trade and adventurism lasted for two centuries between the fall of the western Roman Empire and the First Crusade, and it nearly brought about the overthrow of Christianity in Europe (as the Muslims had been close to doing earlier). The benefits to those left at home were considerable. The period produced unprecedented wealth. ❏

ABOVE: a detail from a drawing by Halvfdan Egedins in Snorri Sturluson's *Sagas of the Norse Kings*.

A Viking Burial

In the year AD 921, a peripatetic Arab named Ahmad bin Fudlan came across Vikings who had settled on the banks of the Volga river. They were trading with Constantinople: furs and slaves for gold, silver ornaments and silks. A chieftain died while he was with them, and his account of the funeral is an antidote to some of the romantic nonsense that has been written about the Vikings.

When the chieftain died, Ahmad reported, his maidservants were asked: "Who will die with him?" The first to volunteer was immediately put under guard in case she changed her mind, not that she gave any indication of wishing to do so.

The elaborate formalities began with the division of the chieftain's estate into three equal parts. One went to his family, the second to cover the cost of the funeral, and the last on drink. The boat in which the chieftain was to be despatched was drawn out of the water and decorated with quilts and cushions. Ahmad then met "the angel of death"; he described her as "dusky, hale, strongly built and austere". Austere she might well have been, for it was her function eventually to kill the carousing maidservant.

The chieftain's body was removed from the temporary grave where it had lain for 10 days. Ahmad had a good look at it. "I saw that he had gone black, because of the cold", he said; but otherwise "the corpse had in no way altered." The body was dressed in finery and propped up on cushions in a tent erected on the boat.

"They now brought liquor, fruit, and herbs and put them by him, then they brought bread, meat, and onions, and threw them down in front of him. They brought a dog, cut it in half, and threw it into the boat, then brought all his weapons, and put them by his side. After that they took two beasts of burden, drove them along until they sweated, then cut them up with swords and threw their flesh into the boat. The girl who was to be killed, meanwhile, was going up and down, entering one tent after another, and one man after another had intercourse with her. Each one said to her, 'Tell your master that I only do this for love of him.'" The girl was later taken to the boat, where she handed over her bracelets and anklets to the "angel of death" and the two girls who had been guarding her. They were joined by men carrying shields and pieces of wood.

RIGHT: a romantic view of a Viking (1828).

Farewell drinks and songs followed until, Ahmad wrote, "I saw that she had become bewildered and wished to enter the tent."

The old woman followed her into the tent, whereupon "the men began beating the shields with the pieces of wood so that the sound of her screams should not be heard. Six men then entered the tent, and all of them had intercourse with her. They then made her lie down by the side of her dead master, and two took hold of her hands and two her feet. The "angel of death" put a rope done into a noose round her neck, and gave it to two men to pull. She came forward with a large, broad-bladed knife and began thrusting it in and

out between the girl's ribs in place after place, while the two men strangled her until she died."

Walking backwards, the next of kin then went naked to the boat and lit kindling which had been placed beneath it. "At this moment, an awe-inspiring gale got up, so that the flames of the fire grew stronger." One of the Vikings chose to compare the funeral arrangements with what he had heard about Islamic rites. "You Arabs are stupid," he remarked to Ahmad, "because you take your dearest and most honourable men and cast them into the dust, so that creeping things and worms eat them. We burn them with fire in a twinkling and they enter Paradise the very same hour." Then, according to Ahmad bin Fudlan, "he laughed heartily." ❑

KINGS AND CHRISTIANITY

Constant battles for the throne and the arrival of Christianity in a stubbornly pagan land were the unlikely precursors to Norway's "Period of Greatness"

With Snorri Sturluson, Norwegian history begins to speak for itself instead of relying on outsiders who observed or passed on fantastic tales about the land and its people. Sturluson's epic *Heimskringla (Sagas of the Norse Kings)* is a work of genius.

He visited Norway only twice, but working on his remote saga island of Iceland he compiled an almost inconceivable mass of information beginning in prehistory and continuing until 1177 (two years before he was born), by which time the Vikings had been tamed, Christianity had taken hold in Norway and the country had endured a century of civil war.

Amusing tale

Although Sturluson was himself a foreigner, he drew on the oral history of the skalds at the courts of the Norwegian kings. He was obviously a discriminating historian, although never one to exclude an amusing tale because he did not believe it: "It is the way of skalds, of course, to give most praise to him for whom they composed, but no one would dare tell the king himself such deeds of his as all listeners and the king himself knew to be lies and loose talk; that would be mockery, but not praise."

There are no fewer than 2,000 names of persons and places in his saga and he gives his readers a vivid sense of what was happening, as it were, at home. But Sturluson's unlucky recompense was to be put to death by the King of Norway's men in 1241.

Sturluson introduces the Norwegian royal line in the person of Halvdan the Black, a king troubled by his inability to dream. He consulted Torleiv the Wise, who said he had suffered from the same complaint and had cured it by sleeping in a pigsty. The king followed his example "and then it always happened that he dreamed."

More prosaically, Halvdan was descended from the Swedish Ynglinger family who ruled in Uppsala. His branch had moved to Norway

about a century before the Viking period, when the concept of Norway as an entity existed only in the term *Norovegr*, or North Way, the coastal stretch from Vestfold to Hålogaland.

A king dreaming in a pigsty might seem to belong to mythology rather than history, but he was real enough. The Oseberg ship unearthed in

Vestfold in 1904 proved to be that in which his mother, a Danish princess, was buried. When Halvdan died, his body was chopped up so that the pieces could be more widely distributed to bring good luck to the recipients.

Female demands

Halvdan's son, known as Harald Hårfagre (Fair Hair), was to become the first ruler of a united Norway. It was said of this subsequent unification that he was put up to it by a woman whom he wished to take to bed. Her reply to his proposition, conveyed by messengers, was that she could not possibly "waste her maidenhood" on a man who ruled over a kingdom that com-

---

LEFT: one of the oldest stave churches, Borgund.
RIGHT: Harald Hårfagre (*circa* 1200).

pared so unfavourably in size with those in Denmark and Sweden. His messengers nervously reported her comment but were relieved by the philosophical way in which he took it: "She has reminded me of those things," he said, "which it now seems strange I have not thought of before."

Harald advanced north from Vestfold to improve his conjugal prospects. He made contact with the powerful Earl Håkon, whose interests extended south from Trøndelag, the region surrounding what was eventually to become Trondheim. The cold facts, never as interesting as Sturluson's version, are that Harald and

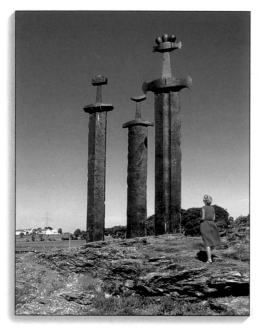

Håkon saw the mutual benefits of trade but first had to suppress unruly Viking bands along the coast who would have disrupted it.

Harald needed assistance and set the precedent for cooperation between the Norwegian and English thrones by turning to Athelstan, King of England. As a pledge of friendship, accompanied by some mutual chicanery, he initiated what was to become another quite common practice: he sent his infant son Håkon to be fostered at Athelstan's court.

Harald's campaigns sent many of his dispossessed opponents into exile in Iceland, Shetland, the Orkney Islands and the Hebrides. The decisive battle was at Hafrsfjord, near present-

day Stavanger, in southwestern Norway in about AD 900. The victory made him, Sturluson says, the first king of the Norwegians, and also won him the postponed hand of the "large-minded maid", who proceeded to bear him five children. As a love story, however, the conclusion is not completely satisfactory. Sturluson writes: "They say that when he took Ragnhild the Mighty…, he had divorced himself from nine other women."

Too many children

The awesome number of royal progeny was to prove a constant source of havoc in the matter of choosing a successor. The English chronicler Roger of Hoveden wrote: "it is the custom of the kingdom of Norway… that everyone who is recognised to be the son of any King of Norway, even though he be a bastard and born of a serving wench, can claim for himself as great a right to the kingdom of Norway as the son of a wedded king and one born of a free woman. And so fighting goes on incessantly between them…"

Harald Hårfagre's umpteenth son, but the only one by Ragnhild, was the wretched Erik Bloodaxe, who advanced his succession by murdering all but one of his legitimate half-brothers. The exception was Håkon, the boy who had been fostered by King Athelstan. Erik had none of his father's authority and the united kingdom quickly degenerated into squabbling petty kingdoms ruled by various of Harald's bastard sons. On Håkon's return from England, Erik was forced to flee in the opposite direction, ending up as King of Northumberland.

First Christian

Håkon den Gode (the Good) was more successful than Erik at holding hostile factions together. Before he died, he was acknowledged as king over the whole coastal area from Oslo to Hålogaland. He was a notable reformer of law and defence; he was also the first Norwegian Christian king, having been baptised while in England. He imported an English bishop and missionaries with a view to converting his countrymen; but that wasn't easy.

Nowhere was resistance to Christianity more forcibly expressed than in Trondheim, which was then against any form of imposed authority whether by Håkon or, as they had just convincingly demonstrated, by the rival King

Øystein of Oppland. Øystein, to some "the Mighty" and to others "the Evil", had offered them as king a choice between one of his thralls, known as Tore the Hairy, or his dog, Saur. They chose the dog. "Then they bewitched the dog with the wit of three men", sufficient to enable the hound to communicate through a mixture of barking and speech. It was into this unorthodox regal set-up that Håkon tried to introduce Christianity. He urged people to "believe in one God, Christ, the son of Mary,

SAUR, THE DOG KING

According to *the Sagas of the Norse Kings*: "The king lived in a palatial kennel and was carried 'when it was muddy' on the shoulders of its subjects."

ioners would drink themselves into extinction and, by instructing them in the cultivation of fruit and vegetables, hoped to persuade them to consume at least some solids. In the end the missionaries realised that pious sobriety was unattainable. The best they could hope for was to have the toasting converted to Christian saints rather than pagan gods. They provided a long list of saints' names and it seems that some of their parishioners were content to drink to them with undiminished frequency and pleasure.

and give up all blood offerings... and fast every seventh day". From the typical audience "there was straightaway a mighty uproar", followed by devious ploys to trick Håkon into eating a morsel of horse flesh on a day when he was self-righteously fasting or make him participate in a toast to one of their pagan gods.

Håkon's imported missionaries despaired. Their targets would not deviate from drinking to pagan gods morning, noon and night. They were concerned, too, that their potential parish-

LEFT: the monument at Hafrsfjord, where Harald Hårfagre first united Norway.
ABOVE: traditional Norwegian houses with turf roofs.

Missionaries' fate

The missionaries had less luck in suppressing traditions like blood sacrifices (usually animals but occasionally humans). In Trondheim the obdurate response to the message they preached was to send out four ships looking for tiresome missionaries: they "slew three priests and burned three churches; they then went home".

Even when Christianity was finally adopted in Norway, much of the old religion lingered until the Reformation and beyond. The early Christian clergy, for instance, ignored papal injunctions about celibacy. The medieval stave churches are another case in point. Their intricate construction resembles nothing if not the keel of a Viking ship, and they are festooned with dragon heads and scenes from heathen mythology. Many of these churches lasted into the 19th century, when they finally succumbed beneath a torrent of Pietism.

On the military front, Håkon was under constant threat from Erik Bloodaxe's avenging sons coming over from Northumberland. In defeat they turned to their uncle, the Danish King, Harald Bluetooth, who wanted to regain old Danish territories at the mouth of Oslofjord. At a decisive battle in 960 Håkon was defeated and killed. With him, for the time being, went Christianity's immediate prospects in Norway.

Unlikely convert

Christianity had to wait for Olav Tryggvason, later King Olav I and a monument in Norwegian history, for its next champion. Sturluson says he was a great sportsman who could walk on the oars along the outside of a ship, "smote equally well with both hands" and could hurl two spears at a time. By the age of 12 he was a full-blooded Viking, cruising the Baltic in command of five longships and later moving west to terrorise the English coast. His personality changed through a chance meeting in the Scilly Isles, where he was resting after some strenuous atrocities. A wise old man took him to one side and explained the True Path. Transformed

overnight, Olav returned to England "and now went about peacefully, for England was a Christian country and he was also a Christian".

He was not so peaceful when converting his compatriots at home. Those who opposed him "he dealt with hard; some he slew, some he maimed and some he drove away from the land". In the circumstances, it is understandable that a man who was elected to argue theological niceties with the king stood up only to develop "such a cough and choking in the chest that he could not bring forth one word and he sat himself down".

Olav Tryggvason was unlucky in love. In proposing marriage to the wealthy Queen Sigrid of Sweden, he insisted she would first have to be baptised. She demurred: "King Olav was very wroth and answered hastily, 'Why should I wed thee, thou heathen bitch?'" reinforcing his point with a smack in the face. "That may well be thy death", she observed: so it proved.

She was a crafty enemy. Her wealth attracted a procession of proposals from minor kings, which she found irksome. King Swein Forkbeard of Denmark, son of Harald Bluetooth, was the type she preferred, and as soon as they were married she talked her husband into an alliance with the Swedish King Olav the Tax Gatherer against Norway. A great sea battle ensued, at the climax of which Olav, who was being assisted by King Boleslav of Poland, was forced to jump overboard. He was never seen again and the victors, including the gratified queen, divided the spoils among themselves.

First saint

The man who would soon restore Norway's integrity had, like Olav Tryggvason, embarked on a naval career at 12. Olav Haraldson, later St Olav, was in England when the same Swein Forkbeard landed his forces and was responsible for the then King of England, Ethelred, being castigated ever more as "the Unready".

Olav allied himself with Ethelred in an anti-Danish war which came to a head at London Bridge across the River Thames. The Danish forces looked, and probably felt, impregnable on their fortified bridge, but they reckoned without Olav's well-built Vikings. Having fastened ropes to the piles under the bridge, they heaved at the oars and brought the whole thing down. Several churches in England are still dedicated to St Olav for this remarkable feat.

A formidable enemy

Olav laid the foundations of the Church, even in petulant Trøndelag, but antagonised many potential rivals, none worse than the expansionist King Canute of Denmark and England, who invaded in 1028 with overwhelming forces. Olav fled to Kiev until he learned that the earl whom Canute had appointed to rule Norway was dead. He returned to regain his kingdom but miscalculated his level of support in Trøndelag and was killed.

Olav was elevated to sainthood and his body placed in the church of St Clement in Trondheim (later to be moved). In spite of his insensitive missionary zeal, the memory of Olav kept

for the Byzantine emperor in Constantinople and saw service in Syria, Armenia, Palestine, Sicily and Africa. He was an enterprising warrior. During one siege he faked his own funeral and, emulating the Trojan Horse, his men persuaded the townspeople to open the gates to admit his coffin which, they promised, would work powerful magic to their benefit.

All of this was immensely profitable because the mercenaries were entitled to keep as much treasure from captured palaces as they could grab with both hands. An oblique memorial to Norwegians like Harald who served with the Varangians exists on the great Piraeus marble

alive the notion of a united and independent Norway through the troubled centuries ahead.

King Canute's kingdom fell apart after his death, the Scandinavian component reforming into three distinct and generally hostile kingdoms. Norway was ruled first by Magnus I and then by Harald Hårdråda.

Noble mercenary

Harald was typical of the young nobles who were forced to look abroad to enrich themselves. He signed up as a Varangian mercenary

lion which the Venetians carried away after their conquest of Athens in 1687 and which now stands at the entrance to the Arsenal in Venice. Very faded, but still visible, is an example of Varangian graffiti: a runic inscription etched into its flanks.

Harald consolidated the kingdom of Norway. Troubled as Norwegian kings invariably were by the people of Trøndelag and its capital, Trondheim, he founded Oslo in 1048 as a counterbalance. He provided the town with a patron saint, Hallvard, whose main claim to sainthood seems to have been the refusal of his body to sink after being thrown into a fjord with a stone around the neck.

LEFT: detail of the carving on Borgund stave church.
ABOVE: runic inscription on a Viking monument.

Defeat in England

As King Canute's sovereignty over England (1017–35) was still within living memory, it was possibly inevitable that a confident Harald would develop similar ambitions. In any case, there had been so much toing and froing between the west coast of Norway and Britain that the affinities between them were as close, or closer, than those between scattered settlements in Norway. Harald therefore probably felt he was exercising a natural right in his invasion of England.

His approach was from the north but his army was stopped at Stamford Bridge, in present-day North Yorkshire. Some historians

taneously acclaimed kings who were all minors. One died young, Sigurd went off to the Holy Land to earn his title, "the Crusader", and Øystein mixed Viking raids with improvements to fisheries, harbours and roads and the establishment of monasteries. Sigurd had the throne to himself after Øystein's death, though he continued to be confronted by the complicated rules of succession throughout his reign.

These battles to occupy the Norwegian throne went on and on. There were brilliant interludes under a king like Sverre, but more often than not the succession was a squabble between the powers behind official contestants

argue that the English army's rush north to meet Harald weakened its ability to resist William the Conqueror when he materialised in the south.

After Harald's death in this abortive conquest of England, he was succeeded by his sons Magnus and Olav the Peaceful, the latter founding the towns of Bergen and Stavanger before being succeeded by his son, yet another Magnus, but in this instance unforgettably "the Bareleg" because, after visiting Scotland (which he dearly wanted to annex), he took to wearing a kilt.

Magnus's death produced the familiar pattern of multiple heirs, in this case three simul-

who might be children not yet six years old. With the stability of Håkon IV's 46-year reign and that of his son, Magnus the Lawmender, however, Norway achieved its 13th-century "Period of Greatness".

Cultural awakening

Money was spent on cathedrals and churches, the arts flourished and Norwegians assiduously studied and followed European fashions. This cultural awakening was to some extent through the creation of a wealthy upper class and the consolidation of state and Church. It was not so beneficial for the peasants; riches were not evenly spread, and the number of independent farmers dropped significantly as they defaulted on mortgages, leaving the Church and big landowners free to repossess their land.

Norway's overseas empire contributed to a sense of greatness. Jämtland in Sweden was Norwegian, as were the Orkney and Shetland Islands. In 1262 Iceland accepted Norwegian sovereignty, as did Greenland. It was the period, too, which saw the growth of towns like Bergen with a rich trade in dried fish from the north. Foreign trade, to begin with, was mainly with Britain but it then tilted towards the Baltic coast, especially Lübeck and the merchants of the Hanseatic League. The Germans had plenty of corn but a shortage of fish; a perfect trade balance with Norway.

The Lübeck merchants grew ever more powerful because of Norway's almost total reliance on them. They were allowed to buy property in Bergen and settle there. If their demands were not met, they simply threatened to cut off corn supplies. Reliance on imported food was effectively costing the country a degree of independence, an unsettling vulnerability which persists in the current national obsession about subsidising agriculture wherever it is remotely possible (and refusing to join the European Union in order to continue to be able to do so).

The Black Death

A galley arriving in Sicily from the Far East in October 1347 brought the Black Death to Europe. Within a couple of years, a third of the European population was dead. The plague was carried north to Bergen in 1349 in the hold of an English ship. The effect on isolated Norwegian farming communities, especially, was catastrophic: farms which had been painfully created in conditions difficult at the best of times were reduced to waste, and in some cases remain so to this day.

The estates generating the wealth which was the necessary platform for general economic development could not be maintained while labourers dropped dead. The nobles who survived were reduced to scratching a living out of the land like everyone else. The effect of *force*

COURTLY BEHAVIOUR

The court of King Magnus the Lawmender was a polite affair, with a prescibed set of rules relating to court etiquette.

majeure acting as a social leveller assumed a pattern in Norwegian history which cannot be discounted in explaining the easy-going classlessness which pertains today.

The decimation of the nobility removed the impetus behind the normally turbulent activity around the Norwegian throne. Unchallenged, two successive kings sat out long peaceful reigns, a foretaste of the comparative stability about to be foisted on all Scandinavia in the late 14th century through the cunning manipulation of Margareta, widow of King Håkon.

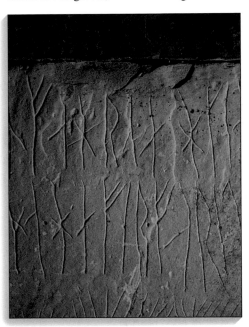

A Danish princess, Margareta was married to Håkon at the age of 10 and was thus steeped in the machinery of monarchy. She has been credited with "the greatest personal position ever achieved in Scandinavia" and was sometimes addressed as "Lady King". She first persuaded the Danes to accept as king her son Olav, then aged five.

With mother active behind the scenes, Olav also took over the crown of Norway at 10, and not long afterwards inherited the claim of the dispossessed Folkung dynasty in Sweden. He died suddenly at 17 and Margareta found a suitable substitute to don the united crowns in Erik of Pomerania, her five-year-old nephew. ❑

LEFT: the Ring of Brodgar, Viking remains on the Isles of Orkney off the northeastern tip of Scotland.
RIGHT: runic inscription in Orkney.

THE 400-YEAR SLEEP

A long spell under the control of its more powerful neighbours brought Norway
mixed fortunes and, ultimately, something to celebrate – a constitution

The union of the three crowns was formalised at a coronation in the Swedish town of Kalmar, close to the then border with Denmark. The date, appropriately, was Trinity Sunday, 1397. The coronation was performed by the Danish and Swedish archbishops; Norway was represented by the Bishop of Orkney. Although

While taking steps to undermine the authority of the nobility, Erik also tried to squeeze the Hanseatic merchants for money. Their response included an attack on Copenhagen, where they were seen off by 200 examples of a new invention, the cannon. He was less successful when the merchants retaliated with a blockade. Those

there may have been an attempt to draft a constitution which would have united the three realms forever under a single king, the rules of succession that were adopted left a gaping loophole. Erik of Pomerania was given full rights to dispose of the crown as he saw fit, a recipe for reversion to the old royal uncertainties after his death.

End of the union

In the event, the union collapsed in his lifetime. His greatest difficulty was paying for the court and administration in Copenhagen. The united crown had no significant estates of its own; the nobility did and was comparatively well off, but it was not inclined to surrender its wealth.

hardest hit were the nobility and wealthy merchants who, holding Erik responsible for their misfortune, conspired to dethrone him.

Erik retreated to the island of Gotland in the hope that they would change their minds. Norway would have done so, but the Danish nobles wanted to make a fresh start. The invitation went to Christian of Oldenburg, who thereupon rose from the title of count in an obscure part of Germany to found a dynasty which was to last for more than four centuries. Sweden resisted the choice, but Norway went along with it.

Christian I was almost as short of money as Erik had been. His attempts to make up shortfalls were notoriously at the expense of Norway, the weaker partner. Expected to hand over 60,000 guilders as a dowry for his daughter Margaret's marriage to the heir to the Scottish throne, he mortgaged the Orkney Islands to Scotland for 50,000. When the time came for the wedding, he was still 8,000 guilders short, and so mortgaged Shetland as well. To put 8,000 guilders into perspective, he spent three times that on a trip to Rome a few years later (which he had to borrow from the Hanseatics). The Scots gloated over the deal; not merely the trifling price but that Margaret "deemed it a greater thing to be queen in Scotland than daughter of a king who wears three crowns".

Treacherous murder

Norway's resentment at such exploitation eventually boiled over. On the turn of the 16th century, Knut Alvsson, a Swedish-Norwegian nobleman, led an uprising which created a potentially independent state stretching from Oslo to Bergen. Danish troops were sent to put a stop to it. The outcome, however, was thoroughly dishonourable. Alvsson had established himself in Akershus Castle in Oslo. He was invited to negotiate under a flag of truce and promptly murdered. In the poem *At Akershus*, Ibsen called his death a blow to Norway's heart.

Norwegian resentment at the treatment meted out to Alvsson was exacerbated by punitive taxes to pay for Christian II of Denmark's wars with the restless Swedes. Norwegians were not altogether sorry to see him toppled and bundled off into exile, but they were not ready to extend a welcome to his successor, Frederik I.

Norway was nominally Roman Catholic and there was little interest in the forces of the Reformation which lay behind the tussle for the Danish throne. The country did not have the urban bourgeoisie who elsewhere were the first to adopt Lutheranism. Norway's peasant culture was deeply conservative, not to say backward, so much so that many scholars classify Norway as "medieval" until the early 16th century.

It could be said that the Reformation, when it reached Norway, was the first of the great European cultural swathes that had any real impact on the country. Feudalism passed it by (never a Norwegian knight in armour rescuing damsels

in distress) as did the Renaissance. Most of rural Norway remained doggedly in its past, Christianity providing only a veneer on what were fundamentally old pagan ways.

A new leader

It was at this point that a new Norwegian leader emerged. He was Olav Engelbrektsson, the Archbishop of Trondheim (or Nidaros, as it was then known). Olav raised an army with a view to getting Christian II back. The exiled king was able to muster a fleet with Dutch help and in 1531 set sail for Oslo. A storm scattered the fleet so that only a small part of it went into

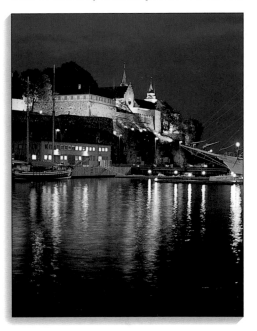

action against Akershus Castle. The attack was futile. Christian was captured and imprisoned, and the Norwegians were forced to acclaim Frederik I as their king.

Christian II was still in prison when Frederik died and was replaced by Christian III, a Protestant. He rounded up the Danish bishops and then ordered the Archbishopric of Trondheim to be abolished, if necessary by force. Olav thought of resisting but, having weighed up the likely repercussions, fled to the Netherlands.

Any further hope of Norwegian independence was squashed by Christian III's 1536 edict demoting the country to the status of a Danish province: "and it shall henceforth neither be nor

---

LEFT: the main entrance to Nidaros Domkirke (Cathedral), Trondheim.
RIGHT: Akershus Festning (Fortress), Oslo.

be called a kingdom in itself." The humbled status was intended to last in perpetuity; in the event it lasted for less than 300 years, culminating not in independence but in an 1814 takeover by Sweden after Norway had become a coveted prize bobbing between its more powerful neighbours.

The loss of political sovereignty under Denmark could not obliterate Norway's separate identity at once. People went on speaking the same language as before and local administration retained many traditional features, but the creeping effects of the Reformation, and Christian III's determination to Danicise Norway, could not be postponed forever.

The Danish influence

Most of the new Protestant clergy were Danes. The revised version of the Bible was in Danish and so were the hymns. Official jobs were invariably given to Danes, who conducted them in the Danish language and reported back to the administration in Copenhagen.

With the spread of schooling and therefore literacy in books imported, naturally, from Denmark (the first printing press was late in arriving in Norway), the anomaly arose of people speaking one language among themselves but reading, albeit with characteristic Norwegian pronunciation, writing and conducting all official business in another. The result was a hybrid

Dano-Norwegian and the genesis of a language dispute which has not been settled to this day.

Norway won a measure of Danish respect in the latter's frequent wars with Sweden, in which the Norwegian contingents acquitted themselves well. Denmark began to realise that Norway could only be governed in its own way. Sweden was forever peering enviously over Denmark's shoulder at Norway. Too much antagonism could result in Norway accepting a more attractive offer of union with Sweden.

A valuable asset

The Norwegian economy began to recover from its long decline, partly as the result of vast shoals of herring which materialised off the coast and partly because of the invention of the water-driven saw, which made exploitation of the timber forests lucrative. Christian IV was far more positive about Norway than his predecessors. He visited the country at least 30 times, making a special trip on learning of the discovery of silver at what is now Kongsberg. He supervised the founding of the town, hence the name, which translates as "King's Mountain". He founded and attached his name to Kristiansand, as he did "Christiania" to the new city built on the site where the former Oslo had burned down in 1624.

Nevertheless, Christian ran the country as if it were a private company. He cracked down on the Hanseatic traders, making them take out Norwegian citizenship, if they had not already done so of their own accord, or leave. Foreigners from other parts were encouraged to bring to Norway their skills, enterprise and, best of all, their money. Under his encouragement, former trading posts became towns in places like Drammen, Moss, Larvik, Mandal and Arendal.

The Norwegians did not always receive these foreigners with uncritical joy. In 1700, for example, a simple fight between two men in Arendal escalated into a brawl which pitched all 900 resident foreigners against everyone else. It lasted a week. Nevertheless, a population which had been reduced by the Black Death to something like 180,000 picked up under Christian's energetic policies, reaching 440,000 in 1665 and nearly 900,000 by 1801.

Not all of Christian IV's successors shared his delicate touch with regard to Norwegian sensibilities. There were periods when the Danish crown was autocratically absolute, and respite depended on having an independently minded Stattholder, the crown agent with responsibility for Norway.

Ulrik Frederik Gyldenløve, the illegitimate son of Frederik III, conscientiously protected his Norwegian charges. He intervened to save peasants from the more rapacious taxes sought by Copenhagen, and he built up the Norwegian armed forces so that at Kvistrum in 1677 they were able to humiliate a far larger force of Swedes. Peter Wessel Tordenskiold became a great

THE DEVIL'S DRINK

The legacy of the zealous Pietism that arrived in Norway in the 18th century can still be felt today, especially when it comes to alcohol.

lous. Gripped by a kind of manic fundamentalism, they despised their folk culture and, particularly in the 19th century when Pietism was still going strong, were encouraged to tear down the ornately carved, wooden stave churches. Confirmation and attendance at church on Sunday were made compulsory.

Looking around them, the Pietists were appalled by the realisation that in their midst, or anyway within the national boundaries, there were still heathens. Thomas von Weston, a superb linguist,

naval hero for many daring feats, the best of which was sailing a small squadron up a fjord (Dynekilen) and destroying a Swedish fleet.

Hellfire and brimstone

As Norway belatedly shed the mantle of medievalism and got to grips with Protestantism, it adopted the faith as zealously as it had once defended paganism. The rural areas, especially, embraced Pietism, real hellfire-and-brimstone stuff which persuaded peasants that their austere existence was actually abominably frivo-

took it on himself to remedy the situation among the Sami (Lapps). Hans Egede went further afield to save souls in Greenland and, although he worked tirelessly, it took him eight years to win his first Innuit convert.

On the other hand, when a liberal wind blew in Copenhagen, it was also felt in Norway. For example, when Christian VII went mad the affairs of state fell into the hands of his physician, a German named Johann Friedrich Struensee. He believed in unrestricted trade, freedom of the press and so on.

Norway was gratified to see the abolition of a trading system which placed a fixed and artificially low value on Norwegian iron imported

LEFT: an old rose-painted *stue* (living room).
ABOVE: a traditional, rural Norwegian Sunday.

into Denmark, whereas Danish corn exports to Norway were sold at whatever the market would bear. Correcting the imbalance helped, but prospects of additional economic reforms ended abruptly when it was discovered that Struensee had been having an affair with Caroline Mathilde, the wife of his deranged patient, and was executed.

One-man enlightenment

Against a backdrop of Pietism and the death penalty for sexual irregularity, one of the first rays of the Enlightenment shone through in the person of Ludvig Holberg. He was born in

Nelson attacks

Co-existence between Denmark and Norway was traumatised from the unlikely quarter of Napoleon Bonaparte. Britain had fallen out with Denmark (and hence Norway) over the Danish alliance with Prussia and Russia. A total of 149 Danish and Norwegian vessels were seized in British ports; in response, a Danish force marched into Hamburg and appropriated British property worth £15 million.

Nelson moved on Copenhagen with a powerful fleet. Danish and Norwegian crews manning a line of blockships put up a spirited defence, and after a six-hour battle Nelson

Bergen but later became a resident of Copenhagen, a playwright, historian and satirist (in Latin) who, according to the distinguished historian T.K. Derry, "in his own generation had no obvious superior in range of intellect except Voltaire". Holberg's impressive output included 26 plays for the newly founded Copenhagen theatre between 1722 and 1727.

Holberg never returned to his home town of Bergen after leaving at the age of 21, and it is a pithy comment on the difficulty of drawing a clear line between specifically Norwegian and Danish history during the four centuries when the two countries were so closely tied that both countries now claim Holberg as their own.

urged the Danish Crown Prince Regent to capitulate, failing which he would have to destroy the blockships "without having the power to save the brave Danes who have defended them". The Prince agreed.

A few years later Napoleon insisted that Denmark-Norway join his continental system and close their ports to British ships. A large British fleet demanded the handing-over of the Danish navy, which Napoleon sorely needed after losing his at Trafalgar, and when this met with refusal, Copenhagen was bombarded with at least 14,000 rounds over three days.

British troops occupied the capital for six weeks, after which they went home with the

Danish fleet and vast quantities of naval stores. The enormity of such an attack on what was a neutral country put Denmark and Norway firmly into Napoleon's camp, a position which required them to join him in attacking Sweden.

The division thus rendered between Sweden and Denmark was bound to have serious consequences. The impotent "pig in the middle" was Norway. The inevitable was set rolling in 1810 when Sweden's King Karl XIII appointed as his heir (of all people, considering the events which had just passed) Jean-Baptiste Bernadotte, one of Napoleon's marshals. Bernadotte improved his Swedish credentials by changing his name to Karl Johan and succeeded to the throne in 1818.

Karl Johan conceived a plan whereby Russia and Britain would support Swedish claims on Norway. They agreed, with the result that Norwegian ports were blockaded to secure a "voluntary" union with Sweden. The Danish Crown Prince Christian Frederik tried to rally Norwegian loyalty, among other things by agreeing to let Norway have the national bank it had long craved. In the end, the decision did not rest in either Norwegian or Danish hands. Union between Sweden and Norway was imposed by the Peace of Kiel (following Napoleon's defeat at Leipzig) in 1814.

Battle for the throne

Christian Frederik was not going to surrender Norway without a struggle. He entertained the idea of getting himself popularly acclaimed as king (he thought his chances best in Trondheim) but the feeling among the population at large was that the Danish line had renounced its sovereignty and the Norwegians were now entitled to choose their own king.

In April 1814, an assembly of 37 farmers, 16 businessmen and 59 bureaucrats met in Eidsvoll to decide what that future should be. The constitution they prepared was signed on 17 May, still the biggest day of the year in Norway. On the same day a new king was elected; it was the tenacious Christian Frederik. Sweden would have none of it. The Norwegians fought well in a one-sided contest but Christian Frederik soon had to sue for peace. Karl Johan stepped forward to occupy his double throne. ❑

> **EIDSVOLL CONSTITUTION**
>
> On 17 May 1814 Norway became a "free, independent and an indivisible realm" according to the new constitution, but it would take a further 91 years for these words to become a reality.

LEFT: the old mining town of Røros, Sør-Trøndelag.
ABOVE: a northern graveyard on Andøya, Vesterålen.

UNION WITH SWEDEN

Through such artists as Ibsen, Grieg and Munch, the voice of an increasingly restless and independent-minded Norway could be heard beyond its own borders

Divorce from Denmark was followed by a quarrel over the division of joint assets and liabilities. The assets were Iceland, Greenland and the Faroes which, Norway claimed, were Norwegian colonies long before marriage with Denmark. The liabilities were the Danish-Norwegian national debt.

Who owed what? The Norwegian position was not only that Denmark alone should shoulder the burden but that compensation was due to Norway for centuries of exploitation. Assuming powers granted under the Treaty of Kiel which had brought about the new union, Karl Johan declared that Norway would pay off some of the debt. The matter of the colonies was not finally resolved until 1931, when the International Court at The Hague found in favour of Denmark.

Two kingdoms

Friction between Karl Johan and the Norwegian half of his kingdom was present right from the start: he envisaged a gradual merging of the two kingdoms, while Norway was determined to consolidate the independence ratified by the 1814 constitution.

A constitutional battle took place over a bill to abolish all noble titles and privileges. Again and again the Storting presented the bill – and the king refused to sanction it. The constitution said he could refuse a bill only twice; the third time it automatically became law. Karl Johan objected strongly to this limitation on his authority which did not exist in Sweden.

A fundamental principle was at stake and the dispute was not to be resolved easily. Indeed, it remained the biggest bone of contention for the life of the union and, as much as anything else, was the author of its eventual dissolution. Norwegian pride was prickly. Merchant ships could fly the Norwegian flag close to home but not in waters notoriously under the sway of North

African pirates. Sweden had bought off the pirates but the immunity extended only to the Swedish flag; if Norwegian ships wanted to take advantage of it, they had to switch flags.

Sweden's dogged refusal to allow Norway its own diplomatic and consular representation abroad was not only an insult but a practical

handicap because the Norwegian merchant fleet was well on its way to becoming, by 1880, the third largest in the world. Its far-flung crews wanted and needed a purely Norwegian diplomatic service.

Oslo once again

Karl Johan was adept at making a timely concession to court popularity, and the welcome he received on visiting Christiania in 1838 was probably sincere, as was the public grief when he died six years later. Although changing Christiania's name back to Oslo obliterated a Danish memory, the capital was, and is, content to leave its main street named after Karl Johan.

LEFT: Eidsvoll, where the Norwegian constitution was signed on 17 May 1814.
RIGHT: King Karl Johan XIV.

The Great Exodus

One thousand years after the first Norwegian Vikings turned their longships towards the west, pushing out as far as North America, a second wave of Norwegians began to cast their eyes in the same direction.

The motives of these new emigrants were similar – lack of opportunity and poverty – but they had none of the warlike excitement of the earlier exodus. These new "Vikings" sought a place where they could work and prosper in peace rather than a place for exploration and conquest.

Yet the first emigrant boat, the 16-metre (54-ft) sloop *Restauration*, crammed full with 52 crew and passengers, must have been scarcely more seaworthy than the superbly built longships. But these early "sloopers", who sailed from Stavanger in July 1825, were idealistic and highly motivated. The leader, Lars Larsen Geilane, was a Quaker and there were members of the religious Haugeans sect among the crew. Their intention to found a classless society where they could follow their own religion had been further encouraged when the previous year another Norwegian pioneer, Cleng Peerson, returned with reports of the promised land.

The *Restauration* reached New York in October of the same year and these farming people, mostly from Rogaland, lost no time in settling on land bought for them by Cleng Peerson at Kendall on the shores of Lake Ontario. This settlement became a staging post on the road to Illinois, where many Norwegians made their homes.

When the *Restauration* left in 1825, Norway's population was only one million, yet the next three generations sent 750,000 Norwegians to North America, reflecting a population increase at home rather than an emptying of the Norwegian countryside, though early industrialists began to campaign against such a dribbling away of potential labour.

The early "sloopers" had more in common with the Pilgrim Fathers who left Plymouth in the *Mayflower* two centuries earlier than with those emigrants who came after them. The main motive among the second and later waves of country people, was good land and good farming prospects rather than religious or political repression. To be an *odelsbonde*, who owned his own land, was to be a free man and the goal of every Norwegian peasant. The American merchant fleets were also eager to make use of skilful Norwegian seamen.

The newcomers prospered and regular letters home, reports, and Norwegian visitors from the New World increased the fever. The letters were printed in newspapers all over the country and one or two mid-Western American states began to use agents to encourage emigration.

By the middle of the 1830s new emigrants and some of the original "sloopers" had moved on to Illinois. Forty years later, their numbers had increased to more than 12,500. The 1862 Homestead Law, which granted land to immigrants, turned the early trickle into a steady flow, and Cleng Peerson founded Norwegian settlements in Iowa.

For many patriotic Norwegians it became *de rigueur* to help the expansion. The great violinist Ole Bull had a well-intentioned but crashing failure with a planned settlement, "Oleana", in Pennsylvania. He was too far from his Norwegian farming roots. The soil was ungrateful, communications impossible, and Bull lost more than $40,000.

Later, Norwegians also settled in Canada; but by the 1930s emigration had dwindled to a trickle. Yet the Norwegian influence was strong in the places where they settled. Today, the overt "Norwegian-ness" may have gone, but anyone who doubts it still exists need only read Garrison Keillor's winsome tales of life around Lake Wobegon. ❑

LEFT: this boy, aged eight, crossed the Atlantic alone in 1907 after his mother died.

His successor, Oskar I, immediately tried to placate Norway through gestures such as his title which, locally, became King of Norway and Sweden, rather than vice versa. He also agreed to a new flag which gave equal prominence to the Swedish and Norwegian colours.

Norwegian politics in the 19th century were dominated at first by the Venstre party which carried the banner of separatism and rallied against the royal veto. Its leader, Johan Sverdrup, was a lawyer who worked at creating an alliance between urban radicals and wealthy farmers. Their interests were too divergent, however, and the party split, leaving room for

The farmers' grip on the national heart-strings, and purse, has never been relinquished.

Putting peasants on a pedestal, however, did not ameliorate the hard facts of life. Emigration to the United States began in 1825, although statistics reveal the irony that emigration was highest when the economic conditions at home were good, and lowest when they were bad. Perhaps it was a case of being too poor in the lean times to pay the fare. In 1882 a record 29,000 Norwegians left, and by 1910 there were more than 400,000 people of Norwegian birth in the United States, their numbers growing right the way through to World War I.

the strong labour movement which characterised most of the 20th century.

It dawned on poorer farmers and peasants who had previously let the land-owning and merchant classes get on with government, that their special interests, especially a reduction in taxes, could be advanced only if they too became involved in the political process. They were assisted by a general mood in the country of national romanticism, a Nordic adaptation of the French philosopher Rousseau's belief in the nobility of savages. The Norwegian peasant farmer was portrayed as the salt of the earth.

ABOVE: emigrants leave Stavanger for the New World.

The arts flourish

The rise of nationalism throughout Europe produced in Norway an unprecedented, and subsequently unequalled flowering of the arts. Henrik Ibsen (1828–1906) and Alexander Kielland (1849–1906), giants among an extraordinarily talented assortment of writers – not forgetting composers, such as Edvard Grieg (1843–1907), and the painter Edvard Munch (1863–1944) – presented the world with a clearer insight into Norway than was available from the best-selling romantic writers.

It may be worth summarising, for strong stomachs, the plot of one such work, *Thelma: A Norwegian Princess*, by Miss Marie Corelli, which ran to no fewer than 47 editions. Sir Philip Bruce-Errington encounters a crazy dwarf who lives in a cavern illuminated by antique Etruscan lamps. Sir Philip and the dwarf converse comfortably in English but that does not prevent Sir Philip from being amazed by the dwarf's intellect, when he correctly guesses his nationality.

Sir Philip then makes the acquaintance of old Olaf Guldmar, Princess Thelma's father. He is a wretched peasant farmer who is also fluent in English. Sir Philip is understandably full of admiration and respect when he discovers Olaf's library. It contains, for example, the

which appeared in the *Spectator* magazine in 1872 about a previously unheard of Norwegian poet named Ibsen who had written "short songs of irregular measure after the manner of Heine". The poet wrote a note of thanks to the writer, Edmund Gosse, adding "I shall consider myself most fortunate if you decide to translate one or more of my books", a modest hint that he may have written more than poems.

Poet and playwright

At home Ibsen and others like Bjørnstjerne Bjørnson (1832–1910) were leading lights in agitation against Danish domination in the arts.

works of Shakespeare, Byron, Keats, Plutarch and Chapman's translation of Homer. It turns out that he is an accomplished Latin scholar, although in religious belief still a devout pagan, "by Valhalla!" being his favourite oath.

Not a moment too soon, Olaf feels death coming on and, following custom, is carried aboard his vessel which is set on fire and pushed out to sea. "He raised his arms as though in ecstasy: 'Glory! – joy! – victory!' And, like a noble tree struck down by lightning, he fell – dead."

That the reality of Norway might be different from the picture conveyed above was first mooted, at least in England, by a short article

The campaign included, for example, that Danish actors should no longer be employed on the Norwegian stage.

Henrik Johan Ibsen was born in the small town of Skien in Telemark *(see page 207)*. His father's financial indiscretions plunged the family into poverty, and Ibsen was apprenticed at an early age to a chemist in the even smaller town of Grimstad. His first poems, with titles like *Resignation*, *Doubt* and *The Corpse's Ball*, give a clue to the majestic gloom – punctuated, nevertheless by delicious wit – of his later work.

After working in the theatre in Bergen, he joined the Christiania Norske Theater (in Oslo), which had been founded to promote specifically Norwegian theatre. He fared miserably with one failure after another, poor health and no money. In the depths of depression he began to question the deplorable position of the creative artist in Norwegian society and that, ironically, put him on the road to better things. *The Pretenders*, first performed in 1864, was a great success and helped him to a travelling scholarship. He went abroad, first to Italy, and did not live in Norway again for another 27 years.

> **IBSEN ABROAD**
>
> According to George Bernard Shaw, Ibsen's influence in England "is almost equal to the influence which three revolutions, six crusades, a couple of foreign invasions and an earthquake would produce."

The plays for which he is best remembered were produced from about 1877 onwards. The first of these, *Pillars of Society*, broke new ground in dealing with the untruth and humbug of a small provincial town. In creating any number of great female roles, Ibsen touched on subjects that audiences and critics were not ready for. If his work was controversial at home, it was considered outrageous when eventually it travelled abroad. According to *The Daily Telegraph* in London the first overseas production of *Ghosts* was "positively abominable... a dirty act done publicly, a (lavatory) with all its doors and windows open ... gross, almost putrid indecorum ... crapulous stuff".

There were other points of view, however, like that of the essayist Havelock Ellis and of George Bernard Shaw who summarised Ibsen's importance to the English theatre with: "The Norman conquest was a mere nothing compared with the Norwegian Conquest."

While the Norwegian element in the work of the great playwright Ludvig Holberg in the previous century could hardly be told apart from the Danish, there was no ambiguity about Ibsen. As a curious footnote, however, Ibsen once wrote to a friend in England saying that "there are very strong traces in me of Scotch descent. But this is only a feeling – perhaps only a wish that it were so."

Battle of wills

Ibsen's strong sense of national identity was mirrored in the political events swirling around him. Problems within the union with Sweden came to a head in 1905 over the long-running dispute about diplomatic representation. The government wanted its own consular service; King Oskar II refused. The government then argued that, if it resigned and the king was unable to obtain an alternative government, his royal power would effectively have lapsed. It would then revert to the Storting, which would choose a new king. The Storting agreed to this plan.

Oskar was hurt and the Swedish government outraged. Neither would have been placated

by a plebiscite which showed 368,208 in favour of breaking away from Sweden and only 184 against. The "compromise" reached in 1905 was in truth a surrender to Norwegian demands: Oskar's abdication and Norwegian independence. The king's parting shot was that no member of his house would be allowed to accept the vacated throne even if it were offered. This was only in part petulance. Oskar was privately convinced that an independent Norway was bound to collapse and whoever was then king would thus be discredited. When that happened, an unsullied member of his house would, of course, be standing by to answer the call. That call was never heard. ❏

LEFT: an early drawing of Oslo's Stortinget (Parliament).
RIGHT: King Oskar II.

AN INDEPENDENT MODERN COUNTRY

Invaded by Germany, then caught up in the Cold War, Norway has passed
through difficult times to emerge as an international peace-broker

The Prime Minister who led Norway to independence was Christian Michelsen, a Bergen solicitor who founded one of the biggest shipping companies in Norway and was by 1903 a member of the government. In the meantime, he had formed a breakaway group in Bergen of "liberals" from the Radical Left.

Michelsen's initial modest aim was to settle the issue of whether Norway should have its own consuls abroad, which would finally destroy the union with Sweden; but by 1904 he was warning the Swedes not to assume that if negotiations failed this time, they could be resumed. Michelsen had recognised the way Norwegian public opinion was running and the support the cause was getting from such famous Norwegians as the explorer Fridtjof Nansen (who later became Norwegian Ambassador in London) and the writer Bjørnstjerne Bjørnson. Soon Michelsen was heading a cabinet that included ministers from a wide range of parties and of many shades of opinion.

With independence established in 1905 and King Håkon VII on the throne, Michelsen quickly left the stormy waters of politics for a calmer and more profitable life in his shipping business, though he remained an active elder statesman until his death in 1925.

No foreign policy

In the long years of struggle, Bjørnson had claimed that "the foreign policy of Norway should be to have no foreign policy", and immediately after independence, the aim of all parties was to avoid entanglement in the affairs of the Great Powers. But, despite its determined neutrality, World War I had the ironic effect of throwing Norway and Sweden back into one another's arms. "A new union, not of the old sort, but a union of heartfelt understanding", was the Swedish king's description, "to maintain the neutrality of the respective kingdoms in relation to all the belligerent powers."

Norway did well out of its neutrality, at least for the first two years of the war. Germany was willing to pay top prices for all the fish Norway could supply, which attracted British attention and led to a secret agreement, backed by the threat to cut off supplies of British oil and coal, under which Britain would buy most of the fish itself. Norway, in return, would not export vital copper pyrites to Germany, but otherwise it was free to trade with both sides.

Those lucky enough to get a share of this trade, and of the domestic black market, flaunted their overnight fortunes in such a way that workers on fixed wages, which were forever falling behind rampant inflation, became rebellious. Employers retaliated with lockouts, and the government was forced to introduce compulsory arbitration.

German submarine warfare put a damper on profiteering. Most of the Norwegian merchant fleet was under charter to Britain and by the end of the war half of it, together with 2,000 crew members, was lost. In absolute terms only Britain lost more of its shipping. The intervention of the United States also made matters worse. The Americans demanded big cuts in trade with Germany before agreeing to make supplies available to Norway.

At the end of the war the neutral countries had little say in deciding the terms of peace. Despite its heavy losses the Norwegian merchant navy received no compensation in the shape of ships from the confiscated German navy, and it was 10 years before injured seamen and the families of those killed received any compensation from the German government.

THE NANSEN PASSPORT

Devised by Fridtjof Nansen, this "passport" offered those people made stateless by World War I a means of official identification.

neutral countries just two months after the League was founded to seek membership.

Norway, temperamentally against alliances, was fiercely divided and it was not until 1920 that the Storting finally voted for membership of the League, Norway's first real move into internationalism. Nansen, who had been so influential in the struggle for Norwegian independence, now had international links to the US, the Soviet Union and elsewhere, and became active in the League, particularly in the slow repatriation of nearly

Nansen and the League

During the war the Scandinavian monarchs had met to discuss and set up committees to review the position of neutral countries when hostilities ceased. Under Fridtjof Nansen, Norway formed an Association for the League of Nations and drafted a potential constitution. But, as the war ended, the great powers were not inclined to take much notice of mere neutrals. They themselves laid down the rules and allowed the

PRECEDING PAGES: a factory in Christiania (Oslo) producing iron stairs (*circa* 1895).
LEFT: King Håkon VII.
ABOVE: the Royal Family with their ski instructor.

half a million prisoners-of-war from Russia. He later donated his own Nobel Peace Prize money for similar work for Russian and Armenian refugees. He was still working on this at the time of his death in 1930.

But in 1920, of the Storting's 20 votes against membership of the League of Nations, 16 came from the steadily growing Labour Party which, at the time, took most of its principles and goals from the ideas behind the Russian Revolution.

Briefly in credit

Although Norway was one of the creditor nations when the war ended, the cavalier business atmosphere of the war years carried over as financial recklessness, if not ignorance. In very short order the country was further into debt than it had so recently been in credit.

By 1921 conditions had deteriorated into a full-blown economic depression with more than a million tons of shipping laid up, free-spending local authorities in difficulty and, unthinkably to Norwegians, one of the biggest banks going bankrupt in spite of secret state support.

The rise of Labour

Storms and controversies over prohibition caused the downfall of three different cabinets. The steadily growing Labour Party became

A lock-out at Norsk Hydro produced not only the most notorious incident in the history of Norwegian industrial relations (police and troops fighting demonstrators) but also the rise to prominence of a figure as shameful in Norwegian memory as anyone since Erik Bloodaxe.

The defence minister who ordered the troops in was Vidkun Quisling, and he was soon accusing Labour of plotting an armed revolution. Quisling was largely discredited in his own country by 1939. At that time he was in Berlin for reasons that were soon to become very clear.

By 1933, the economic crisis was so bad that the unlikely alliance of the Labour Party with

more revolutionary in its beliefs, and passed a resolution reserving the right to use "revolutionary action in the struggle for the economic liberation of the working classes". The point having been made, militancy declined and by the end of the decade the Party had turned its attention back to parliamentary rule. In the 1927 elections, in spite of fragmentation, it became the biggest party in the Storting.

The Wall Street crash of 1929 compounded the economic misery. A third of all trade unionists were already out of work when employers tried to reduce wages which, in spite of nearly a decade of economic turmoil, were still very high compared to most European countries.

the Agrarian (Farmers') Party put a Labour Prime Minister into power. He was Johan Nygaardsvold, with lengthy experience in the Storting. He was Prime Minister from 1935 with a direct responsibility for creating employment and, by 1939, the average day's wage had risen by 15 percent.

Precarious neutrality

When World War II broke out in September 1939 Norway proclaimed immediate neutrality, but had taken almost no precautions to defend herself. Perhaps Nygaardsvold was too immersed in his economic renaissance. He remained Prime Minister until 1945 but in the recriminations and resultant inquiry that followed the end of the war, he was deemed partly to blame for not making adequate preparations.

The first warning signs came from the Allied side, with Britain complaining that its ships were being sunk by Germany in Norwegian territorial waters. Also, German ships were being given free access to strategic iron-ore from the port of Narvik. The ancient Norwegian fleet was in no position to keep territorial waters neutral, so the British suggested mining them.

The dilemma was highlighted by the well-

UNPREPARED

When World War II broke out, Norway called up just 7,000 men and its coastal defences were only half-manned.

government asked why Norway had been unable to prevent German abuse of its neutral waters, and Germany posed the same question, but the other way round.

Invasion by sea

Britain unilaterally began laying mines along the Norwegian coastline and, on the very day Norway lodged a protest – 8 April 1940 – German forces were on the high seas bound for Norway. Once the invasion was under way, the German minister in Oslo sent a note to say that Germany was only occupying a

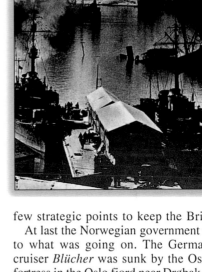

known *Altmark* affair. The *Altmark*, an auxiliary to the battleship *Graf Spee*, was on its way to Germany with 300 captured British seamen when it sought refuge in Norwegian waters near Egersund. The British Royal Navy was alerted to its presence and charged into the fjord to rescue the men while two small Norwegian vessels looked on, making vain protests. The Norwegian government complained to Britain about violation of its neutrality. The British

LEFT: the meeting between Vidkun Quisling and Adolf Hitler prior to World War II.
ABOVE LEFT: strategic map from World War II.
ABOVE RIGHT: the struggle for Narvik, 1941.

few strategic points to keep the British out.

At last the Norwegian government woke up to what was going on. The German heavy cruiser *Blücher* was sunk by the Oscarsborg fortress in the Oslo fjord near Drøbak, and two creaking Norwegian destroyers boldly took on a much larger German force at Narvik.

The Storting granted the government full powers "to take whatever decisions might be necessary to ensure the best interests of the country", the point on which many a debate would later hinge. On 10 April the Germans showed their hand. Quisling, whose National Unity party commanded all of 1.8 percent of the electorate, was their choice as new prime

The Heroes of Telemark

The most celebrated act of resistance in Norway during World War II was the sabotage of the Vemork heavy water plant at Rjukan, in Telemark, in February 1943. No visitor to Rjukan, dwarfed and darkened by mountains all round, could fail to be awed by the audacity of the saboteurs. More importantly, the production of heavy water in the plant, if it had not been stopped, could conceivably have aided the German development of

an atomic bomb. The operation was originally planned for a joint force of Norwegian volunteers and British commandos in two towed gliders. It ended disastrously when both gliders and one of the aircraft towing them crashed 160 km (100 miles) from Rjukan.

The next attempt was an all-Norwegian affair. "Gunnerside", the code name for six men who had been trained in Scotland, parachuted on to a frozen lake where they were supposed to join up with "Swallow", an advance party on the ground. The first person they bumped into was a reindeer hunter. He was later released with food and money on the promise that he would reveal nothing. Once the parties had linked up, they skied to the ridge above Rjukan for the perilous descent on foot. They slithered down, up to their waists in snow. Just after midnight, the covering party took up positions while the six-man demolition team cut a chain on the gates and crept forward to the basement of the concrete building where the most vital equipment and the heavy water storage tanks were located. All wore British uniforms and were agreed that no lights would be carried; weapons would be unloaded to avoid the accidental discharge of arms and anyone captured would take his own life.

As the basement was locked, the best way in appeared to be a funnel carrying cables and piping. Two of the men went through it. The solitary Norwegian guard was astonished, but agreed to lead them to vital components.

"I had placed half the charges in position when there was a crash of broken glass behind me," one of the pair wrote later. The other members of the team, not realising that their leaders had managed to get in, had decided to smash in through a window. With the rest of the charges laid, the six began a rapid withdrawal. They were nonplussed by the co-operative guard who, understandably getting out as well while the going was good, implored to be let in again. He had forgotten his glasses!

The request was granted, but the delay meant that the party had only gone a few yards when there was what members later variously described as "a cataclysmic explosion" and "a tiny, insignificant pop".

Five members of the parachute team reached Sweden after a 400-km (250-mile) journey on skis in indescribably difficult conditions; the sixth stayed on for another year. Of the Swallow party, an irrepressible character named Claus Helberg had the liveliest time. He was chased through the mountains by German soldiers whom he encountered, but escaped after an exchange of shots. Then he fell over a cliff and broke an arm. The next morning he walked into a German patrol but had a good enough story to be taken to a hotel to await treatment. Most of the hotel guests (but not the injured Norwegian) were turned out of their rooms to make way for Reichskommissar Joseph Terboven (the Nazi who ruled Norway) and his entourage. Later, and through no fault of his own, he was bundled along with the remaining guests "into a bus and sent off to the Grini concentration camp". Helberg jumped from the bus and escaped. In due course he turned up in Britain, reporting for further duties. ❑

LEFT: Kirk Douglas in the film *The Heroes of Telemark*.

minister. The government, which had moved itself from Oslo to Trysil, repeatedly refused to comply, and its defiance was repaid with a German bombing attack on the meeting place.

Norway's only hope against such lopsided odds lay in the Allies. From Britain's point of view, Narvik was the key because of the iron-ore traffic. The British Royal Navy went into action against German naval units in the area and destroyed them. A combined force of Norwegians, British, French and Poles fought to regain control of the city itself and on 28 May succeeded in doing so.

Earlier, on 14 and 15 April, other Allied troops had landed near Trondheim. They were joined by small Norwegian units. They put up a plucky fight but, practically without any air cover against the Luftwaffe, took a pasting from above. Towns where there was a British presence were bombed to ruin: Åndalsnes, Namsos, Steinkjer and Mosjøen.

The fight for Norway was overshadowed, however, by the German steamroller in western Europe and, with what were seen to be greater needs there, the Allied forces withdrew, leaving Norway alone.

The king and government, evacuated to the north and ready to fight on, decided that the best course of action was to decamp to Britain. On 7 June 1940 they boarded a British cruiser.

Reprisals begin

A Nazi, Josef Terboven, was despatched to Norway as Reichskommissar. Quisling was appalled; he had expected to be appointed Führer, in which capacity he would then conclude peace with Germany and mobilise Norwegian forces on its side. Terboven had little time for Quisling, but the latter had friends in Berlin who arranged to have him appointed "Minister President". As such, Quisling ordered all children between the ages of 10 and 18 to join his version of the Hitler Youth. His plans for the Nazification of the civil service, courts, all professional bodies and trade unions were in every instance fiercely rejected.

Resistance met with grim reprisals. Two

RIGHT: Vidkun Quisling inspecting German troops in Berlin.

THE "SHETLAND BUS"

The old Viking character was alive in the small boats that regularly made the crossing between Shetland and Norway, keeping links open with the exiled king and government in Britain.

---

trade union leaders, Viggo Hansteen and Rolf Wickstrøm, were shot; the rector of Oslo University was arrested. A steady flow of prisoners, including 1,300 uncooperative teachers, arrived at Grini, the concentration camp established outside Oslo.

The most summary reprisals were meted out to members of the military underground, Milorg, a nucleus of survivors of the 1940 fighting augmented by volunteers and armed by clandestine shipments from Britain.

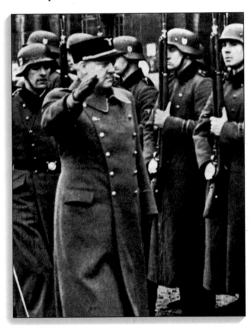

Telavåg, a village near Bergen, was razed to the ground when the German's discovered it to be an assembly point for a clandestine ferry service, the "Shetland Bus", between Norway and Britain. The village men were deported to Germany, the women and children interned. A group of 18 men waiting in Ålesund for the trip to Britain were found and shot. The most famous of the resistance operations was conducted against the heavy water factory at Rjukan in Telemark.

Celebration party

The final chapter of the Occupation was played out by German troops retreating from Finland through Finnmark in northern Norway. They adopted a scorched-earth policy which utterly destroyed many towns and villages. The inhabitants were herded into fishing boats to find their own way to the south.

The Germans were still very strong in Norway while their forces elsewhere capitulated – the army alone numbered 350,000. Fears that the whole country might be put to the torch were laid to rest only when they surrendered on 7 May 1945. The gates of Grini were thrown open and thousands streamed out to join what was undoubtedly the biggest street party ever held in Oslo. It was still going strong a week later when Crown Prince Olav returned, five

only now being replaced, and many of the small northern towns still have an austere anonymity.

Rising standards

Fast economic expansion and many crash programmes led to large investment and overemployment, but it provided a rising standard of living that climbed faster and farther than most countries in Europe. By the early 1960s Norway used more electricity per head than any other country in the world and only three people in every thousand in remote areas had no supply. The mercantile marine had made good its wartime shipping losses by 1949 and

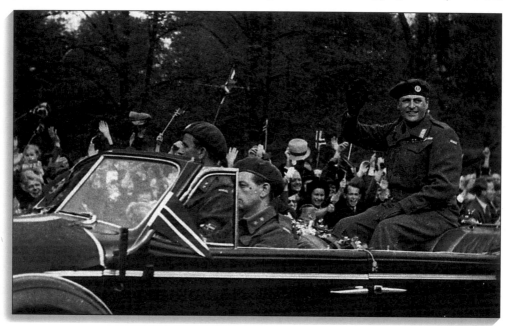

years to the day after his reluctant departure.

Cleaning up after the war concontrated on Quisling's prosecution. Charges were brought against 50,000 people, many for petty crimes rather than full-scale collaboration. The courts were not unduly harsh, perhaps sensing that participation in Quisling's so-called "NS" would remain a stigma. Some 25 were executed, including Quisling and two of his ministers.

After that necessary purging, Norway's most pressing needs were to replace what had been destroyed during the war, and to modernise and expand industry and the economy. The whole of northern Norway had been so heavily devastated that in some cases areas of hasty rebuilding are

tonnage tripled within 15 years. By the 1970s Norway was almost overwhelmed by the riches it was receiving from the oil industry.

All this went along with over 20 years of socialist government, which introduced comprehensive social welfare services, Scandinavian style, and much state control of industry. But this was no far-left Labour Party in the style of its post-World War I predecessors, and many shared its belief in an equal society and care for all.

In keeping with similar parties in Sweden and Denmark, post-war Norwegian socialism had been middle-of-the-road, led first by Einar Gerhardsen, who had been a prominent Resistance worker, then Oscar Torp, and Trygve Brattel. In recent years, the best-known Norwegian prime minister, ranking high in international esteem, has been Gro Harlem Brundtland. She was appointed Prime Minister for the time in 1981. At 41, she was the youngest person ever to hold the office, and the first woman. In total, she held the post for more than 10 years before stepping down in 1996. In 1998 she became Director-General of the World Health Organization. In 2001, however, the Labour Party, which had dominated Norwegian politics for 65 years, suffered a historic defeat. The new

BRUNTLAND REPORT

Norway's Gro Harlem Brundtland was responsible for "Our Common Future", the United Nations' report on world environmental issues.

International links

In 1945 Norway was one of the founding signatories of the United Nations, and a former Norwegian Foreign Minister, Trygve Lie, became its first secretary-general. Lie held the office during the first hopeful years and continued to do so into the Korean War, in which United Nation troops took an active fighting role for the first and last time. Norway provided and staffed a field hospital in Korea. Since then some 32,000 Norwegians have worn a UN blue beret. Norway has continued its com-

centre-right government has pursued a policy of privatisation and concentrated spending on health, education and pensions.

The attitude of King Olav V, who reigned between 1957 and 1991, also helped to keep Norway tranquil. King Olav took his father's motto of "All for Norway". When he died in 1991 his son Harald V succeeded him to the throne. Like his father, he is interested in sports and liked by his people.

LEFT: Crown Prince Olav (later King Olav V) returns to Norway at the end of the war.
ABOVE: for years Lenin's likeness looked across the border from Russia.

mitment to internationalism and peace, notably as broker in the 1993 Israeli-Palestinian peace proposals. Like the other Scandinavian nations, it has concentrated very much on human rights, humanitarian help and environmental issues. The important role played by this small country has not gone unrecognised: at the end of 2000, Norway was elected by the General Assembly to serve as a member of the Security Council for a two-year term commencing in 2001.

Joining NATO was more problematic. Norway saw its role as bridging the Cold War divide, and the country had no particular reason to fear Russia. Unlike Sweden, Norway had never been at war with Russia. The Russians had recently acted as liberators in Finnmark, and the two countries were, in fact, negotiating joint occupation of Spitsbergen.

Nevertheless, for most of the war years Trygve Lie had been advocating an alliance with the great Atlantic Powers for his "seafaring people", rather than with any power in Europe. The fate of Czechoslovakia, a country which also saw itself as a bridge-builder until the Iron Curtain came down behind it, convinced the doubters that Norway's security depended on more tangible Western links than would be afforded by Swedish-style neutrality. As NATO's most north-easterly outpost, with a short 196-km (122-mile)

border with Russia, Norway inevitably walked a tightrope between the super powers. Soviet "merchant ships" visited the northern sea coast and unaccountably needed lengthy, unspecified repairs which kept them in harbour for months. Ships of the Soviet Northern Fleet, based on the Kola peninsula, were a common sight in the North Atlantic when crossing to Iceland.

There were never any major incidents, and, long before *glasnost*, Norway turned a philosophical face to its massive neighbour. Since the break-up of the Soviet Union, Norway has been more concerned about the environmental threat presented by out-dated nickel works, nuclear power stations and nuclear waste from decommissioned submarines and other vessels of the former Soviet Northern Fleet.

Maintaining independence

The debate over whether to join the European Community aroused great passions, especially among farmers and fishermen who believed that membership would end their subsidies. The Storting was generally in favour of applying for membership along with Denmark and Britain, partners in the European Free Trade Association (EFTA), but the first approaches were rebuffed by an imperious General Charles de Gaulle.

A referendum was organised in 1972 to gauge public opinion on whether another attempt ought to be made. There was never any doubting where the farmers and rural Norway as a whole would stand. In the event, the country opposed joining by a vote of 52.5 percent.

In 1993 the anti-European Centre Party of farmers gained ground but not enough to stop Gro Harlem Brundtland taking the Labour Party back to power. Sweden and Finland having voted to join Denmark in the European Union, she felt confident enough to hold another referendum on membership in 1994, warning that, with oil and gas revenues rapidly declining, Norway could no longer afford to stay out in the cold. But again the country voted no, by an even narrower margin than in 1972. Having been ruled by Denmark, Sweden and the Nazis, Norwegians seemed determined to hang on to every shred of their hard-won independence.

Although the opposite sides of the 1994 EU debate were unyielding, the situation normalised fairly quickly once the vote was over, but the issue continues to be hotly debated with poles indicating a swing towards a "yes" vote. Meanwhile, the Agreement on the European Economic Area (EEA), signed by the EU and EFTA countries in 1992, ensures Norwegian participation in the future of the EEA, gives it access to the EU market and opens the door to further co-operation.

In 2001, Norway signed the Schengen Agreement allowing citizens of other Schengen countries to travel without passports. The centre-right government elected in September 2001 has had to relax the immigration laws in the face of labour shortages at home. So, Norway is gradually becoming more outward looking. ❑

LEFT: Mother Teresa receiving the Nobel Peace Prize in 1979.

Norway and its Neighbours

I f you walked into a room and met three Scandinavians, it would be hard to tell which was the Norwegian, which the Dane and which the Swede. They look alike, have similar interests, and seem to speak the same language, even if the accent is somewhat different.

The written languages, all based on Old Norse, are so similar they are easily understood by all, and Scandinavian Air Service, the airline shared by the three countries, solves communication problems by allowing its crews to use their own language. This works well when a crew is Norwegian, but less well with Danes and Swedes who sometimes find each other incomprehensible.

This Scandinavian family is often taken to include Finland, though the Finns are of a different race with a language related to Hungarian – and that only marginally. In any event, all four countries are part of the Nordic group, which includes Iceland, the autonomous territories of the Faroes, Greenland and the Åland Islands in the Gulf of Bothnia.

Like all families, Scandinavians have the usual squabbles, jealousies, misunderstandings and false images of one another that come out of close proximity. To other Scandinavians, Norwegians are "blue-eyed" or naive, often the butt of innocuous jokes, yet both Swedes and Danes are astonished to learn that similar jokes are told by Norwegians against them. The family analogy continues in that the Danes tend to look on Norway as a younger brother, with all that that implies.

Sweden, with which Norway shares a 1,700-km (1,000-mile) border, is often looked on by Norway (and to a lesser extent by Denmark) as an elder brother, with allegations of arrogance and insensitivity from the smaller countries and a tendency for the larger to think it "knows best". But since Norway discovered oil in 1969, the big-brother attitude has taken a knock, and left Sweden looking at Norway with a degree of wonder and envy. The image of Norway as the junior partner is partly due to the fact that, after 500 years ruled first by Denmark then Sweden, the present Norwegian state is less than a century old, though Norway has been a nation for as long as any Scandinavian country.

RIGHT: conscripts undergoing winter training in the far north of the country.

Norway's only non-Nordic neighbour is Russia. The two countries co-exist without much friction on Spitsbergen (Svalbard), the remote northern islands, best known for coal, bird and plant life, and the sealers and whalers of former days.

In the days of the Soviet Union they were at odds over their joint border in the far northern Barents Sea, where the two countries are face to face on a dividing line more than 1,700 km (1,000 miles) long. Norway favours a border on the median line equidistant between the two countries, but their Russian neighbours have wanted to adopt a sector principle. The area under dispute is as big as Belgium, Switzerland and Austria com-

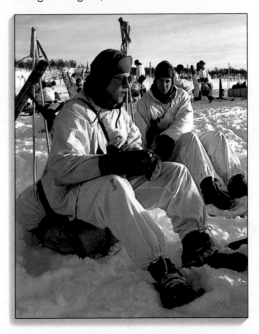

bined, and the Russian proposals would give Russia control of larger fish stocks and oil reserves.

During World War II, when only Sweden was neutral, the Scandinavian countries did their best to help one another, although neither Norway nor Sweden has yet managed to forget that Sweden allowed German troops to pass through its country on their way to attack Norway. Many Finnish children left for homes in Sweden, and that country also became an escape route from Norway. At the end of the war, Norway, Denmark and Iceland became members of NATO, Sweden continued to be non-aligned, and Finland (stuck in an uneasy position between the eastern and western blocs) declared itself neutral. ❑

WHO ARE THE NORWEGIANS?

Ask a visitor what defines a Norwegian and you might get a general description of a Scandinavian. While some of the stereotypes ring true, differences abound

One character in a Hans Christian Andersen story proclaims: "I'm a Norwegian. And when I say I'm Norwegian, I think I've said enough. I'm as firm in my foundations as the ancient mountains of old Norway... It thrills me to the marrow to think what I am, and let my thoughts ring out in words of granite."

Andersen was, of course, a Dane, and he was teasing the Norwegians, as their Scandinavian neighbours are apt to do. In much the same way as Italians are satirically reduced to being tearful opera and ice cream fiends, and Frenchmen become obtuse philosophers in onion necklaces, so the typical Norwegian is portrayed as a simple, stubborn peasant who from time to time needs a comforting pat on the head. The country's refusal, in 1972 and again in 1994, to join other Scandinavian countries in the European Union confirmed this view to many.

Naturally enough, Norwegians see themselves rather differently. A Gallup poll once asked 200 people from each of 12 countries to rank themselves in terms of culture, food, living standards, beauty, *joie de vivre*, and national pride. The Norwegians gave themselves top marks in virtually every category. This sweeping victory for the home side was surpassed only by the conceit of the American entry.

Generous hospitality

The Norwegian character is of course far more complex than Andersen would allow or Gallup could measure. It is sometimes said that Norwegians are xenophobic. While this may be an exaggeration, it is certainly the case that they do not accept outside criticism. Yet the hospitality shown towards foreign visitors far exceeds the demands of mere good manners. An English visitor arriving late was whisked off spontaneously to a wedding party in Oslo. As the only foreigner among 200 guests, he was

disarmed when the bride's father, advised of his surprise presence, gave away his daughter in English. Although the younger Norwegian guests were, as usual, fluent in English, some older ones were left in the dark, but they thoroughly approved of the gesture.

The same English visitor, immobilised by

skis around his neck after capsizing on a narrow cross-country ski trail, brought down a party of local skiers who descended on him too fast and too late to stop. The victims of this pile-up were disgruntled until they made sense of his choked apologies, in English of course, at which point they tried to make him feel that, in the circumstances, the violent introduction was an unexpected pleasure, not to say privilege.

Other signs of welcome are given without thinking. A visitor in the house is the signal for lighting candles, probably a throwback to the days when, compounded by the long hours of winter darkness, houses shuttered against the cold were rather gloomy. Until quite recently,

---

PRECEDING PAGES: 17 May, National Day; fishermen at Verdens Ende; Royal Palace guards.
LEFT: a passion for sport.
ABOVE RIGHT: shopping on Karl Johans gate, Oslo.

most of Norway's population was thinly scattered across a vast landscape in a patchwork of tiny communities, so visitors invariably arrived after a long and exhausting journey, sometimes on skis. The assumption was that they arrived hungry, and restorative food and drink still appear as if by magic. A planned meal for guests requires elaborate place-settings, and includes food that bears little resemblance to the normal low-calorie diet of everyday life.

Visitors will not be allowed to leave without a tour of the house and a look at the family album. The Norwegians are attentive hosts who

nature of life in such a community: mutual support in adversity weighed against a suffocating lack of privacy at other times.

The Ten Commandments

The lesser-known Aksel Sandemose wrote Ten Commandments for village life, the essence being humility bordering on self-abasement. They included: "You must not think that you are worth anything; you must not think that you are better than anyone else; you must not think yourself capable of anything worthwhile; and you must not think that you are in any way exceptional."

expect very little in return – common courtesy, and some appreciative comments about their warm welcome as well as the tasteful interior decoration of the house. Norway's vaunted standard of living is a relatively recent phenomenon, thanks mainly to a prosperous offshore oil industry.

The more enigmatic aspects of the Norwegian psyche – including the Nordic gloom which descends after a drink too many – have been famously scrutinised by a native, Henrik Ibsen. He was brought up in small communities and, during a long exile, turned his critical eye on the experience. One of the themes running through Ibsen's work is the double-edged

Jingoistic chest pounding of the sort noted by Hans Christian Andersen is derived to some extent from Norway's peculiar position as both one of the oldest, if not the oldest, nation in Europe and at the same time one of the youngest. It is the oldest in the sense that the Norwegians can trace an unbroken line of descent from people who inhabited their territory in prehistoric times, a homogeneity whose origins predate the beginnings of Western civilisation in the Aegean.

Yet the present state of Norway was reconstituted only in 1905, which makes it younger than many of the junior members in the United Nations, themselves pasted together by the imperial powers in the 19th century. Having been relegated to a back seat in Scandinavian affairs for hundreds of years, these distant descendants of the illustrious Vikings need to pinch themselves – or blow a trumpet – as if they nervously expect to wake up and discover that their independence was a cruel dream.

Norwegians enjoy amazing longevity. They manage to look remarkably healthy all their lives, and the octogenarian grandmother whizzing by on skis is not a myth.

> ### FLAG HAPPY
>
> Many houses have flagpoles and every household possesses a flag which is hoisted on the slightest pretext, if only to indicate that the owner is in residence.

in foreign waters, relegating it to no more than a patch on a much larger Swedish flag. The flag flown on Norwegian shipping was, like separate consular representation and the establishment of a national bank, a perennial bone of contention before independence.

Norwegians would be distressed at the thought of their revered flag being desecrated as a pair of underpants or on shopping bags. Their dignity as a sovereign state is not to be trivialised. The Swedish king who reluctantly oversaw Norway's independence

In any case, there are Norwegians alive who can remember, or have had drummed into them, the euphoria of liberation from their domineering Scandinavian partners.

Free to show the flag

Well-deserved national pride makes Norwegians ardent flag-wavers. This could be construed as a rude gesture to the Swedes who, under the union, decided when, where and how the Norwegian colours were to be shown

---

FAR LEFT: still cutting the grass by hand at 89.
LEFT: a great-grandmother with her 19th grandchild.
ABOVE: enjoying the September sun.

predicted that bureaucratic incompetence would soon have Norwegians begging to be returned to the fold. The response, even now, is a reluctance to admit (to outsiders) that they are capable of making a mistake, as if to do so would vindicate the Swedish king.

As long as authority was vested in foreigners, Norwegians did not regard it too highly. On assuming it themselves, however, authority was allowed to assume the aura of divine right, before which loyal citizens should willingly prostrate themselves.

Norwegian history is full of swings from one extreme to another. Pagans who held out against Christianity until a surprisingly late date became, and in some cases remain, doggedly fundamentalist after seeing the light. However, a nation which was once thought to be in danger of drinking itself to death has by no means buried the bottle. Drinking alcohol is now restricted mainly to the weekend and Alcoholics Anonymous are not the only ones to welcome austere state measures.

Visitors sampling the state television service might wonder, too, at the litany of self-congratulation in almost daily items about the excellence of the health and welfare services. Programmes about children – for example, choirs singing carols at Christmas – are bound

refugees. If proved, the evidence would be difficult to swallow, as it was when statistics revealed that suicides had overtaken the number of traffic deaths in a certain period. Was that not, an apologist ventured, excellent proof of road safety standards?

The Norwegian language(s)

In contrast with these examples of mild paranoia, Norwegians can be remarkably robust where they might be expected to be most sensitive. There is no alarm about the predatory impact of, say, satellite television on a language which hardly exists outside Norway. Far from

to include an unrealistic proportion of Third World immigrants. The way the camera seeks out and locks on to black, brown or yellow faces, possibly in difficulty with unfamiliar tunes and words, seems a rather contrived message to the effect that Norway can show the world a thing or two about liberal decency. This is a role which many are pleased to play; appeals for money by international relief agencies are always met with astonishing generosity, and the country spends more per capita on foreign aid than any other in the West.

Such open-handedness has inevitably attracted abuse, and questions are increasingly asked about the "real credentials" of political

resenting visitors who presume to address them in a foreign language, Norwegians positively relish the challenge, and usually respond with considerable fluency.

Confidence in the hardiness of their language is curiously at odds with its historical background. Language was a burning issue in Norwegian politics until the 1950s, having forced a prime minister to resign in 1912. The long-running controversy started as a form of agitation against Danish rule, throughout which Danish was the language of the civil service, schools and the Church. For a long time after the Reformation the revised Bible was available only in Danish, as were all the new hymns.

Denmark got its first printing press in 1480 but Norway had to wait until 1643. Until then books were imported and in Danish.

When reading aloud, Norwegians modified standard Danish through the use of their own pronunciation and intonation. This mixture eventually produced a hybrid known as *bokmål* (book language).

The search for a native language

The 19th-century nationalists still saw it as fundamentally Danish, however, and wanted a national language which was authentically Norwegian. Unfortunately, there was no single

the theatre, and if Norwegian had to be spoken, a Danicised pronunciation was fashionable. These tendencies eroded as intellectuals like Ibsen lent respectability to the campaign for the revivification of a purely Norwegian language.

In 1929 *bokmål* and *nynorsk* were recognised as dual official languages, the hope being that they would drift towards a blend which would be known as *samnorsk*. The names of cities and towns lost their Danish connotations. Christiania, for example, reverted to a good old Norwegian name, Oslo. The reformers also tackled the habit of referring to the number 25 as "five-and-twenty". It became "twenty-five".

Norwegian substitute, because the language had developed many distinct dialects. Rather than choose one dialect at the expense of the others, the language reformers concentrated on developing a composite.

The early language reformers included Ivar Aasen and Knut Knudsen, the latter a schoolmaster driven by his pupils' frustration in trying to work out Danish spelling. They worked on what became known as *landsmål* or *nynorsk*, but their efforts were not unreservedly welcomed. Danish was the language of society and

LEFT: winter skiing in the Nordmarka.
ABOVE: summer on a Telemark beach.

Progress towards *samnorsk* was given a nudge in the 1950s with a proposal to have school textbooks converted into it. There was such an outcry, however, that the government backed down. Subsequent policy has been to treat the two languages even-handedly, still hoping that they will one day converge. In spite of attempts to shore up *nynorsk* through radio and television, it looks as if it is losing ground.

Individualistic tongue

Educated speech is distinctly that of the southeast, although that does not prevent country dwellers on a visit to the capital, say, from laying on their regional accents thick for effect.

The Bergensere (people from Bergen), at the heart of the *nynorsk* area, are certainly proud of their individualistic tongue.

The regional fragmentation at the heart of the language debate extends to most facets of cultural and economic life. While Norway has since Viking times been a single nation, it has been a confederation of many parts. Norway can be divided north–south, east–west or a dozen different ways. Like the Renaissance, the Industrial Revolution hardly intruded, so there was not the rapid urbanisation which occurred elsewhere. Trondheim, Bergen and Oslo were towns rather than cities. A later creation like

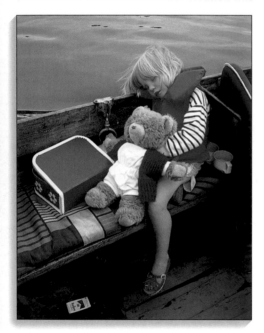

Stavanger owed its existence to the arrival of vast shoals of herring, which were the basis of jobs, trade and other prerequisites of a cash economy. Most of Norway remained rooted in subsistence agriculture.

Preserving old necessities

Rural families tended to be isolated and self-sufficient. Their lives depended on agriculture, and the land was not good enough to support more than a family or two in a single valley. Separated from their neighbours by mountains which were ironically easier to cross in winter (on skis) than in summer, they effectively lived in different worlds. There were hardly any vil-

lages where tradesmen could be found and paid in cash. The versatile family managed on its own, a resourcefulness which still runs in the blood. It is not unknown for young couples living in Oslo today to solicit the help of friends to build their first home with their own hands.

The modern Norwegian makes a virtue out of what used to be necessity. The ideal *hytte*, as a country cabin is known, is isolated. It will probably have electricity, but running water may be considered effete. Visitors who decide, sensibly, to rent a *hytte* will almost certainly come round to the view that water drawn from a stream is not merely an exercise in rural nostalgia but also doubly delicious. In winter there is the added joy of first having to drill a hole through the ice to reach it.

Messing about in boats

The old necessities carry over to the passion for owning a boat. On summer evenings, Oslo fjord is alive with boats, a pattern repeated everywhere. Although Norwegians are said to grow up on skis, messing about in boats is equally ingrained. Both used to represent basic transport in a land where road and rail construction costs billions because of the mountainous terrain and deep fjords. Although the country is now well served in both departments, the boat was once both a tool of daily life as well as a source of recreation.

Modern Norway has the reputation of being an enlightened, progressive state on the Scandinavian model, but it does Norwegians no disservice to recognise the Viking beneath. A man found sitting in a hole on the snowbound Oslo golf course said with a twinkle that his ancestors had devised a system of digging holes which, taking into account the direction of the wind, provided an emergency – and actually quite comfortable – refuge in the event of snowstorms. He felt he was doing his bit, preserving some of his heritage for posterity. He put his palms to his temples and waggled his outstretched fingers.

That the Vikings wore horns is doubtful, if not an outright fallacy, but only the most churlish observer would wish to deny someone who saw sport in sitting in a hole in the snow a certain degree of historical licence. ❏

LEFT: at the end of a day on the fjord.
RIGHT: traditional *bunads* worn for church on Sunday.

EPIC EXPLORERS

Whether because of exile, scientific exploration, or wanting to be the first,
Norwegian explorers have travelled the world from North to South Pole

Although exploration is most often associated in modern times with rocket journeys into space, the names of at least two Norwegian explorers are as evocative now as at the time of their epic achievements: Roald Amundsen (1861–1930) is forever remembered as the man who beat Captain Scott to the South Pole; and Thor Heyerdahl (born 1914–2001) for the *Kon-Tiki* expedition.

Their fame steals some of the limelight which ought to be apportioned to a much larger cast of intrepid Norwegians, beginning with Bjarni Herjulfsson who, in 986, lost his way while sailing from Iceland to Greenland and ended up, according to an ancient saga, as the first European to sight the American continent. On Bjarni's return, Leiv Eiriksson borrowed his boat to investigate the mysterious sighting and became the first European to set foot on the American continent.

Early migrations

A 19th-century Norwegian explorer, Fridtjof Nansen (1861–1930), set the pattern for the investigation of human migration. He established his reputation in 1888 with a hazardous crossing of Greenland from east to west. A few years later he was excited by the discovery near the southern tip of Greenland of some wreckage whose origins were traced to the New Siberian Islands. How had it got there?

Nansen determined to find out. His vessel, *Fram*, was designed to lift herself under the crushing pressure of the drift ice in the Arctic Ocean. She was set adrift off the New Siberian Islands in September 1893 and, two years later, emerged near Spitsbergen – but without Nansen. He had left the ship in charge of his second-in-command in a heroic but vain attempt to reach the North Pole with dog-drawn sledges. He and his companion survived a win-

ter in Franz Josef Land, living in an ice hut and eating whatever they could shoot. They reached safety on practically the same day as *Fram*, and Nansen's six volumes of findings are the basis of the science of oceanography.

Such was Nansen's fame that, when war threatened between Norway and Sweden over

the dissolution of their union, he was sent to London and Copenhagen to win support for the Norwegian cause.

The purpose of the 1947 *Kon-Tiki* expedition was to test a theory about the origins of the Polynesian people and culture *(see page 162 for details on Kon-Tiki Museet)*. Heyerdahl demonstrated that a balsawood raft set adrift off the coast of Peru could eventually – it took him about four months – reach the Tuamotu archipelago 8,000 km (5,000 miles) to the west. In the 1960s he successfully conducted a similar experiment – the *Ra* expedition – to discover whether West African voyagers using their traditional rafts may have reached the West Indies before Columbus.

PRECEDING PAGES: the *Fram* stuck fast in the Arctic ice.
LEFT: Hanssen, one of Amundsen's expedition members to the South Pole, next to the flag.
RIGHT: Roald Amundsen.

Viking explorers

The father of Norwegian exploration, or at least the earliest recorded explorer, is Erik the Red, a man who seems to have had a liking for slaughter. In the 10th century he was banished from Norway to Iceland for murder, and then from Iceland as well for several more killings. Unwelcome anywhere, he sailed west with a shipload of livestock and discovered the world's largest island – a lump of ice, more than 3 kilometres (2 miles) thick in places.

Obviously a keen angler, Erik was so engrossed by the excellent catches to be had in summer that he neglected to collect enough ani-

and in every respect a temperate, fair-dealing man", which would seem to set him apart from his father. His 35-man expedition left Greenland about the year 1000. They landed first at "Markland", a wooded region on the coast of Labrador, and then continued south to "Vinland".

An inscription on a map probably drawn by a monk in Basel in 1440 – about half a century before Columbus sailed to the New World – describes Leiv Eiriksson's discovery of "a new land, extremely fertile, and even having vines... a truly vast and very rich land". Attempts to settle the land were defeated by the hostile natives.

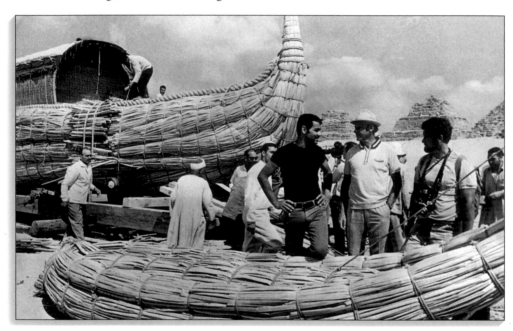

mal fodder for the winter. His livestock starved to death. He resolved to risk violation of his ostracism to collect replacements from Iceland and to persuade others to join him on return. Erik trumpeted his new-found land with the zeal of an unprincipled estate agent. It was so wonderful, he told his audiences, that he had decided to call it Greenland. By 985 he had acquired animals and enticed enough colonisers to fill 25 ships, of which 14 reached the destination.

It was in one of the settlements founded by Erik the Red that his son, Leiv, having heard Bjarni Herjulfsson's strange tale, prepared to find out for himself what it was all about. He was "big and strong, of striking appearance,

American proof

Certainly the existence of "Vinland" was known to Adam of Bremen, a chronicler in the 1070s, and to writers of the sagas, but it was through a typically bizarre quirk of archaeology that Eiriksson's discovery of America is put virtually beyond doubt. Excavations on the site of a Greenland farm which belonged to a member of the "Vinland" expedition produced a lump of coal which proved to be anthracite, a material unobtainable in Greenland but plentiful on the surface in Rhode Island.

The case was strengthened in 1960 by Helge Ingstad, who thought about the likely landing place on the American continent of an expedition from Greenland. Working like a detective, he backed a hunch and at L'anse aux Meadows, on the northern tip of Newfoundland, discovered that six buildings had once stood on the site. Carbon dating proved they were medieval, and the archaeological remains left no doubt that the occupants had been Norsemen.

Race for the Pole

Roald Amundsen had served a rigorous apprenticeship for his famous assault on the South Pole, which came about as a last-minute change

NORTH TO SOUTH

Børge Ousland was the first man to reach both the North (1994) and South (1995) Poles alone on skis without the help of man or beast.

pipped him to the post, in 1910 he secretly went south instead in Nansen's old ship, *Fram*. But not until he reached Madeira did he let anyone know what his intentions were.

Amundsen decided to dispense with all scientific work in his sprint to the South Pole. Scott had a head start but discovered too late that his Siberian ponies were useless in the conditions. He and his team had to pull their sledges. Amundsen took a shorter, rougher route and had the benefit of dog teams. In the event, he beat Scott by a month.

of plan. Although he had taken part in a Belgian expedition to Antarctica his first interest was the Arctic. He was stuck for two years off King William Island in a seal-hunting boat, *Gjøa*, and applied his time to studying the Innuit inhabitants and making reckonings on the magnetic pole.

Amundsen knew about Captain Scott's ambitions to reach the South Pole but he himself was more concerned in reaching the North. Nevertheless, faced with the shattering disappointment of the news that Robert Peary had

LEFT: Thor Heyerdahl's *Ra* under construction in Egypt.
ABOVE: Monika Kristensen.

The dispirited English team perished on their return, and this unlucky fate took some of the lustre off Amundsen's feat. At last, though, the director of London's Royal Geographical Society, which had backed Scott, paid tribute to Amundsen's effort as "the most successful polar journey on record".

To the overwhelmingly male-dominated ranks of Norwegian "explorers" it is refreshing to add the names of Liv Arnesen (born 1953), who, in 1994, was the first woman to reach the South Pole alone, and Monika Kristensen (born 1950) who led a South Pole expedition in 1986–87, following in the footsteps of Roald Amundsen. ❑

FOLKLORE: SAGAS AND FOLKTALES

Among the treasures of Norwegian heritage are its legends and sagas. This form of popular story-telling is an important part of the national psyche

The Norwegian word for folktale, "*eventyr*", crops us as early as the 12th century in the form "*ævintyr*", borrowed from the Latin word "*adventura*", meaning event or strange occurrence. These folktales were imaginative stories passed from one storyteller to another, and depicted relationships expressed in fantastic and symbolic terms. Narrators were often clergymen who used folklore as a moralistic vehicle. The folktale style was, above all, objective: however fantastic the subject, the narrative was always realistic and believable.

COUNTRY LEGENDS

A constant topic in Norwegian legend is its landscape. Many of the stories connected with the sea involved mythical creatures, the best known of which are the Lake Mjøsa monster and Draugen, the personification of all who have died at sea. In lakes and rivers lives the sprite Nøkken *(Nixie)*. Many mythical creatures inhabit the mountains and forests, and tales about landmarks created by trolls exist all over the country. Marks left by trolls show their size, such as the Giant Cut (Jutulhogget) in Østerdal.

▽ **PAGAN RELIGION**
Lom stave church in Gudbrandsdal, dating from around 1200, is decorated with carved dragons and fantasy creatures entwined with tendrils of vine.

◁ **TROLLS**
The immoral troll's ambition is to wield power over mortals, but they are stupid and easily duped.

△ **THE GOLDEN BIRD**
Theodor Kittelsen's illustration of a Norwegian folktale, *The Golden Bird*, is from the collection of legends and sagas by Asbjørnsen and Moe.

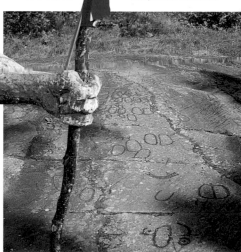

THE GOLDEN AGE OF LITERATURE

On 17 May 1814, after almost 300 years of Danish rule, Norway signed the constitution at Eidsvoll. This event heralded a revival of the Norwegian language that spanned the remainder of the century. Per Christen Asbjørnsen (1812–55) and Jørgen Moe (1818–82) were part of this "golden age". Inspired by the German Brothers Grimm and Norwegian Andreas Faye, who published *Norske Sagn* (Norwegian Legends) in 1833, Asbjørnsen and Moe set about compiling the first collection of Norwegian folktales as *Norske Huldre-Eventyr og Folkesagn* (Norwegian Ghost Stories and Folk Legends). Their first volume appeared in 1845, the second edition in 1852. Asbjørnsen went on to publish an illustrated version, commissioning some of the best Norwegian painters of the time, including Erik Werenskiold (above) and Theodor Kittelsen. Asbjørnsen and Moe's collections have become classic Norwegian folktales; Kittelsen and Werenskiold's illustrations have given the troll its visual image.

◁ **CHRISTMAS CHARACTER**
The Norwegian version of Santa Claus, *Julenissen*, is a mixture of the Nordic *nisse* (the mischievous gnome) and St Nicholas.

▽ **MYTHS AND MONSTERS**
Stories about fantastical beasts form the largest group of Norwegian folktales. They often lurk in bottomless lakes and terrorise the forest.

◁ **BRONZE AGE TOTEMS**
The Bronze Age rock carvings at Leirfall (Lerfald), near Hegra include totemic figures performing pagan rituals linked to hunting seasons.

▷ **ANCIENT GRAFFITI**
The prehistoric rock carvings (*c.* 4500 BC) on the Lista peninsula indicate early ship-building skills and a sea-faring culture.

OFF-THE-SHELF MONARCHY

Imported from Sweden in 1905, Norway's popular monarchy has passed through various trials on its way to the very heart of the nation

For the chronically under-employed off-shoots of European royalty, the rash of new states in the 19th and early 20th century brought blessed job opportunities. Their prospects were reduced by republican tendencies and other disappointments: Albania offered its throne to the England cricket cap-

tain, who declined, but in 1905 Norway's criteria were less capricious. The new state had a long royal pedigree, but it had died out during 400 years under Danish and Swedish rule. While Norwegians saw some advantages in a Scandinavian as king, there was the feeling that a Danish or Swedish monarch would amount to the despised *status ante quo*. In the event, the former considerations outweighed the latter, and an invitation went to Prince Carl, second son of the future King Christian IX of Denmark and grandson of Sweden's King Karl XV.

Prince Carl, then 33, was married to Maud, Princess of Wales and daughter of England's Edward VII. He insisted first on a plebiscite.

The result was favourable, so on 25 November 1905, having assumed the title Håkon VII, he stepped ashore in Norway sheltering his young son, born Alexander Edward Christian Frederick but quickly renamed Olav, from driving snow. Håkon himself continued to sign letters to friends and relatives in England as "Charles".

Republicanism survived in Norway. Politicians complained that the cost of the monarchy was too high. The royal apartments in the palace were scarcely habitable to begin with and the government would pay only half the repair costs. Frugality was paramount. By watching expenses as carefully as he observed constitutional niceties, Håkon gradually won over the sceptics. Left-wing doubts ceased in 1926 when he called on the Labour Party to form a government.

The king worked hard at not being a foreigner. He travelled widely and impressed his subjects with a dignified modesty. The crown prince needed no encouragement to make up the perceived deficiency in the family tree. Although born in England, he felt at home and proved it by winning prizes on the Holmenkollen ski jump, as daunting a test of Norwegian authenticity as there could be. He also represented Norway as an Olympic sailor, another huge plus to his sea-minded subjects.

Resistance in exile

World War II was the supreme challenge. Implacably opposed to Hitler, King Håkon had to contend with the local clamour for neutrality. "I must be careful... not to say too much," he wrote to Queen Mary, his sister-in-law in London, "so that my ministers cannot say I am more English than Norwegian." He would abdicate rather than bow to German demands for recognition of the Quisling government. Running the gauntlet of the Luftwaffe, he escaped to England. His work, and that of the crown prince, with the Norwegian exile movement inspired dogged resistance at home and cemented a bond which gave the king a tumultuous reception on his eventual return to Oslo.

Håkon died in 1957 at the age of 85, and became known as Håkon the Good. His only child, who succeeded as Olav V, inherited the same unassuming manner, evident in his endearing discomfort while delivering the traditional New Year's Eve television broadcast, and the affection in which his father was held.

When he died in 1991, the people's grief was genuine. It was not just the passing of an old man, but personal sorrow at the loss of one so dear to many.

Changing with the times

King Olav V was succeeded by his 44-year-old son, who assumed the title of Harald V. Harald had been raised to carry out his royal duties, while maintaining strong personal ties with the people and his own time. King Olav's announcement in 1968 that Crown Prince Harald wished to marry a commoner triggered a heated debate on the future of the monarchy. The decision was made by King Olav himself after consultations with the government. The response was favourable and the majority of the population immediately accepted Sonja Haraldsen as queen. She quickly became inseparably linked with the national unity symbolised by the royal family.

King Harald has made a name for himself as a competitive sailor. In 1987 he won the world championship with his new yacht *Fram X*, which was a gift from the Norwegian business community on his 50th birthday. Both King Harald and Queen Sonja are involved in various outdoor sports, as is their daughter, Princess Märtha Louise (born 1971), who has achieved considerable success in the equestrian field.

Public face, private lives

The king was less than amused when, in 1994, Princess Märtha Louise's interest in equestrian sports extended to being cited as co-respondent in a British divorce case as a result of an alleged affair with a married show jumper. Not that it caused much of a stir in the Norwegian press, which has tacitly agreed not to encroach on the private lives of the members of the royal household. This privacy was somewhat tested with Crown Prince Haakon's choice of bride in 2001:

LEFT: King Harald and Queen Sonja with their son and daughter. **RIGHT:** King Harald at a skiing event.

single mother and anthropology student, Mette-Marit Tjessem Høiby. Like his father, Haakon has chosen to "marry the girl he loves rather than love the girl he marries". The partnership may have added fuel to the flames of republicanism, but in a country in which nearly 50 percent of babies are born out of wedlock, it is not so remarkable.

> **PERSONAL PROTECTION**
>
> When an American reporter found King Olav V travelling alone on the train and asked whether it wasn't a security risk, the king replied "not with four million bodyguards!".

Haakon and his sister were educated at state schools. The crown prince then embarked on naval training and later on crossed the Atlantic to study political science at the

University of California, Berkeley. His preparation as a future head of state has continued as a trainee at the Norwegian Ministry of Foreign Affairs in Oslo. In 2002 Princess Märtha Louise married a commoner, Ari Behn, in 2003 the couple had their first child, Maude Angelika.

All this fits in perfectly with the egalitarian outlook that pervades Norwegian society. Like the flag and the 17th of May celebrations, the Norwegian monarchy symbolises independence from the almost 400-year rule under first Denmark and then Sweden. What often appears to be fervent nationalism is in fact no more than national pride and a desire to hold on to a hard-earned self-determination. ❏

THE SAMI: PEOPLE OF FOUR NATIONS

Behind the popular image of the Sami with their colourful costumes and large herds of reindeer lies a rich complex culture that is an important part of modern Norway

The Sami (or Lapps, as they are sometimes called despite its derogatory overtones) have lived in Norway from time immemorial. Traces of their presence stretch back more than 8,000 years. The name Sami comes from the Sami *sápmi*, denoting both the people themselves and their traditional territory. Samiland extends from Idre in Sweden and adjacent areas in Norway south to Engerdal in Hedmark; to the north and east it stretches to Utsjoki in Finland, Varanger in Norway and on to the Kola peninsula in Russia. It covers a larger area than Norway and Denmark combined, and the population is cautiously estimated at 70,000, of which around 45,000 live in Norway, mainly in Finnmark.

Norwegian Sami divide roughly into three groups. The Mountain Sami are the most widespread, ranging from Varanger to Femunden. They live mainly by breeding reindeer. The River Sami live around the waterways in the interior of Finnmark and have turned increasingly to agriculture and animal husbandry, though hunting, fishing and berry-picking still add to their income. The third group, the Sea Sami, is the largest, making a living from fishing and farming in a lifestyle that differs little from that of other northern Norwegians.

Ancient culture

The Sami people have been very successful in conserving their rich cultural heritage and many unique traditions. Not the least important is the Sami language, which derives from the Finno-Ugric branch of the Uralic family and is closely related to the Baltic Sea-Finnish languages.

From ancient times, the sea has been of great importance as an abundant source of fish, and of seal to provide them with valuable hides and skins. Walruses, with their precious tusks, were also highly prized, particularly by the Sami craftspeople who produced all sorts of tools and

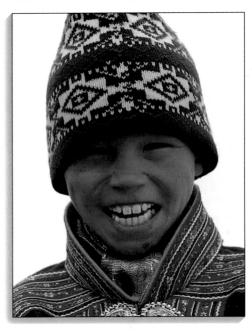

utensils including needles, buttons, spoons, cups, and a variety of musical instruments.

Samiland is a mighty land, rich in lakes, rivers, small streams, grandiose mountains and boundless hills, which in some places reach as far as the Atlantic coast. Besides fishing, hunting also used to be important and there was much game, big and small. Squirrels, martens, foxes, even bears were all hunted, but the most important animal was – and to a certain extent still is – the reindeer. About 10 percent of Norway's landmass is used for reindeer grazing (mostly in Finnmark). While the economic value of this industry is minor on a national scale, it is important both financially and culturally to the Sami, with about 40 percent of the population living from herding reindeer.

Very few of the truly nomadic Sami people are left. Most Sami have settled down in the sense that they have a permanent address but move with their herds to the high ground in the summer. During late summer and in the autumn

---

PRECEDING PAGES: children in Kautokeino, Finnmark, ready for confirmation.
LEFT: traditionally Sami women love smoking pipes.
RIGHT: a Sami boy.

the reindeer are driven down to the woods near the foot of the summer mountain pastures where there is plenty of lichen. There they stay during winter, roaming in freedom until the spring when it is time once more to move up the mountain to the high slopes, now covered with succulent, nourishing vegetation.

Brilliant colours

Many visitors to Norway come north to Sami-land and to the beautiful *fjell* (mountains) in search of untouched nature. Mosses and lichens give a gentle splash of colour to the vast land, and grasses, especially sedges, are abundant here. At the beginning of summer the rare, pale Pasque flower *(Pulsatilla vernalis)* is in bloom and the cinnamon rose *(Rosa majalis)* gives colour to the rocky hillside and the edges of the bog. Carpets of mountain avons *(Dryas octopetala)* are characteristic of soil that is rich in calcium, as are many other species, often with names that begin with *fjell*.

Perhaps the colours all around them have been a source of inspiration for the traditional Sami costume. In days gone by, this dress was for daily use; now it is kept for festivals, weddings, funerals and other important occasions. Easter is *the* big feast, particularly in Kautokeino, with tradi-

SINFUL SINGING

Of great importance when trying to get inside the world of the Sami people is to understand the importance of the *yoik*, a kind of primitive singing comparable with unaccompanied humming or melodic scanning. To outsiders, it is particularly difficult to grasp since the words can be isolated or subordinated to melody and rhythm, followed by long sentences of meaningless syllables, such as *voia-voia*, *ala ala*, or *lu-lu-lu*.

The *yoik* probably originated as a way of keeping reindeer quiet and at the same time frightened wild animals away. But it is also used as entertainment, when people are gathered together. In Finnmark, *yoiking* has grown strong and each Sami has his own personal melody. Traditionally, a young Sami boy will compose his own *yoik* for the girl he is courting. However, today a suitable *yoik* can be composed to order for almost any occasion.

Like many other Sami traditions, the *yoik* was forbidden by the missionary Christians. At a time when the only decent song was a hymn, the *yoik* was seen as sinful. But a *yoik* could not be burnt like a troll-drum. Many of the old melodies are still alive, handed on from one generation to the next. With the current spread of world music, the Sami singer Mari Boine is known all over Europe, and her success has brought new life to Sami music and culture.

tional reindeer racing and other events. Then the richly ribboned skirts and frocks, with red their most outstanding colour, are fetched from drawers and chests. These generous ribbons are used as wristbands or cuffs and as "stockings".

There are no bounds to this richness and colour, which makes a magnificent sight. With these lavish dresses go jewellery in silver, exquisitely worked into neck chains and elegant pendants. Another speciality is pewter embroidery, in which very thin threads of pewter are sewn in ingenious patterns on fine bracelets or on bags made of reindeer hide.

The old religion

Like many other people living in close contact with nature, the Sami had, and still have, a religion related to shamanism, in which nature and its forces are of the greatest importance. Beaive (the Sun) and Mannu (the Moon) were the supreme gods; next came Horagalles, the god of thunderstorms. Under these main gods there were many lesser gods and spirit beings, who ruled over fertility and over wild animals and the hunt, as well as over lakes and their fishes and other inhabitants. There were evil spirits as well. One was Rota or Ruta, the demon of illness and death; another was the Devil himself, Fuadno. In many areas Sami religion was related to Norse mythology: Horagalles corresponding to the Norse god of Thunder, Thor.

Christianity did its best to combat and extinguish this popular belief and Swedish Laestadianism did much to destroy the Sami religion. Many of the ceremonial "troll-drums", of great importance in Sami culture but anathema to the would-be missionaries, were burned.

The most effective Christian missionary was King Christian IV. He travelled to Finnmark around the turn of the 17th century and in 1609 introduced the death penalty for Sami who refused to give up their traditional faith. He followed this with an order to build the first Christian church in Varanger.

To go to church regularly was, nevertheless, impossible for many of the nomadic Sami, who had to travel over mountains and vast lakes. It was the great festivals which gathered the Sami together and so it is today: New Year, Easter, Lady Day, and the spring and autumn equinoxes.

In addition, the Sami people count eight seasons, all of them related to their reindeer and these too must be celebrated.

Language revival

Traditionally, Sami culture possessed an extensive oral "literature", including a vast number and variety of legends and fairytales, many of which were written down earlier this century by J.K. Ovigstad in his *Sami Fairytales and Legends*. This literature also includes a distinctive form of poetry designed to accompany the traditional Sami "song" or *yoik (see box left)*..

In the first half of the 20th century, it was

government policy to encourage the "Norwegianisation" of the Sami people and its language. This led to the irony that one of the greatest writers of Sami descent, Mario Aikio from Karasjok, wrote only in Norwegian, though today a number of younger writers are once again using the Sami language.

As happened with many minority languages in recent times, Norway now has a policy of encouraging the Sami language. It is taught from the start of schooling and Sami people can pursue higher education in their own language in various establishments such as the Universities of Oslo and Tromsø, and their their own Teachers' Training College in Alta.

LEFT: a Sami woman at the reindeer round-up.
RIGHT: a character from the Sami theatre.

Karasjok has the De Samiske Samlinger (Sami Museum) while in Kautokeino, where the great Easter celebrations are held, there is the Kautokeino Kulturhuset (Culture Centre).

When the Norwegian Broadcasting Corporation (NRK) planned a second radio channel in the early 1980s, it came up with the unusual idea of placing the first station in the remote north of Norway and beginning broadcasts with the first Sami service, then gradually working its way south.

FALLOUT

In 1986, radioactive pollution from the Chernobyl nuclear disaster hit the Sami hard, both culturally and economically, through contamination of their reindeer, which had eaten polluted lichen.

Towards home rule

The Norwegian Sami have also fought for political control over their own affairs and for the preservation of their way of life which has continued to be eroded by the opening up of the northern areas through improved roads and other forms of communication.

The establishment of national parks, for example, can lead to the protection of wild animals that prey on the reindeer herds and Sami people have been successful in gaining compensation for reindeer grazing areas and recognition of the right to hunt and fish. Sami have also succeeded in curtailing some electricity development projects which would have flooded whole districts and jeopardised the local reindeer economy.

Today, the Sami people have their own Sametinget (parliament), based in Karasjok, which was opened in 1989 with great ceremony. The parliament is an elected body and to vote you must have a grandparent speaking the Sami language or "feel that you are a Sami". Further progress was made in 1990 when Norway ratified the ILO Convention, which dealt with the rights of indigenous and tribal peoples.

The Sametinget deals with all matters pertinent to the Sami people and is gradually being given more autonomy, but so far its power is fairly limited, mainly advisory. It has developed a plan of action for Sami coastal and fjord areas, an agricultural plan, and has participated in a Sami fisheries committee. In addition it has conducted its own studies aimed at boosting local employment (in which tourism is playing an increasingly important role). But the Sami parliament has demanded more self-government. They claim Oslo doesn't understand how life in the Arctic is. A recent law that said only vets could castrate reindeer is given as an example.

Nordic co-operation is also a central part of its activities. The Sami parliaments in Norway, Sweden and Finland decided in 1996 to collaborate through a special parliamentary council. There is now a political adviser for Sami issues at the Ministry of Local Government.

The most contentious issue currently being debated is Sami land rights, and in particular mineral rights. The Sami recognise the enormous wealth that lies beneath the frozen tracts of the Finnmarksvidda (the great Finnmark plain). Major international mining companies are continuously charting the area for mineral deposits and there is talk of Klondyke-like gold deposits. Similarly, international oil companies are continuing to explore the Barents Sea, where major gas fields have already been discovered. But most of the minerals remain underground while the argument about how the profits should be spent remain unresolved. ❑

LEFT: the Sami singer Mari Boine is now known internationally.
RIGHT: an old Sami woman fixing her traditional *lavvu* (skin tent).

BOAT BUILDERS AND ENGINEERS

Travelling around Norway has never been easy. However, Norwegian engineers have come up with some spectacular solutions to speed you on your way

Norway is 1,600 kilometres (1,000 miles) long and has a coastline that resembles a set of jagged teeth, a myriad of islands and more than its fair share of mountains. Added to such geographical difficulties are a harsh climate and a population of only 4.5 million people scattered the length and breadth of the country. In short, a nightmare for those whose job it is to plan and build a transport network.

In the 1980s offshore oil came to the rescue, generating wealth that was used partly to upgrade roads and improve the mountain and undersea tunnels that are so vital in this fierce terrain. Such spending produced some spectacular feats of engineering, but the North Sea bonanza is reaching its peak and so new solutions will have to be found.

In the wake of the Vikings

It is not surprising that Norway has traditionally relied on the sea (which had for so long concealed those oil riches) as its basic means of transport, or that most towns and villages lie along the coast and fjords and have harbours. When roads were still primitive tracks and railways in the early stages of construction, shipping routes for passengers and cargo were already well established. This was the main reason that early tours of Norway seldom penetrated inland but kept to the coast and fjords.

The backbone of the domestic sea transport system was, and still is, the famous Hurtigruten, the coastal express steamers which have linked the numerous communities along the coast for many years. These ships followed the route of the Vikings and were originally a series of unconnected independent services. Many operated only during the summer, anchored at dusk, and did not sail through the night.

It was the Vesteraalens Dampskibsselskab (Steamship Company) that established the first year-round express service in 1893, which

sailed between Trondheim and Hammerfest – without overnight stops. Later, other lines joined in and the Hurtigruten assumed a major role, carrying mail, cargo and passengers, including tourists, from Bergen in the southwest to Kirkenes in the northeast. Today, in spite of the development of other forms of

transport, coastal shipping continues to play an important part in the Norwegian communications network.

From *stolkjaerre* to the car

As new roads and bridges have been built and new tunnels bored, the number of smaller ferry services has steadily declined; but the ferries in the west and north of Norway will continue to play an important role well into the millennium. National Route 1 in west Norway, for example, crosses no fewer than eight fjords between Stavanger and Ålesund.

Until a couple of decades ago, many quite important roads were still unsurfaced. Road

---

LEFT: Tjeldsund Bridge connecting the island of Hinnøya to the mainland.
RIGHT: landing on an Arctic airstrip.

building has never been an easy option in Norway and a lot of highways were narrow and rough, while those which crossed the mountains and *fjells* were closed in winter and regularly damaged by the harsh weather.

Before the car, the principal form of transport was the *stolkjaerre*, a two-wheeled horse-drawn cart without springs which seated two persons. An alternative, a *kalesjevogn*, seated a maximum of six passengers. When the car made its first appearance there was little to

SLOW PROGRESS

As late as 1925 a guide book to Norway still noted that the "normal method of progress along the country roads, from posting station to posting station, is the native cart or *stolkjaerre*."

engineers have risen to the challenge and created new highways with good surfaces, built superb bridges, and blasted numerous and lengthy tunnels.

The Norwegian skill at tunnelling through the solid rock that forms their mountains creates one of the biggest impressions on visitors. Norwegian tunnels are rarely flat or straight, but wind up and down the mountains with gradients, curves and spirals to make for adventurous underground driving. The more dramatic exam-

encourage it. However, gradually roads improved, although it was not until after World War II that the Norwegians took to motoring.

The Norwegian art of tunnelling

Since the 1980s a surge in road building has gained increasing momentum. But even today there are only a few short sections of motorway, and Norway has its own types of hazard, ranging from reindeer on the road to narrow bridges, blind corners and steep gradients.

Minor roads, particularly in the mountains, are frequently unsurfaced while some of those covered with asphalt – especially in the north – suffer from frost heave. But Norway's civil

ples can gain 300 metres (1,000 ft) in a few minutes, replacing roads that once clung to the mountainside in a succession of hairpin bends and steep gradients and which were closed by snow all winter long.

Nothing has deterred Norwegian engineers from tackling the incredibly difficult to the near impossible – such as the tunnel on the road between Skei and Fjærland which lies beneath an arm of the mighty Jostedal glacier. Previously Fjærland was isolated, reached only by ferry. The only hazards now are sheep, which have learned to appreciate the comfort of lying in tunnel entrances where it is cool in summer and warm in winter.

Underwater motoring

Having mastered the skill of tunnelling on land, Norwegian engineers have turned their attention to the seabed and undersea tunnels. One of the most spectacular burrows out from the mainland to Vardø, which lies on a small island off the north Finnmark coast. It is nearly 3 km (2 miles) long and descends 88 metres (288 ft) below the cold waters of the Arctic Ocean.

At Ålesund on the west coast two undersea tunnels, totalling nearly 8 km (5 miles) link the main town to the island of Vigra, where the airport is located, and have cut out the necessity of a ferry crossing. With an eco-

(9 miles) underground from Oslo Sentralstasjion to Lillestrøm: the original budget was doubled when engineers struck a fault through which several lakes in Østmarka began to drain. The initial decision to build the tunnel was based on environmental considerations: the resulting ecological damage is still not fully understood.

Public transport

Public transport makes good use of Norway's road system to reach outlying towns and villages. The bus station in the centre of any town is busy from morning to night – a revelation to

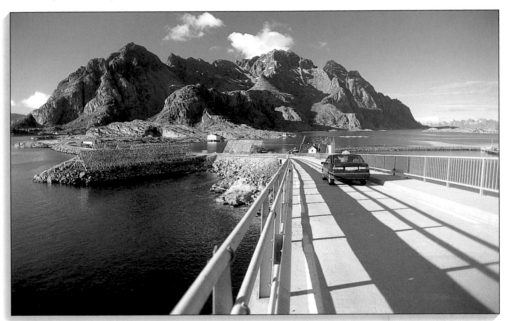

nomical frame of mind, the Norwegians used the rock drilled out of the tunnels to extend the airport's runway.

The cost of these projects is enormous and the pace of the work has made it impossible for the government to contain them within its budget limits; increasingly, these improvements are paid for by tolls. Some complain that tunnel development has got out of hand, and, to a certain extent, this is true. The high-speed rail link to the Oslo Gardermoen Airport travels 14 km

LEFT: a steam train at Voss on what was to become the Oslo-Bergen railway line.
RIGHT: island-hopping in the Lofotens Islands.

those for whom a bus is almost an extinct species. What is more, Norwegian public transport has done a marvellous job of integrating road, rail, ferry and even airline schedules. The ferry waits for the train, and the smaller planes owned by Braathens and others, which carry most of the internal passengers, hop neatly from small airfield to small airfield.

There are also long-distance buses, the most outstanding being Express 2000 which runs between Oslo in the south and Hammerfest in the far north. It takes 25 hours, travelling through Sweden and Finland on the way, and claims to be the longest service of its kind in the whole of Europe.

The slow train

A technical article published in 1850 came to the conclusion that because of the difficult terrain and inhospitable climate "the use of the locomotive is impossible or impracticable". But the engineers proved the writer wrong, although building a railway was slow going. The first line from Christiania (now Oslo) to Eidsvoll opened in 1854, principally for the transport of timber from the Lake Mjøsa region to the harbour at Christiania from where it was exported.

This was typical of how the railways developed piecemeal, with unconnected segments serving a particular industry. The tracks were

not even the same width and, although the question of the gauge was resolved in 1894, it was 1949 before the last line of importance converted to European standard gauge.

The most important rail route in Norway, from Oslo to Bergen, was also one of the most difficult to build and its 470 km (295 miles) did not open until 1909. Now electrified, the Oslo-Bergen line is regarded as one of the great railway journeys of the world. It climbs over the massif of the Hardangervidda, which was conquered by engineering audacity, sheer sweat and a state budget. To protect the line against snowdrifts, the engineers built snow fences, tunnels and snow sheds along the most

exposed stretches: from Utstaoset 100 km (60 miles) of track lies above the tree-line. It includes 178 tunnels, and for many years the Gravhal tunnel was Norway's longest at 5,310 metres (5,800 yds).

At Myrdal there is a spectacular branch line to Flåm, on the Aurland fjord, which descends from 870 metres (2,845 ft) to just 2 metres (6 feet) above sea level in 20 kilometres (12 miles). It is now one of the major tourist attractions of Western Norway. The trains pause midway on the journey so that passengers can see and photograph the spectacular Kjosfossen waterfall. For safety reasons the engine has five independent braking systems.

All over Norway the many gradients and curves on virtually every line, plus the fact that much of the system is single track, mean that train speeds, even today, are not high. A limit on the volume of traffic, because the railways link comparatively small centres of population, also mean infrequent services.

Taking to the air

Just as Norway's natural conditions encouraged the development of coastal shipping, so the same conditions have proved to be made-to-measure for air transport. The thin spread of the population has not inhibited the development of an extensive domestic air network with 50 airports scattered all over the country.

These services are used by five million passengers a year – a ratio of passengers to population which is claimed to be a world record. The domestic and international network is long established and the spur of daunting distances has meant that the Norwegians have brought to aviation much of the same spirit that they brought to the development of shipping.

The major international airline is Scandinavian Airlines System (SAS), a joint operation between Norway, Sweden and Denmark, but the dominant domestic airline is Braathens. Widerøe is the main operator on the "thinner" routes serving many small communities, especially in the north of the country. Short-runway aircraft provide a regular service, even during the harsh winters, and most of the airports are tiny and carved out of what would appear to be, except to a Norwegian engineer, quite unsuitable terrain. ❑

LEFT: satellite communications in the Arctic.

Black Gold

It became clear in the 1970s that vast oil and gas riches lay beneath the ocean floor off the Norwegian coast, and yet the full extent of these resources is still being determined today. Current estimates predict that without major new oil discoveries oil production will gradually decline in the 21st century, but as a major gas exporter Norway can count on a longer perspective.

It all started in 1962 when, prompted by a gas find off Holland, the American Phillips oil company acquired the right to explore in Norwegian waters. Other companies soon followed. After clarification of legal problems and territorial rights with Denmark and Britain, drilling started in earnest in 1966. Four years later, Phillips announced the discovery of a giant oil field, Ekofisk. The 1970s saw a series of major discoveries: French Elf found Frigg; American Mobil found the world's largest offshore oil field, Statfjord; Shell confirmed the giant Troll gas field off Bergen. The wily Norwegians learned quickly and two Norwegian oil companies joined the fray. The state-owned Statoil discovered Gullfaks, and the semi-nationalised Norsk Hydro became the operator at Oseberg.

Oil production at the Ekofisk field started modestly from a floating rig in 1971. Permanent installations and a pipeline to Teesside in north-east England were commissioned in 1975. By the end of the 1970s Norway had built a gas processing plant at Kårstø, near Stavanger, and was exporting dry gas to the rest of continental Europe, and the Norwegian shipbuilding industry was entering a golden age as far as contracts were concerned.

Activities were for some time restricted to areas south of the 62nd parallel, in order to maintain a moderate tempo. Exploration off mid- and north Norway was not permitted until 1980, and even then it was strictly regulated. New finds were soon made at Haltenbanken off Trøndelag. Shell brought the Draugen oil reserves on stream in 1993. Further north, the Heidrun field started production in 1995. After several years of discussing production levels, the offshore industry was finally forced (by low oil prices and an inexperienced centre coalition government) into a 3 percent production cut, with the hope that this would help oil prices rise once again.

To the far north in the Barents Sea, some 50 wells have been sunk. So far no oil has been found,

RIGHT: at work on an offshore oil platform.

but plenty of gas, though as yet these fields are too far from Europe to be commercially viable. Nor is there any agreement with Russia over the demarcation line in the Barents Sea.

The Norwegian state has three sources of revenue from its offshore industry: taxes and duties levied on the oil companies; the state's direct economic involvement; and share dividends from its 100 percent ownership in Statoil and 50 percent ownership in Norsk Hydro. In 1997, the Labour government established an Oil Investment Fund, created from surplus oil revenues. The plan is to invest half of the fund with a view to financing future pension demands, among other things. The

price of oil has a huge impact on Norway's balance of trade. Off-shore oil and gas contribute more than 50 percent of export earnings.

With copious quantities of natural gas, as well as all the country's existing hydroelectric schemes, you would think that Norway would have plenty of energy: but you'd be wrong. With demand already outstripping supply by 10 percent, and bound by the 1998 Kyoto conference on climate change to reduce carbon dioxide emissions into the atmosphere, Norway is having to look elsewhere to regain self-sufficiency in electricity production. Whilst looking into clean ways of burning natural gas, attention is now focusing on such renewable sources as bio-energy (burning wood), heat pumps and solar power. ❑

AN OUTDOOR LIFE

In Norway you are free to roam, through forest or over mountain; but wherever you end up, however remote, you can rely on the homely comforts of a hytte

As a race, Norwegians are quite at home in their wild, unspoilt country, and have a great feeling for its mountains. Composer Edvard Grieg, who did much to capture the Norwegian landscape in his music, wrote with passion of the Jotunheimen range in central Norway: "When I contemplate the possibility of a future visit to the mountains, I shudder with joy and expectation, as if it were a matter of hearing Beethoven's Tenth Symphony." There are higher, more remote, more exotically named countries with more photographically stunning landscapes, yet few can claim a population so attuned to its great outdoors.

One Norwegian in four counts outdoor recreation as a first pastime, and Norwegians excel at sports evolved from outdoor pursuits such as cross-country running or skiing, orienteering and cycling. Everyone, from all walks of life, takes part: urbanite and ruralist, commoner and king tramp the terrain, year round. Foreign visitors, unaware of this, often find the mass migration to the open air unnerving, especially if they arrive on business at Easter or during July, the prime times of the year for moor and mountain, sea and shore.

Free to roam

Centuries of that view evolved into one of the country's shortest laws – the 1957 *Lov om friluftslivet* (Outdoor Recreations Act) – which states succinctly that: "At any time of the year, outlying property may be crossed on foot, with consideration and due caution." The few restraints imposed are for environmental or safety reasons. Camping isn't permitted in the immediate watersheds of drinking-water reservoirs, and bonfires are forbidden during summer dry spells that can turn the taiga to tinder.

This liking for untethered roaming seems an integral part of the national character. Among the country's real-life heroes are Fridtjof

PRECEDING PAGES: walking along a forest trail.
LEFT: at the end of a day's sailing.
RIGHT: climbing a glacier in the Jotunheimen.

Nansen and Roald Amundsen, towering figures of polar exploration around the turn of the 20th century, and Thor Heyerdahl, probably the most widely known Norwegian abroad.

Though on a smaller scale, encounters with nature thread the fabric of everyday life. A family returning from an autumn hike to collect

wild mushrooms for the table will drop into a public mushroom check station to verify the edibility of their harvest. In the winter, city dwellers heading for a ski tour in a nearby forest dial the same snow report number as they dialled the previous summer for the water temperatures at local bathing areas.

Norwegian kindergartens and day-care centres are usually small buildings attached to extensive outdoor playgrounds, designed for day-long activity. Only in extreme weather, defined in most places as below –10°C (14° F), do the kids stay indoors or at home. Coddling in Norway does not include separation from the wrath of the elements. Yet Norwegians see no valour in doing battle with nature. As the British polar exploration chronicler Roland Huntford pointed out, that's more the British psyche: Norwegians are much likelier to meet nature on its own terms and seek or make their own comfort wherever they go.

The *hytte*, a home from home

In a country where winter days are short and nasty weather can crop up any time of the year, comfort translates to secure shelter, often your own. Fully a quarter of the country's households also own a holiday home, or *hytte*. By an accident of etymology, *hytte* translates to "hut",

Following the red "T"

Supreme on that scale are the *hytter* run by Den Norske Turistforeningen (DNT), literally "The Norwegian Tourist Association", with Tourist implying "on foot". Now well into its second century of housing and otherwise providing for walkers, skiers and climbers, DNT and its sibling local tourist associations own *hytter* throughout the Norwegian wilderness. Even the simplest put to rest any thought of a "hut", while the larger make the title ludicrous.

Well-marked walking trails connect the lodges or cabins (two better translations of *hytter*) which stand at crossroads on networks so

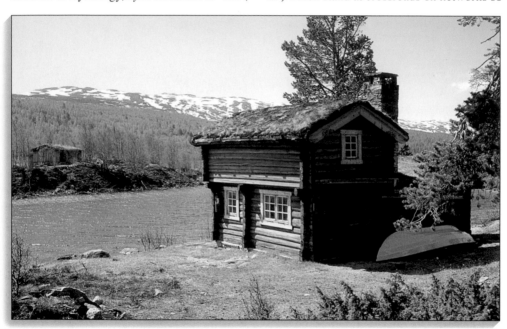

but there the similarity stops. A *hytte* is by no means a rough structure; most are well appointed small wooden houses, and many are larger than their owners' permanent homes.

Those without a *hytte* of their own are frequently related to, or are close friends of, *hytte* owners. Otherwise, there are many paths to the comforts of a *hytte*. Clubs and associations often own one, and one of the standard business "perks" is liberal use of the company *hytte*. Even though holiday flats and time-share apartments are on the increase, the *hytte* still reigns supreme in fulfilling its original intent: to supply comfort in remoter places where it is otherwise unavailable.

extensive that DNT 's trail marker, a red painted letter "T" on cairns, has become synonymous with serious walking. When winter snows cover the cairns, poles in the snow serve the same purpose.

The bulk of the trails and lodges are conveniently in the middle of the triangle bounded by the cities of Oslo, Bergen and Trondheim. A central entry point is Finse, situated above the timber line at 1,200 metres (4,000 ft). Finse's main street is the station platform; there are no cars because there are no roads. When a train has gone and the last passengers have left, Finse returns to normal, a speck in a seemingly infinite expanse of rock, ice and snow.

A few hundred metres from Finse railway station is the DNT *hytte*, with its 114 bunk beds in two and four-person rooms, hot showers, a staffed dining room serving three meals a day, a snack bar and three lounges. Other DNT lodges are still larger: Gjendesheim in Jotunheimen has 129 bunks. The DNT also has unstaffed self-service accommodation. Here you can prepare your own food or purchase from a pantry. You pay upon leaving, by putting money in a box on the wall. The honour system works well.

FARAWAY SO NEAR

So ethereal yet so accessible is Finse that it was chosen as a location for the space adventure film *The Empire Strikes Back*, the sequel to *Star Wars*.

scale of note-worthy mountains where sheer altitude, not challenge, is the main criterion. Though this fact has led to relative anonymity – few Norwegian peaks appear in the classic mountaineering literature – it does mean that you can ascend the equivalent of the Matterhorn or Mont Blanc without having to cope with the problems of altitude.

Most Jotunheimen trails meander from 900–1,200 metres (3,000–4,000 ft) above sea level and there are few or no acclimatisation problems at that height.

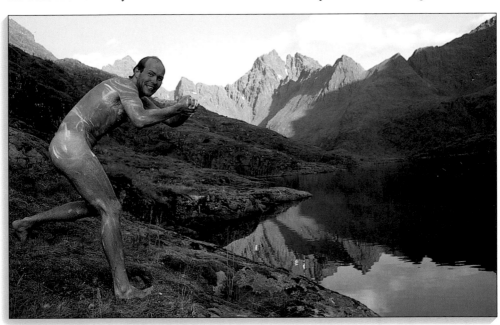

LEFT: a typical *hytte*, in Ottadalen.
ABOVE: going for a quick dip in the fjord.

Accessible mountaineering

To the north of Finse lie the Jotunheimen mountains, the range that took its name from Norse mythology, literally "Home of the Giants". The name is appropriate: peaks jut a kilometre and more skywards from lake-studded, moraine-strewn flats, all above the timber line. Nonetheless, even the loftiest of the Jotunheimen peaks, Galdhøpiggen and Glittertind, which are the highest in Northern Europe with summits more than 2,400 metres (7,900 ft) high, rank low on the international

Some of the glaciers that hewed the Norwegian landscape left offspring. One, Jostedalsbreen (the Jostedal Glacier), is the largest on the mainland of Europe. Jostedalsbreen and its siblings throughout the country are the places to see crampon-shod parties wielding ice axes from spring until autumn. Contact with the ice that shaped their land is currently the Norwegians' fastest-growing wilderness recreation and many centres now organise specialist courses.

Skiing

Skis have been a source of benefit and pleasure to Norwegians for thousands of years, with much of local community life in winter dependent on skis. In the 19th century skiing evolved into a mass sport, urged on by the Morgedal pioneer Sondre Norheim. The first skiing competitions were arranged in the mid 1880s – the term "slalom" originated in Morgedal from the Norwegian words *sla*, meaning slope or hill, and *låm*, depicting the track down it.

Norwegians have practically unlimited access to skiing and skating facilities. About 30,000 km (18,600 miles) – three times the distance between Norway and Australia – of

> ## STONE AGE SKIER
>
> The Rodøy Man, a 4,000-year-old rock carving in Nordland, is evidence that skiing in Norway dates back to the Stone Age.

has decreased somewhat in popularity in recent years. Nevertherless there are some 600 ski-jumps in Norway *(see page 105)*. In the total absence of snow, there is always skating or ice hockey. In winter, municipalities up and down the country convert sports fields and playgrounds into ice rinks by getting the local fire brigade to spray them with water. These are then used for ice hockey and speed skating. When the fjords freeze over, whole families take Sunday "walks" on skates among the rocks and islets.

marked ski trails wind their way through unspoiled scenery. Cross-country skiing in the mountains may be enjoyed until well into May. The winter darkness is no obstacle with some 2,500 illuminated tracks providing for a bit of serious exercise after work.

Alpine skiing has gradually increased in popularity in Norway. Though by no means as universal as cross-country skiing, most communities have a locally prepared piste. Major ski resorts include Trysil in Hedmark, Hemsedal and Geilo in Buskerud, Voss in Hordeland (which is a year-round resort), and, of course, Lillehammer in Oppland, the location of the 1994 Winter Olympics. Ski-jumping

Outdoors in reach

In travelling time, even the remote wilderness areas are close to the bulk of the population: the wilderness itself is still closer. Oslo is bounded on its landward side by Øslomarka, a vast area of forests (larger than Greater London) set aside for outdoor recreation. Likewise, Bergen has its Vidden, Trondheim its Bymarka, Tromsø its Tromsdalen. No Norwegian city is without nearby natural surprises. But to Norwegians, who are as likely to shoulder rucksacks as to carry a briefcase, that's no surprise. ❑

ABOVE: one of the many small harbours along Norway's long coastline.

The Great Ski-Jump

The Holmenkollen Ski Festival is the oldest in the world and one million people leave the centre of Oslo for Holmenkollen during the 11 days of the festival in March each year. At the climax on Holmenkollen Sunday, more than 50,000 people gather at this famous ski-jump hill to watch ski-jumping in the country that invented it. But though the Nordic skiing competitions (cross-country and ski-jumping) and the newer events attract top competitors eager for World Cup points, Holmenkollen is much more than yet another international winter competition. This is very much a citizens' festival, a chance for ordinary Norwegians and visitors to take part in the events.

The idea of sitting or strolling as a spectator all day in the middle of a Norwegian winter might sound like the best way of catching a cold but the excitement is high. Wrapped in boots, anoraks, gloves and hat, with the necessary extra of a warm cushion to sit on, everything is happening and you need no more than a regular quick coffee, best laced with aquavit, to keep out the cold.

Norway was the first country to introduce ski competitions when Norwegian soldiers began to compete as early as 1767 and the first civilian event took place in 1843 at Tromsø. By the 1880s, the Norwegian Society for the Promotion of Skiing already held a winter competition and in 1892, this transferred to Holmenkollen. That year, the longest ski-jump was 22 metres (72 ft). Today, it is more than 126 metres (413 ft).

In the very first days the competitors were all Norwegian but even by 1903 Swedes had arrived, and were soon joined by French and German skiers. Since World War II, foreigners from most skiing countries have taken part – and won. Women first competed in 1947, when Alpine skiing events were introduced, but they weren't admitted to the cross-country race until 1954.

Norway's King Olav V, a first-class sportsman, made his debut on the Holmenkollen jump in 1922, and was a faithful spectator for nearly 70 years. His son, King Harald, has inherited this keen interest in the sport. As long as there is a jump at Holmenkollen, the royal family will watch the events from the royal box.

The fortnight begins with the Handicap Ski Race; next comes the Guards' Race, followed by the Norwegian Members of Parliament – fitter perhaps than their counterparts elsewhere – and local politicians, and cross-country skiing at all levels. On Children's Day more than 5,000 children swarm into the arena, for events to mark the end of the season at the children's ski school, and on Holmenkollen Sunday itself, the Holmenkollen March attracts around 7,000 to 8,000 people, many just ordinary skiers, to ski either 21 or 42 km (13 or 26 miles) through the Nordmarka forest finishing right under the jump.

The atmosphere of Holmenkollen Sunday is electric. They call it Norway's second national day, after Constitution Day on 17 May, and most spectators

arrive early for a large breakfast-cum-brunch at one of the local hotels to keep out the sub-zero cold, before making their way to their seats. First come the children's events and demonstrations of skills such as Telemark skiing and parachute jumping. Next is the finish of the Holmenkollen March which leads up to the climax, the great ski-jump.

The huge crowd packed into the arena hushes as the first skier appears. Up there on the top platform, he looks like a being from another world. The silence lasts until the tiny, bright figure takes off and, in a second, is flying through space with an ease that makes it look simple. Then as skier follows skier in graceful arcs, a roar loud enough to cause an avalanche fills Holmenkollen. ❑

RIGHT: Holmenkollen Sunday.

SPORTING PASSIONS

To Norwegians, sport is almost a religion, permeating every aspect of life, and there is room for everyone, from Olympic champions to Sunday goalkeepers

Put the question "Are you a skier?" at almost any social gathering anywhere in Europe, and you could expect a few positive responses and perhaps a lecture or two on the virtues of the sport. Put the same question to someone you meet of a Sunday afternoon at one of the ski trail lodges in Norway, which you can only reach on skis, and the answers will be quite different: "No, I'm a bank clerk"; "Who me? Never dream of it!".

A way of life

Why the disparity? The answer lies in a tradition that has woven sport deeply into the fabric of Norwegian life. It is even reflected in the language. While English has just one word, "sport", Norwegian has two: *sport* and *idrett*. The Norwegian *sport* is the umbrella word that covers all sporting events, so that a sports journalist in Norway plies exactly the same trade as his or her foreign counterpart. The word *idrett* is reserved for events in which the limits in performance are determined by the capabilities of the human body. Horse riding is not *idrett*, while scuba diving is. There is a further nuance: *aktiv* (active) means a person currently competing in a sport classified as *idrett*.

This explains why, when you ask skiing Norwegians "are you a skier?", you have asked if they currently compete in the sport. Ask often enough, and you unearth the astonishing fact that one Norwegian in three is *aktiv*.

Mad about sport

This amazing statistic reflects the high priority Norwegians give to sport. Oslo has numerous statues of living Norwegians in sporting poses: a statue of King Olav V skiing, near the Holmenkollen ski jump, one of marathon runner Grete Waitz running, of course, at the marathon gate of Bislett Stadium, and statues of speed skater Oscar Mathisen and figure skater Sonja

Henie near the Frogner Park Stadium. All new high-rise flats are obliged by law to include "sports gear storage rooms". Within the Ministry of Church and Education there is a department for "Youth and *Idrett*". City newspapers vie with each other for sales on the strengths of their sports sections, and almost 14 percent

of the Norwegian Broadcasting Corporation's output is devoted to sports.

So pervasive is sport that visitors sometimes ask "Where is the flash, the excitement?" The answer is that the pinnacles are there, as high and sometimes higher than elsewhere, but the surrounding plateau of sporting achievement is so high that it makes the peaks less prominent.

Norges Idrettsforbund (NIF), the Norwegian Confederation of Sports, is the umbrella organisation for 53 separate sports federations with, in total, more than 1.7 million members. It spotlights this fact in its motto "Sport for All", and the pinnacles are grouped and designated "elite". So, for the Confederation and its

LEFT: on the cross-country trail.
RIGHT: a youthful Prince Haakon Magnus shows his skill as a water-skier.

Morgedal and Telemark Revival

For jazz fans, New Orleans is the ultimate magnet, just as Wimbledon is for tennis players. For skiers, the start of it all is Morgedal, in the southern county of Telemark, a hamlet that long remained an entry only found in history books pored over by scholars of the sport of skiing. Today, that has all changed because of a reawakening of interest in the style of skiing called Telemark, which evolved in Morgedal.

In the mid 19th century, there were even fewer people than the 200,000 who live in Telemark today – a hardy breed of woodsmen, small farmers, hunters and traders, who fashioned their own implements including the skis they needed to get about on winter snows. Morgedal is in the mountains, so the ski makers there sought designs that would perform well in the surrounding rugged terrain, both in everyday winter skiing and for impromptu sporting meetings. Among the best in the mid-1800s was Sondre Norheim, a young tenant farmer. He excelled not only in village ski meetings but also in ski-making skills.

Norheim devised bindings (devices that hold ski boots to skis) that were firm and were the first to give the feet control over the skis. He also gave the skis what is known as "sidecut", the slight hourglass profile of a ski seen from above. Sidecut is what enables skis to run true and turn easily, even to this day.

Norheim and his fellow Morgedal skiers used the new designs to perfect new skiing manoeuvres, including ways of turning and stopping on snow, and ways of landing from airborne flights off snow-covered rooftops and natural outcrops. Their fame spread and, by 1868, Norheim and his farmers from Telemark were ready to show off their new skills. He led them on skis for the 180-kilometre (112-mile) journey from Morgedal to Christiania (now Oslo), where the city crowds turned out to greet and applaud the peasant skiers and their miraculous new techniques. This led to the start of the big ski-jumping contest at Husaby near Oslo in 1879, where 10,000 spectators led by the king cheered the skiing pioneers from Telemark. Around the same time, the Telemark skiers established the world's first ski school in Oslo.

In 1902, the first ski-jumping rules committee met to compile criteria for judging the style of competitors at the annual Holmenkollen ski-jump meetings. They honoured the origins of the two most skilful groups by affixing their names to the two turns then executed by ski jumpers to come to a stop after landing from flight. The turn in which the skis are held parallel throughout was named the Christiania, while the bent-knee stance with one ski trailing became the Telemark.

In modern Telemark skiing, the heel is free to lift up from the ski, and turns are steered, with one ski trailing and at an angle to the other. From the side, the manoeuvre looks like a genuflection in motion. Although competitive Telemark ski races are now held on packed slopes, as are alpine ski races, true Telemark skiing is a throwback to the skiing of Sondre Norheim's time. The rebirth of the Telemark turn has revived another old skiing practice – skiathlon – in which competitors must ski-jump, ski through a slalom course, and run a cross-country ski race, all on the same pair of skis.

The name is new, but the combination of manoeuvres dates to the times when the men from Morgedal first mastered the ski-jumping meets in Christiania some 130 years ago. A ski–jumping performance required the competitor to jump through the air, come to a stop after landing, ski back uphill to the top of the ski-jump, and jump again before finishing. ❑

LEFT: Traditionally Telemark skiing uses one stick only.

member associations, competitive sport is both egalitarian and elitist.

International competition

From the broad base of people for whom sport is a major leisure time activity come the elite, competitors who enter the many national championships and represent Norway in international sports meetings. The results speak for themselves. For a country with such a small population, Norway has always been disproportionately strong in sports.

Traditionally, Norwegian competitive prowess has been in winter sports and in sail-

of the profits of the state-run football pools and Lotto, the national lottery.

In addition, the 5,000-odd clubs use extra-curricular activities, such as bingo and local lotteries, to raise up to 40 percent of their income. Wherever you go, you are besieged by young people selling lottery tickets to support the local sports club.

However, recreation-type activities have been gaining in popularity at the expense of more strenuous sports. The Ski Association, Handball Federation and Athletics Federation are losing members while golf, billiards and amateur dancing federations are growing.

ing, but Norwegians have also won international medals in a wide range of events including marathon running, cycling, boxing, wrestling, handball, karate, canoeing, rowing, shooting, weight-lifting, women's football and ballroom dancing.

Such pervasiveness and prowess have their price. The annual turnover in sports, excluding the sports equipment sector, is more than NOK1,400 million (£120 million), and sports are supported through many channels: the NIF receives 90–95 percent of its revenue from central government, and sport receives one-third

ABOVE: the Norwegian football team in action.

Football figures first

As elsewhere in Europe, football is Norway's number one sport, with more than 1,800 clubs and a total of over 280,000 players. It is also the best supported, through funds from the football pools and from the sale of players to the major European leagues, in particular the English Premier League. As a result, a number of English clubs are now well supported by Norwegian fans.

While Norwegian football struggles to drop its amateur status (the population is too thin, too self-engaged, and too busy to generate serious gate money), foreign coaches and eager agents find rich pickings among the home-grown talent.

Individual sports

Number two in the statistics and, its supporters contend, spiritually number one, is the country's traditional stalwart, skiing, with more than 1,500 clubs and a total membership of over 200,000. Together the five skiing disciplines – cross-country, alpine, ski-jumping, biathlon (a cross-country skiing and rifle shooting combination event), and combined (ski-jumping followed by a cross-country competition) – receive as much funding as football. Third in line is gymnastics, with more than 500 clubs and over 100,000 members. Then follow handball, track and field athletics,

orienteering, shooting, swimming, sailing and volleyball. Of these top ten only three, football, handball and volleyball, are team sports. The balance is almost the complete reverse of most countries, where team sports dominate, a possible reflection of the Norwegian mentality.

Grass roots support

The backbone of Norwegian sports is, of course, Norwegian involvement. A great deal of work on sports facilities is local and voluntary. Approximately half of the country's 1.4 million families with children are involved in sports in some way other than direct participation. Father is an official of the local club, and mother helps on the stalls at the annual club flea market. The older children sell club lottery tickets. In fact the whole family helps to run the annual club meets. Most families have one member who is either a certified coach or is training to become one.

One persistent reminder of this involvement is the seeming ubiquity of sports facilities and sports instruction. There are 10,000–12,000 sports centres in Norway, from the most modest local football field to major stadiums and indoor halls. In summer and autumn, they are hatcheries for future football and track-and-field athletic talents. In winter, their iced surfaces swarm with figure and speed skaters and serve as mini-arenas for ice hockey and *bandy*, a related sport played with a ball instead of a puck, to rules more closely resembling those of field hockey.

This high involvement has some drawbacks. In the more popular sports, competition has become so fierce that the criteria for doing well have been elevated to seemingly unattainable heights. Youngsters pushed into competition by overzealous parents can burn out prematurely, and this has become a recognised problem in almost all sports.

Such intense involvement, though, doesn't diminish the everyday enjoyment of sport. Internationally renowned violinist Arve Tellefsen's prime lament is that his infrequent sports ventures – his boyhood skills of ski-racing and football – invariably rate more media coverage than his violin virtuosity. But that doesn't prevent him from putting on a pair of skis or kicking a football at the weekend. ❏

WINTER OLYMPICS

Norway can claim more Winter Olympic medals than any other country apart from the former Soviet Union, and winter sportsmen and women are among the country's heroes. In the 2002 Olympics in Salt Lake City, Norway came second to Germany – winning 11 golds, 7 silvers and 7 bronzes – but ahead of Russia, Canada and the United States. The Norwegain cross-country skier Bjørn Dæhlie has printed his name indelibly on Winter Olympic history with the highest number of individual medals ever. In recent years Norwegian alpine skiers Ketil Andre Aamodt and Lasse Kjus have both won the Alpine World Cup.

LEFT: kayaking in Arctic waters.
RIGHT: climbing a frozen waterfall.

FISHING: SPORT AND SUSTENANCE

Norway's fjords, rivers and coastline are a veritable anglers' paradise. And when it comes to eating fish, Norwegians have a dish for every occasion

To Norwegians, fish is the standby staple. Even in modest markets, the variety of fish and fish products is amazing, and Norwegians look on a proper fresh fish shop as an asset to a community. Fish is both humble fare and holiday cuisine. Fish balls in white sauce are the Norwegian dining-table stalwart, and steamed

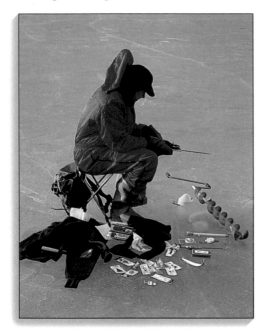

cod is a favourite for Sunday dinners. On festive occasions, herring in myriad forms takes its place with other delicacies such as *gravlaks* (cured salmon), *rakørret* (half-fermented trout), and *lutefisk* (dried codfish marinated in a lye solution, a dish few foreigners appreciate).

It is not surprising that Norway is a country of fishermen of all kinds. The language differentiates between them accordingly: *fisker* means "fisherman", one who lives by commercial fishing; while *sportsfisker* is the amateur variety, an "angler". But there the similarity stops. Angling in Norway is done both for the sport itself and as part of other outdoor pursuits. Fishing tackle is among the paraphernalia of camping trips, just as it is the prime equipment for avid anglers.

The long coastline is a mecca for saltwater angling, yet freshwater angling is the more popular pastime, and there are a quarter of a million fishable inland lakes and ponds. The most common of around 40 freshwater species are trout and char; in the northernmost parts, and in lakes and ponds at higher elevations, they are the only fish. Grayling and pike are more common in larger lakes and rivers in eastern and central areas. Local legends about lakes rich in pike hold that the fish are descended from stocks set out in the late 18th century by the ruling Danes.

Bream, whitefish, perch and carp are found in most lower lakes in the southern part of the country, as well as in eastern Finnmark in the far north. Reliable varieties in saltwater include cod, coalfish, haddock, whiting, halibut, herring and mackerel.

The stars on the angling scene are the Atlantic salmon and sea trout, related varieties which are both popular game and commercial fish. The commercial varieties now come largely from fish farms, but the game fish still swim the rivers until they are two to six years old, migrate to the sea, and then return to spawn in some 400 rivers. Norwegians argue about the best rivers, but five in the northern part of the country stand out – the Alta and Tana rivers in Finnmark, and the Gaula, Namsen and Orkla rivers in Trøndelag, all of which draw anglers from around the world. There, the sport is so popular that you have to apply for licences as much as a year in advance.

Gaining a licence

You need two types of angling licence to keep within the law. The first one is the annual *Fiskeravgift* (fishing fee) that helps to offset the costs of overseeing fishing and the aquatic environment (particularly adding lime to the water). The *Fiskeravgift* can be obtained at the post office and covers freshwater fish and crabs, but not salmon and sea trout. The latter two are, however, included in the annual fishing licence, which is usually twice the cost of the fishing fee. Fishing in sea water is free, whereas fishing in lakes and rivers requires a further local licence. Freshwater fishing licences come from the owners of the fishing rights, usually the property owners along the banks of a river or the shores of a lake, whether private persons or communities. These vary in price, and are valid for specific dates and periods, ranging from one day to several weeks. You can buy them from local hotels, sports shops or tourist offices.

Fly fishing is popular, so much so that Norwegians compete in the sport, including the annual world championships in fly casting.

Other countries do better in fly-casting competition, but the Norwegians pride themselves on their versatility. Lure fishing leads, spoon-hook fishing and trolling are also widespread.

Baiting the hook

Even youngsters start fishing using artificial bait. Theories abound as to why this is so, but the most plausible ascribes it to Norway's location and topography. In the north, there are few insects large enough to use as bait, and worms are hard to find on rocky shores. Minnows and other live fish are prohibited as bait, primarily to curtail the spread of parasites and diseases.

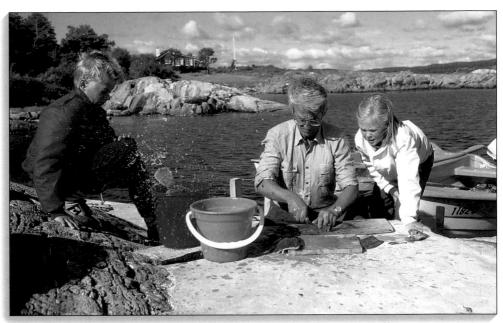

MAXIMUMS AND MINIMUMS

The question of size, whether with a record in mind or to protect juvenile fish, is never far away. Norwegian angling records include 32.5 kg (71.6 lb) for freshwater salmon and 37.5 kg (82.6 lb) for cod caught in the sea. Although trout average 0.5 kg (1 lb), the freshwater trout record currently stands at 15.3 kg (33.7 lb). As for the minimum permissible sizes for keeping caught fish, they are 25 cm (9.8 inches) in length for salmon, sea trout and sea char, and 30 cm (11.8 inches) for all other fish.

LEFT: the strange fascination of ice fishing.
ABOVE: cleaning the catch outside the family *hytte*.

For the same reasons, the transfer of live fish, water, or wet fishing boats or other equipment, from one watercourse to another is prohibited.

Just as winter does not deter Norwegians from walking (they switch to cross-country skis), frozen lakes do not halt fishing. Ice fishing is a prime wintertime hobby, a simple and straightforward form of angling, which requires only a baited hand line or short pole and line, warm clothing, and lots of patience. Ice anglers must hew holes in the ice by hand as motorised augers are prohibited. It's a sport for the hardy, and ice angling contests, such as the popular Ice Fishing Festival at Vangsvatnet in Voss, are for the very dedicated. ❑

THE TRADITIONAL ARTS

Tradition is strong in Norway, especially when it comes to the folk arts; but to an inquisitive eye, that tradition contains some unexpected influences

In AD 793 "dire portents appeared over Northumbria and sorely frightened the people. They consisted of immense whirlwinds and flashes of lightning, and fiery dragons were seen flying in the air. A great famine followed those signs, and a little after that in the same year, on 8 June, the ravages of heathen men miserably destroyed God's church on Lindisfarne, with plunder and slaughter."

So the *Anglo-Saxon Chronicle* documented the destruction of the monastery at Lindisfarne, now Holy Island, just south of Berwick-upon-Tweed in Northumberland in the northeast of England. It was the first major impact on Christendom by the Vikings, the pagan men of the north who were to make their mark on European culture for the next three centuries. But in the end, it was a reciprocal cultural exchange. An early Viking king, Olav Haraldson, converted to Christianity, was baptised in Normandy, and returned to his homeland to introduce the faith. By the year 1030, when he fell in battle, he had firmly rooted Christianity in most areas as Norway's future religion.

Today, the legacy of the Vikings is neither blurred nor buried, but still highly visible in a myriad of forms, collectively termed the folk arts. Wood carving, rustic painting, colourful national costumes and decorative painting are the most obvious forms.

Wood carving

The Viking Age owed its very being to superior sea power. The Viking craft, or longships as they became known, were at once extremely seaworthy and boldly beautiful. They were clinker built (overlapping planks held together with iron rivets) on long keel planks that swept up to a stem at either end. The Vikings carved elaborate decorations on the prows down to the waterline, often with dragon heads and figures.

They also carved elaborate designs on everyday items, from the handles of implements to the lever of the aft-right mounted *styrbord*, or steering board. On land, the details of buildings were similarly enhanced. Pillars were carved, not just at their capitals, but over their entire surfaces. There were ornate friezes, inte-

rior mouldings were decorated and gable ends became display points. Wood carving was a highly developed art, executed primarily for, and partly by, the Viking aristocracy.

Stave churches

By the 12th century, Christianity had supplanted the aristocracy as the prime patron of the arts, and the wooden *stavkirke* (stave church) became the major outlet of wood carving as an art form. About 750 of these magnificent structures were built, most in a 100-year period from 1150 to 1250, and 32 survive to this day, making them among the world's oldest wooden buildings. Their ornately carved

---

PRECEDING PAGES: traditional rose painting.
LEFT: a detail from Tidemand's *The Grandmother's Bridal Crown*.
RIGHT: jewellery on a national costume.

portals serve the same purpose as old book illumination in England. They are one of the country's manuscripts. First, there are the animal heads of Nordic mythology, documenting the remnants of the Viking Age; then the classical tendril of Christian art appears, springing from the jaws of a beast. Finally, tendrils and flowers assert themselves, sometimes solo and sometimes interwoven with other motifs, partly but not completely replacing the beasts. Aside from the stave churches and their various artefacts, these early people decorated chairs, beds, tables, ladles, bowls and other household items with ornate carving. Some of the best-preserved

for peasant pieces of native spruce or pine, the more ornately carved the better.

"Collecting old houses is something of a family mania," says one shipowner (the nearest Norway comes to an aristocracy). "My father, brother and I have been combing the back country for 40 years for handcrafted dwellings and objects, homesteads, barns, cabins and huts complete with their country beds, chests, baskets and cupboards. Each must be unique to its own valley and period."

Typical of the national mania for folk art, this family's collection began simply by bartering with valley farmers for small items, such as

examples of the work of Norwegian medieval artisans are the carved portals, window surrounds and other details of farm buildings.

A passion for the past

The traditions survive to the present day. The timber *hytte* – even the ultra-modern *hytte* built in the 21st century – must have some exterior carving, and the Frognerseteren Restaurant, which was built in 1891 on a hillside overlooking Oslo and remodelled in 1909, is one of the best examples of the more modern dragon style of decorated wooden buildings. Today's nostalgia in home furnishings is not for the lavish designs of the courts of the past, but rather

handcrafted butter and porridge *tine*. These colourful, wooden caskets, often a first gift to a betrothed, form an unbroken tradition from Viking times to the present. Always highly decorated, the *tine* are still used by country lads to show off their carving and rose painting skills.

Rose painting

Much as wood carving evolved from the urge to decorate functional items, the art Norwegians call *rosemaling* or "rose painting" sprang from humble surroundings. The two were often used together: carved building details and household furnishings and implements were frequently painted, both as enhancement of, and in contrast to, the carved wood. The name misleads: roses appear only in a few of the traditional patterns; it would be more correct to term it "rustic painting", which denotes its agrarian roots, far removed from the cities. True *rosemaling* is not limited to flowery designs, although variations of the tendril motif are its strongest themes. It also includes geometric figures, portraits, and an occasional landscape.

The earliest decorations have survived less well than the carvings on which they were painted, so the beginnings of rose painting remain an enigma. The oldest surviving examples date from around 1700, centuries after the necessary paints were first available.

Theories on its origins abound. One school of thought holds that originally it was used to add colour to drab interiors. From medieval times on the typical rural dwelling was an *årestue* (hearth house), a windowless room with an opening in the roof to let the smoke from the open fire in the centre to escape. Rose painting could have been the peasants' reaction to their otherwise grey interior environments.

Another line of thought, with some substantiation in contemporary historical records, is that the peasants emulated the ornate decorations of churches, which were then also the major civic buildings in rural areas.

Imported styles

Whatever its origins, rose painting evolved and, in its own right, became a record of its times. The earlier rose paintings of interiors and household articles clearly show that the art of the Renaissance reached as far as the Norwegian countryside. The colours are the peasant stalwarts, blue, green, red and yellow, but the patterns are definitely imported.

The prosperity of the late 18th century brought more clerics and more functionaries to rural districts and with the new professionals came their belongings, decorated household furnishings and implements. What the peasants saw they replicated as best they could in their own style.

Most were untutored and the commonest way of learning the skills was either from travelling artists or from local practitioners. The

relative isolation of the valleys, cut off from their neighbours by the high mountain ranges, meant that every valley became its own art centre for a particular style of painting.

Too conservative to borrow directly from outsiders, Norwegian farmers carefully extracted only those aspects that fitted their own sense of colour and decoration. Hallingdal farmers were partial to delicate S-curves applied to everything from walls to spoons and bowls. In affluent Gudbrandsdal, the locals carved their decorations into built-in benches and box beds. The most isolated districts, such as Setesdal, have a very simplified *rosemaling* tradition. So indi-

vidual were the styles, today's experts can identify the age and origin of almost any item with uncanny accuracy. Their knowledge is currently much in demand as rose-painted period furniture commands the highest of prices for Norwegian antiques.

Rose painting survives today, like wood carving, as a nostalgic link with the past and throughout the country amateur rose painters keep that link alive. For most it is a hobby with the occasional spin-off of small profits from sales to local handicraft shops. But for some it offered more. One of the antique business scandals of 1989 concerned cleverly faked, rose-painted "antique" furniture.

LEFT: rose painting used to decorate a set of shelves.
RIGHT: Einar Holte at work on one of his famous miniature wooden boats.

The national costume

Norway's *bunad* is as colourful as the national costumes of any country. It is not just worn by folk dancers or for fancy-dress parties, but is in regular use as formal attire at weddings, official ceremonies, and at gatherings on national holidays. Many claim that the *bunad* is Europe's most often worn national costume.

The *bunad* is a throwback to the everyday clothing of times past, and the word itself means simply "clothes". It has developed variations in style, cut, colouring and accessories according to locality and the skills and tastes of its makers. There were costumes for men,

women and children, everyday *bunads* and dress *bunads*. As with rose painting every area of the country had its own style.

Despite these differences, the *bunad* has common characteristics that identify the dress as Norwegian. Women's costumes characteristically have skirts or dresses of double-shuttle woven wool and bodices or jackets of similar or contrasting material worn over blouses with scarves. Sashes, purses, the beautiful silver accessories and traditional shoes and stockings complete the costume. Men's *bunads* are essentially three-piece knickerbocker suits, with matching or contrasting waistcoats, white shirts, long socks and traditional shoes.

Like wood carving and *rosemaling*, the design of a *bunad* is in itself a historical record. For example, those from coastal areas often reveal a stronger Continental influence than those from the remote valleys, where housewives spun, dyed and wove their own woollens to local patterns.

Folk revival

In the mid-19th century, factory-made cloth and garments began to replace homespun products. As people moved from farm to town, the *bunad* seemed to be heading for extinction. It was rescued single-handedly by Hulda Garborg, a prominent author who saw a need to preserve the rural traditions. Shortly before the turn of the 20th century, she founded a *leikarring*, or folk dance group, in Oslo. Folk dances should, she maintained, be performed in folk costumes which led her to compile the first anthology of *bunads*, published in 1903. It was a best seller and Garborg and one of her dancers, Klara Semb, succeeded in starting the folk dance movement and a *bunad* renaissance which continues to the present day.

Although *bunads* are no longer daily wear, the number of known types and varieties is greater than ever. Some, like those from Setesdal, date back 300 years or more. Others, such as the costume from Bærum, a suburb of Oslo, have been designed in the past 40 years.

Its current popularity is matched only by the range of opinions about how it should be worn. Traditionalists contend that a *bunad* from a particular district should be worn only by a person born and bred there. Moderates maintain that correct style outweighs the circumstances of the wearer's birth and upbringing, and the radicals view the *bunad* as a style to be copied piecemeal in modern clothes.

While the standard dark suit has, like in so many other countries, become the bastion of the Norwegian male wardrobe, women still face the dilemma of what to wear for formal occasions. In Norway, a *bunad* is always correct. It is timeless and may be passed on from generation to generation, while the traditional silver belt is often a gift from a father and mother to their son's wife. ❑

LEFT: Hulda Garborg (left) photographed in 1899 dressed in a traditional *bunad*.
RIGHT: the 13th-century Heddal stave church.

TRADITION, NOT HAUTE CULTURE

Norwegian artists, writers and musicians dug deep into the country's
rural past in search of a new national identity

Culture in Norway? Well, certainly it exists, in its own fashion. Just take a look at your fellow travellers in the Oslo Central Station. Half of them trudge around in boots and a backpack; the other half have only the backpack. They are all heading for isolated cabins – Norway's holy *hytte* – far away from the city and its pleasures. The Munch Museum and National Theatre take second place to trekking the highlands, searching mountain valleys for *rosemaling*, the indigenous folk art.

That is all culture certainly, though not of the grand, *haute* culture sort. Although Norway does not foster glittering opera soirées, galas do, of course, occur, a notable example being the awarding of the Nobel Peace Prize. But such parties are just the icing on the cultural cake and ever so slightly foreign, imported glamour (Nobel, after all, was a Swede).

Home-grown culture

Real Norwegian culture is something far more fundamental – folksy, a reaction to foreign domination. As a political entity, Norway was established in 1905 after centuries of Danish and Swedish rule. All Norwegian "dialects" were forbidden by the Danes for official documents and communications. The national constitution, which was drawn up at Eidsvoll in 1814, was in Danish. Such cultural imperialism was crushing to Norwegian self-esteem and national identity.

Ordinary Norwegians were driven away from the centres of power to rural farms. Tradition, folk costume, the old ways became a cultural refuge and eventually the treasuries of Norway's national personality. Culture with a capital "C" was something the overlords brought with them from foreign capitals. And it was something they took away with them when they left. Norway today has no noble families excepting the king and his household.

LEFT: Henrik Ibsen.
RIGHT: murals by Per Krohg and Henrik Sørensen in the main hall of Oslo's Rådhus (City Hall).

While politicians could elect a king and parliament, it fell to cultural workers, especially writers and painters, to revive the national identity. They turned for inspiration to the traditions of those isolated valleys with their ancient farmsteads and their equally ancient verbal traditions, telling heroic sagas about an expansive

Norway of earlier days and of the greatness of native Viking lords.

Henrik Wergeland (1808–45), a richly talented poet and prose writer, became an early and passionate propagandist of this sort of Norwegian nationalism. Following the same call, artist J.C. Dahl (1788–1857) left his studio for the wilds of Norway's hinterland. His shimmering, majestic views of the mountains are major attractions at the National Gallery, which he helped to found in 1836.

On the dark side, the epoch's fears of isolation and rampant anxiety of the future inspired the violent, emotionally charged style of painter Edvard Munch (1863–1944). Death and desolation are his recurring themes most strongly expressed in *The Scream* (1893), *The Kiss* and *The Vampire* (both 1895). Munch's fears of enslavement come so close to the national heart that his works have been enshrined in their own museum in Oslo as well as on an entire floor of the National Gallery.

Equally loud cries for freedom came from Henrik Ibsen (1828–1906) whose poetic drama *Brand* was a spirited indictment of Norwegian authority at home. It put Ibsen on the cultural map for the first time even outside Norway.

At the same time, the close of the 19th century, other authors turned homewards for inspi-

ration. Alexander Kielland (1849–1906) abandoned a promising international career to write about old Norway. Nobel laureate Knut Hamsun's (1859–1952) chilling novel *Hunger* (1890) is an exposé of the abuses of bourgeois Swedish rule. His masterpiece, *The Growth of the Soil* (1917), reflects a deep love of nature and concern for the effects of material conditions on the individual spirit, themes that still dominate Norwegian writing.

Even architects abandoned continental idioms to embrace a native "Viking Romanticism". They began building in heavy timber and turfed roofs. Eaves and gables sprouted carved and polychromed dragon heads. An

excellent example of the style is Troldhaugen, the last home of composer Edvard Grieg (1843–1907). Just outside Bergen, the house fits perfectly into Grieg's unabashed folkloric, wildly romantic style. He titled his creations after national heroes such as the much loved *Peer Gynt Suite* (1876, words by Ibsen).

Over a century ago, new plays by national playwright Henrik Ibsen, works by major authors such as Amalie Skram (1847–1905) and Kielland were front-page news in Oslo, Bergen and Trondheim. Critics and politicians publicly debated new works; plays became issues, even national causes. Literature became the smithy where the nation's identity was being forged.

Dramatist Bjørnstjerne Bjørnso (1832–1910), championed the Norwegian cause, working his entire life to free the Norwegian theatre from Danish influence. While director of Bergen's Ole Bull Theatre (1857–59) and the Oslo Theatre a few years later, he commissioned new, saga-like dramas drawing on Norway's epic past, such as the *Sigurd Slembe Trilogy*. His efforts helped to revive Norwegian as a literary language. He became poet laureate and his poem, *Yes, We Love this Land of Ours,* became a rallying point in the struggle for political independence from Sweden. The poem is now the national anthem of Norway.

New Norse vs *bokmål*

The political and extremely didactic approach in Norwegian literature finally disappeared in the 1980s. But there are still many attempts to emancipate individual languages. Norway has three languages: Sami, used almost exclusively by the Sami (Lapps) in the north; then there are *bokmål* (book language) and *nynorsk* (new Norse), two variations on a theme that have developed since independence.

Bokmål grew out of the gradual exchange of Danish loan words for words discovered in native dialects, by the substitution of Danish syntax with Norwegian, and by turning soft Danish consonants into hard Norwegian ones. It became the official language, used today by about 80 percent of the towns and throughout the entire northern districts.

New Norse is only used by about 15 percent of Norwegian primary school children. It draws heavily on the archaic Old Norse of the central-western dialects. Since this is a language based on rural culture, *nynorsk* suffered because of

20th-century urbanisation, losing ground to *bokmål* – though to complicate matters, *nynorsk* literature is very popular.

New concerns

The 1980s produced a sort of realistic novel, written in sociology textbook style, directly opposed to the older, bourgeois psychology novels, "a die-hard heritage from Hamsun, Cora Sandel and Torborg Nedreaas". Most readable among these "revolution" works are Dag Solstad's (born 1941) trilogy about World War II, *Svik* (Betrayal), *Krig* (War) and *Brød og Våpen* (Bread and Arms). This revival of

problems using "street language" and spoken modes of expression. Løvied's lyrically erotic *Sug* (Suck) rocked the staid Oslo critics but has brought her international recognition. Live Køltzow's (born 1945) third novel, *The Story of Eli*, explores sex roles in society.

The 1990s saw a general literature boom. Whodunnits by Gunnar Staalesen, Kim Småge, Ingvar Ambjørnsen and Anne Holt are well known and popular. The first prize, however, must go to a book on the history of philosophy written for adolescents: *Sophie's World* by Jostein Gaarder. He is quite easily the most famous Norwegian writer since Knut Hamsun.

social realism allowed an author such as Asbjørn Elden (1919–90) to produce essentially modern yet "back to our roots" sagas about the inconspicuous lives of ordinary people, such as his *Rundt Neste Sving* (Around the Next Bend).

Women have come to the fore of Norwegian writing. Cecilie Løveid (born 1951) and Kari Bøge (born 1950) crashed on to the literary scene in the late 1970s with audacious, even shocking works. Ignoring male-dominated social realism, they picked apart purely female

LEFT: detail from Edvard Munch's *The Vampire* (1895).
ABOVE: writer and nationalist Bjørnsterne Bjørnson at the dinner table.

Post-war art

As with other cultural forms, Norwegian art began to drop its nationalist style after World War II. Gone (but certainly not forgotten) were the fairytale illustrations of Theodor Kittelsen (1857–1914) and morbid subject matter of Edvard Munch and in came the modernists. Impressionism inspired such landscape artists as Gladys Nilssen Raknerud (born 1912) and Thorbjørn Lie-Jørgensen (1900–61); expressionism found its place through the likes of Arne Ekeland (born 1908) and Rolf Nesch (1893–1975); and abstract expressionism appeared in the early 1960s through the work of Sigurd Winge (1909–70) and Jakob Weidemann (born 1923).

However, the old nationalist style continued well into the 1950s with such artists as Hjalmar Haalke (1892–1964) and Søren Steen Johnsen (born 1903) and the team responsible for the Oslo Rådhus murals.

There was also the inevitable reaction to the modernists. When Odd Nerdrum (born 1944) applied for a place at the National Academy of Fine Arts he submitted three works; two of these had been long-term projects, but he was selected on the basis of his third work, an abstract image thrown together the night before. With his scepticism towards the establishment and doubts about abstract art reinforced, the

Leading the way

If there is one area where Norwegians have the edge it is in furniture; consider Peter Opsvik's classic TrippTrapp chair for kids or his sculpture-like Cylindra Objects, and architecture, which in recent years has responded to increasing demands for sustainable development. Probably the most internationally renowned Norwegian architect is the "concrete poet" Sverre Fehn (born 1924), whose main materials have been concrete, wood and glass, and Nordic light. In 1997, Fehn became the first Nordic architect to win the American Pritzker Architecture Prize, the "Nobel Prize" of archi-

young Nerdrum turned to the great masters, in particular Rembrandt, in whom he saw "eternal tranquillity". However, his subject matter was always on the controversial side – *Amputation* (1974), *Hermaphrodite* (1976–81) – and it took until the late 1980s for the Norwegian public to catch on to his post-modern classicism.

There is growing interest in the moderns, which had hitherto been the domain of the avant gardist Swedes. The focal point of the Norwegian art calendar is the Autumn Exhibition in Oslo, and in recent years the city has seen the opening of three new contemporary art galleries, all exhibiting the works of national and international artists.

tectural awards, and the award cited "a marvellous, lyrical and ingenious architectural form... both forceful and extremely rational". To see his work visit the Norsk Bremuseet (Glacier Museum) in Fjærland, built in 1991, or the Hedmarksmuseet (Museum) in Hamar.

There is also a wealth of talent to continue the traditions of the prolific sculpture Gustav Vigeland (1869–1943). There are more 20th-century sculptures/statues per capita in Norway than in any other country in Europe: see *inter alia* Joseph Grimeland's Sailors' Memorial, Bygdøy; Arnold Haukeland's "dynamic" structure, Strandpromenaden, Oslo; and Knut Steen's Whaling Monument, Sandefjord.

Norway's Paganini

Norway has a long tradition in music. The skaldic poems of the Viking Age provide a medieval link to the music traditions of Central Europe; Gregorian chants used in the worship of St Olaf are very similar to the Parisian school of the 13th century.

While higher forms of music stagnated during the 450 years of Danish rule, folk music unfolded freely, encouraged by the ecclesiastical centres and travelling musicians of the time.

Norwegian music developed for the first time in the early 1800s, mainly as a result of the union with Sweden and the influence of the Royal Swedish Court, but also because of the international breakthrough made by violin virtuoso Ole Bull (1810–80) in 1834. "The Nordic Paganini", as he was called, became a model for musicians and writers such as Grieg, Bjørnson and Ibsen. The 1870s and 80s became know as the Golden Age of Norwegian music with such prominent composers as Halfdan Kierulf (1815–68), Edvard Grieg and Johan Svendsen (1849–1911). Music took on a national flavour, urged on by Ole Bull's promotion of the Hardanger fiddle and Ludvig Mathias Lindeman's collection of Norwegian folk tunes. Most of the composers of the second half of the 19th century incorporated some element of folk music in their works.

With the end of the union with Sweden in 1905, Norwegian composers found the need to define a national identity, which they achieved by reverting back to the music of the Norwegian Middle Ages. Seeking inspiration in medieval poetry, German romanticism and French impressionism, David Monrad Johansen (1888–1970) tried to create a monumental kind of music based on musical archaisms. This national romanticism continued until just after the war. Germany was out; a new generation of composers went to study in Paris or the United States, consciously aware of the need to internationalise their musical language.

Today, Oslo, Trondheim and Bergen all have philharmonic orchestras, and the latter hosts the Bergen International Music Festival each May.

> **FESTIVAL CULTURE**
>
> Norway has a festival for almost everything, from the midnight sun and trolls to emigration. Music, crafts and national dress abound.

The Norwegians' yearning for culture is most explicit, however, in the myriad of festivals, especially folk festivals, that are organised each year. If you wish to find the real soul of Norway visit the country in May. It's a month when little gets done, much to the chagrin of foreigners who arrive on business. But it's the prime time for observing the patriotic emotions that lie at the centre of Norwegian culture. The month starts with the May Day festivals; but the high point comes on the 17th, Norway's National Day. ❑

> **NORWEGIAN CINEMA**
>
> Based around a unique system of municipal cinemas and the state-run Norsk Film, Norwegian cinema has come a long way from its first feature *The Perils of the Fisherman*, made in 1907. It gained a considerable amount of international attention in the 1970s with such films as Anja Breiens' *Wives* (1974) and Lasse Glomm's *The Second Shift* (1977). The prevailing style of social realism began to fade in the 1980s, and was replaced by a variety of approaches, including Roar Skolman's surrealist *Junior Heads* (1981) and the Oscar-nominated *Pathfinder*, made in 1988 by Nils Gaup.

LEFT: Norsk Bremuseet (Glacier Centre), Fjærland, when first built. **RIGHT:** the novelist, Live Køltzow.

NATURE'S LARDER

Wild nature and a mild climate are the main sources of the ingredients from which Norway's culinary traditions have evolved

Magnificent landscapes and climatic contrasts have helped to create a natural larder from which Norwegians have helped themselves for centuries. Norway's long, varied coastline has provided ample opportunity for harvesting both "wild" and farm-raised fish; the slow ripening process of everything that grows during the light summer imparts an extraordinary aroma to berries, fruits and vegetables; and the animals that graze on the verdant grass provide meat with a distinctive full flavour. Today Norwegian comestibles such as Chinese cabbage, apples, pears, cherries and strawberries are in demand the world over. Although eyebrows are raised when the nation's chefs win international awards, it is not the first time that foreigners have been impressed by Norway's fare.

PAPAL SURPRISE

When papal envoy Cardinal Wilhelm Sabina attended the coronation of King Håkon V in Bergen in 1247, he arrived with apprehension having been forewarned about the food. However, in his speech following the banquet he lavished praise on the meal he had been served. Sadly, the historical record of his speech makes no mention of the menu, but visitors to Norway in the 18th and 19th centuries speak highly of the salmon, fowl, game and strawberries with cream – treats which modern-day tourists may also experience.

▷ **MARKET TRADING**
The famous Bergen fish market was once the place where locals gossiped about the latest catch: now they come here to catch up on the latest gossip.

△ **WILD PASSION**
Cloudberries (or *multebær*) are found in mountain marshlands in late summer/early autumn. Rich in vitamin C, *multer* is used as a jam, a liqueur and in desserts.

◁ **GONE FISHING**
Fish of all shapes and sizes, including cod *(torsk)*, haddock *(hyse)* and plaice *(flyndre)*, are landed daily in the ports

△ **SUPERIOR BREAKFAST**
Probably the most important meal of the day in Norway is breakfast *(frokost)*, with copious amounts of cold meats, cheeses, crispbreads and black coffee.

AKEVITT – THE WATER OF LIFE

Akevitt (aquavit or "water of life") is the national spirit of Norway. The most famous aquavit, Løiten Linie, is matured through a century-old process which includes a sea voyage in oak casks across the equator and back (each bottle carries details of its "voyage" on its label). This story originates from 1840, when the Norwegian ship *Preciosa* rounded Cape Horn; on board was aquavit, which the crew swore had improved in flavour.

Distilled from Norwegian potatoes, this blend of spirit, caraway and other herbs and spices is matured for several months in sherry casks. The result is a smooth spirit of about 45% proof by volume. Norwegians regard Linie as an accompaniment to pork *(ribbe)*; it also goes well with seafood and the Christmas *lutefisk* dish.

▽ **LOFOTEN TRADITIONS**
Klippfisk (dried, salted split-cod) is a major Norwegian export and *rorbuer* (fishermen's huts) now accommodate tourists in Lofoten.

▷ **PRAWN COCKTAIL**
Fresh prawns *(reker)* are a favourite among Norwegians, served with white bread *(loff)*, mayonnaise, lemon and an ice-cold pils.

▷ **MAGIC MUSHROOMS**
Chanterelle mushrooms are found in the forests north of Trøndelag and are a delicious complement to reindeer and game.

WHY DOES EVERYTHING COST SO MUCH?

Norway's high standard of living has its price, but it is not as expensive as it was in days gone by

Let's get this straight right from the start: day-to-day living *used* to be exorbitantly expensive in Norway, about 25 years ago, but there has been a gradual levelling out of prices in comparison with other European

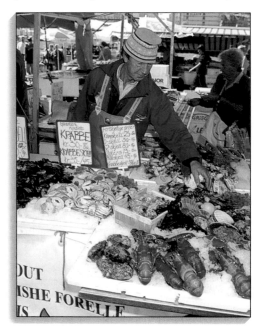

countries. Today, some food items are generally less expensive than elsewhere, such as coffee and butter, but these are the exception rather than the rule. Visitors are often surprised at the relatively high prices for meat and, amazingly enough, fish. Staple vegetables are reasonable; exotic types, for which there is less demand, are expensive. Fruit follows the same pattern. You can find imported apples or tomatoes at normal European Union (EU) prices. To reduce costs, it's worth looking out for *Lavpris* (low price) shops.

Somewhat surprisingly Norway produces a reasonable tomato crop, less because of sunshine and high temperatures and more because

of encouragement from the Norwegian Ministry of Agriculture, which sees independence from other countries as its main aim.

"Made in Norway"

Norway's desire to be self-sufficient has blossomed in unusual areas. The farmers in some tiny valleys in the west of the country live in grand style because their tomatoes, cucumbers, Chinese cabbages or cattle are highly subsidised. Only 3 percent of the land is used for agriculture, so variety is essential.

Cattle farmers are proud of their beef and pork, vegetable farmers praise their organically grown produce; and it's true that meat scandals are unheard of in Norway. But it's equally true that Norwegian tomatoes don't taste of anything much other than water. However, 95 percent of the grain consumed is harvested in the country and cattle is almost entirely reared for the domestic market.

As far as foodstuffs are concerned, the logo "Made in Norway" is therefore more an expression of a political principle than of exceptionally high quality.

Things are changing. The higher standard of living has stimulated a demand for a richly laid table. Admittedly, prices in Norwegian hotels are high – but so is the standard of the breakfast buffet. Anyone sampling a fully laden breakfast table can only start the day in a good mood: fruit juice, smoked salmon, pickled herring, fresh bread, fruit and muesli. This meal can easily get light eaters through the day and save them the expense of lunch.

Taxed to the hilt?

Not so long ago, it was fashionable to blame rich farmers and a false subsidy policy for high taxes. In reality these subsidies are cut each year and more and more smallholdings have been given up.

Income is subject to 30–45 percent income tax. But that's it. Social security, health insurance and pension payments are all included, and even the Church is funded by the state.

Other state revenue comes from oil and gas sales as well as taxes on various luxury items – which explains the high prices for cars, alcohol and cigarettes. Luxury costs money and Norwegians aren't supposed to enjoy luxury items – or at least they should do it in a different way.

> **MONEY BACK**
>
> Often a deposit of NOK 1 is charged when purchasing bottles, either glass or plastic. The money is refunded on return of the bottles.

The debate on cigarette and alcohol prices is an inevitable item in the annual budget discussions and only two of the eight political parties

enlivened by the Christian Democratic Party, which rallies against these vices. Norwegians, however, have long learned to live with the link between vice and illness, have stopped arguing about prices, and drink their beer in peace.

As the alcohol takes affect, and especially if there are visitors present, many Norwegians feel obliged to explain why they are drinking. It is, they will say, because they can't remember when they were last in such good company or, as the case may be, feeling lonely and neglected. Before a dark cloud of

in the Storting vote to reduce these taxes. The rest squeeze yet a little bit more out of them every year.

To drink or not to drink?

Beer and wine prices are also on the increase. As Norwegians resignedly comment: "That's as certain as Christmas comes in December." But what is the reasoning behind this policy? The government insists that the treatment of alcohol and cigarette-related illnesses costs billions. And the budget discussions are also

---

LEFT: Torget, the fish market in Bergen.
ABOVE: weekend market at Youngstorget, Oslo.

Nordic gloom settles on the proceedings the subject is likely to broaden to why Norwegians drink so much, or, not much at all.

The question of alcohol and its corollary, teetotalism, have long been burning issues in Norway and are discussed so keenly that visitors, who are bound to become involved, might like to familiarise themselves with the background.

The climate is often blamed for Norwegian drinking. There may be some truth in this, since long winters used to put a premium on the art of preserving and storing food. Salt was the key, and it was therefore consumed in such quantities that great thirst necessarily followed. At one time, the "normal" consumption of beer and mead was between six and 10 litres (10–18 pints) per day. The aristocracy drank wine from the earliest times.

The 19th century produced a rash of travel books about Norway, and all of them drew attention to a weakness for drink. Even boys of 12 and 14 years, according to the Reverend R. Everest, indulged in the "odious vice", drinking quantities of brandy "that would have astonished an English coalman". Pontoppidan, whose *Natural History of Norway* was published in 1755, admired the Nor-

> ## THE GREAT DEBATE
> Since Norway's independence in 1905, the prohibition issue has been responsible for the downfall of three governments.

wegians: "so hospitable ... liberal ... willing to serve and oblige strangers."

Not, however, when they drank: "When a peasant with his family was invited to a wedding, the wife generally took her husband's (funeral) shroud with her; on these occasions they seldom parted before they were intoxicated with liquor, the consequences of which was fighting, and those battles seldom ended without murder."

Home brew

Although the Norwegians are extremely hospitable they will only offer alcoholic beverages once proper friendship has been established.

Those who like the odd tipple can normally present a well stocked bar but many of these drinks are often home-made. Every large town has shops selling winemaking equipment, so only hosts who travel abroad or live near the coast can offer famous names.

One thing visitors should not expect is the Viking drink of mead. This tradition has nearly died out – because honey is expensive and it's difficult to make.

Statistics prove, it is said defensively, that Norwegians actually consume less alcohol than almost any other European nation. These statistics also reveal that beer and wine have supplanted harder spirits. But unreported numbers are a lot higher: Norwegians like to travel and certainly buy the complete quota of duty-free items.

Also not included in the statistics is "HB", home-made schnapps made from sugar and potatoes. Even in this high-tech age, there are still quite a few moonshine distillers at work, and *sprit* (96 percent raw alcohol) smuggling is big business.

It would be unrealistic to seek reliable information about smuggling along Norway's long coastline, although there may be a clue in the fact that when a strike closed the state-run *Vinmonopol* shops for months on end in 1986, there were no apparent shortages and, as soon as the suppliers had geared up for the unexpected windfall, the price of alcohol went down to levels unknown before or since.

A history of prohibition

The first attempt to curb drinking in Norway, possibly in the world, was made by King Sverre in Bergen in the 12th century. He was the leader of a rapacious bunch of ruffians called the *Birkebeiner*, who might have won the Battle of Fimreite for him against the rival Magnus Erlingsson except that they were too drunk to fight on his behalf. Sverre's attempt failed.

The strident minority in favour of total prohibition saw World War I, in which Norway remained neutral, as an opportunity to press their case further. The excuse was to conserve the raw materials that went into the making of beer and spirits.

When the war ended the restrictions were not lifted; on the contrary, they were extended to cover all alcoholic drinks except wines below a certain, modest strength.

Unfortunately for the prohibitionists, France, Spain and Portugal were among the largest customers for Norway's important fishing industry, and they paid for the fish with wine, none of which qualified under the new regulations for sale or consumption in Norway.

Under pressure from the fishing industry, the limit was lifted just enough to admit the French wine, but the country was also saddled with 400,000 litres (88,000 gallons) of French brandy for which it had no possible use, having given an undertaking not to re-export it. The government immediately declared prohibition permanent, a signal to both Spain and Portugal that it would not be hoodwinked in similar fashion again.

Two years later, they let it be known that 500,000 litres (110,000 gallons) of fortified Spanish wine were nevertheless on their way, shortly to be followed by 850,000 litres (185,000 gallons) of Portuguese. The government resigned rather than face a country awash in untouchable drink. The new government lifted the ban on wine, and in so doing put the skids under national prohibition.

State control

Since 1923 and until the late 1990s the import and sale of wines and spirits had been a state monopoly. Government buyers decided what was to be made available (and the price) in the chain of *Vinmonopolet* shops, as well as in most hotels and restaurants. It was said that by this act the Norwegian state had made itself the biggest single buyer of alcoholic drinks in the world, a painful irony for the numerous prohibitionists who were still beating the drum.

In 1997, however, the Norwegian government made a major concession to the EU by deregulating the import, wholesale and distribution side of the market. The effect of this means that hotels, restaurants and bars may now do business with independent importers, and *Vinmonopol* has been forced to privatise its distribution function. Although maintaining their monopoly on retail sales (and prices), the *Vinmonopolet* shops have slowly revamped their image (they used to be as uninviting as a dentist's waiting-

room), and the stigma attached to walking around with chinking wine bottles in a plain plastic bag is fast disappearing.

One of the results of this, as visitors find out, is that drinks are freely available in major cities, albeit at numbing prices. Today, it is easier to be served a drink in Oslo at 2am than it is, say, in London. Laws affecting the sale of alcohol, however, are decided at the *kommune* level (i.e. by town and rural councils), so outside the cities, and especially on the west coast *bibelbeltet*, it is a matter of luck whether a particular place is completely dry and without a legal drink within 100 km (60 miles).

Paying for the roads

It's no exaggeration to claim that car drivers have financed their own infrastructure. Here, as with alcohol and tobacco, Norwegians believe in the principle of cause and effect, which is paid for through high car prices (Norway doesn't have its own car industry), a large tax on petrol and toll charges: if you want to drive through Oslo (and there are few ways to circumnavigate it), Bergen, Trondheim or Stavanger, you have to pay a toll.

The road system, on the other hand, has been considerably upgraded and now, with numerous bridges and tunnels (including under the sea), reaches the tiniest villages. ❑

LEFT: a *Vinmonopol* shop.
RIGHT: home brewing in the attic.

PLACES

A detailed guide to the entire country, with principal sights clearly cross-referenced by number to the maps

Norway is a long narrow strip of a country, stretching north from mainland Europe far into the Arctic. In the ancient capital of Trondheim, you are 500 km (350 miles) from the modern capital of Oslo, yet only a quarter of the way up the country's jagged coast. Oslo is as far from Monaco as it is from Nordkapp (North Cape), with Norway's northernmost outpost, the islands of Svalbard (Spitsbergen), hundreds of kilometres further on. With a population of only 4.5 million, Norway has, above all else, space.

Yet travel is not difficult. From early times, the Norwegians (as Vikings) were magnificent sailors, and this old way of travel continues today through the Hurtigrute coastal steamers and other ferries that link coastal communities. On land, the Norwegians have achieved in 100 years the seemingly impossible, connecting even the most isolated settlements by building railways, roads and bridges across their fjords and by tunnelling deep into the mountains and under the sea.

This is one of Europe's most beautiful countries. The scenery is dramatic and the land changes constantly, from mountain to sea, fjord to forest. Oslo, Stavanger, Bergen, Trondheim and Tromsø are small manageable cities that make good use of the surrounding countryside. Neither the Norwegian climate nor the people are as chilly as the northern latitudes might suggest. The Gulf Stream warms the western coastline so that the seas are ice-free all the year round, and the great distances and long journeys between villages, towns and farms have encouraged an age-old tradition of hospitality.

In the 1970s, oil brought wealth to Norway and now these stubborn, self-sufficient and deeply patriotic people enjoy one of the highest standards of living in the world.

Norwegians are an outdoor people, and Norway a country where inhabitants and visitors alike can make the most of limitless space for walking, skiing, touring and just breathing in the clear air. As a visitor you are advised to "explore" the amenities on offer, but do not expect all the man-made attractions to be as monumental as the country itself. The relatively small domestic market and short summer season are unable to finance major "Disney-like" attractions, and many of the museums, especially those in rural areas, exist more because of local enthusiasm and voluntary effort than to any supreme tourist policy and national funding. When you see a national heritage symbol our advice is to go and investigate – you'll probably be pleasantly surprised. ❏

PRECEDING PAGES: storm over Borgundfjorden; a "light circle" in the Arctic city of Tromsø; Gamlehaugen.
LEFT: drying fish in the Lofoten Islands.

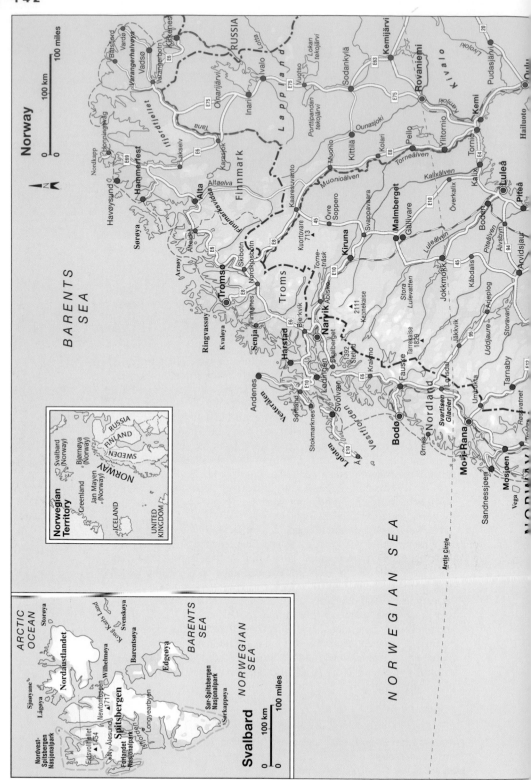

Norway

100 miles
100 km

N

BARENTS SEA

Finnmark

Troms

Nordland

Lappland

RUSSIA

NORWEGIAN SEA

Arctic Circle

Svalbard

ARCTIC OCEAN

Sjuøyane
Storøya
Kong Karls Land
Svenskøya
Nordaustlandet
Barentsøya
Edgeøya

BARENTS SEA

NORWEGIAN SEA

Nordvest-Spitsbergen Nasjonalpark
▲454
Ny-Ålesund
Newtontoppen ▲1717
Spitsbergen
Forlandet Nasjonalpark
Isfjorden
Longyearbyen
Sør-Spitsbergen Nasjonalpark
Sørkappøya

100 km
0
100 miles
0

Norwegian Territory

Greenland
Jan Mayen (Norway)
Svalbard (Norway)
Bjørnøya (Norway)
RUSSIA
FINLAND
SWEDEN
NORWAY
ICELAND
UNITED KINGDOM

OSLO, NORDIC CITY OF LIGHT

Oslo has long since shaken off its dowdy image. Its compact centre is full of street life, with a multitude of galleries and museums. Oslo's fjord, the Nordmarka forest and a Viking ship are just a short ride away

Map on pages 148 & 156

I n the 1880s and 1890s, Edvard Munch drew and painted an Oslo seemingly inhabited by spectres. Men and women were dressed all in black, their hat brims pulled down low, their faces chalk. To him they were like "the living dead who wend their tortuous way down the road that leads to the grave."

This is the Oslo that was, a dour city lacking the vitality of Copenhagen or Stockholm; Munch left it to live in Berlin and Paris. Nearly 100 years later, until the mid-1980s, many of Oslo's cultural attractions were still imported, while native talent left for the brighter lights elsewhere. The only real cultural diversions were a few museums based around explorers and skiers.

Expensive and remote, Oslo also bore another black mark. Nights were meanly trimmed of their fun by laws that severely curbed drinking hours. And so travellers to Norway used to give Oslo no more than a passing nod as they steamed through on their way to Bergen and the more spectacular scenery of the west-coast fjords.

PRECEDING PAGES: outside Oslo's parliament building on National Day. **LEFT:** Gustav Vigeland's great Monoliten. **BELOW:** Aker Brygge.

Coming alive

To call Oslo the Nordic City of Light may be too pat a way of saying that Oslo has come of age. However, in a fairly short space of time it has, and Oslo today – a city that celebrated its thousandth birthday in the year 2000 – bears little resemblance to the dim place that Munch so hated, or even to the Oslo of the early 1980s. Norway, despite all its interest in the past, has awakened to the attractions of city fun. The small capital by the fjord has developed into a metropolis with a revitalised cultural life, not to mention a diverse and lively night life.

Oslo's cultural rebirth in recent years has been in part conscious, in part a natural outcome of infusions of money in the right places. If the talent were to be lured back home, things would have to change dramatically. They did. On the back of the oil boom came more and more money for the arts. Suddenly there was sufficient going on at home to make artists curious enough to return. One famous Norwegian who stayed faithful to Oslo throughout her career was actress Liv Ullman, who frequently returned to play in Ibsen here. Now, the building of a magnificent waterside National Opera House is underway, for completion for 2008.

Best by boat

Oslo is at the head of a fjord shaped like a swan's neck; it is surrounded by low hills. Your initial impression will depend on how you arrive. The ideal way is by boat, for then you get the most complete picture, though arriving by car from the south along the Mosseveien also offers some impressive views. There are a few tall buildings in Oslo, but your view from the fjord will still be dominated by the **Rådhuset** ❶

(City Hall; open 9am–4pm; entrance fee May–Aug, otherwise free; guided tours Mon–Fri 10am, 12pm, 2pm; tel: 23 46 16 00). It is a large, mud-coloured building topped by two square towers, called the "goat cheese" *(geit ost)* by locals because of its resemblance to blocks of locally produced goat's cheese. Opened in 1950 to commemorate the city's 900th anniversary, the building improves on closer inspection. The courtyard is adorned with fantastic figures and symbols from Norwegian mythology; note the **astronomical clock**, the **Yggdrasill frieze** by Dagfin Werenskiold and Dyre Vaas' **swan fountain**. The mosaics inside the main hall are based around more modern themes. The south-facing clock, at 8 metres (30 ft) in diameter, is one of the largest timepieces in Europe.

In defence

Walking south from the Rådhuset, along the fjord, is the medieval **Akershus slott og festning ❷** (castle open May–mid-Sept Mon–Fri 10am–4pm, Sun 12.30–4pm; fortress open Mon–Fri 9am–5pm, Sat–Sun 11am–5pm; Sept–May closes 4pm; grounds open all year; tel: 23 09 35 53). Built originally in 1299, it helped to

Central Oslo

protect Christiania (as Oslo was called until 1925) from marauders throughout the periods of Danish and Swedish rule. The Nazis took over Akershus during World War II and shot several resistance fighters by the old magazine. When the war was over, the traitorous Norwegian chancellor, Quisling, was shot on the same spot. **Norges Hjemmefrontmuseum ❸** (Resistance Museum; open Oct–mid-June, times vary; mid-June–Sept Tues and Thur 10am–6pm, Mon, Wed, Fri and Sat 10am–5pm, Sun 11am–5pm; entrance fee; tel: 23 09 31 38) in the grounds illustrates the intense story of occupied Norway, while the **Forsvarsmuseet ❹** (Armed Forces Museum; open June–mid-Aug Mon–Fri 10am–6pm, Sat–Sun 11am–5pm; mid-Aug–May Mon–Fri 10am–3pm, Sat–Sun 11am–4pm; tel: 23 09 35 82) covers Norwegian military and political history from the Vikings to the present day.

Thrusting up on the opposite side of the Pipervika inlet are the glass, chrome and neon traceries of **Aker Brygge ❺**. Centred around an open-air sculpture court, this modern harbourside development contains shopping arcades, bars, restaurants, food stalls, theatres and galleries as well as outdoor festivals in summer.

In summer, greenery encroaches on Oslo from every side. From the fjord approach you'll see the tops of the trees of **Slottsparken ❻** (Palace Gardens), and several parks stretching north beyond it to the wooded hills at Oslo's back. There your eye will inevitably be drawn to the giant white curlicue of the Holmenkollen ski-jump arched against one of the city's highest hills.

Compact centre

Oslo city centre is large enough to be interesting yet compact enough to get around on foot. The main axis is **Karl Johans gate**, originally designed in 1826 by the royal architect H.D.F. Linstow, it was widened some 30 years later to

Map on page 148

TIP

Buy an Oslo Pass for free admission to the city's museums, free public transport and parking, discounts at shops, restaurants and on car hire. Obtainable from tourist offices and hotels.

BELOW: the Rådhus (City Hall) at night.

A statue of Karl Johan XIV stands on the steps of Det Kongelige Slott, *the Royal Palace.*

become Oslo's answer to the Champs Elysées. Its western end merges into the broad avenue leading to the doors of **Det Kongelige Slottet ❼** (Royal Palace), and the focal point of the National Day celebrations on 17 May. In the east it runs to Jernbanetorget, the location of **Oslo Sentralstasjon** (Oslo S station). To the south, the centre extends to the fjord.

Parallel to Karl Johans gate to the north is **Grensen**, another busy, shop-lined street. The **Oslo Domkirke ❽** (Cathedral; open noon–6pm) dominates the Stortorvet (square) at the east end of Grensen. Completed in 1697, its exterior is of darkened brown brick, while inside artists of the 18th, 19th and 20th centuries have contributed to the cathedral's adornment, including stained-glass windows by Emmanuel Vigeland. Behind Domkirke is **Basarhallene** – a round, colonnaded market with food and handicraft stalls.

Lille Grensen leads south to the **Stortinget ❾** (Parliament; July–Aug guided tours) on **Karl Johans gate**, from where **Eidsvollplass** runs west alongside the old university. Studenterlunden, the small park around the university, contains the main university building, **Aula ❿**, which is decorated with murals by Edvard Munch. The **Nationaltheatret ⓫** (National Theatre) is just opposite Studenterlunden, and Slottsparken is immediately west.

Artistic attractions

Norwegians, with their seagoing past, have always had a fine awareness of faraway cultures. But it has always been hard to entice foreign artists they admired, to their own shores: Norway was too remote, the population too small. Riotously enthusiastic receptions can make up for a lot, however, and that's how Oslo now gets its favourites back year after year. The Oslo Philharmonic, whose home is the

BELOW: inside the Rådhus (City Hall).

Konserthuset ⑫ (tel: 23 11 31 00) on Munkedamsveien, performs with a daz-zling sequence of guest conductors and soloists. Away from the classical, the variety of music to be heard in Oslo's clubs and concert halls is vast, from South American folk music to indie rock; even international rock stars add Oslo to their world tour calendar. In June, the Norwegian Wood rock festival is held at Frogner in Oslo, while every July there is an international jazz festival, and in September it's the Gjøglerne Kommer (The Clowns Are Coming), a performing arts festival.

Map on page 148

Christian's town

The simple need for space to accommodate all these artistic ventures has also played a role in reviving neglected parts of Oslo. It has helped to breathe life back into **Christian IV's town**, "Kvadraturen", an historic area bounded to the north by Rådhusgata and to the south by Akershus Slott, and characterised by old customs and shipping houses and grand open plazas. At one time this area was frequented only by prostitutes and their pursuers. The town's history as a redoubtable part of Oslo is reflected in its former nickname, "Little Algerie" – see the painting in Engebret Café on Bankplassen, an artists' haunt since the early 1900s.

But **Gamle Logen** on Grev Wedels Plass is now a serious concert venue and there's also the **Cinemateket** (repertory film theatre). The **Norsk Arkitektur-museum** (Museum of Architecture; open Mon–Fri 11am–4pm, Wed until 6pm, Sat–Sun noon–4pm; tel: 22 42 40 80) is found in Kongens gate and includes fea-tures on 1,000 years of Norwegian architecture. The **Museet for Samtidskunst** ⑬ (Museum of Contemporary Art; open Tues–Fri 10am–5pm, Thur till 8pm, Sat 11am–4pm, Sun 11am–5pm; entrance fee; tel: 22 86 22 10) is housed in the original Norges Bank (Central Bank) building, on Bankplassen, and has an extensive col-

BELOW: Akerhus Slott (Castle).

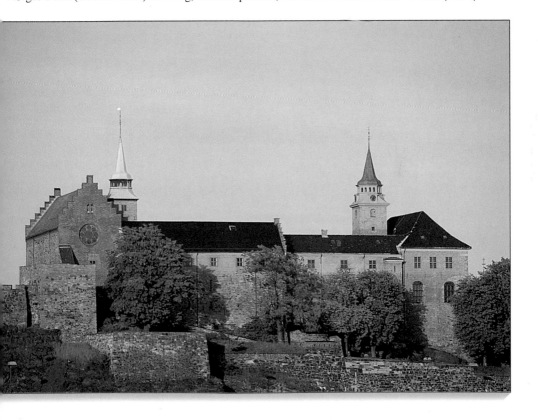

lection of 20th-century Norwegian art. Just around the corner is **Astrup Fearnley** (Museum of Modern Art; open Tues, Wed and Fri 11am–5pm, Thur 11am–7pm, Sat–Sun noon–5pm; entrance fee; free Tues; tel: 22 93 60 60), which focuses on international artists, although it too contains Scandinavian works. Galleries across the city are full of art in every medium, and established museums have opened their doors to the works of contemporary artists. Try the **Stenersenmuseet** ⓯ (Munkedamsveien 15; open Tues, Thur 11am–7pm, Wed, Fri–Sun 11am–5pm; entrance fee; tel: 22 49 36 00), which shows Norwegian art from 1850 to 1970.

Children in Oslo have their own museum of art, Barnekunstmuseet (Lille Frøens vei 4; open Tues–Thur & Sun; closed mid-Aug–mid-Sept). Works by youngsters from 180 countries are on display and artistic activities are a regular feature.

A multitude of museums

The **Nasjonalgalleriet** ⓰ (National Gallery, Universitetsgaten 13; open Mon, Wed and Fri 10am–6pm, Thur 10am–8pm, Sat 10am–4pm, Sun 11am–4pm, closed Tues; tel: 22 20 04 04) is for anyone who has never heard of any Norwegian artist apart from Edvard Munch. The sheer size, if not the content, of the forest and fjord paintings of the Romantic artist J.C. Dahl (1788–1857) will impress you. You'll also see the work of his prolific contemporaries, Adolph Tidemand (1814–76) and Hans Frederik Gude (1825–1903). There is a wonderful series of etchings depicting barn dances, village scenes and festivities. The display of Impressionist works is excellent. And don't forget the Munch room.

A little further north is the **Kunstindustrimuseet** ⓱ (Museum of Applied Art, St Olav's gate 1; open Tues, Wed and Fri 11am–3pm, Thur 11am–7pm, Sat–Sun noon–4pm; entrance fee; tel: 22 03 65 40). It is graced by two earthenware urns at its entrance and has superb displays of Norwegian textile, fashion and furniture design. The most famous tapestry in its possession is the *Baldishol*, dating from 1180, and one of the most popular exhibits is of the royal costumes. On the uppermost floor is a collection of Scandinavian design for the home ranging from bent-wood chairs to streamlined kitchen gadgets.

West along Drammensveien from the National Gallery is the small **Ibsen-museet** ⓲ (Arbiens gate 1; guided tours Tues–Sun, noon, 1pm and 2pm; entrance fee; tel: 22 55 20 09) set in Henrik Ibsen's apartment where he lived from 1895 until his death in 1906.

For the technically minded there is the **Norsk Teknisk Museum** (Museum of Technology, Kjelsåvn 143; open June–Aug 10am–6pm; Sept Tues–Fri 10am–4pm, Sat–Sun 10am–5pm; suburban train, trams 12 or 15, bus 22, 25 and 37 to Kjelsås; entrance fee; tel: 22 79 60 00). This is a great day out for children, with lots of hands-on exhibitions about energy, industry, transport and telecommunications. Nearby is a water mill and weir which feeds the Akerselva river.

Life on the streets

Along with an upturn in the arts, Oslo's streets are tangibly alive, especially in summer: festivals come fast and furious, and the crowds at restaurants and cafés brim over on to the pavement.

Oslo's growth in nightlife owes much to the extending of licensing hours to 3am in the 1990s. The number of **bars** and **clubs** that has sprung up in order to take advantage of late-night traffic is astounding. **Restaurants**, too, have flourished: the influx of immi-

BELOW: in summer everything happens on the streets.

grants has resulted in a variety of ethnic kitchens being opened. Included among these "foreign" restaurants are typical north-west Norwegian fish restaurants, which serve traditional dishes according to age-old recipes.

Norwegians are serious coffee drinkers. There are **cafés** that are simply cafés (*kafé*). Then there are *gjæstgiveris*, pubs, *kros*, *bistros*, *spiseris* and *kafeterias*, which all tend to be a bit more casual than restaurants; in other words, they are likely to serve smallish meals plus snacks all day and into the night. Seattle-style coffee shops are also popular. The world *barrista* (coffee-making in a café) champion is Norwegian and the championships are held in Oslo every year.

Most eating and drinking places start to fill slowly after working hours and turn more boisterous after supper. Bars and clubs are spread throughout the city, and range from underground to upmarket – consult the *What's On* Oslo Guide, or ask someone who knows Oslo. The "in" scene changes every year, but can normally be identified by the long queue in front of the building, which will certainly not disperse until after 1am. Hip places include Onkel Donald Kafe, Universitets Gate 26, and TGI Fridays on Karl Johan.

Evening entertainment

The Norwegians tend to divide their evenings into three different parts. Since eating and drinking in restaurants and bars is expensive, many people invite friends into their homes for a meal, or for "before" drinks (*vorspiel*). The richer crowds may opt for cinemas, theatres or restaurants, after which the real nightlife starts and the high price for a beer is no longer important. From 2am the pubs empty and act three is about to begin. Friends and neighbours (not necessarily the ones who were with you at the beginning of the evening) are invited in and offered the

Map on page 148

The Fram, *Fridtjof Nansen's Arctic exploration boat, took Roald Amundsen to the South Pole in 1912.*

BELOW: enjoying a drink on Karl Johans gate.

TIP

You can save on accommodation and sightseeing by booking an *Oslo Pakken* (Oslo Package) offered by travel agents. A room with breakfast at a choice of 42 hotels and the Oslo Pass are included.

remaining contents of the house bar *(nachspiel)*. Despite all the fun of enjoying Oslo till the last bars close, natives still pull on their boots and head for the hills the next day. Love of nature and folklore are inbred in today's Norwegians.

Come Sunday evening, it's a good idea to book tickets early if you want to see a film, since Sunday is Oslo's favourite time to go to the movies. The price of seats is reasonable and all cinemas show films in their original language with Norwegian subtitles.

There is no English-language theatre but Norwegians are devoted theatre-goers, and companies perform everything in Norwegian, from Eugene O'Neill to Andrew Lloyd Webber. You will find international drama festivals across Norway in summer, which is your only chance to see something in English. However, if there's an Ibsen play on that you know well, it might be worth seeing it in Norwegian – the emotiveness of Ibsen should break through any language barrier.

How to stay solvent

When it comes to budgeting for a stay in Oslo, there are a number of ways to save your kroner. Norwegian hotel breakfasts usually offer a large, help-yourself selection. The better assortments are likely to include toast and crispbreads, cheese, marinated and smoked salmon, herring, cereals, fruit, eggs, juice, tea and coffee. (The *Koldtbord*, which is the lunchtime variation, will have some hot dishes added.) If you can have a hearty breakfast as your main meal of the day, and avoid eating a large evening meal in a restaurant, then you'll manage to keep to a reasonable budget. The most common street snack is the *pølser* – a long, skinny hot dog served either with *brød* (bread) or rolled in a *lompe* (potato pancake). But there are now a lot of cafés, brasseries and pizzerias

BELOW: the rich pattern surrounding Vigeland's Monoliten.

where you can get small to medium-sized meals that won't break the bank. Full meals can be reasonable, too, as long as you don't order a lot of alcohol.

Alas, the high cost of alcohol is near unbeatable, although beer can be purchased before 5pm at most supermarkets for a reasonable price. Bringing in your full duty-free allowance helps, but you can't really tote your own bottle around the streets or in restaurants, so that provides a limited solution. Drinking costs will be high even if you stick to beer, but if you choose wine or spirits, they'll rocket.

In summer, hotel rates are deeply discounted to make up for the lack of business and conference traffic. In winter, you can sometimes do fairly well with weekend rates, but watch out for school and ski holiday weeks when hotels are crowded and rates higher again. Pensions, mission churches and youth hostels are usually reasonably priced. Camping is another option in such an outdoor city as Oslo: the site at Ekebergsletta *(see Travel Tips page 369)* a hilly park suburb with wonderful views over Oslo and the fjord, is 3 km (2 miles) from town.

From Munch to minorities

Combining a museum visit with a stroll is a relaxing and usually a cheap way of spending part of a day or evening. Once you leave behind the bigger hotels and restaurants where business people wine and dine, food and drink prices drop significantly. The exploring suggestions below focus on sights outside the very heart of Oslo; the sights within the city centre area are easily found and fairly close together so no special planning is needed to reach them.

One of Norway's best-known museums is **Munch-museet** ⓭ (Munch Museum, Tøyengata 53; open June–mid-Sept daily 10am–6pm; mid-Sept–May Tues–Fri 10am–4pm, Sat–Sun 11am–5pm; entrance fee; tel: 23 24 14 00;

Map on pages 156–7

BELOW: sculpture and "echo" in the Vigeland-museet.

156

Nordmarka

Strømsdammen Lake · Tryvannstårnet ㉗ · Øvresetertjern · Lillevann · Voksen-kollen · Frogner-seteren · Skogen · 500 · Voksenkollveien · Bogstad camping-plass · Voksenlia · Skimuseet · Holmenkollen kapell · ㉖ Holmenkollen-bakken · Midtstuen · Holmenkollen · Ankerveien · Oslo · Besserud

0 — 750 m
0 — 750 yds

Sørkedalsveien · Borgenveien · Diakonveien · Thulows vei · Nordmarka · Det Internasjonale Barnekunstmuseet (International Museum of Children's Art) · Frøen · Kringkastingen · Grefsen · Gydas vei · Suhms gate · Wilhelm Færdens vei · Kirkeveien

VESTRE GRAVLUND · Volvat · 168 · Colosseum senter · Colosseum kino · Sporveismuseet · Misjons-kirken · Majorstuen · Døvekirken

VIGELANDSPARKEN · Monolitten ㉔ · Frogner stadion · **MAJORSTUEN** · St. Dominikus · 168 · **HEGDEHAUGE**

FROGNERPARKEN · Frogner · Oslo Bymuseum ㉕ · Professor Dahls gate · **HOMANSBYEN** · Prof. Dahls gate

FROGNER · Vigelandmuseet · **BRISKEBY** · Uranienborg · Arno Bergs plass · **Kunstn**

Olav Kyrres plass · Frogner · Gimle kino · American Lutheran Church · **SLOTTSPARK** · Slottet · **DRONNINGS-PARKEN** · Drammensveien

Bygdøy · Oscarshall slott ㉝ · Oscarshallsveien · Universitets-biblioteket · Observatorie terrasse · **RUSELØKKA** · Oslotunnelen

SKILLEBEKK · Rikstrygdeverket · Munkedamsveien · **AKER BRYGGE**

Norsk Folkemuseum ㉜ · Kongen · Ferry port · **FILIPSTAD** · Pipe

Vikingskipshuset ㉘ · Dronningen · Filipstadutstikker · Tjuvholmen · **page 148**

Oslo · Kon-Tiki museet ㉚ ㉙ Frammuseet · ㉛ Norsk Sjøfartsmuseum · **Oslofjorden**

0 — 500 m
0 — 500 yds

Denmark, Germany · Nesoddtangen

One of Oslo's many statues, overlooking the water in Eidsvollplass.

BELOW: enjoying a meal outside, down by the harbour at Aker Brygge.

T-bane Tøyen). A tremendous collection of Munch's work is housed there, all donated by the artist himself. The life of Edvard Munch (1863–1944) was permeated by sickness – a theme reflected in his paintings. Himself a sickly child, both his mother and sister died at an early age from tuberculosis. Festive renderings of gypsy families and blazing autumn landscapes counteract these gloomier works. The famous *Skrik (Scream)* is darkly riveting, as is the *Marats død* series *(Death of Marat*, 1907) in which Munch portrays himself bleeding from gunshot wounds inflicted by an angry mistress. After a series of breakdowns, Munch returned to Norway, having spent most of his adult, artistic life in Paris and Berlin. He sought peace, but continued working, in his cottage at Åsgårdstrand in Vestfold.

The Munch museum is flanked by parks. The one to the east contains the **Tøyenbadet** (public swimming baths), including a lido, water slide and saunas. To the west is the **Tøyenhagen** ⓴ (Tøyen Botanical Gardens) with the Zoological, Mineralogical, Geological and Palaeontological museums at its north end (open all year). In September and early spring, this is the site of Norway's largest traditional circus.

A few streets northwest of Munch-museet, across Trondheimsveien, is the **Grünerløkka** district. It is a former working-class neighbourhood, now densely populated with artists and writers. The most interesting street in Grüncrløkka is **Markveien** ㉑, painted in muted pastel colours and lined with galleries and boutiques. In the courtyard near Markveien 42 is a brick building housing various artists' studios. Parallel to Markveien is Thorvald Meyersgate with many restaurants and bars open until 3am. On long warm summer nights you'd never believe you were so close to the Arctic. Continuing north on Markveien, you'll

Map on pages 156–7

find a cross street called Grünersgate. From here up to Schleppergrellsgate are some magnificent residential courtyards. Peer inside for a look at tranquil urban living in Oslo. **Kampen** ㉒, whose northern limit is Kampenparken (on the southeast side of Munch-museet), is a district of gorgeous wooden houses brilliantly painted in siennas, golds, pastels and vibrant blues. Some of the streets in lower Kampen are overhung by trees and are supremely quiet; look up, too, at the dormer windows above the street corners, hung with macramé and lace curtains.

Directly west of Kampen is Oslo's largest Pakistani neighbourhood, now full of trendy bars and cafés, great restaurants, both Pakistani and international. Oslo's immigrant community has grown rapidly over the past 20 years and now comprises over 30 percent of Oslo's population. Large numbers of Poles come in the summer months for seasonal work, and Norway has accepted many asylum-seekers. While Sweden and Finland have large populations of Romany gypsies, and of Turks who came in the 19th century as fur and skin dealers, one of Norway's oldest ethnic groups is the Tartars, who have been here for centuries.

Vigeland's vision

West of the city centre is **Frognerparken** (park) or **Vigelandsparken** ㉓ (sculpture park; open all year). The park, containing the life's work of the famous Norwegian sculptor Gustav Vigeland (1869–1943), is a 40-minute walk from the centre. One way of getting there would be by continuing on northwest from the Royal Palace to Hegdehaugsveien, which becomes Bogstadsveien – a long, lively street of art galleries and enticing shops – or pick up a bus (Nos 20, 45, 81) or tram (Nos 12 or 15) in the direction of Frogner. Any west-bound

Gustav Vigeland's brother, Emanuel (1875–1948), was a painter. It's worth visiting the Emanuel Vigeland Museum (Grimelundsveien 8, open Sun noon–4pm) to see Vita (Life), *his alfresco decoration of the building.*

BELOW: children on a day out in Oslo.

Nobel's Peace Prize

O ne of the great ironies is that the Swedish armaments manufacturer Alfred Nobel should have been the founder of the world's most prestigious prize for peace. Was it the realisation that his invention of dynamite in 1866 could and had been easily turned from peaceful rock tunnelling to war that led him to include the peace category alongside prizes for physics, chemistry, medicine and literature? Or was his conscience troubled by the thought that his great riches were built on weapons of war? It may have been no more than a tribute to the Norwegian reputation as workers for peace.

Nobody knows what went on in the mind of this introspective, isolated man.

It is almost as strange that when he set up his trust fund, Nobel chose the Norwegian Storting (Parliament) in which to make the

peace award. It was a time when the near century-old union between Sweden and Norway was collapsing. Perhaps Nobel hoped that, by passing the Peace Prize into Norwegian jurisdiction, he might help keep the two nations together. If this was his aim, he failed. The Union was dissolved five years after his death in 1901 and Norway was already a year-old sovereign state at the first ceremonies in 1906.

Except for the Peace Prize, the other five categories are judged in Sweden and presented in Stockholm to those who, in Nobel's words, "shall have conferred the greatest benefit on mankind". The Nobel Peace Prize ceremony takes place in Oslo Town Hall.

Nobel's early instructions were that the Peace Prize should be used to award efforts to reduce the size of military forces and standing armies, but the Prize broadened its remit to the promotion of peace in general. This vague brief can lead to controversy, as it did when the Israeli and Egyptian Prime Ministers, Menachem Begin and Anwar Sadat, received the Peace Prize jointly for their 1978 efforts to open up talks and communication between their two countries. Dr Henry Kissinger's award in 1972 also aroused controversy, particularly when his Vietnamese co-recipient, Le Duc Tho, turned down his own award for their joint efforts in ending the Vietnam war.

However, few begrudged Nelson Mandela and F.W. de Klerk their joint award in 1993.There were no dissenters when the Red Cross received the prize in 1917 for its work amid the battlefield carnage of World War I. The explorer Fridtjof Nansen regarded the Nobel Peace Prize as the greatest of the tributes to his years as internationalist, humanitarian and head of the Norwegian delegation at the League of Nations.

Among the many other recipients were Martin Luther King, Dr Albert Schweitzer, Amnesty International, the Dalai Lama and Kofi Annan. In 1979 Mother Teresa accepted her award in her customary habit and sandals despite the Norwegian winter. Even so her conservative views on abortion led to protests. ❑

LEFT: Alfred Nobel (1833–96).

T-bane from the Nationaltheatret stops at Majorstuen, the end of Bogstadveien, from where it is only a short walk to the beginning of the park.

Map on pages 156–7

Once inside the intricate wrought-iron gates, you'll come across **Vigelandsbroen** (bridge), bedecked with 58 bronze figures of men, women and new-born infants, including the famous *Sinnataggen (Angry Boy)*. Next is *Fontenen (Fountain)*, six male figures raising a giant bowl. Vigeland was obsessed with the cycle of life which he depicts here in 20 reliefs around the edge of the fountain pool. Above the fountain on a raised plateau, and surrounded by 36 groups of granite figures, is **Monolitten ㉔**, a great spire 17 metres (55 ft) high and comprising 121 figures sculpted out of one solid block of a whitish granite. The last of the major sculptures, the *Livshjulet (Wheel of Life)* is a continuum of human figures in a kind of airborne ring dance. The **Vigeland-museet** (open Tues–Sun noon–4pm; entrance fee; tel: 22 54 25 30), containing the rest of his work, is at the southern end of the park. Vigeland spent 40 years of his life designing and constructing the park, all financed by the taxpayer, something which Munch found reprehensible; he made his own feelings clear by donating all his own work to the city.

A living exhibit in traditional dress in Oslo's Folkemuseum at Bygdøy.

A city in the making

Frogner Park also contains the **Oslo Bymuseum ㉕** (City Museum; open June–Aug Tues–Fri 10am–6pm, Sat–Sun 11am–5pm; Sept–May Tues–Fri 10am–4pm, Sat–Sun 11am–4pm; entrance fee; tel: 23 28 41 70). Founded in 1050 by Harald Hardråde, Oslo was originally bounded by the (now subterranean) Bjørvika, Alna and Hovin rivers. It took another 250 years before it attained capital status during the reign of Håkon V (1299–1319). The town had just 3,000 inhabitants at the time.

BELOW: Norwegians are generous in a good cause.

Following a great fire in 1624, Christian IV decided to move the whole conurbation to where Akershus Festning (Fortress) now stands, and the town became known as Christiania or "Kvadraturen". What was the centre is now called **Christiania torv**, where in 1997 a statue of Christian IV's index finger was erected to commemorate the historic event.

With its strict grid plan, Christiania had little in common with medieval Oslo. The greatest change, however, has happened over the past 150 years due to growth in its population. In 1880, Christiania had 120,000 inhabitants; by 1910 the population had doubled. By popular consensus the town reverted to its original name in 1925. From 1945 to 1955, Oslo went through a new period of growth, and surpassed the half million mark in 1997.

Norway's national jump

For **Holmenkollen bakken ㉖** ski-jump and **Skimuseet** (Ski Musuem: open June–Aug 9am–8pm; Sept–May 10am–4pm; entrance fee; tel: 22 92 32 00) take T-bane 1 to Holmenkollen. The jump is only used in February and March, and the crowning event in the ski-jump season is the competition on the second Sunday in March (see "The Great Ski-Jump", page 105). Built in 1892, Holmenkollen is the world's oldest jump, and a national symbol. The adjoining Ski

Away from the city centre, the domestic architecture in some of Oslo's suburbs reflects the tranquil side of urban life.

BELOW: from the top of Tryvannstårnet, Oslo's radio tower, the view stretches to Sweden.

Museum is a monument to "One Thousand Years of Skiing". Very old skis and snowshoes are on display, as well as the trail-worn paraphernalia carried by such intrepid Norwegian explorers as Fridtjof Nansen, who crossed Greenland on skis. A simulator recreates the Holmenkollen jump.

For **Tryvannstårnet** ㉗ (Observation Tower; open June daily 10am–6pm; July daily 9am–8pm; Aug daily 10am–8pm; May and Sept Mon–Thur 10am–5pm; Oct–Apr Mon–Thur noon–4pm; entrance fee; tel: 22 14 67 11), with its lift to a panoramic view of the city, take the T-bane to Frognerseteren (with a restaurant of the same name, famous for its home-made apple pie). The area is thickly forested and popular for walking and skiing. If you choose to go back to Holmenkollen on foot, the walk is signposted and takes 15 to 20 minutes.

Other exploring possibilities are provided by the islands and peninsulas of Oslofjorden, most of which are accessible by ferry from Aker Brygge quay. **Nesoddtangen** is at the tip of a hilly, wooded peninsula jutting from the east side of the fjord. Local artists exhibit at **Hellviktangen Manor** (open May–Sept; weekends out of season; entrance fee), where they serve coffee and waffles on Sundays. The house is surrounded by apple trees and gives directly on to the fjord. **Hovedøya** and **Lindøya** islands have beaches, but the best are on the western edge of Bygdøy. **Gressholmen** and **Langøyene** have free camping and good beaches. **Kalvøya**, on the western side of the fjord near Sandvika, is the site of big outdoor rock concerts in summer.

Bygone days on Bygdøy

Oslo hugs the fjord, and the city limits extend quite far down its sides. Just west of the harbour is the **Bygdøy peninsula**, where the old Viking ships and the more recent explorer ships are kept, and where Norway's maritime past is commemorated (bus 31 or from May–September boat 91 from Rådhusbrygge).

It is home to the **Vikingskipshuset** ㉘ (Viking Ship Museum; open May–Sept 9am–6pm; Oct–Mar 11am–4pm; entrance fee; tel: 22 13 52 80), the **Frammuseet** ㉙ (open June–Aug 9am–6.45pm; Sept–May hours vary; entrance fee; tel: 23 28 29 50), which houses Fridtjof Nansen's polar sailing ship *Fram;* and the **Kon-Tiki Museet** ㉚ (open June–Aug 9.30am– 5.45pm; Sept–May hours vary; entrance fee; tel: 23 08 67 67) which contains, apart from the *Kon-Tiki* raft on which Thor Heyerdahl travelled to Polynesia, *Ra II*, a fragile-looking reed barque on which he travelled to Barbados. There is also a collection of his Easter Island artefacts.

The **Norsk Sjøfartsmuseum** ㉛ (Maritime Museum; open mid-May–Sept 10am–6pm; Oct–mid-May times vary; entrance fee; tel: 24 11 41 50) concentrates on the history of the craft of boat-building.

Also on Bygdøy is the **Norsk Folkemuseum** ㉜ (Norwegian Folk Museum; open mid-May–mid-Sept 10am–6pm; Oct–Apr times vary; entrance fee; tel: 22 12 37 00) and **Oscarshall slott** ㉝ (Castle; open late-May–Sept Thur, Fri and Sun noon–4pm; entrance fee; tel: 22 56 15 39). The folk museum, established in 1894, is an indoor/outdoor museum devoted largely to Norwegian rural culture. The collection of outdoor buildings, including a stave church from Gudbrandsdalen, gives a good idea of what old villages and agricultural settlements looked like. Other exhibits include Ibsen's studio, Sami ethnography, and a pharmacy museum. Oscarshall was built in quasi-Gothic style as a summer residence by King Oskar I.

Map on pages 156–7

Weekends out of doors

A typical city dweller from Oslo spends huge amounts of time outdoors. On workdays, many take their *matpakke* from home (a basic lunch bag stuffed with sandwiches and fruit) and sit outside, weather allowing, between 11.30am and 12.30pm to eat it. (Lunch is eaten later in restaurants, from noon–2pm.) There is a large number of outdoor and pavement establishments, so those without *matpakke* can also lunch out of doors.

The Oslo area gets very warm in summer – the temperature has been known to reach nearly 38°C (100°F) – and very cold and snowy in the winter. So in summer, people are likely to plan outdoor activities after work, anything from swimming, berry-picking, walking, jogging, or cycling at home in the suburbs in the light of the evening sun. Norwegians treasure their space and contact with nature, and many people who work in Oslo live a fair distance from the city; in winter, this means they can get quickly on to the floodlit slopes and cross-country ski trails after work.

Come the weekend, there is a widely followed pattern for the 48 hours. Friday night is usually a night out on the town. This may begin after dinner and a change of clothes at home, especially for younger people, who don't start to fill the bars until well after 10pm. Saturday morning is given over to shopping, followed by gardening or watching football, and Saturday evening tends to be dinner or a party at someone's home. No matter how wild or calm the Saturday

BELOW: a statue of Camille Collett, one of Norway's earliest female writers, in Slottsparken.

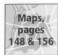

Maps,
pages
148 & 156

night, Sunday is *tur* day. The *tur* is a walk or ski-tour, and a formidable tradition. Depending on a person's age, fitness, and the number of accompanying children, the *tur* can be anything from a one-to six-hour affair. The *matpakke* provides lunch in the forest. Some walks will include café stops in one of the 70-odd cabin lodges in the **Nordmarka** area of Oslo; if not, coffee and hot chocolate come along in a vacuum flask. Home then to change for an early dinner, then it's off to the cinema. And thereby hangs a weekend.

Nordmarka

There is a great swathe of forest due north of the city centre. Larch, birch, pine, aspen and several deciduous species dominate; the colour contrast in autumn is worth a special trip. Den Norske Turistforening (Touring Association) at Stortingsgate 28 has free sketch maps of most routes in these areas; maps 1 to 12, the *"Oslo og Omegn Turistforening"* series, cover the Oslo region; they also sell more detailed survey maps. Access to these routes from the centre is easy and cheap via public transport. For **Grorud** and the **Lillomarka** area (northeast of the city centre), take either T-bane 5 (destination Vestli) or bus 30 from Jernbanetorget. Trails begin just west of the Grorud T-bane. Due north is **Grefsen**, along a suburban train line (information from Trafikanten at Oslo Sentralstasjon), tram 11, 12, 15 or 17 (Grefsen/Kjelsås), or bus to Grefsenkollen.

BELOW: out sailing on Oslofjorden.
RIGHT: a traditional "loft" house (food store) in the Folkemuseum at Bygdøy.

For walks in the **Holmenkollen** area and northwest, part of the Nordmarka, take T-bane 1 to Frognerseteren (not to be confused with Frognerparken) and stay on until the end of the line. You can even rent a sled *(archebrect)* there to take on a 3-km (2-mile) long downhill trail (the Corkscrew). The Touring Association can recommend trails or, even better, ask a Norwegian to recommend a favourite *tur*.

The trails are signposted, but if you get lost, seek help from other walkers. (See the *Oslo Guide* on the website www.visitoslo.com for other recommended routes.)

Many of the forest trails circumnavigate lakes, so a swimming break may be included if it's hot. Come winter, there's skiing (even at night on floodlit trails), skating and sledging to add to the general flurry of activity on a Sunday. If good snow cover has been established, walking trails double as cross-country skiing trails. However Holmenkollen is strictly professional and a very dangerous jump for amateurs.

Something to take home

Handicrafts, textiles, woollens and pewter are favourites for visitors in Oslo. **Basarhallene**, one of the few "older" shopping areas at the back of the Domkirke, has a wonderful jeweller's, Elias Sollberg, and a hat shop. Adjacent are two big department stores, Glasmagasinet across the way (Stortorvet 9) and Steen & Strøm at Kongensgate 23.

Oslo City and **By Porten**, next to Oslo Sentralstasjon, and **Aker Brygge** on the waterfront are three major malls. Grensen is the street for bargains, while Lille Grensen has stalls selling everything from sausages to skateboards. Hennes & Mauritz has a bargain basement on Kirkeristen. Every Sunday there is a big art market in the warehouses around the Blå concert hall off Nordregate. ❏

AROUND OSLO AND ITS FJORD

The charms of Oslofjorden may need some searching out, for this is Norway's industrial heartland, but it is rich in natural beauty and Viking history, and the surrounding area echoes to its pulse

At dusk the islands of Oslofjorden look like hunched prehistoric animals about to sink into a subaquatic sleep. In the colder months, the sky at sunset grows from lavender to purple while the islands turn slate-grey, then ominous and black. Summer sunsets bring twisted pink clouds underlit by a huge red sun that drops only briefly behind the fjord's western cliffs before rising again in the east.

Daytime along the 100-km (60-mile) long fjord reveals a high concentration of industry down both the eastern and western sides. With Oslo at its head, the fjord is the capital's workhorse, its roads travelled by juggernauts with cargoes of timber and oil, its ports and waterways busy with yachts and barges. Outside its working ports, Oslofjorden is a magnificent expanse of water stretching into the Skagerrak. Sprinkled liberally with islands, skerries, natural marinas and swimming beaches, the fjord is popular with Oslo residents in summer.

The lungs of the city

Akershus, **Vestfold** and **Østfold** are the three main counties to touch Oslofjorden. Akershus county contains the Oslo conurbation, the national Gardermoen airport, plus a broad swathe of agricultural and forest land reaching to Sweden. At its northern reach lies the Mjøsa lake town of Eidsvoll, where the Norwegian constitution was signed and the modern state born in 1814. Østfold (east) and Vestfold (west) spread down from Oslo like a pair of lungs. Some of Scandinavia's oldest ruling families were found buried in Vestfold along with several sunken Viking ships loaded with booty, while Østfold is rich with ancient rock paintings and stone circles.

Both of these counties contain provincial cities of major historic significance: Fredrikstad in Østfold, a magnificent fortress town, and Tønsberg in Vestfold, the oldest extant Scandinavian city, founded in 872. Remains of **Kaupang**, the oldest Nordic town yet discovered, were found a couple of kilometres from Tønsberg and are now in Oslo's Historisk (Historical Museum). Corroboration of its early existence appeared in a world history by England's 9th-century monarch, King Alfred the Great. Larger towns usually have an old section closely packed with superbly crafted wooden houses. Halden, near the Swedish border in Østfold, and Larvik in Vestfold, are the southernmost points on the fjord, each accessible within a couple of hours from Oslo.

Despite its rich history and good travel links (not to mention its seafood festivals), the Oslofjord area gets few tourists from outside Scandinavia. The scenery isn't as dramatic as the west coast's. There are, however, more habitable islands than in any other fjord,

PRECEDING PAGES: old wooden houses on Oslofjorden. **LEFT:** a summer's evening on the fjord. **BELOW:** Moses with the Ten Commandments, Drøbak church.

Around Oslo and its Fjord

0 ———————— 20 km

0 ———————— 20 miles

many with sports centres and hotels offering everything from tennis to wind-surfing and swimming. Inland is sloping countryside punctuated by forests, orchards and tilled fields which appeals to cyclists.

Walker's paradise

There are fantastic walks in the **Oslomarka** (the forests surrounding Oslo) accessible by bus, train or tram. Much of the **Nordmarka** ❶ (the area to the north of the city) is privately owned by timber barons who have kept it open to the public and, in any case, Norway's "Outdoor Recreations Act" permits every-body to cross outlying property on foot. The *"Oslo og Omegn"* maps (Oslo Nordmark map, summer or winter, free from Den Norske Turistforeningen at Storgata 3, Oslo; weekdays only; tel: 22 82 28 00) cover the Nordmarka's net-work of cleared trails. Around Grefsen, south of **Maridalsvannet**, is a luxuri-ant parkland (tram 11 and 12 or bus 37 to Grefsen, Grefsenkollen, Kjelsås). Maridalsvatnet is a tremendous lake fed by a series of charming clearwater brooks. **Sognsvann**, the lake west of Maridalsvatnet is at the end of T-bane 5.

By car you can explore further. If you're a fan of Norwegian rural architec-ture you'll have your fill in outer Akershus. Take route E16 in a westerly direc-tion towards Tyrifjorden and at Sundvollen turn right and follow the toll road into the **Krokkleiva** district. The paths cross wooded hills 400–500 metres (1,300–1,600 ft) high. **Kongens Utsikt** ❷ (The King's View) gives panoramic views across Steinsfjorden and Tyrifjorden.

Afterwards, rejoin the E16 northbound, direction Hønefoss. Leave it before Hønefoss to pick up Road 241 northeast from Bråk, and then strike east on to Road 242. South of this road is a **wilderness** of pine marshland, secluded lakes, oak forests and stream-bordered fields (map Oslo Nordmark – Nordre Del). There are some NOK 10 tolls (10 krone coins only), but when you see how wild the area is you'll appreciate the fact that there are any roads here at all. Road 4 south returns you to Oslo and the junction with the E6; northbound it leads to Gjøvik on the western side of Lake Mjøsa.

Birthplace of the state

If you go east from the junction of Road 4 and the E6 along Road 170 you come to the small village of **Fetsund**, just past Lillestrøm, and the **Fetsund Lenser** (open June–Aug Tues–Fri 11am–4pm, Sat–Sun 11am–5pm; May and Sept Sat–Sun only 11am–5pm; tel: 63 88 75 50), a logging museum celebrating the industrial activity on the banks of the Glomma river. The museum includes a nature trail and boat trips to the North Øyeren Nature Reserve, a haven for migratory bird species. The café here specialises in serving grilled *gjedde* (pike) in burger form.

Heading northeast, a road to the left will bring you to **Sørumsand** ❸, where there is a narrow-gauge "Tertitten" railway (open Dec, July–mid-Sept Sun only 11am–3pm; tel: 63 86 81 50). From here, Road 171 will bring you back to the E6. Travelling north you come to the unusual landscape of **Raknehaugen** (burial site; open all year) at Jessheim near **Garder-moen** ❹. Continuing in a northerly direction, at the

On the northern out-skirts of the capital, Oslomarka (Oslo's fields) contains 2,500 km (1,550 miles) of ski trails, 110 km (68 miles) of which are illuminated at night. Trail use is free and there are lodges and cafés along the way.

BELOW: inscription at Skjeberg, Østfold.

The Norwegian Constitution was signed in 1814 in this wooden manor-house near Eidsvoll, home of the Ankers family.

southern end of Lake Mjøsa is **Eidsvoll** ❺, about 80 km (50 miles) from Oslo. Eidsvoll is a lake town of old wooden houses and churches, and nearby, on the other side of the E6 at Eidsvoll Verk, is a national landmark: the **Eidsvolls-bygningen** ❻ (memorial building; open June–Aug 10am–5pm; May–Sept 10am–3pm; Oct–Apr by appointment; entrance fee; tel: 63 92 22 10), a mini-museum to the Norwegian Constitution which includes the room where the document was signed. The nearby **Eidsvoll Bygdetun** (Rural Museum; open June–Aug) consists of a collection of 26 old farm buildings and a World War II museum all set in beautiful countryside. Then tour Lake Mjøsa on the old paddle steamer *Skibladner*. The round trip takes 12 hours, with the halfway point at Lillehammer *(see page 183)*.

Tranquil countryside, sleepy shore

Heading south out of Oslo on the east side of the fjord, the quiet way to Fredrikstad is via the old **Mossveien**, which hugs the fjordline as near as topography allows. Having taken the E6 or E18 out of the city, turn right off the main road at Vinterbru and head for the tip of Bundefjorden. Take the road signposted to Nesoddtangen and you will come across a signpost to **Drøbak** ❼.

The village of Drøbak was once a fishermen's settlement. Fishing vessels still arrive here and sell fresh prawns and fish on the quayside. Places of interest include the **Follo Museum** (Heritage Museum; open mid-May–mid-Sept Tues–Fri 11am–4pm, Sat–Sun noon–5pm; entrance fee; tel: 64 93 99 90) and **Oscarsborg Festning** (Fort; tours in summer; tel: 64 90 41 60) out in the fjord from where gunfire sunk the German cruiser *Blücher* in 1940 (guided boat trips from the harbour). Another point of pride is the cross-timbered

BELOW: Drøbak, a fishing port on the Oslofjord.

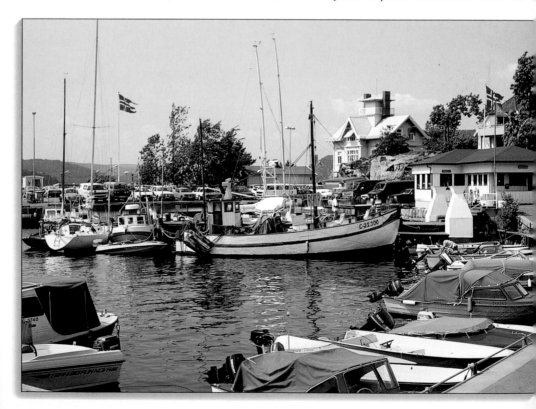

Drøbak Kirke from 1776 (open all year). The church has an elaborately carved model of a ship, a common piece of church decoration in seafaring towns. Rococo touches include wooden busts of Moses and Aaron. Gospel and jazz concerts are held here in summer.

Map on page 170

Artist centre

The road out of Drøbak takes off just before the ferry terminal, from where small car ferries run every half hour or so to the Hurum peninsula. Soon the road passes through fertile farmland and forest, first to Hvitsten and then to **Son** ❽ (pronounced *soon*), a fetching artists' village hugging the edge of a sheltered sound. The surrounding countryside and shoreline here provided inspiration for the likes of Theodore Kittelsen and Edvard Munch.

The **Son Kystkultursenter** (Coastal Heritage Centre; open mid-May–mid-Sept Tues–Sun; tel: 64 95 82 13) explains how this one-time Dutch freeport (the original name was Zoon) has thrived variously on timber, ice and fishing. The unusual elevated building at the edge of the marina is the last remaining fishing-net-drying structure in the Oslo fjord. **Gallery X** and **Bakgården** are showrooms for local artists (open all year), while La Riviera next door is an excellent French restaurant with an authentic wood-burning oven. Son is a popular summer resort for boating enthusiasts and on a summer's evening, with a cold beer in hand, there is no better place to watch the sun set behind the billowing sails of a myriad of yachts.

South to Østfold

Østfold is a long funnel through which tourists from Sweden pour. Despite its industrial towns such as Halden, Sarpsborg and Moss, Østfold buzzes with out-

Knut Hamsun, the Nobel prize-winning novelist, once lived in the Reenskaug Hotel in Drøbak, and the town became a rich source of material for his 1920 novel, Konene ved Vandposten (Women at the Pump).

BELOW: the view over Halden from the fortress.

door pursuits: canoeing and cycling are popular, and the area is dotted with hiking and skiing centres. There are also golf courses, and the Mysen race track. Then there's the draw of the fjord. Jeløy peninsula is the site of **Galleri F15** (open all year; entrance fee) at **Jeløy **, which has fjordside trails and stupendous lawns. Exhibitions are laid out through a light-filled house. Its cafeteria is a beloved coffee pit-stop. Down the coast, the royal yacht *Norge* is anchored at **Hankø**, Norway's regatta centre.

Old centres

**Fredrikstad ** is a gem among Østfold towns, and Scandinavia's only completely preserved fortress town, dating from 1567. The cobbled streets of Gamlebyen (old town) were laid by prisoners; wooden stocks face the former prison, now a bank (but with the prisoners' room preserved). And its restaurants and galleries keep their old facades. The stately Rådhus (Town Hall) was designed by the architect who built Oslo's Stortinget. The old-style Victoria Hotel serves fine meals; game is a speciality.

History and prehistory figure largely in Østfold's attractions. The **Oldtidsveien** (Highway of the Ancients), Road 110 between Fredrikstad and Skjeberg to the west, has 3,000 to 4,000 year old runic paintings and burial sites like **Hunn**, covered with stone circles.

Halden **, situated south of Skjeberg and close by the Swedish border, is dominated by **Fredriksten Festning (Fort; open May–Aug 10am–5pm; entrance fee; tel: 69 18 54 11), a largely intact ruin with many of its buildings serving as small themed museums, including a historic pharmacy (1870), bakery and brewery. The streets below were laid out along the cannons' blast lines to give the fortress's defenders freedom to fire. In summer a passenger boat makes regular trips along the inland waterway system, navigating through the massive Brekke locks, which rise to 26 metres (85 ft).

Throughout Østfold, St Olav's Day (29 July) is celebrated with a great show of folk costume, music and dance. One of the best displays is at the **Borgarsyssel Museum** (open all year; entrance fee) in **Sarpsborg ⑫**, north of Skjeberg. Sarpsborg is the site of one of Østfold's two youth hostels, on Tune lake (the other is at Moss), and it has brewery tours and trips on the jazz boat *Krabben*.

Across to Vestfold

There is much shared history between Østfold and Vestfold. It was the fast action of troops on both sides of the fjord that led to the sinking of the *Blücher*, scuppering Hitler's plans for an easy invasion.

The Moss-Horten car ferry connects Østfold and Vestfold in less than an hour. The **Marinemuseet** (Naval Museum; open May–Sept noon–4pm; Oct–Apr Sun noon–4pm; free; tel: 33 03 33 97) at **Horten ⑬** documents this event and hundreds of others in displays bulging with weird and wonderful artefacts including a full-size submarine open to the public. Multiply the experience a hundredfold if you meet retired Commander Steinar Sandvold here. There are also museums of photography and veteran cars in Horten (both open all year; entrance fee).

Heading southwards, tranquil **Løvøy** island has a solemn medieval stone church. This was Viking country, and **Borre Nasjonalpark ⑭** (open all year; free access to grounds), en route to Tønsberg, contains enormous turf-covered humps concealing Viking kings' graves. Borre also has an extensive network of

Map on page 170

BELOW: in summer, berry-picking in the garden or forest is a popular activity.

Learning to sail on Oslofjorden.

trails, and the largest collection of Iron Age burial sites in Scandinavia. Keeping to the coastline along Road 311, **Åsgårdstrand** ⑮ is the site of **Munchs Lille Hus** (Munch's Little House; open June–Aug Tues–Sun 11am–7pm; May–Sept; entrance fee; tel: 33 08 21 31), where the artist lived when he returned to Norway from abroad. Munch painted *Three Girls on a Bridge* here. Åsgårdstrand Hotel is the town's only hotel. In summer a great gush of activity emanates from here: boat trips, barbecues, and the Åsgårdstrand Festival, when there are dance and piano concerts – and a great Wiener schnitzel barbecue. You can spurn these organised activities to cycle, swim in the fjord, fish in Borre's lake, or watch the fishermen come in each afternoon with the fresh catch.

Viking burial

Between Åsgårdstrand and Tønsberg is **Oseberghaugen** ⑯ (burial mound), the most important Viking site yet discovered (open all year). Oslo's Vikingskips huset (Viking Ship Museum) contains the finds, including the 20-metre (65-ft) arch-ended wooden ship. Only the mound itself, near Slagen church, remains, but as a symbol Oseberghaugen has a subtle, magnetic power.

Just south is history-rich **Tønsberg** ⑰, established in the 9th century and said to be Norway's oldest settlement. On the 65-metre (200-ft) high **Slottsfjellet** are the fortress remains and tower. The main street, Storgata, is flanked by Viking graves. These were excavated and incorporated, under glass, into the ground floor of the new library. Across the street are the walls of one of only two medieval round churches in Scandinavia. The most renowned king to hold court in Tønsberg was Håkon Håkonson IV (1240–63). The ruins of his court can be seen on Nordbyen, a street with old houses hunched along it. A more

BELOW: one of the many popular bathing sites around Oslo's fjord.

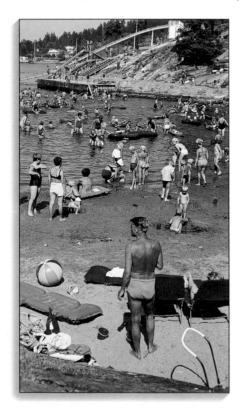

recent native son is Roald Amundsen, the polar explorer. Less known outside Norway is Svend Foyn, the Tønsberg whaling captain who invented the explosive-powered harpoon.

The steamship *Kysten I* (built 1909), moored on Byfjorden near the old customs house, does a three-hour islands tour. North of the *Kysten*, you can pick up Nordbyen which will bring you back into town.

To the south of Tønsberg, along the eastern side of the fjord, the islands of **Nøtterøy** and **Tjøme**, and the skerries, are fantastic summer hangouts. **Rica Havna** is on a gorgeous natural haven carved from rock. **Verdens Ende** (World's End) is, naturally, at the end – but for a few boulders – of the chain. Verdens Ende boasts a near 180-degree view of the sea. The old lighthouse here is a beautifully simple structure made of stone.

On the other side of Tønsbergfjorden lies **Sandefjord** ⑱, once the whaling capital of the world. The sea still dominates life here. One of the main industries is marine paint production. The town centre is compact, and the cosy old Kong Carl Hotel is one of its more handsome buildings. Near Badeparken are the former spa and the old town, along Thaulowsgate. Preståsen is the hilly park above it. Top Airport, with flights to Europe every hour, is located here.

Just outside Sandefjord are **Gokstadhaugen** (burial site; open May–Sept; guided tours; entrance free to grounds), in which the Gokstad ship, now in the

Map on page 170

Vikingskiphuset (Viking Ship Museum) in Oslo, was discovered in 1880; and **Vesterøy** peninsula, ideal for walking, biking and boating. It's a supremely peaceful place – the film star Liv Ullman's summer house is in the vicinity.

Larvik was home to two legendary boat lovers: Thor Heyerdahl, and Scotsman Colin Archer, designer of the polar ship *Fram*. Archer's first house was at Tollerodden, on the fjord. At Larvik's back is the huge Lake Farris.

There are many fine waterside spots around Larvik, such as **Mølland** beach, stacked with sea-rounded pebbles, and **Nevlunghavn**, an exquisite fishing cove tucked around the bay west of Stavern. The fish and shellfish festivals in the Larvik area are renowned. Hotels often host them; the Grand in Larvik has both excellent seafood and a superb "wild" menu including pheasant, ptarmigan (arctic grouse) and elk in their seasons. Inner Vestfold's rivers run with salmon and trout. **Brufoss** is a favourite anglers' haunt (accommodation and day licences available, tel: 33 12 99 20). In winter, this is a popular downhill ski district. You will find a number of ceramic works which offer tours in outer and inner Vestfold and, in common with Østfold, every little hamlet seems to have an art gallery.

Knut Steen's Whaling Monument at Sandefjord.

Local pride

People who live around Oslofjorden have a strange modesty-pride complex. They are the first to point out the area's shortcomings – smallish mountains, the stink of the pulp and paper plants – but once these are out of the way, the superlatives begin to flow. The birthplaces of the most intrepid explorers are here, as are the best sailing races, the warmest summers, the finest archaeological discoveries, the best drinking water, summer resorts… the list goes on; for when it comes to this part of Norway neither the modesty nor the pride is false. ❑

BELOW: a refreshing beer in historic Tønsberg.

THE HEART OF NORWAY

Away from Mjøsa and its lakeside towns, central Norway extends east into the wilds around the old copper-mining town of Rorøs, and north towards the quintessentially Norwegian Dovre Mountains

Map, pages 182–3

Norway's heartland is centred on the counties of Oppland and Hedmark, and is characterised by three main features: Lake Mjøsa, the country's largest lake; the great massif of Dovrefjell to the north; and the long slanting valleys of Gudbrandsdalen and Østerdalen. In this widest part of Norway, these great valleys lie straight and narrow from southeast to northwest, their rivers like veins cutting between the mountain ranges. Alongside the rivers are fertile farms, which climb up the valley sides to forests. Then, above the tree-line come the bare slopes of tussocky grass and rocks, a playground for skiers and walkers.

Despite Norway's busy network of rural buses, it can be difficult to get into some of the remoter corners; but this region makes wonderful country for touring by car. Each new vista is more magnificent than the last as the road climbs, dips and circles. Nevertheless, for some of the higher plateaux, it can be simpler and quicker to push further into the wilderness by train, which stops at many small stations along the main line between Oslo and Trondheim – almost as spectacular as the famous Oslo–Bergen route in the west.

Mjøsa and Mjøsabyen

Lake Mjøsa ❶ also lies southeast to northwest some 160 km (100 miles) north of Oslo. One of the best ways to enjoy the lake and its surroundings is a trip on the old paddle steamer **SS Skibladner** (May–Sept; varying tours on alternate days excl. Sun; tel: 61 14 40 80). Built in 1856 as a continuation of Norway's first railway line between Oslo and Eidsvoll, she now plies the lake carrying tourists and is based in Hamar on the east of the lake.

Around Mjøsa lies some of the most fertile agricultural land in Norway and throughout the gently undulating countryside are large farms, encircled by thickly forested hills. Where Lake Mjøsa is at its widest, some 17 km (10 miles) across, is the attractive island of **Helgøya**. At its southern tip, the island has a burial mound, part of the historic Hovinsholm, a Royal estate from Viking times until 1723.

Three main towns lie along the lake: Hamar and Lillehammer are on the eastern shore and Gjøvik on the west. A bridge across the lake about half way between Hamar and Lillehammer links the municipalities and, in a commercial sense, has combined the area into what has been christened **Mjøsabyen**.

In the Middle Ages, **Hamar ❷** was the centre of Roman Catholicism in Norway and the seat of the bishop. It enjoyed great prosperity and had an impressive cathedral. Hamar's downfall came in 1537 when the Danes carried off the bishop, and 30 years later

PRECEDING PAGES: the opening ceremony of the 1994 Winter Olympics, Lillehammer. **LEFT:** a decorated *stabbur* (food store) from 1863. **BELOW:** Hafjell, near Lillehammer.

Heart of Norway

0 ————— 50 km
0 ————— 50 miles

N

NORWEGIAN SEA

when the Swedes burned the town to the ground. Now the cathedral ruins at Domkirkeodden (Cathedral Point) are part of the **Hedmarksmuseet** (open mid-May–mid-Sept; entrance fee). Not until the 19th century and the coming of the railway did Hamar regain a measure of importance, as a railway junction with a locomotive building works. The works have gone, but the **Jernbanemuseet** (National Railway Museum; open May–Sept; entrance fee; tel: 62 51 31 60), established in 1896, serves as a reminder. A highlight of this large collection is the early steam engine, *Caroline*, built by George Stephenson in 1861. There are regular excursions on a narrow-gauge railway.

The rather unusual "Viking ship" Olympic **skating arena** (open all year; entrance fee) was built for the 1994 Winter Olympics, which were held in and around the Mjøsabyen towns.

Seven of Norway's eight distilleries are located in the region. About 18 km (11 miles) east of Hamar towards Elverum is the **Løiten Brænderi** (guided tours; entrance fee; tel: 62 59 49 10), which is famous for Løiten aquavit.

Sandvig's collection

The largest of the three Mjøsabyen towns is **Lillehammer ❸**, situated at the northern end of the lake where it narrows to become the River Lågen and crosses Gudbrandsdalen (valley). Lillehammer is known as the capital of Gudbrandsdalen and came to the attention of the world as the site of the 1994 Winter Olympics. A downhill skiing area on nearby **Hafjell** and 500 km (300 miles) of cross-country skiing tracks were built for the occasion. Other facilities included an ice-hockey and speed-skating rink at **Gjøvik**.

For summer visitors, the biggest attraction is Norway's remarkable open-air museum, **Maihaugen** (opening times vary; entrance fee; tel 61 28 89 00). Some 120 buildings have been brought into the 40-hectare (100-acre) site from all over Gudbrandsdalen, including a stave church and two farms. The museum was the life work of Anders Sandvig. A dentist by profession, he came to Lillehammer in 1885 suffering

The old paddle steamer, Skibladner, *on Lake Mjøsa travels between Hamar, Eidsvoll, Gjøvik and Lillehammer during the summer months.*

BELOW: Odalen man's best friend, a *fjording* (Norwegian horse).

from tuberculosis and with a life expectancy of a mere two years. Whether or not it was the interest of the museum he founded in 1887 which kept him going, Sandvig lived for another 65 years and died in 1950.

Sandvig is the town's only honorary citizen with his statue prominent in the market place. Apart from the buildings, which range from the medieval to the 19th century, Maihaugen has some 30,000 artefacts, all collected by Sandvig, and the many demonstrations of old skills and rural crafts give the museum a real sense of being alive.

For the motoring enthusiast, the **Norsk Veg Museum** (Museum of Vehicle History; open all year; entrance fee) at Fåberg, to the north of Lillehammer on the E6, has everything from horse-drawn sleighs, gigs and carioles to motor cars. There are some unusual examples, including steam and electric vehicles, a strange six-wheeled Mustad and a 1922 Bjering, which seated two people in tandem and could have its front wheels replaced by skis in winter. There is also the Troll, the last car to be manufactured in Norway, which ended its production run of 16 vehicles in 1956.

Artistic light

The quality of light in Lillehammer and its surroundings has attracted many artists to the area, including Fredrik Collett, Lars Jorde, Alf Lundeby, Einar Sandberg, Kirsten Holbø, Erik Werenskiold and Henrik Sørensen. As a result, the town has an impressive art gallery, the **Kunstmuseum** (Art Museum; open June–mid-Aug: Tues–Sun 11am–4pm; mid-Aug–May: Mon–Sun 11am–5pm; free), which includes works by Jacob Weidemann, and Norway's most famous artist, Edvard Munch.

One of Lillehammer's most revered names is Danish-born Sigrid Undset, winner of the 1928 Nobel Prize for Literature, who took up residence at nearby Bjerkbæk in 1921.

At **Aulestad ❹** (open May–Sept; entrance fee; tel: 61 22 41 10), about 11 km (7 miles) from Lillehammer, is the home of another notable Norwegian author and playwright, Bjørnsterne Bjørnson (1812–1910), one of the writers who inspired the nationalist movement in the 19th century. He wrote Norway's national anthem, *Ja,vi elsker dette landet (Yes, we love this land of ours)* in 1870, promoted Norwegian plays in the theatre in preference to Danish and won a Nobel Prize for Literature in 1903. His house is just as it was when he died.

Alongside these literary attractions, Lillehammer has not neglected its younger visitors. On the outskirts of the town, at Øyer, is **Lilleputhammer** (open May–Sept; entrance fee) with its quarter-scale version of the centre of Lillehammer as it was in 1900. You walk down the main street, peer in the shop windows and find some are open to the public. There is also the popular **Hunderfossen Familiepark ❺** (open May–Sept; entrance fee) north of the town, which features the world's largest (fibreglass) troll; Norway's figure of fable is said to have an evil disposition and a face as gnarled as the mountains and rocks where they have their homes. Nearby is the **Huseskogen bob track** (tel: 61 28 98 00), built for the 1994 Winter Olympics and which offers dry runs for tourists during the summer.

Østerdalen

To the east of Lake Mjøsa lies **Østerdalen**, which cuts through the mountains on a line roughly parallel to Gudbrandsdalen. At times the valley is narrow, with seemingly endless forests on either side, broken only occasionally by patches of farmland. The valley starts at **Elverum ➏** in the south and continues northwards for 250 km (150 miles) becoming broader and more open further north. Throughout its length flows Norway's longest river, the **Glomma**, kept company by the railway and the E3.

Elverum is one of the essential crossroads of Norway, and lies at the junction of many valleys, with routes to Hamar to the west, Kongsvinger to the south and Trysil to the northeast. It has the well-preserved **Terningen bastion** built in 1673, and a climb to the top of the water tower provides a good view. The town's most famous episode is commemorated in a monument to the fierce battle fought in April 1940, which delayed the German army for long enough to allow the king and members of the government to escape further north before finally crossing to Britain to continue the fight in exile.

Built for the 1994 Winter Olympics, Hamar's ice rink was designed along the lines of an upturned Viking ship.

By far the most important of the town's attractions are two major museums. The **Glomdal Museum** (open June–Aug; entrance fee), opened in 1911 on a large natural site, has 88 old buildings of many kinds, brought in from Østerdalen and Solør. The indoor exhibition is divided into three sections – the farming year; transport and communication; and handwork and crafts – and it shows what life was like in Østerdalen from 1870 to 1900. There is also a collection from the Neolithic age and Viking era, as well as an open-air theatre.

The **Norsk Skogsbrukmuseum** (Forestry Museum; open all year, entrance fee) encompasses forestry, hunting and fishing. The main building also has

BELOW: Lake Mjøsa at sunset.

exhibits devoted to geology and wildlife, and children usually head for the aquarium. The outdoor collection is mainly situated on the small island of Prestøya in the middle of the Glomma River.

Early skiing

To the northeast, **Trysil** ❼, in Hedmark near the Swedish border, is a popular winter sports area. It has the distinction of being home to the world's oldest ski club, the Trysil Shooting and Skiing Club founded in 1861. In summer, Trysil is a centre for paragliding, rafting, canoe tours and mountain tours with pack dogs to carry the luggage. But it goes without saying that almost anywhere in the heart of Norway you only need to go a short way for the sort of outdoor recreation that mountain, river and lake can provide.

North from Elverum along the E3 there are few places of any size or importance, but the whole of this area is well off the tourist track and ideal for exploration. At **Koppang**, about half-way along the length of Østerdalen, you can take an alternative route north, along Road 30 past the long thin Storsjøen (lake), rejoining the E3 at **Tynset**. Northwest of Tynset, you come to Kvikne and near it the rectory at Bjørgan, the birthplace of Bjørnsterne Bjørnson.

Alternatively try Road 219 which turns west at **Atna**, some 30 km (20 miles) north of Koppang, for a drive into the foothills of the wild and mountainous region of **Rondane**, where the peaks rise up to 1,800 metres (6,000 ft) high. At Enden, the road is joined by Road 27, which has taken the parallel route north from Ringebu. Called the **Rondevegen** ❽, the road climbs steeply from Gudbrandsdalen to some superb views of the Rondane Mountains. After coming this far, it is well worth continuing from Enden to Folldal, past the great peaks

BELOW: as this selection shows, each area has its own design of *bunad*, Norway's traditional national costume.

Map, pages 182-3

that include Rondeslottet at 2,178 metres (7,144 ft) high, with the **Rondane Nasjonalpark** (National Park) to the west. Established in 1962, this was Norway's first national park and offers a wide range of trails of varying difficulty.

Road 27 ascends to nearly 915 metres (3,000 ft) before reaching **Folldal**, itself one of the highest permanently inhabited communities in Norway. The community's history begins from when copper was discovered in the area in the 18th century. Although the mine is no longer worked, the mining company is still based here to serve a new mine at Hjerkinn about 30 km (20 miles) away. The old Folldal mine, and some of its buildings, now form a **museum** (open all year; entrance fee) with guided tours in summer.

Along the copper road

From Folldal, if you head east you return to the Glomma River valley and the E3 at Alvdal, all connected to and part of the system of valleys and rivers that spread out from Østerdalen. Along the way abandoned mine works indicate how important minerals were and, to some extent, still are to this area. North of Alvdal, rail, road and river head northeast, through Tolga and Os – which is the start of the **Kopperveien** (Copper Road) – before coming to the old copper-mining town of **Røros** ❾ *(see page 188)*. Here, you can visit the old smelter in the **Rørosmuseet** (open all year; entrance fee), the impressive **church** (open June–Sept: Mon–Sat; Oct–May: Sun only; entrance fee), and a disused mine at **Olavsgruva** (open all year; entrance fee) out east along Road 31.

Røros is also a junction for roads which lead through an eastern wilderness with little habitation: the first is Road 31 to the Swedish frontier, only 45 km (30 miles) away to the east, past several lakes, some artificial, dug to provide water

The unsung heroine of the Gudbrandsdalen valley is Anne Haav, the farm maiden who first made the uniquely Norwegian geitost (goat's cheese) in the 19th century.

BELOW: autumn colours come early on the fjords.

Røros and the Old Copper Country

Røros was the archetypal company town with life and society revolving around the mining of copper. Isolated, exposed, nearly 600 metres (2,000 ft) above sea level and surrounded by mountains and enduring winter cold, its existence was entirely due to the discovery of copper, which was first mined here over 300 years ago and was worked until 1972. The town was hardly beautiful, and slag heaps (slegghaugen) and the smelter (smelthytta) provided the backdrop to the miners' houses. These were usually small and overcrowded, but many workers also possessed a small patch of land and one or two animals as a source of food.

Further away from smelter and slag lived those higher up the company pecking order – in the executive area. By some miracle, Røros escaped the fires which so often laid waste to the wooden buildings of Norwegian towns.

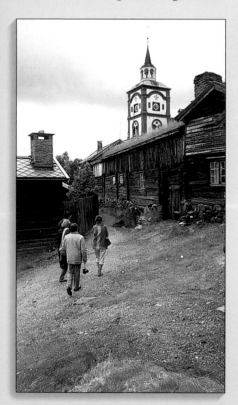

Today, Røros has a unique townscape and almost the entire older part of the town is preserved by law. Doors, windows and colour schemes all have to conform, buildings have to be lived in and there is strict control of advertising signs and notices. As a result, Røros is in a time warp, retaining much of its mining town atmosphere, and is on the UNESCO World Heritage list.

The most noticeable feature in Røros is the stone church – "the pride of the mining town" – which was dedicated in 1784 and replaced a wooden one built in 1650. The interior reflects the mining society, with paintings of clergymen and mining officials. Prayers were said every Sunday for the company and its directors.

The smelter was the heart of the copper-mining company and the focal point of the town. Its bell was rung at the start and end of each shift and is still there today. The smelter has been restored as a museum: the exterior still resembles the building as it was in 1889 but the interior is now given over to a series of exhibitions depicting life in the town, mining techniques in Europe in the 18th and 19th centuries, cultural features of the southern Lapp society and aspects of Røros society and its environs.

One of the most interesting elements in the museum is the series of working models to one-tenth scale which demonstrate the arduous methods called for when the only power available was water, horses and human muscle. In the past it was usual to make such scale models to see if a new technique or piece of equipment would work so today's replicas are following an old tradition.

Thirteen kilometres (8 miles) from Røros is Olavsgruva (the Olav mine), which was opened as a mining museum in 1979. A guided tour takes visitors 50 metres (165 ft) below ground. Up until 1880, when dynamite was introduced, the miners used the heat from wood fires stacked against the rock face to crack the rock. Back on the surface, the bare and bleak scenery surrounding the mine, even in the summer sun, is the most telling way to emphasise the wretched existence of those early miners. ❑

LEFT: both Rorøs church and the town's characteristic turf roofs are now preserved.

for mining operations; another north to Ålen (Road 30) which has a small open-air museum, then through the fast-flowing gorge of the Gaula river until the valley broadens out near Støren; yet another is an alternative route to Fæmund Lake, Norway's third largest, which offers good fishing.

Map, pages 182–3

Peer Gynt country

After Østerdalen, **Gudbrandsdalen** is the second-longest valley in Norway. The Lågen River runs its full length and the valley stretches for 140 km (90 miles) northwest from Lillehammer to Dombås, the starting point for climbing trips into the Dovre rock formation. This huge plateau is very popular with walkers, not least because it is framed by impressive peaks such as the **Snøhetta** 2,286 metres (7,498 ft).

Perhaps because it was surrounded by mountains, which emphasised its sense of identity, the Gudbrandsdal valley has a long tradition of folk dancing and folk music; it is famous for its wood carving and rose painting, and you can find good craftwork to take home. North of Lillehammer at **Ringebu ❿**, you can visit the 13th-century **Ringebu Stavkirke** (Stave Church; open late May–Aug; entrance fee). Built of enormous upright timbers, it has a statue of St Laurentius, crucifixes and a baptismal font all from medieval times.

Peer Gynt, as depicted by P.N. Arboe.

Vinstra ⓫ is the heart of what is known as "Peer Gynt country" after the legendary figure first written about by Peter Asbjørnsen in the 19th century. Asbjørnsen walked the country gathering material for a book of Norwegian folk tales, *Norske Folkeeventyr*, which he published with his friend, Bishop Jørgen Moe, in 1844. Though Peer (or Per) Gynt is legendary, he is real enough to Norwegians as a marksman, ski-runner and something of a braggart who

BELOW: low-lying farmland offers rich pastures.

Map, pages 182–3

was often economical with the truth. Yet the character inspired the poet and dramatist Henrik Ibsen to write the play *Peer Gynt* (1867) and Edvard Grieg to compose his *Peer Gynt* Suite No 1 (1888). Each summer the play is performed along with Greig's music in the amphitheatre at Golåvatnet southwest of Vinstra. One of the so-called Gynt cottages serves as the tourist information office in Vinstra (tel: 61 29 47 70). In the cemetery at **Sødorp**, 2 km (1 mile) away, is a monument to this curious icon of Norwegian folklore.

Today, Peer Gynt is a handy legend to use in the promotion of tourism, hence the creation of the **Peer Gyntveien**, a minor road which goes round in a huge semicircle through Golå and returns to the E6 at Tretten. It reaches an altitude of over 900 metres (3,000 ft) and presents a near continuous panorama of desolate mountains and lakes – stark but appealing. There are a number of mountain hotels in this area which are popular in both winter and summer.

Scottish visitors may want to stop at **Kringen** to see the memorial to a battle of 1612, when an army of Scottish mercenaries was defeated by local farmers. Despite their defeat, the Scots (said to be Sinclairs) have another memorial in the checked cloth used in one local costume, which looks remarkably like Sinclair tartan.

Solid as a rock

BELOW: Dovrefjell.
RIGHT: Maihaugen open-air museum, Lillehammer.

Travelling north from Vinstra, the E6 passes through Otta (where Road 15 heads off west to the western fjords) on its way to Dombås. Here it turns northeast, accompanied by the railway, and climbs up and over **Dovrefjell** ⑫. To many Norwegians, the Dovre Mountains represent the strength of their country, something that brings their nation together. With admirable brevity, they sum it up in the old phrase "*Enig og tro til Dovre faller*" ("United we stand until the Dovre Mountains fall").

The train stops at small stations such as Fokstua, Hjerkinn, Kongsvoll and Drivstua to disgorge walkers with boots and backpacks. The summit of Dovrefjell is at Hjerkinn, reputed to be the driest place in Norway, and for the rest of the way it is all downhill across the **Dovre Nasjonalpark** (National Park) en route to Oppdal. Dovrefjell is one of only three places in the world where you find musk ox in the wild.

Oppdal ⑬ looks up towards the Dovre plateau, and to Trollheimen *(see page 286)* to the northwest. In winter, it is a centre for skiing and in summer for walking, fishing, rafting and riding. The cable car takes walkers and skiers high above the village.

Not far from Oppdal, off Road 16, a small path leads to a peaceful place with trees and uneven mounds which are Viking graves. This is **Vang**, once the centre of the community until the railway brought Oppdal to life. There are 758 graves dating back to the early Iron Age. A track branches off to **Gjevils-vassdalen** and its lake. It is here that Anders Rambech, an 18th-century country attorney and one of the negotiators of the 1814 Constitution, built **Tingstua**. Today the wooden building is a popular upland inn. Small and simple though it is, the inn has been favoured by Queen Sonja who made it her base for walking into Dovrefjell. ❑

Map, pages 182–3

PEAK AND PLATEAU

Whether on foot or by car, the peaks of Jotunheimen and the flat rocky expanse of the Hardanger plateau both mesmerise and stun the senses with their sheer size and magnificence

Jotunheimen ("Home of the Giants"), which includes Norway's mightiest mountain range, and Hardangervidda (*vidde* means "highland plateau") together form an extensive area of outstanding natural beauty. Centres of population are few, places of interest are also thin on the ground, but of superb scenery – mountains, glaciers, lakes and rivers – there is an excess.

The attraction of **Hardangervidda** resides in its wide open spaces. On average 900 metres (3,000 ft) above sea level, it lies south of Jotunheimen with three main valleys – Begnadalen, Hallingdalen and Numedalen – cutting across it. The centre of the plateau with its lakes and streams (a paradise for anglers) forms the source of the mighty Hallingdal and Numedal rivers. There are a number of magnificent waterfalls in the area, including **Vøringfossen** *(see page 238)* and **Valursfossen** , which drops 90 metres (300 ft) into Hjelmodalen. To the south, Hardangervidda broadens out from **Hallingskarvet**, a rocky wall rising to a height of 1,700 metres (5,700 ft).

Crossing the plateau

Hardangervidda is in many ways unique as Europe's largest mountain plateau, covering an area of 10,000 sq km (3,860 sq miles), nearly a third of which lies within the **Hardangervidda Nasjonalpark** ⓯. The flora and fauna of the plateau is Arctic and hugely varied: several thousand reindeer roam freely, around 120 species of birds breed on these upland moors, and there are in excess of 400 different species of plants, an abundance due to the two distinct climates of Vidda – the gentle western coastal climate and the harsher inland climate of the east. There are tracks and trails galore and isolated cabins provide basic overnight accommodation.

The **Oslo–Bergen railway line** ⓰ cuts across Hardangervidda keeping Road 7 company as far as Haugastøl, where it goes north of the Hardangerjøkulen through **Finse** ⓱ *(see box, page 194)*, Myrdal and Mjølfjell. The road takes a different course, heading southwest across the wide, empty landscape with distant views of mountains, passing lakes and streams, before making a dizzy descent to sea level via a series of brilliantly engineered tunnels to Eidfjorden.

Travelling northeast from Haugastøl, both road and railway are initially dominated by Hallingskarvet. The immediate surroundings become somewhat softer as you reach **Geilo** ⓲, which has a good strategic position at the head of the Hallingdal valley and the gateway to Hardangervidda. Though it lies at a height of 800 metres (2,650 ft) above sea level, Geilo has grown into one of Norway's most popular winter sports resorts with 18 lifts, 34 well-groomed downhill runs

LEFT: view from the top, Jotunheimen.
BELOW: keeping traditional tunes alive.

Apart from Torpo
Stavkirke, other stave
churches worth
visiting in Buskerud
county are to be found
further south at Uvdal,
Nore, Rollag and
Flesberg.

and 220 km (135 miles) of cross-country tracks. With its range of hotels, Geilo has also become popular as a summer holiday centre and as a base for exploring the region by car (although the choice of roads is limited), on foot or horseback. In summer it still looks like a typical winter resort minus snow, with its spread out, slightly unfinished appearance.

From Geilo, Road 40 goes southeast past **Hol Bygdemuseum** (Rural Museum; open June–Aug; entrance fee) which takes the usual form of a collection of old buildings. In this case it includes the Mostugua from 1750, the Hågåstuga from 1806 and a mill from 1774. Road 40 continues along the eastern edge of Hardangervidda before it follows the Numedal valley to Kongsberg.

Road 7, meanwhile, continues northeast to Hagafoss where **Road 50** turns off it towards Lake Strandavatn. It leads along the north side of the long, clear lake dotted with small mountain huts. The landscape soon changes, however, allowing a magnificent view, and a summer skiing centre is located nearby. Suddenly the road begins to descend through a series of tunnels, including spirals, until the motorist is decanted into the Aurlands valley which continues to the village of Aurlandsvangen at the head of Aurlandsfjorden.

After being separated by Strandfjorden, Road 7 and the railway meet up at Ål ⓓ, where the Norwegian-German artist Rolf Nesch (1893–1975) lived and worked for 25 years. The **Nesch Museum** (open all year; entrance fee) contains the largest exhibition of his work in the country. **Torpo** has no museum but a stave church (open June–Sept; entrance fee) which is the oldest building in Hallingdal. It dates back to the second half of the 12th century and has a splendid painted ceiling from the 13th century. The motifs include scenes from the life of St Margaret, to whom the church is dedicated.

BELOW: summer
skiing in
Jotunheimen.

FINSE

To the south of the Jotunheimen lies the hamlet of Finse, the high-point at 1,225 metres (4,000 ft) on the Oslo–Bergen railway line. Its high street is the station platform; trains are the local traffic, as there are neither cars nor roads. It's a small speck in a seemingly boundless expanse of snow and ice, and a gateway to some of Norway's most beautiful wilderness.

Finse has the country's largest *hytta* (holiday lodge) for hikers and skiers, and a hotel. It is the starting point for two giant trail networks, stretching as the crow flies 225 km (140 miles) north to the Jotunheimen and 100 km (60 miles) south to Hardangervidda. In summer the region offers more than 5,000 km (3,000 miles) of T-marked hiking trails. At Easter-time, 2,000 km (1,240 miles) of ski trails are marked by poles in the snow.

The *hytta* are one of the great secrets of Norwegian hiking and skiing. You need only carry a light sleeping bag, because they have comfortable bunk beds, and meals are provided in most. The majority of *hytta* are owned by Den Norske Turistforening (DNT; tel: 22 82 28 00). You need not be a member to stay in a DNT *hytta*, but the cost of membership is soon offset by the discounts offered on accommodation. Trail use is free.

Just past Gol, Road 7 turns southwards towards Nesbyen, Norway's oldest outdoor museum. Founded in 1889, the **Hallingdal Folkemuseum** (open Apr–Oct; entrance fee) has 22 buildings, the earliest – Staveloftet – dating from 1340. All come from different parts of Hallingdal. Some interiors are rose painted and the exhibition building houses collections of furniture, textiles and weapons.

The two other roads at Gol both lead the traveller through more attractive scenery. Road 52 goes northwest along the Hemsedal valley through **Hemsedal**, another winter sports centre with 13 lifts, 26 runs and 90 km (55 miles) of cross-country tracks. The church (open Mon) has an altarpiece from 1775 and a painting of *The Last Supper* from 1716. From the village a minor road goes past a small open-air museum near the village of Ulsåk and, further on, a private toll road winds its way across superb scenery to Ulnes on Road E16. This is the **Utsiktsveien ⑳** (Panorama Way; summer only), a popular route which links the Hemsedal and Valdres valleys. Although narrow and rough in parts, it lives up to its name, threading its way between lakes and providing fine views of the Skogshorn, known as the "Queen of the Hemsedal".

Home of the Giants

The **Jotunheimen** was, in Norwegian mythology, the home of trolls and giants and it is here that the mightiest mountains are to be found. In the east is the **Jotunheimen Nasjonalpark ㉑** which includes the two highest mountains in the country: **Galdhøpiggen** at 2,469 metres (8,098 ft) and **Glittertind ㉒** at 2,452 metres (8,043 ft). In west Jotunheimen is another group of crevassed mountains, the **Skagastølstindane**, which reach 2,000 metres (8,000 ft). The

Map, pages 182–3

BELOW: the mountain massif of the Jotunheimen.

southern part of the Jotunheimen has some major lakes, including Gjende, which is particularly beautiful with its greenish glacier water and flanked by impressive peaks. Other major lakes are Bygdin, Tyin and Vinstri, while glaciers add to the superb natural attractions.

Northern approaches

The northern border of Jotunheimen is the Otta River valley, which acts as a natural boundary. From **Otta** in the east the river and Road 15 go through fertile countryside, with farms and forests, but beyond **Lom** the scenery gradually changes. The green and lush surroundings give way to forests and rocky outcrops and the river grows more turbulent. Eventually at the tree line the scenery becomes bare and inhospitable.

    Grotli, which consists of little more than a large roadside hotel, cafeteria and souvenir shop, marks the beginning of Lake Breidalsvatnet. Shortly afterwards at Langevatnet, Road 63 turns off and becomes a spectacular mountain road which skirts Djupvatnet and then descends steeply to Geiranger. Road 15 continues on its course through 15 tunnels until it reaches Stryn on Innvikfjorden. An alternative to Road 15 from Grotli is the old **Road 258 ㉓**. Some 26 km (16 miles) long, it climbs to a height of 1,139 metres (3,736 ft) and although narrow and unsurfaced in parts provides a thrilling journey. West of the summit it passes a summer ski centre and **Snowland**, a summer activity area for the family – with snow thrown in.

    Between Otta and Grotli there are only two roads that go south, bold enough to penetrate the heart of Jotunheimen. Road 51, the most easterly, leaves the Otta–Grotli road at Randen and heads into the **Valdres** region. It starts by climb-

Ridderspranget (Knight's Leap) was so named after the Valdres knight Sigvat Kvier kidnapped Ivar of Sandbu's betrothed. Sigvat, hotly pursued by Ivar, and with the beautiful woman in his arms, escaped by jumping the River Sjoa at this spot.

BELOW: fish-farming in Sunndalsfjorden.

Map, pages 182–3

ing into an area of upland pastures with a distant backdrop of mountains. A further climb to Darthus brings **Ridderspranget ㉔** (Knight's Leap) close at hand, where the River Sjoa is channelled into a narrow gorge.

Lakes lie scattered across to the west while beyond can be seen the peak of Glittertind. The most important stretch of water is **Lake Gjende ㉕**, long and narrow and curving slightly to the southwest. Beyond Bessheim there are more inspiring views and this scenic feast continues for kilometre after kilometre.

Bygdin lies between two lakes: Lake Bygdin which stretches like a long finger pointing to more distant mountains in the west; eastwards is the major expanse of Lake Vinstri. There are boat trips on several of the lakes and Lake Bygdin has northern Europe's highest scheduled boat service, in waters 1,060 metres (3,477 ft) above sea level.

The heart of the Valdres

Between Bessheim and Bygdin the road reaches its highest point – 1,389 metres (4,557 ft). From here it descends, first to the tree line, then to more gentle scenery at **Beitostølen**. This winter sports resort got its first ski lift in 1964 and now has eight lifts, 16 runs and more than 325 km (200 miles) of cross-country tracks. It is a typical village of its kind with several hotels – very popular for cross-country skiing – and with a school for disabled and blind skiers, who plunge down the slopes with unbelievable confidence.

Fagernes ㉖ is in the centre of the Valdres area. The focus of attention is the large **Valdres Folkemuseum** (open all year; entrance fee) which features some 80 buildings built between 1200 and 1900. Of particular interest are a 16th-century tapestry, medieval chests, a collection of antique silver, folk music

The River Sjoa is good for white-water rafting.

BELOW: the visitors stare at the goats, and the goats stare back.

Map,
pages
182–3

Mountain seter
(summer farms)
in autumn.

BELOW: summer
on Lustrafjorden.
RIGHT: Borgund
Stavkirke near
Flåm.

instruments and hunting weapons. On a modern note, Fagernes has one of Norway's newest airports, opened in 1987. This area is also scattered with **stave churches** including Hedalen, Reinli, Lomen, Høre, Øye, Hegge and Garmo.

In one direction the E16 goes southeast through the Begnadal valley and eventually to Hønefoss. In the opposite direction the road goes west through more exciting scenery on the southern edge of Jotunheimen. At Tyinkrysset a road goes off to Øvre Årdal on Årdalsfjorden while the E16 turns south, descending through forested scenery to **Borgund** ㉗. Apart from the stave church at Heddal in Telemark, the one at Borgund is regarded as the most typical and best preserved in Norway. Built in 1150, it is dedicated to St Andrew.

At **Sæbø** a **minor road** goes to **Aurlandsvangen** ㉘. It starts to climb almost immediately through lush scenery but this gradually changes as the narrow road ascends higher and higher, unfolding a series of stunning panoramas until the summit at 1,305 metres (4,284 ft). It then begins an increasingly steep descent to the village of Aurlandsvangen. "Breathtaking" is an over-used description but on this road it is justified, especially the view over Aurlandsfjorden from several thousand feet above it. Not for the fainthearted.

Across Sognefjell

The second route south from the Otta–Grotli road is Road 55 from Lom to Lustrafjorden, which is the part of Sognefjorden farthest from the sea. **Lom** ㉙ is a typical Norwegian "junction" village with its two or three hotels, shops and garages, but it also has a fine stave church. The **Fossheim Steinsenter** (Stone Centre; open all year) in Lom contains stones, rocks and gems from all over Norway and it has a collection of minerals from Jotunheimen, while the

associated **Norsk Fjellmuseum** (Mountain Museum; open May–Sept; entrance fee) focuses on mountain life throughout Norway.

Starting out from Lom, you drive through the deceptively placid Bøverdal valley, passing small farms and villages, but the view gradually changes as it gains height and the mountains become more noticeable. At **Galdesand** there is a toll road to Juvashytta, which is the nearest point by car to the Galdhøpiggen mountain.

At 640 metres (2,100 ft) is **Elveseter** ㉚, one of Norway's most unusual hotels. The Elveseter family has owned the property for five generations, gradually converting it into a hotel but retaining many of the old buildings. The oldest is from 1640 and has survived as a wooden building because of the dry mountain air. The first visitors arrived in the 1880s, but it was the opening of the Sognefjell road in 1938 that led to the expansion of tourism.

The road continues its upward ascent past the isolated Jotunheimen Fjellstue to the summit at **Krossbu** at a height of 1,400 metres (4,590 ft) amid superb mountain scenery. From there, make the steep descent to **Turtagrø** where the hotel (which is about all there is to Turtagrø) is a popular base for walkers and climbers; continue the downward course to softer surroundings at Fortun and, a few miles on, to sea level, at the end of **Lustrafjorden** at Skjolden. ❏

TELEMARK AND THE SOUTH

Map,
pages
204–5

Norway's southern coastline is a magnet for summer visitors with its beaches and picturesque seaside towns. Inland, the scenery is starker and life in the mountain valleys lingers in the past

A s they are proverbially advised to do "when in Rome", visitors to Oslo – or, equally, to Stavanger and Kristiansand – could usefully do what the locals do for recreation. The fundamental choice is either mountains and lakes, in which case they steer a course for **Telemark**, or the sea, which draws them to **Aust-Agder** and **Vest-Agder**, jointly known as Sørlandet (south land).

Locals would usually travel in their own cars, a definite advantage in trying to make the most out of Telemark but not so necessary on the coast, along which it is possible to leapfrog from port to port on ferries which are sufficiently frequent to permit an improvised itinerary.

Oslo, Kristiansand and Stavanger, the principal cities along the southern rim of Norway, have good connections, including flights, so they all serve as practical starting or finishing points for a tour, and you can combine Telemark and Sørlandet on one of several coach excursions. One from Oslo, for example, covers nearly 1,200 km (750 miles) by road and ferry and lasts five days.

Designed by a king

In 1639 King Christian IV of Denmark-Norway had the sort of whim which is the privilege of kings and very few others. He wanted to found a town and name it after himself. In the event, the choice of the site where **Kristiansand** ❶ now stands was not entirely capricious. It was an admirable base from which to control the approaches to both the North Sea and the Baltic. The town had to be fortified, and much survives of the first of many forts to be built on the site, **Christiansholm Festning** (fortress; open May–Sept 9am–9pm; tel: 38 07 51 50). Through nearly three turbulent centuries, however, none of the forts ever fired a gun in anger (not until 9 April 1940), and gradually Kristiansand changed from being a military town to a trading and administrative centre.

Kristiansand has had its problems: with witches, one of whom confessed (in 1670) to having flown to Copenhagen to pour poison into the mayor's ear; fire (in 1734); syphilis (in 1782); and a "privateer" period (1807–14) marked by such wholesale swindling, bribery and corruption that it caused "violent upheavals in the economic life of the country".

Present-day Kristiansand has managed to put all that behind it. It is a pleasant city, laid out in squares according to Christian IV's directive, and the sort of place which invites visitors simply to stroll about. The weather is more reliably sunny than anywhere else in Norway, the port and central market are always busy, the **Kvadraturen** is a picturesque quarter of old wooden houses, and one never has to look far for a spot to sit down and watch the world go by. "A total

PRECEDING PAGES:
Norway's Sørlandet
(south land) is rich
farming country.
LEFT: Brevik on the
Telemark coast.
BELOW: a farmer
assesses his grain
harvest.

Southern Norway and its Fjords

0   20 km
0   20 miles

N

NORTH
SEA

HARDANGERVIDDA

Hardangervidda
Nasjonalpark

Hordaland

Rogaland

Vest-Agder

Setesdal

Haugesund

Stavanger

Sandnes

Egersund

Lyngdal

Kristiansand

Mandal

Lindesnes
Fyr

Hanstholm

of more than 10,000 seats in cafés and restaurants" is the city's proud claim.

The city's zoo **Kristiansand Dyrepark** (open all year, times vary; entrance fee; tel: 38 04 97 00), which includes the miniature town of Kardemomme By, is "the most visited family park in Norway". The fictional town is out of a popular children's story by Torbjørn Egner and besides the large zoo there are water chutes and other attractions. Just north of the centre the **Ravnedalen Nasjonalpark** (National Park) is set in attractive, hilly grounds. The **Gimle Gård** (mansion; open mid-June–mid-Aug noon–4pm; May–June and mid-Aug–Oct Sun noon–5pm; entrance fee; tel: 38 09 02 28) across the River Otra is a magnificent symbol of 19th-century Norwegian capitalism. It was built by a shipping and trading tycoon, Bernt Holm, and passed down the family (with a five-year interruption while it was occupied by the German army) until finally it was bequeathed to the town and opened to the public in 1985. The **Setesdalbanen** (Railway Museum) with its narrow-gauge steam railway (departures July: Tues–Fri and Sun; June and Aug: Sun only; times vary; entrance fee; tel: 38 15 64 82) is a short way north of the city.

Dutch port

About 45 km (28 miles) west of Kristiansand is **Mandal** ❷. A busy port long before Christian IV felt the urge to build Kristiansand, it suffered from the competition afterwards. A 1799 traveller remarked that "the houses are jammed together so tightly that a careless pipe-smoker at any open window could spit into his neighbour's parlour." This is due to the nostalgia of foreign residents: Dutch who were there to trade, and Scots. The point known as **Kastellet** is where a wealthy Dane, who once reached into his pocket to make a personal loan to the notoriously empty-pocketed King Frederik IV, installed cannon to keep pirates away from his estate.

The nearby lighthouse at **Lindesnes Fyr** ❸ (open all year; entrance fee to museum) marks the southernmost point of Norway, and in bad weather is buffeted by ferocious

A possible sighting of the Seljord Monster, as depicted here in an early illustration, draws many to the small Telemark village of Seljord.

winds. The small islands 5 km (3 miles) offshore are often mentioned in ancient Norse sagas as a refuge for Vikings ships waiting for better weather before turning the corner into or out of the Skaggerak. **Farsund**, a little further up the coast and once a privateer centre, has suffered the misfortune of being destroyed by fire so often that there is hardly a building left pre-dating the 20th century. Nevertheless, the relatively modern houses are painted white and present a pleasing spectacle.

The region is rich in rock carvings and ancient sites including, near **Vanse**, the remains of nine Iron Age homes surrounded by 350 burial mounds. Lomsesanden, a popular beach on the Lista peninsula, is all of 10 km (6 miles) of white sand. The last town before Vest Agder rises to meet Rogaland is the small port of **Flekkefjord**, known for its Hollenderbyen (Dutch Town), a historic area with Dutch-style white houses lining narrow streets. This is mountainous country which, apart from necessitating the construction of some of Norway's longest railway tunnels (there are 46 between Flekkefjord and Kristiansand), has created several waterfalls, especially around Kvinesdal.

Coastal journey

The principal centres along the coast east from Kristiansand are, in order, Lillesand, Grimstad, Arendal and Risør. **Lillesand ❹**, apart from being a pretty holiday town with a pleasant selection of cafés and restaurants around the harbour, has a special place in Norwegian history as the centre of an 18th-century revolt led by a farmer named Lofthus, a Robin Hood figure who travelled to Copenhagen to confront the Crown Prince with a long list of grievances. On his return he collected a force of 2,000 men and caused panic among the Danish "establishment" in the coastal towns. The house where he was finally arrested still stands; he spent the rest of his life in chains. The **Lillesand Bymuseum** (town museum; open mid-June–mid-Aug Mon–Fri 11am–3pm, Sat 11am–2pm, Sun noon–4pm; entrance fee; tel: 37 27 04 30) tells the whole story.

BELOW: a statue of Henrik Ibsen in Skien.

Grimstad ❺ is indelibly associated with Ibsen. It was here that he served his apprenticeship to a chemist. Ibsen was an unhappy young man and Grimstad, though a pretty place, must have contributed (together with Skien, where he was born) to his searing exposure of goings-on in small Norwegian towns. His works caused a scandal at the time, but years have healed the wounds and he is commemorated in the **Ibsen House/Grimstad Bymuseum** (Town Museum; open June–mid-Sept Mon–Sat 11am–5pm, Sun 1–5pm; entrance fee; tel: 37 04 46 53) which holds the largest collection of Ibsen memorabilia in Norway.

Arendal ❻ is full of character, every ounce of which was needed to thwart King Christian's plan to close it down and transfer the inhabitants to his pet project, Kristiansand. One of his successors, Frederik IV, visited Arendal in 1704 and was puzzled about dinner with the local priest who "went to great trouble to explain in detail how the rite of circumcision was performed by the Jews". Arendal prospered in the 17th and 18th centuries as a conduit for timber shipments abroad, including much of the timber used for the rebuilding of London after the 1666 Great Fire. In 1863, Arendal itself was struck by fire, losing the houses on stilts which had earlier given it the nickname of "Little Venice" but, overflowing on to a number of small islands, it retains its lovely setting. An unusual and recent addition to its attractions is a museum meticulously created by unpaid volunteers out of the contents of a pottery factory that went out of business a few years ago. Located in the Regency-style Kløcker's House (1826), the enthusiasm of the staff at the **Arendal Bymuseum** (town museum; open mid-June–mid-Aug Tues–Fri 9am–3pm, Sat 10am–2pm, Sun noon–4pm; entrance fee; tel: 37 02 59 25) is infectious. The **Rådhus** (Town Hall), previously the home of a merchant, is said to be one of the largest wooden buildings ever constructed in Norway.

Risør, the most easterly town in Aust Agder, was also threatened by the creation of Kristiansand. Its traders were forced to maintain residencies in the new city but they kept their links with their home town. Mary Wollstonecraft, an English visitor in 1795, noted an addiction to tobacco. The men never took their pipes out of their mouths and absolutely refused to open a window. The women, she decided, dressed like tarts or, as she put it, "sailor girls in Hull or Portsmouth". Many of these women were probably Dutch since it was fashionable among young seamen to bring wives back from the Netherlands, the main trading partner. In Risør, as in other parts of Sørlandet, children may still be given distinctly Dutch names.

The ice canal

The capital of Telemark is **Skien ❼**, which was the birthplace, in 1828, of Norway's greatest playwright, Henrik Ibsen. His home, **Venstøp**, forms part of the **Telemark Museum** (Brekke Park; open mid-May–Aug 10am–6pm; entrance

Ibsen completed his first play, Catalina, *in 1850 while still serving his apprenticeship to the chemist in Grimstad. Soon after, he left behind his provincial existence and headed for Oslo.*

BELOW: Kragerø, summer home of Edvard Munch.

fee; tel: 35 52 35 94) and has become a national shrine. Skien holds an Ibsen festival every August with concerts and plays, but originally came into existence on the industry producing stone projectiles for military slingshots, even stranger than another industry which prospered in the nearby village of Ulefoss until the close of the 19th century, namely the production of ice. Ice was easily transported along Telemark's natural waterways, which were later rationalised into a canal system.

The impressive **Telemarkskanal** ❽ (canal) stretches from the Telemark-sjærgården, an unusual skerry formation that stretches out from Oslofjorden along the southern coast, to the foot of Hardangervidda. Eight sets of locks raise boats a total of 72 metres (225 ft) up to Flåvatn, which in turn runs into Kviteseidvatn and Bandak all the way to Dalen. Completed in 1892, the canal cuts 110 km (70 miles) into the interior and is now used by pleasure boats such as the *M/S Victoria* and *M/S Henrik Ibsen* (both open May–Sept; tel: 35 90 00 30).

The canal is littered with attractions, including **Vrangfossen** (waterfall) above Ulefoss, and with places to stay. The best way to keep abreast of what's on is to visit through www.visittelemark.com or telephone 35 90 55 20).

Interior isolation

Throughout Telemark one senses an older Norway lurking just beneath the surface. The upper districts were, until recently, impenetrable except on skis; travel in winter being easier than in summer. Isolated communities were not inclined to take orders from interfering outsiders, although a lot of water has passed under the bridge since the people were described (in 1580) as "shameless bodies of the Devil whose chief delight is to kill bishops, priests, bailiffs and superiors – and who possess a large share of all original sin".

Inside the silver mine at Saggrenda not far from Heddal.

BELOW: typical "Sørlandet houses" near Farsund, Vest Agder.

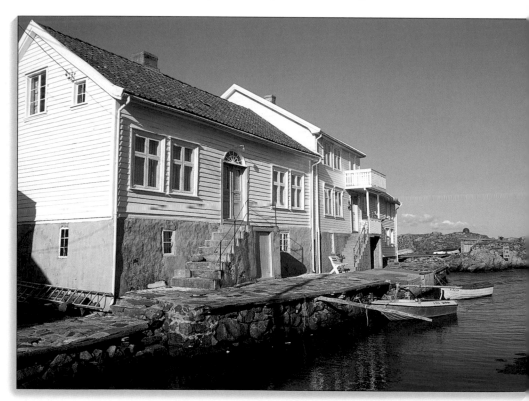

A finger of Telemark reaches the sea at Kragerø, not far from the mouth of Oslofjorden, but the province is associated in most minds with the inland terrain, which inspired an eccentric farmer named Sondre Norheim to turn the pedestrian business of plodding about in snow on two planks into the sport of skiing. His discovery of the delights that could be achieved with planks that were properly shaped and had heel bindings made him overlook his domestic chores. It is apparently true that, when he ran out of firewood in winter, he simply hacked off another piece of his house and put that on the fire *(see "Morgedal and Telemark Revival, page 108)*.

Morgedal, where Norheim lived (he later emigrated to America) deserves to be called the cradle of skiing but it is now only one of dozens of skiing centres in the province, many of which have ski-lifts to complement the traditional cross-country courses which do not need mechanical contraptions. Norheim's statue is a feature of the **Norsk Skieventyr** (Norwegian Skiing Adventure Centre; open mid-May–mid-June 11am–4pm; mid-June–mid-Aug 9am–7pm; late Aug 11am–4pm; entrance fee; tel: 35 05 42 50), located near to Kviteseidvatn and the canal.

Rural arts

Visitors with their own transport in Telemark can hardly go wrong: pick any of the winding roads that head inland and the scenery is bound to be breathtaking.

For those who do not have a car, the waterways are a wonderful alternative: Skien is on a main canal line from Oslo and a good place to pick up boats going north through Sauherad to Notodden (Road 36 then 360 covers the same route). Schedules change according to season – in some parts the boats press on with

Map, pages 204–5

BELOW: the popular bathing beach at Mandal.

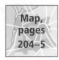

Map,
pages
204–5

the help of a small ice-breaker – so it is advisable to check with the tourist office (tel: 35 90 00 20) in Skien. West of Notodden, along Road 11, lies **Heddal ❾** with its famous **Stavkirke** (open mid-May–mid-June 10am–5pm; mid-June–mid-Aug 9am–7pm; mid-Aug–mid-Sept 10am–5pm; entrance fee; tel: 47 35 02 04 00), the largest in Norway. Built between 1147 and 1242, it has a richly carved doorway with animals and human faces. But Heddal is more than that. The Telemarkers are masters at expressing nature through art and nowhere is this more evident than in the rose paintings in the Ramberg room of the **Heddal Bygdetun** (farmhouses: open mid-June–mid-Aug 10am–5pm; entrance fee).

Further on, Road 37 branches off to the north past Lake Tinnsjø towards **Rjukan ❿**. The stretch between Rjukan and Rauland is particularly lovely and can be covered by public bus. Keep an eye open for highly decorative wooden houses and double-storey barns, sometimes bigger than the house itself, with a ramp leading to the upper floor.

The attraction of Rjukan itself is the heavy water plant, now the **Norsk Industriarbeidermuseum** (Norwegian Industrial Workers Museum; open May–Sept daily 10am–4pm; entrance fee; tel: 35 09 90 00), but in 1943 the target of a daring sabotage attack by the Norwegian resistance *(see "The Heroes of Telemark", page 54)*. The town library, incidentally, has a good collection of literature about the operation. Rjukan is generally rather gloomy because the sun is nearly always blocked off by surrounding mountains. On top of those mountains, though, another world of vast vistas opens up, and it is said that on a good day it is possible to see one-sixth of Norway. You can take Northern Europe's oldest cable car (open June–Aug; weekends only Sept–May; entrance fee; tel: 99 51 31 71) from Krosso to the top of Gvepseborg at 860 metres (2,800 ft) for just such a view.

BELOW: collecting the honey in summer.
RIGHT: *Lindesnes fyr* (lighthouse) on the southernmost tip of Norway.

Medieval life in the 20th century

An alternative route inland is Road 39 from Kristiansand, which climbs up the Otra valley and runs north along **Byglandsfjorden** to **Setesdal**. Until modern times this area was very remote. The inhabitants sent their timber down to Arendal by pushing it into a river, which plunged 700 metres (2,300 ft) over a distance of about 150 km (90 miles). They preserved their own almost medieval way of life, including a distinct dialect, dress and cuisine, into the 20th century.

Setesdal is a haven for those in search of rural culture. The most famous dwelling is **Rygnestadtunet**, a 16th-century windowless tower of three storeys with an amazing collection of relics, such as leather hangings depicting St George's battle with the dragon. The tower was built about 400 years ago by Vond-Asmund who, on discovering that his fiancée was about to marry someone else, snatched her away from the wedding procession. From the upper floor of his fortress, he fired off arrows at anyone who approached and in so doing killed at least four people. His descendants still farm in the area. Rygnestadtunet is part of the **Setesdalmuseet ⓫** (Heritage Muesum; open all year; entrance fee; tel: 37 93 63 03), which is 15 km (9 miles) to the south.

If you feel in need of light relief after all this, you can visit the Sommarland family park at **Bø** (open June–Aug; entrance fee; tel: 35 06 16 00). ❑

FJORDS

*The Norwegian fjords are a defining feature of both country
and culture – the difficulty is to decide on a favourite*

To create a fjord, take a mountain and a river, and mix in an Ice
Age many thousands of years ago. To describe the fjords is to
find yourself running out of superlatives: the deepest water, the
highest mountains, the narrowest, the most beautiful, the stillest,
the most peaceful... each fjord has its own special characteristic,
from the Sognefjord (the longest) to the Geiranger, which many people think the most beautiful. But who would argue? With so many
fjords, everybody is entitled to their own opinion.

The fjords gave Norway its great seafaring tradition. From the
early Vikings who found Scotland, Iceland and the rest of Europe
easier to reach than the area around Oslo, to the modern traveller
who chooses a ship as the most comfortable way to travel this magnificent coastline, the sea has provided the link.

The fjords begin at Stavanger in the south, now Norway's oil
capital, not far from Preikestolen, the great slab of rock standing a
dizzy 600 metres (2,000 ft) above Lysefjorden. They stretch north to
the Hardanger, one of the largest in the country and an early favourite
where the old traditions of music and storytelling influenced travellers
such as the composer Edvard Grieg. On the way, they encompass
Bergen, the fjord capital; Sognefjorden and Nordfjorden, in an area of
glaciers, lakes and mountains massifs; Storfjorden, parts of which
bite far into the land; and, finally, the calm of the Geiranger.

From their high mountain sides, waterfalls cascade into the fjords,
and small farms cling to every ledge and hectare of green. The fjords
are beautiful, timeless, and everyone's idea of the soul of Norway. ❏

PRECEDING PAGES: passing through Trollfjorden, in the Lofoten Islands,
is a delicate operation for the Hurtigruten ship.
LEFT: small coastal freighter at Femrissundet (sound) in the north.

ROGALAND

This often overlooked corner of the country contains many delights, from the picturesque fishing harbour of Egersund to an eagle's-eye view over Lysefjorden from the top of Preikestolen

Map, pages 204–5

Many people believe that Norway's fjord country begins at Hardangerfjorden and the city of Bergen, and stretches north. If so, they are missing all the southern fjords and islands, where Norway first became a nation. Today this area of Rogaland is centred on Stavanger, the centre of Norway's international oil industry, and contains some of the fjord country's most spectacular natural sights: what a pity to miss Preikestolen ("the pulpit"), a flat slab of rock swooping some 600 metres (2,000 ft) up from Lysefjorden, which offers a 180-degree view over *fjell* and fjord.

Rogaland has the mildest climate in Norway and the beauty of the coast is unsurpassed. These coastal and outer fjord areas have the highest average temperature in the whole country, but pay the penalty for their closeness to the sea in unexpected showers and a higher rainfall. In winter, thanks to the Gulf Stream, there is little snow and the fertile fields are green for most of the year.

Starting in the south

By air, the way in is Stavanger's international airport at Sola, or you might come by express boat from Bergen in just under three hours. From the south, the main road is the E39, which crosses into Rogaland south of the old town of **Egersund ⑫**, now Norway's largest fishing harbour. There is also a coastal route (the scenic Road 44), which hugs the coastline all the way north to Stavanger. At the southern corner of this route, small fjords bite into a rough, rocky coast, which lead to green valleys and a myriad of shining lakes.

The best view of Egersund's sheltered harbour, with its dozens of yachts both big and small, is from the top of the lighthouse. The town itself has a fine **cruciform church** (open June–Aug; entrance fee) from 1620 (renovated in the late 18th century) and the **Dalane Folk Museum** (open June–Aug; entrance fee; tel: 51 46 14 10) which includes the **Egersund Fayance Museum** (displaying painted earthenware crockery, which was once the town's main industry).

Inland is the waterfall **Fotlandfossen ⑬**, and further north on the E39 you come to the southern end of **Ørdalsvatn**. From here, Rogaland's last remaining inland waterway boat, *Ørsdølen*, sails the 20 km (13 miles) to Vassbø at the far end of the narrow lake. Near there you can have a simple home-made meal before the boat returns. A few miles further on is Vikeså, where Road 503 to Byrkjedal runs past **Gloppedalsura**, where the boulders are as big as houses.

The flat and fertile country above Egersund is Norway's main area for the production of meat, dairy products, poultry and eggs, but it was not always as peaceful as it is today. In AD 872, it was the scene of

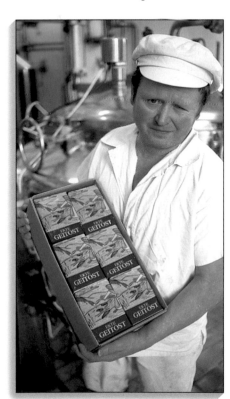

LEFT: Preikestolen, one of Rogaland's best-known landmarks.
BELOW: goat's cheese made at Egersund.

the **Battle of Hafrsfjord** , where King Harald Hårfagre (Fair Hair) won his final and most important battle to unite the warring Norwegian kingdoms. That battle is marked at the edge of Hafrsfjorden, the near circular fjord to the south-west of Stavanger, where three huge sculptured swords rise out of the ground.

In 1977, by royal decree, a narrow strip some 70 km (43 miles) long, from Raumen Island at the southern end to **Tungenes Fyr** ⑮ (lighthouse; open June–Aug; entrance fee) northwest of Stavanger, became **Jærstendrene Land-skapsvernområde** ⑯ (Protected Landscape Area), which includes offshore islands. Raumen itself is one of eight bird sanctuaries where, at different times of the year, you can find turnstones, ringed plovers and knots taking a brief rest on the long flight to or from southern Europe or Africa; offshore are win-tering eider and long-tailed ducks, and the islands provide nesting places for seabirds, often in protected areas closed to visitors during the breeding season.

In the eight botanical reserves you can find such delights as the spear-leaved fat hen saltbush, and the rare marsh orchid growing in the reserve near **Ogna** ⑰. There are also four geological sites and no less than 150 monuments listed and protected. But this does not mean that Jærstrendene is given over solely to flora and fauna. **Beaches** with white-gold sand are popular picnic spots and, though the water can be chilly, this does not deter swimmers.

Bicycle land

Sandnes on Sandfjorden is Norway's "bicycle town", where the famous DBS bicycles are made and, whether this is the reason or not, where cycling is pop-ular and you can hire bikes to explore the surrounding countryside. Another delight for youngsters is **Kongeparken** ⑱ (open June–Aug daily 10am–6pm; May and Sept Sat–Sun only 10am–6pm; entrance fee; tel: 51 61 71 11), Norway's biggest leisure park, not far from Sandnes at the little town of Ålgård. At 80 metres (260 ft) long, Kongeparken's Gulliver is hard to miss. Inside, Gulliver's body is full of unusual play-things and the park has Scandinavia's longest bob-sleigh ride.

In many of the mountain areas around the fjords, waterfalls cascade hundreds of metres below. One of the most famous is **Månafoss** ⑲ on the Frafjord, the innermost finger of the Høgsfjord, reached by Road 45 south from Ålgård to Gilja. At Gilja, turn down the steep road to Frafjord, which gives a fantastic view of the fjord. There are directions to Månafoss in the car park at the foot of the mountain.

Fjords once more

The **Ryfylke area** ⑳ northeast of Stavanger is true fjord country, one of the least-known parts of Nor-way despite the drama of its scenery. In the south, due east of Stavanger, Ryfylke starts with **Lysefjorden** and stretches north past long narrow lakes that once were open fjords, until it reaches **Vindafjorden**, **Saudafjorden** and **Suldalsvatn**.

Although he never saw it, Victor Hugo described Lysefjorden in *The Toilers of the Sea* as "the most ter-rible of all the corridor rocks in the sea". Hugo prob-ably meant "awesome" and that the fjord still is. Every

BELOW: Månafoss waterfall.

visitor to Norway should try to walk out through heather moor and scrubland to stand on the top of **Preikestolen** ㉑, a rock platform high above the fjord. On the way you might see golden eagles, willow grouse, ptarmigan and other birds as well as reindeer and the angular shape of an elk. The great height of Preikestolen gives a view towards Stavanger and the fjords to the west, and upwards to the treeline and the rocky heights above. Everywhere there are lakes, waterfalls and rushing torrents.

From the village of Forsand at its mouth, Lysefjorden is 40 km (25 miles) long and, at its innermost end, has one of Europe's most remarkable feats of civil engineering: the road to the hydro-electric power station (closed Mon; entrance fee) at **Lysebotn**, which is hidden hundreds of metres inside the mountain. This road, which seems to defy gravity, snakes up and down more than 750 metres (2,500 ft) with 27 hairpin bends and connects Lysebotn to Sirdal and Setersdal to the east along the Lyseveien. If you dare to keep your eyes open as the bus takes its near perpendicular route down, the view is magnificent.

Near the end of the fjord on the south side towers **Kjerragfjell** ㉒, an enormous granite mountain around 1,100 metres (3,550 ft) high. Lie on your front and look down through the wedge cut out of the mountain plateau to the fjord below. To get there takes about two hours' walking from several spots along the Lyseveien.

Inshore islands

The sheltered bay north of Stavanger, and the outer islands such as Karmøy, protect Ryfylke's inshore islands from the North Sea. Christianity flourished early here under the protection of the bishops of Stavanger and the islands have many

Map, pages 204–5

Wedged between two rocks, the famous Kjerragbolten offers a breathtaking vantage point from which to view Lysefjorden below.

BELOW: Gulliver at Kongeparken.

*Sandvesanden beach
on the island
of Karmøy.*

churches. In summer, the 12th-century **Utstein Kloster** ㉓ (cloister; open Easter–Sept, closed Mon; entrance fee) on **Mosterøy** makes a beautiful setting for concerts which are mostly classical. It offers the traveller a refreshing break on the way from Stavanger to Boknafjorden. The cloister's setting, acoustics and the palpable sense of history give these concerts a very special atmosphere.

The many **lighthouses** are not only landmarks for islanders and seafarers but make excellent bird-watching sites, with the hunched outlines of cormorants and other seabirds on wave-washed rocks below. The waters around these peaceful islands are a sea kingdom for sailors of all kinds with enough coastline to give every boat a bay to itself and many yacht harbours. Most of the island grocers also provide boat services and it is easy to hire rowing boats and small craft with outboard engines.

Northeast highlands

Here fjords, lakes and rivers are rich in fish and fine for sailing and canoeing, and all these inland, eastern areas of Rogaland have good cross-country skiing tracks in winter as well as some fine alpine slopes. Among the best holiday areas is the **Suldal district**, stretching from Sand on the Sandsfjorden, along the River Suldalslågen (river) – where the rushing waters have produced huge salmon (the largest so far weighed almost 44 kg (75 lb) – to the long, narrow Suldalsvatn. At the Sand end of Suldalslågen is **Laksestudioet** ㉔ (open daily mid-June–mid-Aug 10am–6pm; mid-Aug–mid Sept noon–4pm; entrance fee), an observation studio, built under a waterfall where visitors look through a large window at the salmon resting before their next leap up the fish ladder on the way to their spawning grounds. Where river meets lake is **Kolbeinstveit Museum** (rural museum;

BELOW: Utstein Kloster (cloister) on Mosterøy.

open June–Aug Tues–Sun 11am–4pm; entrance fee; tel: 52 79 72 84) with the old Guggedalsloftet Bygdetun (farm) which dates back to the 13th century.

From Sand, a bus follows the line of the river to the giant **Kvilldal** ㉕ station, opened in 1982 by King Olav, who chiselled his signature into the mountainside, a popular royal tradition in Scandinavia. On the way to this cavernous power station the bus stops at the **Lakseslotte** ㉖ (Salmon Castle) at Lindum, built by Lord Sibthorp in 1885, when the British "salmon lords" looked on a few weeks in Norway as part of the fishing season. River and lake still draw anglers from many countries and the castle is a popular guest house.

From Stavanger and Jæren, ferries and express boats reach this fjord country and its islands, and it is easy to combine bus and ferry. Vindafjord, Saudafjorden and Suldalsvatn look up to 1,500-metre (5,000-ft) peaks that lead the way to the great mountain massif of Hardangervidda, in the next county north, Hordaland. In summer you can take the exciting **old mountain road** north from Sauda to Røldal; the new road has tunnels to keep it open all year. At Røldal, and on the road from Suldalsvatn, you pick up the **Opplevelsesrute** ㉗ (Discovery Route, E134), which has come over the Haukeli mountains from Telemark, and you can continue along until it becomes Road 13 towards Odda.

Back to the coast

The sea route north to Bergen is one of the most popular ways to see the northern coast. By taking an express boat (a cross between a catamaran and a hydrofoil) you can drop off at any of the harbour stops and stay a night or a week according to your whim. **Karmøy** ㉘, the island at the south of the outer islands chain, is big enough to merit its own boat service, which goes to **Skudeneshavn**

Map, pages 204–5

While on Karmøy, pay a visit to the Fisheries Museum at Vedvågen, with its saltwater aquarium. The building was designed by the Norwegian firm of architects, Snøhetta, winners of the competition to design a National Opera House in Oslo.

BELOW: typical "seahouses" in Skudeneshavn.

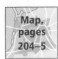

Map,
pages
204–5

BELOW: young buskers in Haugesund during the Film Festival.
RIGHT: fish market on the island of Utsira.

in the south, an idyllic old port with white, wooden houses along narrow streets (tours from **Mælandsgården Museum**; June–Aug). The north of the island is linked to the mainland just south of Haugesund, the first sizeable coastal town north of Stavanger, fast becoming prosperous through oil.

Karmøy's known history dates back to saga times, when it was the "Northway" shipping lane that gave Norway its name. Harald Hårfagre made his home at **Avaldsnes** ㉙ after the battle at Hafrsfjord. Also here is **St Olaf Kirke** (church) which was built between 1248 and 1263 by King Håkon Håkonson and restored in 1922 as the parish church. Near its north walls stands St Mary's Sewing Needle, a strange 6.5-metre (21-ft) high stone pillar leaning towards the church wall. Legend tells that the Day of Judgement will come when the pillar touches the wall; many priests are said to have climbed the pillar at dead of night to pare away the top to make sure that the day is not yet nigh.

Roman connections

On the west coast at **Ferkingstad** are historic boathouses with walls made of stone blocks 1.5 metres (5 ft) thick. Further north on the west coast, outside the town hall at **Åkrehamn**, stand two stone pillars from the Iron Age. Crossing to the east coast, near the town of **Kopervik** are burial hills and mounds and stone pillars. The largest burial mound, Doøa Hill, was restored in 1978 and, though it has not yet been fully excavated, it dates back to the Bronze Age. Further north, on the mainland side of the bridge to Haugesund are **Dem Fem Dårlige Jomfruer** (Five Bad Virgins), stone monuments some 2.5 metres (8 ft) high, where excavations in 1901 revealed a Roman bowl dating from AD 300–400.

Haugesund has long been a centre for fishing, shipping and farming. Today its harbour is filled with pleasure boats; the town has also become a festival and congress centre and plays host to the International Trad Jazz Festival and the Norwegian Film Festival (both Aug; dates and prices vary).

Numerous fjords and lakes cut into the roughly shaped peninsula, like a piece of well-nibbled cheese, ideal for fishing, sailing, rowing, canoeing, diving and walking. Further out to sea a boat trip to the idyllic group of islands of **Røvær** ㉚, around 10 km (6 miles) to the west, occupies a half or whole day and offers shore fishing, interesting flora and fauna and, in summer, a wharfside café.

For the adventurous, *M/S Utsira* (tel: 52 72 50 55) provides a daily service to the island of the same name ㉛, familiar from European shipping forecasts and Norway's western outpost. The 90-minute journey out makes a wonderful tour for bird-watchers, as does the island itself. Fishing is also excellent and Norwegian saltwater fishing is free to holders of a national licence *(see pages 112–13)*. Day licences for lakes and rivers are available: contact Haugesund Tourist Office, tel 52 72 50 55.

To the north of Haugesund, the **Espevær** ㉜, a fishing village situated at the mouth of Bømlafjorden River, is well endowed with its own heritage sites. The village itself is one of the best-preserved sites in Norway; there is a maritime and fisheries museum, as well as a bathing house. ❏

STAVANGER

Once the port from which thousands emigrated to the United States, today Stavanger attracts an international crowd – and cuisine – as the centre of Norway's thriving oil industry

Map on page 226

Strange though it may seem in a city which has devoted nearly 1,000 years to the sea, the best way to arrive in Stavanger is by overnight train from Oslo. As the dawn arrives, the train slips along the side of the fjord with black mountain peaks outlined on either side, past the huge latticework of oil rigs and drilling towers which have made Stavanger Norway's oil capital. Enormous though they are, somehow they do not intrude on the landscape because the size and grandeur of mountain and fjord dwarfs even these industrial giants.

Stavanger has been lucky because the sea has always been good to the city. As one source of prosperity disappeared, another arose. Shipping, fishing and trading have taken the city's ships and people all over the world, and brought seamen to Stavanger, to give it an easy-going relationship with other nations. Today, Norway's fourth-largest city is as international as ever: nearly a tenth of its 110,000 inhabitants are foreigners.

International eating

This international community has demanded high standards and Stavanger has good restaurants, hotels, entertainment and a cosmopolitan atmosphere out of all proportion to its size. As well as the traditional **restaurants**, which specialise in good Norwegian food, there is a choice of Indian, Italian, Greek, Portuguese, Mexican and Japanese, and at least half a dozen Chinese restaurants. The city also has an annual food festival and a gastronomic institute.

Restaurants, and particularly alcohol, are expensive in Norway, but a great many cafés, bars and pubs have sprung up, sometimes with live music, plus a handful of youthful discos, which do not necessarily serve alcohol. In the **fish market** on the quayside, where fresh crabs eaten on the spot are the favourite buy, and at the **fruit and flower market** nearby you will hear many languages, and in the heart of Stavanger's shopping streets behind the market almost all the assistants speak English.

Apart from the oil prosperity, Stavanger is also the principal town and seat of government of Rogaland.

An American connection

In the 19th and early 20th centuries Stavanger was the exit port for Norway's extensive emigration programme to the United States *(see page 44)* – there are more Americans of Norwegian descent than there are Norwegians. Not surprisingly, therefore, the city is host to **Det Norske Utvandrersenteret Ⓐ** (Emigration Centre; open Tues 9am–7pm; tel: 51 53 88 60), where Norway's emigration history is documented and commemorated. For a fee, genealogical researchers will help you to find your Norwegian

LEFT: Stavanger's past prosperity was based on sardines.
BELOW: winter in Stavanger.

TIP

See Stavanger
Museum's five sites in
one day for the price
of a single ticket.
Stavanger Museum
itself, the Canning
Museum, Maritime
Museum, the royal
residence of
Ledaal and the
19th-century manor
house, Breidablikk,
are all included.

roots. In June the centre arranges the Emigration Festival with exhibitions, concerts, folk dancing, a crafts market, seminars, fjord cruises and city sightseeing. The highlight of the festival is the re-enactment of the 1825 sailing of the *Restauration*, the boat which carried the first emigrants across the Atlantic.

The smell of sardines

The *iddis* (the colloquial name, meaning sardine label, for a person from Stavanger) claims to be the oldest true Norwegian, dating from 872 and the Battle of Hafrsfjord, which took place just south of the city, and in which King Harald Hårfagre won his final battle to unite the kingdom.

When work began on the Domkirken (Cathedral) in 1125, Stavanger was simply a cluster of small wooden houses at the end of the narrow inlet called **Vågen**. It was chosen as the heart of the bishopric, nevertheless, because it was the only recognisable settlement along this southwestern coast. From then on Stavanger was the most important town in the area. It grew slowly; the population was only 2,000 at the start of the 19th century, but had jumped to 30,000 by 1900.

In the 18th and 19th centuries, the city depended on fishing and maritime trade and faced the world with an unbroken row of wharves and warehouses dedicated to these industries. Around the 1870s, at a time when fishing and shipping were beginning to face decline, the fishermen turned their attention to brisling (small herring), which were cured and canned in the town and sent as Norwegian "sardines" all over the world.

At one time Stavanger had as many as 70 canneries and nearly three quarters of the population worked in the industry. In the first half of the 20th century, the smell of oily fish hung over the town, permeating every breath. But Stavanger

BELOW: an oil rig
under contruction
dwarfs the city.

Stavanger

0   100 m
0   100 yds

never doubted the value of that smell. When, on a particularly odiferous day, a cheeky youngster wrinkled a disdainful nose, a mother would say: "Don't scorn it, that's the smell of money." It was, and Stavanger thrived on sardines until, after World War II, that all-pervasive tang began to fade along with the demand for sardines. For nearly 20 years, Stavanger knew difficult times. Then, in the late 1960s, came oil – once again the sea had provided. Visit the modern, interactive **Norsk Oljemuseum ❸** (Norwegian Petroleum Museum, Kjeringholmen; open June–Aug daily 10am–7pm; Sept–May Mon–Sat 10am–4pm, Sun 10am–6pm; entrance fee; tel: 51 93 93 00) for an insight into this valuable source of energy.

Present-day reminders

Many traces remain of these fluctuations in the city's fortunes. From the late 17th and early 18th century is **Gamle Stavanger ❸** (Old Stavanger): more than 180 early 19th-century, white, wooden buildings looking down towards Vågen, with cobbled streets lit by old-fashioned street lamps. But this is no museum. There may be a preservation order on the exteriors, and the owners take pride in keeping them in character, but the interiors have every comfort and gadget that modern Norwegians expect, and Gamle Stavanger is one of the most coveted areas in Norway to live in.

Artefacts from Stavanger's old canning industry are kept in the Hermetikkmuseet (Canning Museum).

Nor have the canning factories been lost. Many are converted into modern offices, without destroying their scale and shape, and buildings that once canned sardines may now be the headquarters of an international oil company. One factory at Øvre Strandgate, near the harbour, has been preserved in its original state as the **Hermetikkmuseet ❹** (Canning Museum; open June–Aug daily 11am–4pm; Sept–May Sun only 11am–4pm; entrance fee; tel: 51 52 65 91). In

BELOW: Gamle (Old) Stavanger is still a living community.

Stavanger waterfront at night.

the big open room with its curing ovens, the guides describe the life of the people who worked long hours in the intricate process of threading the sardines on to long rods, smoking, then packing them, almost all of it being done by hand. On Tuesday and Thursday from mid-June to mid-August you can sample freshly smoked brisling for yourself, cooked in one of the original ovens.

Even nearer the harbour and the centre of the town is the **Sjøfartsmuseet** ❺ (Maritime Museum; open Sun 11am–4pm, other days by appointment; entrance fee; tel: 51 84 27 00) in one of the old mercantile houses on Nedre Strandgate, with its warehouses towards the sea. It traces the history of Stavanger's maritime links over the past 200 years. Today, large windows have replaced the warehouse doors and you turn your head from the history behind you to the modern town outside. On the Nedre Strandgate side of the museum, away from the harbour, is the general store, full of the provisions and supplies that it would have held before World War II. Upstairs, where the owner lived, is an office just as it might have been when a crewman called in during the 1930s in search of a berth, or the skipper came to pay his respects. The flat shows the comfortable life of a shipowner in the late 19th century.

On the other side of the harbour facing the Maritime Museum is the site of the original Viking settlement. The **Valbergtårnet** ❻ (tower; open Mon–Sat all year; entrance fee; tel: 51 89 55 01), built in the 9th century as a fire lookout, is the best point from which to get a view over the whole city.

Centre of worship

BELOW LEFT: old wooden houses.
BELOW RIGHT: Stavanger Domkirke, the only remaining building from the city's medieval past.

The heart of modern Stavanger is the area around **Breiavatnet**, the small lake in the middle of the city, near the oldest and biggest building, the beautiful 12th-century **Domkirken** (open mid-May–mid-Sept daily; mid-Sept–mid-May Wed–Sat, times vary). Construction began in 1125 by Bishop Reinald of Winchester in the Anglo-Norman style. It can claim with justification to be among the best-preserved medieval cathedrals in Europe. Alongside is the **Cathedral School** built in 1758 on the 12th-century foundations of the Bishop's Residence.

Inside, this stone cathedral has a feeling of austere strength in the massive pillars which contrast with the elegant arches of the chancel and a remarkable tapestry (made by Frida Hansen in 1927) in the vestibule. Both chancel and vestibule were rebuilt after 1272 in a style similar to the Scottish Gothic of the times, a reminder of Stavanger's international connection even in those early days. One of the finest pieces in the cathedral is Andrew Smith's ornate 16th-century pulpit.

Even earlier is **Jernaldergarden**, the Iron Age farm at **Ullandhaug** (open daily; entrance fee; tel: 51 84 60 71), about 2 km (1 mile) or so to the southwest of the centre. Here archaeologists unearthed and then reconstructed part of the farm to show three houses, parts of a cattle track and the original encircling stone wall from AD 350 and 550. This was a golden age in Norway, and the city's **Arkeologisk Museum** (Archaeological Museum; open June–Aug Tues–Sun 11am–5pm; Sept–May Tues 11am–8pm, Wed–Sun 11am–3pm; entrance fee; tel: 51 84 60 00) is gradually furnishing the houses to show how people lived then.

From Ullandhaug, it is worth visiting the nearby **Botanisk Hage** (Botanical Garden; open daily; entrance fee) which has a herb and perennial garden with more than 1,500 species from all over the world. Rogaland is rich in birds and fauna and the **Stavanger Museum** (open June–Aug daily 11am–4pm; Sept–May Sun only 11am–4pm; entrance fee; tel: 51 84 27 00) has an excellent exhibition, not only of Rogaland wildlife but also displays of cultural history and the history of fishing, which covers the industry and its creatures, including whales and seals.

Water buses

The inhabitants of the city jump on to a boat as unconcernedly as most of us jump on a bus. There are tours to the islands and fjords and fast ferries north to Bergen, where business travellers sit in their city garb alongside holidaymakers' picnic boxes and fishing gear. Fjordline operates between Newcastle (England), Stavanger and Bergen, and Sola International Airport has flight connections to several European capitals as well as a busy domestic service.

Outdoor activities

The city is right on the doorstep of the Jærstendene Landskapsvernområdet (Protected Landscape Area), which stretches 70 km (43 miles) down the southern coast and its offshore islands, with nature reserves and silver sand beaches, ideal for swimming and picnicking. Sport at any time of the year is good: swimming, sub-aqua diving, sailing, wind-surfing and fishing. There is an active hiking club plus tennis and horse riding in Jærstendene. In winter you can have the best of both worlds. Thanks to the Gulf Stream, Stavanger remains mild and the fields around the city are rarely covered by snow, yet it is not much more than an hour from good ski slopes. ❑

Map on page 226

Chemical analysis has confirmed that the copper used to cover New York's Statue of Liberty came from one of the old Visnes copper mines on the island of Karmøy northwest of Stavanger.

BELOW: much of Norway's food is grown in the area south of Stavanger.

HORDALAND

An inspiration to generations of Norwegian artists, the mighty Hardangerfjorden lies at the heart of this region, which mixes wild coasts with sheltered islands, and spring blossoms with fjord waters

Map on page 234

N obody knows how many hundreds of islands lie off the coast of Hordaland. Deserted skerries, green islets, prosperous small harbours and busy communities stretch out along the coast like a knotted skein, from the southern island of Bømlo to the beautiful small island of Fedje not far from the mouth of Sognefjorden.

Many of the inner islands around the fjord capital, Bergen, are linked by bridges and causeways in a pattern of islands and sea that seems all of a piece with the many branched fjords, including the famous Hardangerfjorden. Inland, the further east, the higher the ground becomes until it reaches Hardangervidda, the great mountain plateau which stands 1,300 metres (4,500 ft) above sea level.

The beginning of Christianity

The southwest district of **Sunnhordland** has islands, skerries, sounds and straits, good harbours and sheltered bays. Though the North Sea is its neighbour, the climate is surprisingly mild. The main islands are **Bømlo**, **Stord** and **Tysnesøy**, and even so close to the sea they have a variety of scenery. An upland ridge on Stord reaches nearly 750 metres (2,500 ft) and the view stretches east to Hardangerfjorden and the white sheet of the Folgefonn Glacier, and south towards Haugesund. Everywhere are sails of all colours, the white wake of an express boat from Stavanger to Bergen and the smaller trails of pleasure craft.

Stord also makes a good paddling-off point for sea canoeing, either from island to island, or into the mouth of the Hardanger. It is an "oil island" too, where the gigantic outlines of oil platforms take shape, some rising nearly 380 metres (1,250 ft) out of the water.

The sagas tell that in 1024 St Olav first introduced Christianity to Norway in these islands. Today, an annual outdoor performance (late May or early June; tel: 53 42 07 90) of the historical play *Mostraspelet*, held at **Mosterhamn ❶** on Bømlo dramatises this ancient saga. Nearby is a stone cross erected in 1924 on the 900th anniversary of the arrival of Christianity, and Mosterhamn has the **oldest stone church** in Norway (open all year; entrance fee) built around 995–1100. The church bells bear images of St Olaf.

Gateway to Hardangerfjorden

The mouth of the Hardanger fjord is as beautiful as anywhere in the fjord itself, but the irony is that Sunnhordaland as a whole tends to be overshadowed by the fame and drama of Hardangerfjorden. Too many visitors travel through quickly on their way to other places. The discriminating know it deserves a longer look. **Leirvik** on Stord is a good starting point with short ferry connections to most of the surround-

PRECEDING PAGES:
a cruise ship in Eidfjorden.
LEFT: sea wake.
BELOW: blossom time below the Folgefonn Glacier.

ing islands and to the mainland. It is also the location of the **Sunnhordland Folkemuseum** (open all year; entrance fee) which was established in 1913 as the local history museum. To the south, the ferry to **Valevåg** puts you on the right track for **Ryvarden Fyr** (lighthouse; open Apr–Dec) at the mouth of Bømlafjorden, the home of the innovative composer Fartein Valen (1887–1952). There is also a museum, art gallery and café at nearby Møstrevåg.

To the east, a ferry to Sunde on the mainland brings you to where the cold waters of Hardangerfjorden begin to seep into the warmer tides from the west and the lovely 17th-century **Baroniet Rosendal** (Rosendal Barony; open May-Sept; entrance fee) in **Rosendal ❷**, the only one of its kind in Norway, which largely lost its aristocracy with the departure of the Danes. The manor house was built in 1665 by Ludvig Rosenkrantz. He is buried in the nearby medieval Kvinnherad Kirke (church), snuggled into the shelter of a rock face and once owned by the Barony. The Barony today has a peaceful park and a large carefully tended rose garden and is held in trust by Oslo University. Throughout the summer there are lunchtime concerts, and the **Rosendal Music Festival** during May and June.

A national inspiration

Hardangerfjorden is part of the Norwegian legend, the fjord that gave its name to Norway's national musical instrument, the eight-stringed Hardanger fiddle, and provided inspiration for the composer Edvard Grieg (1843–1907), the musician Ole Bull (1810–80) and, indirectly, for the 19th-century nationalist movement that eventually led to Norway's independence. Among these mountains and fjords, Grieg and Bull travelled on foot and horse, learning old melodies and dipping into centuries-old cultural traditions and customs.

Tourism came to the Hardanger district back in the 1830s when the poet Henrik Wergeland (1808–45) wrote about "wonderful Hardanger", and foreign as well as Norwegian artists, scientists and other travellers began to arrive; first in a trickle, then in a flood when, 30 years later, the steamers began to run regularly from Bergen or Stavanger.

Like the visitors of today, they came to Hardanger for its waterfalls, for the secret beauty of smaller fjords that lead almost to the massif of Hardangervidda, and for glaciers and mountains that rarely lose their snow-caps, contrasted with orchards lining the fjordside. Nearly half a million fruit trees grow here, turning the fjord pink and white in spring as the blossom reflects in the deep, still water. At blossom time the waterfalls are in full spate, shooting over the sides of the mountains, and the Hardanger has two of Norway's highest and best known: Skykkjedalsfossen, which falls 300 metres (1,000 ft), and Vøringfossen, lower but famous for its beauty.

Crossing to the north side, Road 49 runs along the sunny side of Hardangerfjorden towards the fjord villages of **Norheimsund** and **Øystese ❸**. Alternatively, they can be reached through day or longer excursions from Bergen either by boat or road (E16 and then Road 11). Both of these villages offer excellent trips for exploring the fjords by car and ferry, and marked paths here and at **Kvamskogen** further inland make

Map on page 234

FJORD NORGE
FJORD NORWAY

Hordaland is at the heart of Norway's fjord country.

BELOW: the beautiful Vøringfossen (waterfall) lies at the end of Eidfjord.

for safe walking. But take time out to visit the **Ingebrigt Vik Museum** (open June–Aug; entrance fee) at Øystese, one of Norway's most distinctive museums containing virtually all the works by the sculptor of that name.

Not to be passed by is the **Hardanger Fartøyvernseter** (Hardanger Ship Conservation Centre; open all year) at Norheimsund where conservationists are patiently restoring the wooden craft that made Norwegian boat-building famous. They range from small rowing boats to the Centre's most prestigious restoration, the *M/S Mathilde*, a 22-metre (73-ft) Hardanger yacht launched in 1884. This superb yacht has regained her former splendour under the guidance of Kristian Djupevåg (who also restored Roald Amundsen's yacht, *Gjøa)* and it has the world's largest authentic yacht rigging. The *Mathilde* sleeps 25 passengers in bunk benches or hammocks and is available for cruises and day excursions, when she can take 50 people to sail fjord and sea as they might have in bygone days.

Jondal ❹, on the other side of the fjord, is the entrance to the Folgefonn glacier, and the **Folgefonn Summer Ski-centre**. The safe but exciting road to the new ski centre is clear from June to September. With snow all year round, there are three mobile ski lifts, alpine and cross-country skiing tracks (you can hire all the necessary equipment), a cafeteria and guided walks on the glacier.

Jondal itself has a country museum, in the old **Lensmannshuset** (Sheriff's House; May–Sept; entrance fee), and Hardanger Cathedral (the largest church in the Hardanger region). Not far away at **Herand** you will find Bronze Age rock carvings and, at Herandsholmen, Hardanger's first guesthouse which opened in 1754. By now, into the inner fjords, the road suddenly turns sharply southeast along the short straight sides of Utnefjord to Utne village, part of Ullensvang *kommune*, which also includes both sides of Sørfjorden.

Edvard Grieg used to visit a small hytte *poised on the edge of Hardangerfjorden near to the village of Ullensvang where, with piano and writing desk at hand, he would compose surrounded by the beauty of the Norwegian fjords.*

BELOW: the old fjord village of Utne.

Five generations

When the fjords were West Norway's main "roads", **Utne ❺** was an important junction between east and west and had the first post and telegraph offices in Hardanger, in 1836 and 1876 respectively.

Two establishments in Utne which sum up Hardanger life over the past centuries are the **Hardanger Folkemuseum** (open daily, closed winter weekends; entrance fee, for details see below), and the **Utne Hotel** (tel: 53 66 69 83), founded in 1722, the oldest hotel in Norway still in operation. Since 1787, five generations of the same family have owned the hotel. It first became famous internationally during the time of Torbjørg Utne (1812–1903), known with affection as Mor (Mother) Utne. Her picture hangs on the sitting-room wall. The family is represented today by her great granddaughter, Hildegun Aga Blokhus. It has always been a favourite spot for artists who have donated many paintings and the hotel also holds exhibitions of national costumes and characteristic embroidery.

Since it opened in 1911, the Hardanger Folkemuseum has collected old houses and farm buildings for its outdoor museum, formed into a "cluster farm" as it would have been before the Norwegian agricultural reforms in the middle of the 19th century. Along the shore are old boathouses and a merchant's shop, which was in use in Utne not all that long ago, and an orchard preserves many old varieties of fruit which have now disappeared from other parts of the Hardangerfjord. Inside, the museum has a modern exhibition, other rooms showing old crafts and folk art and the famous Hardanger fiddle, and changing exhibitions on special fjord themes.

Past Utne, the fjordside road turns due south into the **Sørfjorden**. Once you are used to the narrow road and would like to enjoy the magnificent view,

Map on page 234

BELOW: traditional wedding at Voss led by a fiddler and toastmaster.

*A traditional
"children's
wedding" at Voss.*

you should stop at **Agatunet** ❻ (open May–Aug; entrance fee), the farm of a 13th-century local sheriff. From the Middle Ages to the recent past, Agatunet grew into a nine-family village with a cluster of some 30 buildings. Today, the families no longer live there but the buildings have been preserved.

On the eastern side of Sørfjord, a short ferry ride away, is the area's main amusement park, Ferieparken at **Kinsarvik** ❼. A favourite with children, it has a water chute, trampoline, a miniature zoo, a boating lake, and lends out surf boards, water mopeds and water skis. Kinsarvik was also part of the main east-west route and its market place attracted merchants from both sides of Hardangervidda to exchange bog iron and furs for sea salt. The **old stone church** is said to have been built by Scottish builders around 1200, and has a 17th-century pulpit painted by Peter Reimers. Until Utne Kirke (church) was consecrated in 1896, Kinsarvik had for centuries drawn its congregation from all around the fjords, and many worshippers arrived in church boats.

Falls, farm and forest

Heading northeast from Kinsarvik on the E13 and then Road 7 you will find one of the area's most beautiful stretches of water, **Eidfjorden** ❽. It cuts far into the dramatic landscape which includes the **Hardangerjøkulen** and below it **Skykkjedalsfossen** ❾, Norway's highest waterfall, and **Vøringfossen** ❿, which falls 150 metres (490 ft) down into the wilds of Måbødalen. There is a path at the top overlooking the fall which is not for vertigo sufferers. Alternatively, you can walk down to view this great outpouring from below, and fitness fanatics might welcome the challenge of the age-old packhorse track up Måbøfjell, with 1,500 steps and 125 bends. From June to August look out for signs to

BELOW: snowman outside Vangskyrkja (Voss Church).

the **Måbødalen Kulturlandskapsmuseum** (Cultural Landscape Museum; open June–Aug; guided tours available) which provides a network of trails all sign-posted and with information boards explaining the various points of interest. The public barbecue areas make fabulous picnic stops.

Above tiny Simadalsfjord is **Kjeåsen** ⓫, a mountain farm which claims to be the world's most isolated settlement. It lies like an eagle's nest 620 metres (2,000 ft) on near vertical rock above the distant waters of the fjord. Those feeling strong and brave can tackle the old path to the top and marvel that this was how the villagers struggled up with their every need. For frailer spirits it is possible to reach Kjeåsen by car through a magnificent new tunnel. Inside the mountain is the **Sima Kraftverket** (Hydro-Electric Power Station; open June–Aug; entrance fee) which arranges guided tours three times a day.

Crossing Eidfjorden at Brimnes you enter a farming and forestry district. Instead of taking the E13, take a right turn onto Road 572 which will bring you to **Ulvik** ⓬. Artists and other visitors have been coming here for longer than almost any other place in Hardanger and the village has permanent exhibitions by artists such as Tit Mohr (born 1917) and Sigurd Undeland (1903–1983). No one should miss the fine examples of **rose painting** in Ulvik's 19th-century church, painted in 1923 by Lars Osa (1860–1958).

Hang-gliding to skiing

Continuing on in a loop back to the E13 you come to **Voss** ⓭, which lies next to a lake, **Vangsvatnet**, in the middle of rich farmland. The Voss *kommune* (district) makes full use of its surroundings to attract visitors. In summer they come for touring, fjord excursions, mountain walking, parachuting, hang-gliding and paragliding from **Hangurfjell**, and fishing and watersports on Vangsvatnet. In winter, everything changes and Voss becomes one of the best centres for alpine and cross-country skiing of the more energetic touring variety.

Voss is also a good place for mountain touring and sport fishing in the 500-or-so lakes and innumerable mountain rivers and streams, with the Vosso river famous for the size of its salmon. Even in summer the high mountains call for boots or very strong shoes and plenty of extra clothes – temperatures drop quickly; this applies in all upland areas.

The top station of the **cable car** up Hangurfjell gives one of the best prospects of Voss in its bowl-shaped valley. As the ground drops away below, the two gondolas, "Dinglo" and "Danglo", take only four minutes or so to lift you 610 metres (2,000 ft). On a sunny day, a coffee on the platform outside the cafeteria is magnificent, with the occasional excitement of a paraglider soaring into the sun and over Vagnsvatnet, spread out below.

At the beginning of World War II, Voss was badly damaged by German bombing and not much remains of the old town centre except the **Vangskyrkja** (church; open June–Aug daily), which dates back to 1277. The inside is certainly worth seeing with a colourfully painted ceiling liberally adorned with flying angels. Outside, a great stone cross stands in a field south of the church which, according to legend, was raised two centuries before the church was

Map on page 234

Apart from its artistic associations, the village of Ulvik has the unlikely privilege of being where the first potatoes were grown in Norway, back in 1765.

BELOW: moonrise over the island of Fedje.

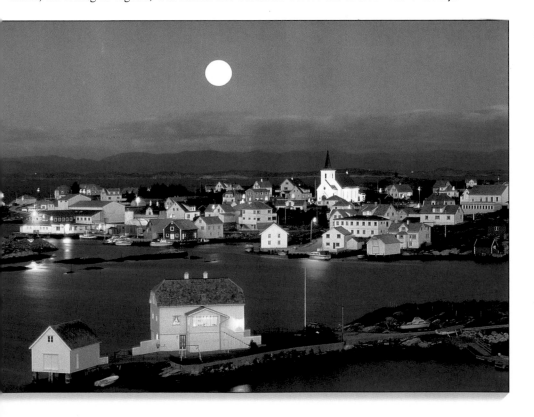

built by the proselytising King Olav Haraldson. The church walls are 2 metres (7 ft) thick and the wooden octagonal steeple is unique in Norway.

Below Hangurfjell, about half an hour's walk above the town, is **Voss Folkemuseum** (open all year; tel: 56 51 15 11), a collection of 16 old wooden buildings standing in traditional form around a central courtyard. The houses date from 1600 to 1870 and contain implements and furniture in use until 1927, incredible though it may seem. Yet somehow, despite the heavy farm work and meagre evening light, farm people like these managed to produce some beautiful embroidery, wood and other craft work. One of the most delightful is a traditional wood carving of a Voss bridal party riding to church, with the bride's horse led firmly by her father as though he feared she might gallop away. The carving is by a local sculptor, and is based on a bronze relief in the little park below Voss station in which the main figure, the bridal fiddler, is the legendary Ola Mosafinn who died in 1912.

Artistic tradition

Voss has long been a centre for artists and musicians, and their monuments are scattered around. The 1957 Sivle monument marks the centenary of the birth of the author and poet Per Sivle (1857–1904), who grew up on the mountain farm of Sivle, in the great Stalheim Skleive (gorge); the monument behind Voss church commemorates three Bergslien artist brothers, Brynjulf, Nils and Knut; near Voss Fine Arts Society is a memorial to actor Lars Tvinde, born and bred on the farm of Tvinde, which lies below the Tvindefossen (a waterfall to the north of Voss); and on the same road the 1958 Sjur Helgeland Memorial commemorates another local fiddler and composer.

BELOW: midday snack at the Hangur ski centre.

This artistic tradition continues and Voss is one of the best places to hear the Hardanger fiddle and see the old dances performed in beautiful costumes. On the main street is a shop where you can see, or even buy, the ornate silver belts and jewellery that go with the traditional Norwegian costume.

Around Bergen and north

From Voss the E16 is the quickest way to Bergen. Back in the city, Bergen's islands are linked so closely together that sometimes it is hard to realise that you have crossed water, but islands such as **Askøy** and **Osterøy** to the north of Bergen have their own character, and the area round the **Bjørnafjorden** (the Bear fjord) to the south is particularly mild and green, and full of boats of all sorts.

After an hour's drive to the long narrow island of **Sotra** ⓮, which shelters the city from the North Sea, there is no doubt that this is a different world. Sotra is a good base for sea canoeing in and out of its small offshore islands and rocks and, in good weather, as far as the open sea to combine canoeing with ocean fishing. In any case, shelter is never far away.

North of Bergen is a second island district, **Nordhordland**, that stretches as far north as Sognefjorden and includes the islands of Holsnøy, Radøy and Sandøy. At weekends, it is a favourite area for Bergensere who go sailing, swimming and fishing.

Although this region depended on ferries for a long time, today taking the car is no problem: most of its fjords and sounds can be crossed via modern suspension and pontoon bridges.

In Nordhordland the sea can be at its wildest, smashing against the western coast, yet the area has been inhabited for some 8,000 years. Håkon den Gode (the Good) is buried at **Seim** ⓕ, near Knarvik (around half an hour from Bergen by express boat). Another rare reminder of the Vikings is a beech wood, also at Seim, 1,000 years old and the northernmost beech wood in Europe.

Today, fish farming is important to Nordhordland, which exports vast quantities of salmon and trout all round the world, and the fish farmers are now attempting to rear cod, halibut and other species. Some fish farms are open to the public. There is good sea fishing for cod and coalfish, and special rosy-coloured trout inhabit many of the lakes. Diving and sub-aqua fishing, as well as treasure-hunting, are easy in these transparent waters. Oil is a modern, though not conflicting industry in this widespread area with the night gleam of the light from Mongstad one of the few reminders of this large refinery.

Dangerous waters

Most remote of all, and a target for both sailing picnics and holidays, is the island of **Fedje** ⓕ, an important navigation point for many centuries with two 19th-century lighthouses still in use today. In these ever-changing waters, Norwegian sea laws insist that all ships must carry a Norwegian pilot, and all tankers destined for Mongstad refinery are navigated from here through the unreliable waters. Stay overnight on Fedje in one of the guesthouses in Kræmmerholmen or in the Pensjonat there and sample the idyllic bird and flower habitat. ❑

Map on page 234

BELOW: the Stalheimskleive (gorge) was the scene of fierce fighting during World War II.

NORWAY IN A NUTSHELL

If you have only a day to spare in this region, this tour which, but for the lack of an island or two, might well be called "Hordaland in a Nutshell", covers many of the sights. Organised by Norwegian State Railways and the private Flåm Utvikling AS line, it runs throughout the year and combines bus, ferry and train *(see page 360).*

The tour starts with a train journey from either Oslo or Bergen to Myrdal and can be done in a day in the summer months (in winter an overnight stop is necessary). From Myrdal it sets off on one of the steepest train journeys in the world, the 50-minute panoramic trip down 850 metres (2,800 ft) of mountain gorge to the pretty village of Flåm, stopping – thanks to one of the five separate sets of brakes – to photograph the torrent of Kjosfossen and to pick up passengers at one or two of the tiny stations.

The next leg is by ferry, which travels through Aurlandsfjorden and Norway's narrowest fjord, Nærøyfjorden, whose rocky sides are twice as high as the water is wide, to Gudvangen. From here the journey continues by bus to Voss, skirting Oppheim Lake. In summer the bus makes the hairpin ascent to the Stalheim Hotel. The hotel parapet looks down over the great depths of the Stalheimskleive (gorge). A tortuous descent leads to the fjord.

BIO-DIVERSITY AND SUSTAINABILITY

About 20,000 years ago Norway was covered in ice and barren tundra. But, as the climate changed and ice melted, flora and fauna began to thrive

The first species to arrive in Norway, following the melting of the glaciers, were the Arctic animals such as reindeer, fox, wolf and wolverine. Trees came later, accompanied by a rich flora and fauna including bears, lynx, elk, marten, hare, beaver and otter, and small rodents including the lemming. The forests were filled with grouse, owls and woodpeckers. The lakes provided a habitat for geese, grebes, ducks and cranes; shadowed closely by birds of prey. The coastline teemed with kittiwakes, guillemots, auks, puffins, cormorants and gulls. The coastal waters were awash with arctic fish such as cod, haddock and halibut, and the rivers offered spawning ground for salmon, trout and char. Perch, powan, pike and grayling joined the eco-system via the freshwater Baltic. Mankind entered the scene about 10,000 BC, with a strong hunting instinct. Whales, seals, lynx, bear and wolf almost became extinct, replaced by sheep and about 200,000 domesticated reindeer.

FROM PREDATOR TO PROTECTOR

Today large areas of Norway have been designated as national parks to protect special habitats and support bio-diversity. Hunting is strictly controlled: wolves are regularly sighted in East Norway and the last of Europe's wild reindeer, about 15,000 in total, are now found on the Hardangervidda. Norway promotes sustainable management of ocean resources and has resumed commercial whaling based on studied whale counts. The elk, on the other hand, has benefited from commercial deforestation and numbers have grown.

▽ **WATER BIRDS**
The clownish-looking puffin *(Fratercula arctica)*, with its parrot-like bill, is an expert diver and adroit fisherman.

▷ **WORKING MAMMALS**
Reindeer often serve as a substitute to cattle or horses and are used to draw sledges and logs. They thrive on lichen moss.

▷ **WILD CATS**
The Eurasian, or Northern lynx *(Felis lynx)*, is an agile climber and often hides in trees ready to pounce on small animals and birds. Lynx are also highly valued for their fur.

◁ **BEAR NECESSITIES**
Brown bears *(Ursus arctos)* are now restricted to the Nordland region. A protected species, many bears are electronically tagged.

◁ **LORD OF THE FOREST**
The European elk *(Alces alces)* may stand up to 2.4 m (8 ft) high. The males' flattened, broad antlers are shed each year after the mating season.

COMMERCIAL WHALING

Norway was once a great whaling nation: northern towns grew up around the prosperous whale oil industry. Electric lighting sent the whaling industry into decline but, by then, the global whale population had been decimated, leading to international legislation.

Still, Norway continues to hunt in order to maintain its coastal communities and has recently introduced a DNA registry for all whale meat sold, to prove it was caught legally. The hunt is held in summer when fishing activities are low and much effort goes into teaching and pursuing correct hunting methods. But high concentrations of toxins have led to a whale blubber mountain.

◁ GREAT WHALES
Although Norway is one of the few countries to pursue commercial whaling, sightings are now rare. Minke and beluga whales are more common in Spitsbergen.

△ ARCTIC KING
The polar bear (Ursus maritimus) is Europe's largest predator and chooses his habitat where there is an abundance of seals.

▷ MOUNTAIN GIANT
The musk ox (Ovibos moschatus), once close to extinction, is found in Arctic regions and feeds on grass, moss and sedge.

BERGEN

With its relaxed atmosphere, stunning setting and vibrant cultural life, Bergen is an appealing mix of the cosmopolitan and the outdoors, with easy access to the western fjords

Map on page 248

There's always a sense of symmetry and order about a city built on hills. If it also stands on a peninsula and has a harbour at its heart, it is bound to be beautiful. Bergen, the capital of West Norway, has all these things. Built on seven hills, the city grew outwards from the coast and harbour in the quaintly named Puddefjorden and spread across the steep slopes and over the bridges that link islands and headlands.

The best place to get a feel of this natural shape is to take the newly modernised funicular, **Fløibanen ⒶⒶ** (every half hour, May–Aug 7.30am–midnight; Sept–Apr until 11pm; fee), that climbs more than 300 metres (1,000 ft) in just eight minutes from the centre to **Fløyen**, high above Bergen. On the downward journey, you seem to be tipping headfirst into the city.

At the top is the lovely old-fashioned building that houses Fløyen Restaurant, built in 1925, and the start of eight marked walking routes, the longest no more than around 4 km (2½ miles), though this does not mean they do not contain steep hills through woods and open moor.

A leisurely coffee or lunch on the verandah of the restaurant gives a chance also to drink in the superb view over hundreds of islands, many with the small *hytter* (wooden cabins) and a couple of boats tied up to a landing stage that sums up a Norwegian's ideal summer. All around are mountains and hills that cradle the city – Fløifjellet, Damsgårdfjellet, Løvstakken, Sandviksfjellet, Rundemånnen, Blåmannen, and the highest of them all, **Ulriken** at around 600 metres (2,000 ft) reached by a cable car (every seven minutes, summer 9am–10pm; winter 10am–5pm; fee). The Ulriken mountain café is open when the cable car is running. There is a double-decker bus connection with the cable car from Torget, the site of the famous Bergen fish market.

A long tradition of international trade has made this city the most outgoing in Norway and given the Bergensere a jauntiness in their walk that hints at generations of sailors, quick wits, worldliness and a sense of their own worth. Bergensere are certain they are the best, secure in the knowledge that, although Olso may now be the capital, it is historically a mere toddler compared with Bergen.

Olav Kyrre's city

King Olav Kyrre is credited with founding Bergen in 1070 at Torget. But it would be naive to believe that, long before, the perfect natural harbour and sheltered fjords were not a home for people who depended on the sea. During the 13th century, Bergen became the first capital of a united Norway, and a great ecclesiastical centre, with a cathedral, 20 churches and chapels, five monasteries and two hospitals for the

PRECEDING PAGES: Bergen harbour. **LEFT:** "Jacob", the street sign for Jacobsgården. **BELOW:** Fløibanen on its way up Fløyen, one of Bergen's seven hills.

Bergen

0 _____ 250 m
0 _____ 250 yds

poor. Bergen lost its capital status to Oslo during the Middle Ages, but still dwarfed the new capital. In medieval times, it was the biggest city in the Nordic countries and, until 1830, the largest in Norway. Today, with a population exceeding 230,000, it is roughly half the size of Oslo.

Much of this early size and success came when Bergen was chosen as the hub of the medieval German Hanseatic League in the north. Their trading base on the north side of **Vågen** became the power house of all trade on the northwest Norwegian coast. But the Hansa began to grow too powerful all over Scandinavia and, at last, Norway broke the tie that kept the west in thraldom.

The perils of fire and war

As in all wooden cities, fire has swept through Bergen on many occasions, often devastating it. The result is that the oldest surviving buildings are noticeably built of stone, and the present streets, following the last fire in 1916 when a gale fanned the flames to an inferno, are wide and designed as fire breaks.

During World War II, Bergen was a centre of the resistance movement and many young people from the town took the perilous route out through the islands to Scotland. There they trained for resistance work and then smuggled themselves back to West Norway to become members of sabotage groups. The actions of the movement are commemorated by the **Theta Museum** in Bryggen (open mid-May–mid-Sept Tues, Sat and Sun 2–4pm; entrance fee; tel: 55 55 20 80).

Yet the major disaster of this unhappy period came not directly from war but through accident caused by war. In 1944 a Dutch ammunition ship in the harbour blew up, damaging many of the oldest buildings on the northern promontory, including Håkonshallen and Rosenkrantztårnet. Anti-German feelings ran high at that time. The famous **Tyskebryggen** (quay named after Hansa merchants) has been tactfully renamed **Bryggen ❸**.

Starting with the past

The earliest archaeological remains are in **Bryggens Museum ❻** (open May–Aug daily 10am–5pm; Sept–Apr Mon–Fri 11am–3pm, Sat noon–3pm, Sun noon–4pm; entrance fee; tel: 55 58 80 10), past the Hansa houses on the north side of the harbour. The museum contains the medieval remains uncovered during archaeological digs between 1955 and 1972. There are also many artefacts and re-creations of medieval rooms. Together it gives a picture of the time when Bergen was a small fishing and sailing community that clung to the shallow slopes above the shore.

Nearby is the oldest building still in use, **Mariakirken ❼** (St Mary's Church; open late-May–Aug Mon–Fri 11am–4pm, closed Sat–Sun; Oct–Apr Tues–Fri noon–1.30pm; entrance fee in summer; tel: 55 31 59 60), built in the early years of the 12th century and justly proud of its rich baroque pulpit. The only other medieval churches to survive periodic fires are the present **Domkirke ❺** (Cathedral; open Tues–Fri 11am–2pm; tel 55 31 04 70), once dedicated to St Olav but now a blend of many different periods, and **Korskirken ❻** (the Church of the Holy Cross; open Mon–Sat 11am–3pm), most of it now

BERGEN

Serving as the starting point for numerous tours and cruises, Bergen is known as the "gateway to the fjords".

BELOW: trolls guard the entrance to a souvenir shop.

National Day celebrations in Bergen.

in the Renaissance style of the 17th century. The latter two are relatively close to the harbour and all three merit a visit.

Holmen was the site of **Bergenhus**, the old timber-built royal palace used when Bergen first became a capital. At a time of much building in the 13th century, it was converted to a fortified stronghold of stone, and the restored remains are close to where the original cathedral and bishop's residence stood. There are two particularly notable buildings: **Håkonshallen** (open mid-May–Aug 10am–4pm; Sept–mid-May daily noon–3pm, Thur 3–5pm; entrance fee; tel: 55 58 80 10), built by King Håkon Håkonsson between 1247 and 1261, which was used for the wedding of King Magnus Lagabøte (the Lawmaker), who was Håkon's son and co-ruler; and **Rosenkrantztårnet** (open May–Aug 10am–4pm; Sept–May Sun only noon–3pm; entrance fee), which was the work of a Danish governor of Bergenhus, Erik Rosenkrantz, who grafted it on to Håkon's original "Keep of the Sea" in the 1560s.

Håkonshallen is the largest secular medieval building still standing in Norway. When both it and Rosenkrantztårnet were badly damaged in the 1944 explosion, Norwegian historians took the opportunity to reconstruct them as closely to the originals as possible. Today, Håkonshallen makes a magnificent concert hall. Rosenkrantztårnet is now a museum, with both permanent and special exhibitions.

The power of the Hansa

In summer, guides from Bryggens Museum also conduct tours through the row of **Hansa houses** that line Bryggen. These Hansa homes and warehouses were all built after the great fire of 1702, which destroyed many buildings, and they are on the UNESCO World Heritage list. One key to understanding the Hansa way of life is a visit to the **Hanseatiske Museum** (open June–Aug 9am–5pm;

BELOW: Bergen's sheltered harbour.

Sept–May times vary; entrance fee; tel: 55 31 41 89), furnished in the style of the time when the merchant had his accounting room within the main office on the first floor. This small room enabled him to keep an eye on the liquor room next door. The adjoining room, decorated with a Royal Cod, distinguished by a bump on its head and said to bring luck, served as dining and sitting room for merchants and apprentices. On the floor above are the apprentices' tiny box beds, one above the other. The sleeping quarters were tiny, but importantly retained heat. Although apprentices were merchants' sons, sent to learn their business with a colleague, they were locked into their "prisons" each night.

As a fire precaution – all too often in vain – no heating was allowed in these Hansa houses and the Germans must have suffered torments of cold in the biting damp of a Bergen winter. No wonder that **Schøtstuene** ❿ (open June–Aug 10am–5pm; May and Sept 11am–2pm; Oct–Apr Sun only 11am–2pm ; entrance fee; tel: 55 31 41 89), the assembly rooms nearby, were so popular during winter when trade was slack and few ships were in the harbour. The long central table held both beer jugs and the Bible, exemplifying the two religions of the Hansa. In a drawer was the cane used to discipline the apprentices who had their schooling there. The "rules of the club" adorn one wall, written in Low German (old Northern dialect).

At Elsesro, further out along the coast road, past Bergenshus and the North Sea quay, is **Gamle Bergen** ⓚ (Old Bergen; open May–Sept 9.30am–4.30pm; guided tours only, every hour; entrance fee; tel: 55 39 43 00), the obligatory open-air museum beloved of Scandinavia. Here there is a collection of 40 wooden buildings from the 18th and 19th centuries, the interiors decorated to show different styles. Along the cobbled streets, guides in traditional red calf-length costumes and black shawls lead tours which range from the French

Map on page 248

Historic wooden sign in Gamle (Old) Bergen.

BELOW: Torget, the city's famous fish market.

TIP

Buy a *Bergen Kortet* (card), valid for 24 or 48 hours, and enjoy free admission to many museums, free travel on city buses and on the funicular to Mount Fløyen, plus numerous discounts. Available from the Tourist Information Office and hotels.

Empire splendour of the official's drawing room to the tiny house where the seamstress plied her diligent needle in the 1860s. Nearby is the popular **Sandvik Sjøbad** (bathing area) which looks out over Byfjorden to the city.

Back along Vågen, a short ferry trip from below Rosenkrantztårnet to the Nordnes peninsula gives a good opportunity to view the beautiful lines of the sailing ship *Lehmkuhl*, which trains youngsters in sailing techniques and gleams with polished brass. A short walk towards Nordnes point reveals another castle, **Fredriksborg** (no visitors) and further north is **Nordnes sjøbad**, which includes a heated outdoor pool. Here, too, is **Bergen Akvariet** (Aquarium; open May–Aug 9am–7pm, feeding times noon, 3pm and 6pm; Oct–Apr 10am–6pm, feeding times noon and 3pm; entrance fee; tel: 55 55 71 71), which gives the feeling of having dipped below the surface of the sea.

Morning market

Early each weekday morning, **Torget** is the site of Bergen's fish, fruit and flower market. Customers engage the fishermen in serious conversation about the day's catch, watched by an interested circle, and the stalls sell *gravlaks* (cured salmon), lobster and *klippfisk* (dried cod). This busy scene is the heart of Bergen, where there is always something going on and where people linger to watch the transactions or peer into the boats tied up at the quay after a night's fishing.

Just south of the fish market is another square where people like to linger, **Torgalmenningen**, housing many of the city's best shops. The square also holds the **Sailors' Monument**. Carved figures march round the base of this memorial dedicated to all Norwegian sailors who lost their lives at sea. Alternatively, just up the hill from the fish market in another old section of the city is the **Gamle Rådhuset** (Old Town Hall). Originally built as a private house in 1558, it was presented to the town in 1562 and served the city for several centuries until, in 1974, the city administration moved to an inelegant high-rise modern block. Another attractive old building in the area is the **Hotel Victoria**.

BELOW: underwater at the Bergen Aquarium.

Museum cluster

Bergen is a good walking city and, if you fix your eye on the tall steeple of **Johanneskirken** (St John's Church; open Tues–Fri 10am–2pm), a short walk up Vest Torggate from Torgalmenningen takes you to the top of **Sydneshaugen**, near the university area and the site of a clutch of museums: the **Naturhistorisk Museum** (natural history museum; open mid May–Aug Tues–Sat 10am–3pm; Sun 11am–3pm; entrance fee; tel: 55 58 29 20) standing in the fine **Botanisk Hage** (botanic garden), the **Historisk Museum** (cultural history museum), and the **Sjøfartsmuseum** (maritime museum; open June–Aug daily 11am–3pm; Sept–May Sun–Fri 11am–2pm; entrance fee; tel: 55 54 96 00) which traces the history of this seafaring area from the Old Norse period to the present day.

The university area consists of beautiful merchants' villas from the turn of the 20th century, and is where the Arctic explorer Fridtjof Nansen spent the early years of his career. It was also a base for the father of weather forecasting, Vilhelm Bjerknes.

Famous names

It is not surprising that this lively city, with its close European links, should have been the birthplace of many famous people. It was also a strong base for 19th-century nationalism which culminated in 1905 in Norway gaining its independence from Sweden. The prime minister who led Norway then was Christian Michelsen, whose home **Gamlehaugen** (house open June–Sept Mon–Fri 10am–1pm; gardens open all year; entrance fee; tel: 55 92 51 20) at Fjøsanger is now the residence of the king when he is in Bergen.

Nationalism had strong roots in the 19th-century revival of Norwegian culture, led by the playwright Henrik Ibsen, the violinist Ole Bull, the composer Edvard Grieg, and writers such as Bjørnstjerne Bjørnson. Though Ibsen and Bjørnson were not natives of West Norway, Bjørnson was for a time director of Bergen's **Den Nationale Scene ®** (National Theatre) founded by Ole Bull in 1850, and Bjørnson's statue stands on the steps in front.

The virtuoso violinist Ole Bull's contribution to Norwegian culture came through his wanderings in the villages of West Norway and the great Jotunheim mountain plateau east of the fjord country. Here he collected many old folk melodies which were played on the Hardanger fiddle, the area's traditional instrument. Later, Grieg transcribed some of these folk tunes for piano, saving them from being lost. He also founded Norway's National Theatre and hired a young Henrik Ibsen as a writer.

Every year, thousands of visitors come to look round Grieg's summer home at **Troldhaugen ❺** (open May–Sept daily 9am–6pm; Oct, Nov and Apr Mon–Fri 10am–2pm, Sat–Sun noon–4pm; mid-Jan–Mar Mon–Fri only; entrance fee; tel: 55 92 29 92) some 8 km (5 miles) south of Bergen on a high point above the fjord. Here Grieg found peace to compose in his *hytte* (holiday lodge).

Edvard Grieg (1843–1907).

BELOW: a dragon boat procession along Bryggen.

Fantoft stavkirke (stave church), in the Paradis district of Bergen, was brought from its original home on Sognefjorden in 1879. It burnt down in 1992 and has since been meticulously rebuilt (open May–Sept).

BELOW: view from the top of Fløyen.

The house is just as Grieg left it; his manuscripts are scattered around and even his piano is in working order in the comfortable drawing room. In the past, this room was the venue for many musical evenings; today, if you are lucky, the curator will play some of Grieg's music for you. The size of the room inevitably limited the size of the audience and in 1985 Troldhaugen opened a special **Chamber Music Hall**, with a turf roof seating 200, built into the hillside so that it is barely visible among the tall trees. The floor-to-ceiling windows behind the stage provide the audience with a lovely view of the composer's hut and Lake Nordås. The latest addition is the **Edvard Grieg Museum** close to the concert hall and villa.

Troldhaugen is a wonderful setting for a concert and a continuation of the summer evening tradition when Grieg and his wife, Nina Hagerup, a Danish singer, would entertain their friends in the quiet garden outside the drawing room. Any bus for the Fana district goes to Hopsbroen, then a 15-minute walk leads to Troldhaugen; many city excursions also include Troldhaugen.

Ole Bull built his home on the island of **Lysøen** ❶ (open mid-May–Aug Mon–Sat noon–4pm, Sun 11–5pm; Sept Sun only noon–4pm; entrance fee; tel: 56 30 90 77) in 1873, when his fame had long spread throughout and beyond Norway. Bull turned the island into a park with woodland and walking routes and the house itself is unlike any other in the country. Made of traditional Norwegian wood, the decorated and screened balcony and the pointed arches of the windows on the front of the building have an almost Moorish flavour, and the tower topped by a minaret is reminiscent of St Basil's in Moscow's Red Square. To get there, take the bus marked "Lysefjordruta" from bus station gate 19 or 20. The ride takes 50 minutes and stops at Beuna Kai. Then take the Ole Bull ferry, which leaves every half hour on the hour. By car, take road 553 and head south

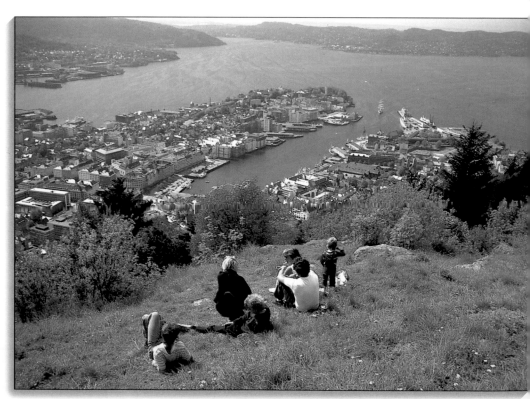

in the direction of Fana. It's a good idea to combine the visit to Lysøen with a stop on the way at **Lysekloster**, the ruins of a 12th-century Cistercian abbey, a daughter monastery of Fountains Abbey in Yorkshire, England.

Map on page 248

Artistic legacy

Whether as a result of the fame of people such as Bull and Grieg, Bergen has a lively artistic and cultural life – hence it was honoured as one of the European Cities of Culture 2000. The **Bergen International Festival of Music**, held each May and early June, attracts international artists and thousands of visitors. At the end of the 1970s, the festival led to the building of a new concert hall, **Grieghallen ⓤ**, with marvellous acoustics. The outside of the building looks remarkably like that of a concert grand piano, perhaps as a tribute to the composer whose name it bears. This is the heart of the 12-day festival but the whole city is involved, with events in Håkonshallen, Troldhaugen, Lysøen and Mariakirken.

Bergen also has several strong art collections, mostly centred on **Lille Lungegårdsvann**, the octagonal lake in the middle of the park, not far from the statues of Edvard Grieg, and of Ole Bull playing his violin, and near Grieghallen. Here are the **Bergen Billedgalleri ⓥ** (Bergen Art Gallery; open June–Aug daily 11am–5pm; Sept–May closed Mon; entrance fee; tel: 55 56 80 00), with a large collection of Norwegian painting over the past 150 years; **The Rasmus Meyers Samlinger Collection ⓦ**, which also specialises in Norwegian paintings with many by Edvard Munch; and the **Stenersens Samling ⓧ**, with works by Munch, Picasso and Klee amongst others – all part of the newly refurbished Bergen Art Museum.

Bergen is also strong in private galleries, many of which specialise in modern painting. Shops often offer opportunities to see traditional crafts. Best known is

BELOW: a concert in the ornate music hall of Ole Bull's house on Lysøen.

Map on page 248

Husfliden (on Vågsalm), which has richly decorated Norwegian costumes, textiles and woodwork, including the famous *rosemaling* (rose painting). For Norwegian glass try **Irgens** in Markeveien and Bergen's **Glasmagasin**.

Tradition in action

During the summer (mid-June to late August) the open-air stages at Lille Lungegårdsvann and Torgalmenningen are used almost daily for music and dance performances. Folk dancing and music from rural Norway are particularly popular with the Bergensere and visitors alike. Nearest to the real thing is **Fana Folklore** (summer, tel: 55 91 52 40), in the district of Fana to the south. This is designed as a country wedding with typical Norwegian food, such as *rømmegraut*, a rich celebration "porridge" which bears little resemblance to the breakfast variety, cured mutton and sausage, flat bread and other traditional dishes.

To experience Fana Folklore, travel by bus from Festplassen to **Fana Kirken**, the 800-year-old church, for a recital of hymns and melodies by the organist; then on to **Rambergstunet**, and a welcome by the *lur*, an instrument similar in sound to a coaching horn, and then to the long trestle tables for the wedding fare, accompanied by folk dancers weaving and jumping in the prescribed steps that almost died out during the 19th century. There are also displays by children and songs accompanied by one of Norway's *langleik*, a one-string zither.

Outdoor city

The most popular pastime is **sailing**. Not far behind are sea fishing and swimming. Or you could simply take a fjord cruise. Try the Norway-in-a-Nutshell bus, train and boat tour for a great overview of the area. The hills above Bergen, just 10 minutes away from the centre, are ideal for walking, and **Sandviken Ridesenter**, not far from the Gamle Bergen Museum, organises horse riding tours.

For something different, try a night at **Travpark** (Thur, from 6pm; tel: 55 39 68 00) at Åsane, around 16 km (10 miles) from the city (bus 285). This is a peculiarly Scandinavian sport. The atmosphere is electric as the horses and their drivers race round the track.

Apart from the gardens at Troldhaugen and Lysøen, the Norwegian Arboretum at **Milde** (open daily), founded in 1971, is busily planting up shrubs and trees from many parts of the world, and this pretty area along the shore has rocky gorges, hills and a small lake. The Fanafjord also provides good swimming. To get there take the bus to Mildevågen, and then a 15-minute walk to the arboretum.

Too many people make the mistake of allowing only a day or even half a day for Bergen at the start and end of a visit to the western fjords, which doesn't give the city a chance. It is much better to use it as a base for a fjord holiday, combining the cosmopolitan delights of the city with the splendid scenery of the fjords. Bergen has plenty to do and see, or you can simply spend some time just soaking up the atmosphere down by the busy harbour. But, take an umbrella; on average, it rains 219 days per year ☐

BELOW: Ole Bull nicknamed his house "the Little Alhambra".
RIGHT: old houses in the maze of narrow lanes behind Bryggen.

THE MOST BEAUTIFUL VOYAGE

Map on page 262

This is one of the great sea journeys of the world: from Bergen to the end of Norway and back again, the vessels plying the Hurtigruten are mail boats, freight ships and passenger liners in one

The ship slips out of **Bergen**'s hill-ringed harbour at 10.30pm, day in day out, all year round. In winter, it has been dark for hours and passengers linger no longer than to wave goodbye to the lights of the city before scuttling below to the warmth of saloon and cabin. In summer, it is a different matter: the deck is crowded as the big steamer sweeps out towards the fjord, leaving behind the small houses where the Hansa merchants once lived.

The coastal express heads north through Byfjorden and Hjeltefjorden, past the islands of **Askøy** and **Holsnøy** for the open sea, at the start of a trip of 1,250 nautical miles round Nordkapp (North Cape) and then to Kirkenes near the Russian border, crossing the Arctic Circle en route.

Nowadays, this coastal voyage has become one of the most popular journeys for visitors, but it is much more to the Norwegians themselves. From earliest times, this long and beautiful coast has been the main link in Norway for communication and trade, connecting communities hundreds of kilometres apart; the western and northern Norwegians once regarded Scotland and Iceland as being easier to reach than the region around present-day Oslo. In winter, it was the only way to travel because the Gulf Stream kept, and still keeps, the seaways open all year round.

PRECEDING PAGES: sunset at sea. **LEFT:** resting on the aft deck. **BELOW:** the view from on board *M/S Nordlys* between Rørvik and Brønnøysund.

The swift route

The first steamship, the *Prinds Gustav*, set out from Trondheim to Tromsø in 1838. In time, other steamers also began to ply between the coastal towns and in 1893 a local steamship company, Vesteraalens Dampskibsselskab, opened the Hurtigruten (literally "swift route") between Trondheim and Hammerfest, in the far northwest. As the line extended to Bergen and Kirkenes, several ship-owners became involved. Following various mergers, just two companies now run 11 ships (ranging from the grand old *M/S Harald Jarl* to the *M/S Nordnorge*, built in 1997) for a round trip that takes 11 days from Bergen and back. Shorter trips are available.

The Hurtigruten makes 34 ports-of-call along this ever-changing coast, some at places no bigger than a handful of houses around the harbour, with local people waiting on the quayside to collect a car or a container, to greet friends who have hopped a short distance between small towns where the alternative is a long difficult drive, or just as a social occasion where locals wave to the passengers looking down from the rails when the stop is too short to go ashore.

Part of the charm is watching a working ship going about its business: the efficient mooring as the crew shout down to the dockers; the crane winching over a

Hurtigrute

0   100 km

0   100 miles

tractor which has been chained fast to the deck during the voyage; and the nervous face of its owner as a car is winched up.

From October to May the first stop for going ashore is **Ålesund ❶**, one of the three Møre towns. It has all the natural design of a town built round a harbour and, because of a disastrous fire in 1904, it was rebuilt all of a piece, with the wooden houses in an Art Nouveau style, carefully preserved and painted in brilliant colours. From June to September, the vessel heads north to **Molde** instead of Ålesund. The high point of the tour is descending Trollstigen's (Troll Road's) 11 hairpin bends .

The next main stop is **Trondheim ❷**, further up a magnificent coast with 87 peaks, snow-capped for much of the year. When it was the ancient capital of Norway, Trondheim was called Nidaros, and **Nidaros Domen** (Cathedral) is a national shrine; it contains a memorial to King Olav Haraldson, who became St Olav the Holy after his death at the Battle of Stiklestad. The Trondheim stop is long enough for a morning tour of this historic city, with its busy harbours and bays, and wide streets lined with small wooden houses and old warehouses. From May to September, the tour also visits the Museum of Musical History at Ringve.

Early next morning, as the ship steams north again, it crosses the **Polarsirkel ❸** (Arctic Circle) and sails into "the land of the Midnight Sun". From April to September passengers board a smaller vessel at Grønøy to navigate the narrow Hollandsfjord inland. The tour then alights at the foot of the spectacular Svartisen, Norway's second-largest glacier. On the way south, at the Arctic Circle crossing, "King Neptune" joins the celebrations on deck to award Arctic Circle certificates.

Hamsun's Nordland

Into the **Lofoten Islands ❹**, the ship is now in Nordland, the territory of one of Norway's most famous writers, Knut Hamsun. Hamsun named the old trad-

Map on page 262

ing centre of **Kjerringøy** "Sirilund" in his novels, which describe the surprisingly outward-looking lives of these northern fishing and trading families around the turn of the 20th century. A Hamsun novel, particularly *The Wayfarers*, is a good accompaniment to a voyage that illuminates his own characters and their thinking, and gives an insight into life in these northern lands today.

On deck, as the steamer weaves in and out of the islands, bird-watchers find it difficult to go below even to eat or sleep, in case they miss one of the numerous seabird colonies, the congregations of colourful exotic ducks in winter harbours and, particularly, the comical little puffins in their hundreds of thousands.

Between **Solvær** and **Stokmarknes**, the ship makes a brief detour into **Trollfjorden**, something no big cruise liner could do because the sheer faces of rock and scree press close in this narrow fjord. This, too, calls for a celebration and the ship's chef serves a special Trollfjorden soup to the accompaniment of Grieg's most troll-like music and the arrival of a troll to delight the passengers. In winter, ice makes entry impossible, but instead there is the endless fascination of the **Aurora Borealis** (Northern Lights) – sometimes white spears, at others a brilliant blue-green aura across the sky, or a multi-coloured spectacular that gleams and sparkles. The high mountains of the fjord country further south have disappeared by now but, during the brief light of a winter day, the low slanting sun picks out the white cones of snow-covered hills.

There is time to see the Norwegian Crown Jewels on display in Trondheim's Nidaros Domkirke (Cathedral).

Watching the seasons go by

In spring and autumn, the 11-day journey feels like a voyage through the seasons. Leave Bergen in May, when the fjord valleys are brilliant with blossom, and the hills and mountains of the north will still be white as snow flurries

BELOW: a steamer dwarfs the dockside at Øksfjord.

Map
on page
262

Arriving at Sortland.

BELOW: heading
north near Skjervøy.
RIGHT: late evening,
during the midnight
sun, north of Bodø.

scurry across the fjords and mountains. The return journey is the reverse: just as the north is beginning to slip out of its winter grip, the swift Norwegian summer marches north and will have already reached Bergen and the mountains around it, and it could be warm enough to lie out in a sheltered corner of the deck as the ship nears the end of its long journey.

The northern city of **Tromsø** ❺, set on an island in a rugged landscape, has a relaxed cosmopolitan atmosphere that fits with its nickname "Paris of the North" and can be enjoyed in its numerous restaurants and street cafés. It has the most bars per capita in Norway, with a bustling nightlife. Among the stops are **Tromsø Museum** and the **Ishavs** (Arctic) **Cathedral**, which has the largest stained-glass window in Europe. Returning south to Tromsø in summer, there is time for a midnight excursion by cable car to the summit of **Mount Storsteinen**. At 410 metres (1,350 ft) above the sea, there is a wonderful sunlit view of coast and country.

Into Finnmark the ship sails past a coast of scoured hills and watercourses with forests along the valleys, to **Hammerfest**, Norway's most northerly town. In summer, the steamer, working ship or not, makes a concession here and slips through the Margerøy Sound to Honningsvåg and the start of an excursion by coach to **Nordkapp** ❻ (North Cape) – a highlight of any visit to Norway.

North Cape also marks a change of direction to the east across the very top of Norway on the way to **Kirkenes** ❼, 5 km (3 miles) from the **Russian border**, a coast where the place names begin to show Sami (Lapp) and Finnish origins. Kirkenes itself is a mining town in a strange no-man's land between East and West, which is also influenced by the local Sami culture. A bus then passes through Kirkenes and heads for Storskog and the Russian border.

Nowhere missed

Heading south, after visiting Tromsø, the vessel takes in a brief sightseeing tour at Harstad before moving on to **Trondenes Church**, the world's northernmost medieval church and, at 750 years old, the historical centrepiece of Trondenes. After a visit to Trondheim, passengers take in a short tour of the beautiful coastal fishing town of Kristiansund then arrive at Molde to experience the panoramic views of the Romsdal fjord and the Romsdal alps. On the way south again, the ship stops by day at the places it visited when northbound passengers were fast asleep below decks, so nowhere is missed. Nor is it generally a rough voyage: the Hurtigruten hugs the coast or weaves in and out of islands that shelter the ship from the excesses of the Atlantic Ocean and the Norwegian Sea, even in the far north.

Although the network of small aircraft linking scattered communities has done much to reduce its traffic, the coastal steamer is still there when airports are closed and roads blocked. For supplies and deliveries to distant industries and traders, ships are invaluable and can carry things too big for the plane. Even so, with the ever-increasing tourist traffic this emphasis is likely to change somewhat in the future. For now, though, the "swift route" along Norway's jagged coastline continues to be a unique mix of the workaday and the spectacular. ❑

FROM SOGN TO NORDFJORD

The presence of the last Ice Age is felt strongly here, in the shape of the great Jostedal glacier; but humans have also left their mark, in the form of ancient rock carvings and a plethora of stave churches

Map on page 234

From a seat in one of the small planes that somehow contrive to land on the narrow strips along the fjords or the tiny green patches between the mountains, it looks an impossible territory. Yet the land that runs from Sognefjorden in the south to Nordfjorden to the north has all the features that made Norway famous: the world's longest and deepest fjord, Europe's largest glacier and Jotunheimen, Scandinavia's greatest mountain massif.

The large *fylke* (county) of Sogn og Fjordane lies between a zigzag coastline drawn by the waters of the North Sea and the start of Jotunheimen's heights. Narrow fingers of water push inland from the main fjords to reach far into the mountains, and waterfalls tumble hundreds of metres into the fjord below. The force of all this water feeds powerful hydro-electric power stations, tucked away inside the mountains. Aluminium plants also make use of the spouting waterfalls to generate power and, among other things, produce the road barriers for many of Europe's mountain roads.

In the past, fjord, mountain and valley could be near impassable in winter. Today, though journeys often take longer than elsewhere, travel is made easier thanks to the network of ferries, tunnels and bridges. From Bergen, an express boat (a catamaran with water jet engines) reaches deep inland as far as Sogndal on Sognefjorden, almost half-way to Sweden.

LEFT: Flåm village.
BELOW: St Olav's Kirke (once the English church) in Balestrand.

Deepest and longest

At 200 km (120 miles) long and 1,300 metres (4,260 ft) deep, **Sognefjorden** ⓱ is unmatched anywhere in the world. After British visitors discovered it in the 19th century, royalty too endorsed the fjord's delights. As Crown Prince, Edward VII came over from Britain as early as 1898, and Kaiser Wilhelm II was on holiday in Sogn when he learned of the assassination of the Archduke at Sarajevo which triggered World War I.

In spring, the fjord is pink and white when this apparently ungrateful soil puts up umbrellas of fruit blossom in orchards and gardens. In the warm summer days, far above the fjord, cattle and sheep cling to the small grass plateaux around the mountain farms or *seter* where once women and young girls spent the summer making cheese. The majority of the 100,000 people in the county still make their living by farming or fishing, forestry and fruit growing.

On both sides of the fjord small villages cling to every square metre of land, each with its own atmosphere. **Balestrand** ⓲ has been a favourite since the 19th century and has an English church, St Olav's, founded by one of those fearless Victorian Englishwomen who travelled the world. German artists from the Düsseldorf Academy were also quick to appreciate the beauty of Sognefjorden and built Swiss-style houses, decorated

TIP

In summer, guides
from the Jostedals-
breen National Park
Centre, 20 km (12
miles) east of Stryn,
lead tours and glacier
explorations to differ-
ent offshoots of the
great Jostedal (details
tel: 57 87 68 00).

BELOW: a solitary
boat on
Sognefjorden.

with dragon heads in deference to their hosts' Viking past, to add to the charm of this picturesque village. The area is renowned for having a particularly mild climate and lush vegetation; across a small neck of water at **Dragsvik**, a local pastor-botanist planted exotic trees which thrive in the sheltered bay.

Ice spectacle

A narrow side-fjord leads to the little community of **Fjærland** (road connections here were not completed until 1986), a dairy farming centre near the two southernmost offshoots of the great **Jostedalsbreen** ⓳ (Europe's largest glacier). Nestling at its base on a large, flat esker deposited thousands of years ago is the **Norsk Bremuseum** ⓴ (Norwegian Glacier Museum; open June–Aug 9am–7pm; Apr–May and Sept–Oct 10am–4pm; entrance fee; tel: 57 69 32 88). In 2005 the museum will include a new wing devoted to natural and artificial climate change.

Tourists come to Fjærland every year to climb (or merely gaze at) the awesome glacier. From a distance, the concrete and glass building designed by Norwegian architect Sverre Fehn looks like part of the glacier itself. The museum includes a special cinema for viewing panoramic shots of Norwegian glaciers.

The ferry from Dragsvik runs to **Vangsnes** on the south side. From there, it is only a few kilometres to **Vik** ㉑ and the 12th-century **Hopperstad Stavkirke**, with dragon heads on the outside and rich decorations within. Vik also has a stone church, **Hove Kirke**, only 20 years younger than Hopperstad (both open May–Sept; single entrance fee). On the way back, stop at the statue of the heroic Norwegian explorer, Fridtjof Mansen, a gift from Kaiser Wilhelm II in 1913.

Going east from Balestrand, a short crossing takes you to **Hella** ㉒ and past the glistening arc of **Kvinnfoss** (Lady's Waterfall) close to the main road. At the

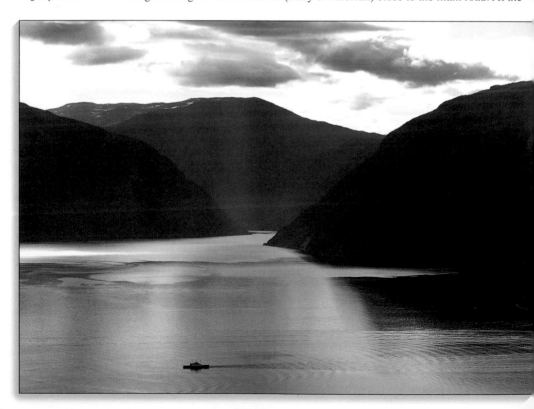

head of the fjord, **Sogndal** is the centre for trade and administration in an area of forestry and farming. The pretty little town swells considerably during term time because it is also a centre for education, with university colleges and Norway's oldest folk high school. To the north, farms are dotted along Sognadalen's narrow lake. This is a popular spot for walking in summer and skiing in winter.

Kaupanger Stavkirke (open June–Aug; entrance fee), a little further along Road 5, was built in the 12th century; its plain dark wood exterior has been restored, and it is a lovely place to listen to the organist's summer recitals. **Sogn folkemuseum ㉓** (open May–Sept 9am–6pm; otherwise 9am–4pm; entrance fee; tel: 57 67 82 06) was set up in 1909 as a living museum with animals, including 35 houses and farm buildings, to show how people lived in Sogn from around 1500 up to the present. The museum is used as a setting for folk music and dancing.

Standing tall beside the fjord at **Nordnes** is a stone to mark the Battle of Fimreite in June 1184. That was when King Sverre and his peasant Birkebeiner (so-called because of their birchbark leggings) defeated King Magnus Erlingsson and the nobility, a turning point in Norwegian history.

Taking a break on the Flåm to Myrdal mountain railway.

Cool, green waters

In **Luster ㉔**, to the northeast of Sogndal, is **Urnes Stavkirke** (UNESCO World Heritage Site; open June–Aug 10.30am–5.30pm and by appointment; entrance fee; www.lustertourist.com), thought to be the oldest stave church in Norway and linked with the coming of Christianity. Also within easy reach is yet another icy tongue from Josterdal glacier, called **Nigardsbreen**, where one of the delights is a boat trip over the ice-cold, green waters of a glacier lake.

South of Sogndal, Sognefjorden ends in the two most easterly fjords leading to Årdal and Lærdalsøyri, lovely valleys with mountain farms, plenty of opportunities for walking, climbing, or fishing in upland lakes and streams. The **Norsk Villakssenter** (Wild Salmon Centre; open June–Aug; entrance fee) at **Lærdalsøyri ㉕** provides an observation pool for wild salmon. Lærdal's one-time importance as an east–west trading route is evident at Gamle (Old) Lærdalsøyri, an area of beautifully restored 18th and 19th-century listed building (open May–Sept; entrance fee).

BELOW: Urnes Stavkirke (Stave Church), high above Lustrafjorden.

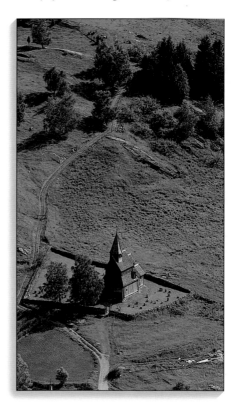

Aurlandsvangen, Flåm and Gudvangen lie along the innermost recesses of the fjord, which stretch south from the main fjord like an upside-down "Y". **Nærøyfjorden ㉖** to the west is the narrowest in Europe, and both provide the most dramatic fjord cruise in West Norway, the mountains pressing so close that you wonder if the boat will squeeze through. Also not to be missed is the **mountain railway ㉗** from Flåm to Myrdal, which spirals up the steep mountain gorge (*see "Norway in a Nutshell", page 241*).

Life on the lake

If from Balestrand instead of heading inland you turn northwest, along Road 5/13 towards Förde and the coast, you come to one of the regions many lakes – **Jølstravatnet** – that penetrate the foothills of the high tops in the east and feed into the fjords in the west. On the south side lies the farm **Astruptunet ㉘** (open

The replica Viking knarr *(freighter)* Saga Siglar *in Sognefjorden before leaving for a two-year, round-the-world voyage.*

BELOW: sunset lights up the slopes of Sognefjell.

May–Sept; entrance fee; tel: 57 72 67 82), home of the artist Nikolai Astrup (1880–1928) who found themes for his art in his own surroundings. Astruptunet is just as it was during the painter's life, though the barn has been replaced by a new art gallery with a permanent exhibition.

From Jølstravatnet, it is easy to reach **Grovebreen** (glacier), some 1,600 metres (5,250 ft) high, and Haukedalsvatn to the south is quite close to the far side of the glacier. Walkers can reach the great icefields of Josterdalsbreen. A series of valleys, lakes and fjords link these high plateaux into the Nordfjord system to the north.

After leaving Jølstravatnet the Jølstra, said to be one of the best salmon rivers in the area, drops hundreds of metres by the time it reaches **Førde ㉙** on Fördefjord. Here you find the main **Sunnfjord Museum** (open June–Aug; entrance fee; tel: 57 72 19 35), a collection of 25 restored buildings, 17 of which are reconstructed as a farmstead from around 1850.

Along the coast

The best view of Sunnfjord's hundreds of islands is from the high peaks in the east, though the coast itself is by no means flat. **Bleia** rises straight from the north side of Fördefjord to more than 1,300 metres (4,300 ft), the summit of the Sunnfjord Alps, and many of the islands have high peaks. These islands stretch the length of the coast, from Fensfjord and the island of Sandøy, north to Vestkapp (West Cape) where the Hurtigrute (coastal steamer) turns northeast to its next stop at Ålesund.

It's an odd thought that **Florø**, the only community in this large county big enough to be called a town, should lie on the remote edge of the sea, but not so strange when you remember that Norway has always depended on the sea for food, trade and transport. The **Sogn og Fjordane Kystmuseet** (Coastal Museum;

mid-June–Aug Mon–Fri 11am–6pm; Sat–Sun noon–4pm; Sept–mid-June until 3pm; entrance fee; tel: 57 74 22 33) in Florø has a fine collection of old boats. This most westerly town had its birth in the herring industry which flourished in the middle of the 19th century. Today, it still depends on the sea for fish, while oil and gas fields away to the west have, nevertheless, turned Florø into an oil centre.

Map on page 234

Offshore sights

There are many places to see: rock carvings at **Ausevik**, southeast of Florø; the nearby island of **Svanøy** with the ancient stone cross of St Olav, covered in runic inscriptions, a manor with an old garden and magnificent trees; there is a Romanesque medieval church on **Kinnøy**, where the Kinna Play, *Songen ved det store djup (The Song of the Great Deep)*, is performed by the county theatre group and local people, and draws thousands to the island each June.

To the north of Fløro, at the mouth of Nordfjorden, is the island of **Bremangerlandet** ㉚ with its **Vingen carvings,** which are even older than Ausevik's and show the lives of the fishing-settlers of Nordfjorden. Further north, the village of **Måløy** on **Vågsøy** is one of Norway's largest fishing and trading ports, and at Raudeberg fish of all kinds are salted and dried. But size is relative, and industry does nothing to detract from the rural quietness of this hilly island. Måløy features the Allied Monument, a 6-metre (20-ft) high granite obelisk raised in memory of 52 Allied soldiers who died during the Måløy raid in 1941.

North of Vågsøy and Raudeberg is **Silda**, a tiny island for sea-anglers, divers and bird-watchers. It has fewer than 80 inhabitants, no cars and, on an islet in the middle of the harbour, a restored fish salting works serves a feast of seafoods. On the nearby island of **Selje** ㉛ are the medieval ruins of **St Sunneva Kloster**

In summer, it is possible to see sea eagles along the coast of Sogn og Fjordane. This is the farthest south that this magnificent bird of prey builds its nest.

BELOW: the sturdy *fjording* (fjord horse), typical of the region.

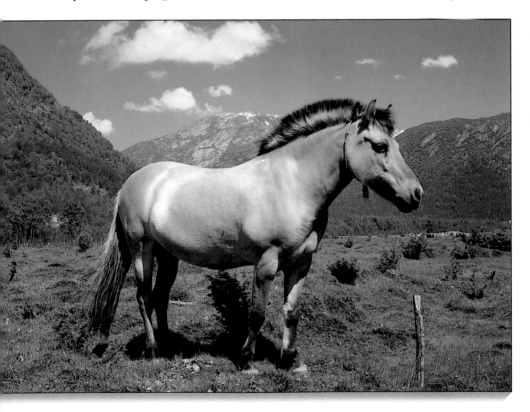

(Monastery). On the northernmost tip is **Vestkapp** where winds blow fiercely. Its closest neigbouring land is the Shetland Isles off the north of Scotland.

Inland along Nordfjorden

Nordfjorden is 100 km (60 miles) shorter than Sognefjord. With so many side-fjords, lakes and valleys it is easy to get into the mountains or make the journey up **Briksdalsbreen** ㉜, one of the most beautiful glaciers in the fjord country. Even better is that you can climb up to the base of the glacier in the two-wheeled farm carriages, *stolkjaerrer*, pulled by small, sturdy, cream-coloured *fjording* (fjord horses; details: Briksdalsbreen Tourist Information, tel: 57 87 68 00).

Hornindalsvatnet is Europe's deepest freshwater lake. Following the melting of the ice at the end of the last Ice Age, the Hornindal valley flooded to a depth of 514 metres (1,686 ft).

The traditional home of the *fjording* is the Eid district, centred around **Nordfjordeid**, where Nordfjorden proper has already divided itself into Eidsfjorden and Isefjorden. **Eid** ㉝, which is also connected to the coast by Road 15, is famous for **Firdariket**, the seat of the last Viking chief, and the town has traditional white-painted buildings. The church, which dates from 1849, is decorated with beautiful **rose paintings**.

To the south of Eid, Road 1 crosses Utfjorden and then runs along Gloppenfjorden, which ends at **Sandane** ㉞, the main town of Gloppen, the biggest farming district in the whole county and also a large fur-breeding centre. The **Nordfjord Folkmuseum** (open June–Aug; entrance fee) started in 1920 with five turf-roofed houses but now has more than 40 historic buildings, including a mountain *seter*. At the fjordside is a 100-year-old **sailing barge**, *Holvikjekta*, the last of the traditional freighters that served coast and fjord. There is also a fine adventure centre, **Glopen Camping og Fritidssenter** (tel: 57 86 62 14), which offers a week's programme of riding, canoeing, wind-surfing, mountain

BELOW: summer swimming in the cold fjord waters.

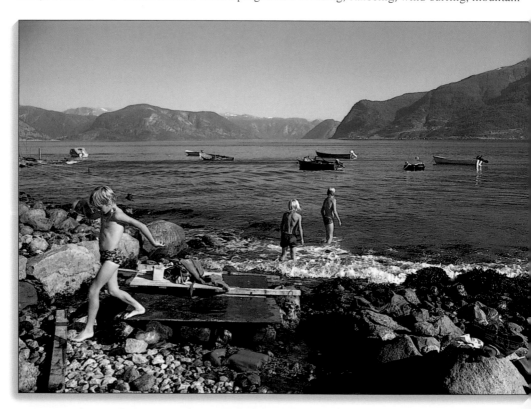

and glacier walking, mountain cycling and sight-seeing to various beauty spots.

Continuing east along Road 15 from Eid you come to Hornindalsvatnet, which leads to Grodås, sited where the ground begins to climb. Hornindal valley has long traditions in handicrafts and folk music, and musicians wear the black breeches, or the long black skirt and green bodice of the area. The most famous artist was Anders Svor (1864–1929), first a wood carver and then, after a time at the Copenhagen Academy of Art, a sculptor. The **Anders Svor Museum** (open all year; entrance fee; tel: 57 87 90 00) contains more than 400 of his sculptures.

Map on page 234

Fjord end

Further east you reach the Inner Nordfjorden, where the fjord system ends at **Stryn ㉟**, **Loen** and **Olden**, the start of three spectacular valleys stretching up to the northwest edges of the Jostedalsbreen. Nowadays, three tunnels out of the Stryn valley cut right through the mountain to the renowned Geirangerfjord to the north. Stryn is famous for summer skiing on the northeast of Strynsvatn, where the ground rises to Tystigbreen. Until you watch, it is hard to imagine skiers in swimsuits with deep tans, but there they are enjoying every moment.

Loen suffers from severe rockfalls. In 1905 a piece of the Ramnefjellet mountain fell into the lake and caused a flood wave 50 meters (164 ft) high that killed 63 people. Oldedalen is the route to Briksdalsbreen (glacier) from the Briksdalsbreen Fjellstove; go by horse-carriage or on foot, and then a half-hour walk leads to the great cascade of ice which hangs above the ice flows and the green waters of the glacier lake. Small birds flutter over the water and, in olden times, farmers from eastern Norway drove their cattle over these great icefields down into the kindlier valleys of the west. ❑

BELOW: the Briksdals glacier, part of the great Jostedalsbreen.

MØRE AND ROMSDAL

Map on page 278

The county of Møre og Romsdal has a bit of everything: a jewel of a fjord, Geirangerfjorden; the Art Nouveau Ålesund; the peaks of Trollheimen, Home of the Trolls; and delightful islands to spare

or nearly a century the coastal steamers of the Hurtigrute have called at Åle-sund, Molde and Kristiansund along the sea route that leads to Trondheim and the north. This part of Norway's jagged coastline is 6,000 km (3,730 miles) long; more than 10 percent of the county's population lives on islands. It's scarcely surprising then to learn that, even today, the sea is still the great provider for Møre og Romsdal. Prospecting and providing for the oil industry are the most important activities, and North Sea oil and gas are likely to become even more significant as Norway seeks new fields.

Looking at the jumble of coastline, islands and fjord mouths on a map, it is sometimes hard to distinguish where sea and islands end and fjord and mainland begin. Yet move inland and half the area lies above 600 metres (2,000 ft). In the southeast, the highest peaks reach more than 1,800 metres (6,000 ft). The county is divided into three municipalities: **Sunnmøre**, **Romsdal** and **Nordmøre**, of which the main centres are Ålesund, Molde and Kristiansund.

Sea trade has always been important and, from the Middle Ages, the accolade for a settlement was to be given *kaupang* (market) status. At that time there were just two: Borgundkaupangen, 5 km (3 miles) from the centre of Ålesund, in Sunnmøre; and Veøykaupangen, in Romsdal. Both were centres for north–south and east–west trade routes on sea and land. Today buses 13, 14, 24 and others marked Møre from Ålesund will take you to the **Sunnmøre Museum** (Open Air Museum and Coastal Heritage Site, Borgundkaupangen and Medieval Age Museum; varying opening hours; common entrance fee; tel: 70 17 40 00).

Rare harmony

Ålesund ❶ is Norway's largest fishing town but best known for its Art Nouveau architecture, built in 1904 after a great fire which destroyed the centre and which gave rise to the Norwegian saying: "I've never heard anything like it since Ålesund burnt down."

First to the rescue came the Norvegophile, Kaiser Wilhelm II of Germany, who sent four ships laden with supplies and building materials (the stained-glass windows in the gable end of the **church** were an inauguration gift from the Kaiser). With help and donations from all over Europe, the people of Ålesund completed the rebuilding of their town by 1907 in the now carefully preserved Art Nouveau style. **Ålesund Museum** (open all year; entrance fee; tel: 70 12 31 70) features exhibitions on the 1904 fire and subsequent rebuilding.

Towers, turrets and medieval-romantic frontages, often with more than a trace of Nordic mythology, give the town a harmony which extends to the painted wooden warehouses along **Brosundet**, the deep inlet of the inner harbour. Until the 1950s, Ålesund was a

PRECEDING PAGES: around Olden. **LEFT:** looking down into Geirangerfjorden. **BELOW:** Art Nouveau detail on a door in Ålesund.

Hauling the catch aboard just off the island of Rundøy.

veritable gold mine for fish, fishermen and their boats, and *klippfisk* (traditional Norwegian split, dried cod). But as fishing changed so did Ålesund, which added fish processing and fish farming. Many former warehouses are now offices and restaurants, pleasant places to try out one of the more unlikely local specialities. These include bacalao, a dish created in Portugal from Kristiansund's export of *klippfisk*, and the more traditional brennsnute, a potato and meat stew.

From the top of the 418 steps up **Aksla** hill in the centre of the town – if the climb doesn't leave you breathless, the view certainly will – you can see over several islands, now all linked by 12 km (8 miles) of deep underground tunnels. With great practicality, the builders used the rock from the tunnels to extend the airport on the nearby island of **Vigra**.

Every book and brochure that describes the county's thousands of islands shows similar happy pictures of people in, on or under the sea, and anglers with magnificent catches. There are sea caves, tunnels and bird cliffs, little harbours, campsites, clean, white beaches and *hytter* (holiday lodges) to rent. Some have relics of the Vikings, many have summer festivals. What these sea islands have to offer is almost unlimited: the difficulty is which to choose.

Bird island

The island of **Runde ❷**, 67 km (42 miles) southwest of Ålesund, is not to be missed. Runde attracts professional and amateur naturalists from all over the world. More than 200 bird species have been recorded but this small island is best known for breeding birds, which line the cliffs in their hundreds of thousands. When they fly, it looks as if a gigantic swarm of insects has darkened the sky. One of the best ways of seeing the island is by taking a four-hour tour on board the *Charming*

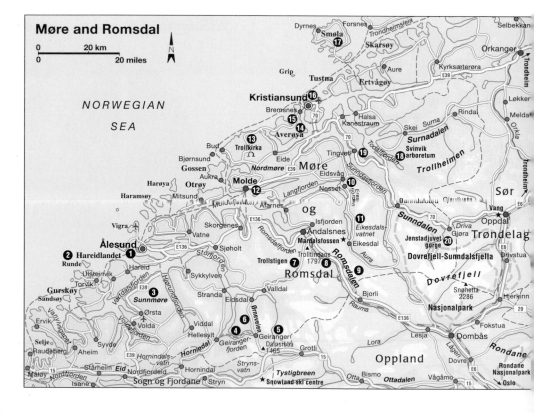

Ruth, which departs from Ulsteinvik harbour daily from June to August. As a bonus, in the waters round the island are interesting wrecks; not so long ago divers found a cache of gold from a Dutch ship, *Ackerendam*. An express boat/bus connection that takes 2½ hours leaves from Ålesund at 8.30am weekdays.

Map on page 278

Gateway to the Geirangerfjord

South from Ålesund between the Vartdalsfjorden and the Hjørundfjorden, the **Sunnmøre mountains ❸** plunge straight into the fjord near Ørsta, one of the early targets for the many British climbers who first made Norway's mountains known to the world.

One way of sampling the full range of Norwegian cuisine is to visit Ålesund in August, when it plays host to the annual Den Norske Matfestivalen (Food Festival; tel: 70 15 76 25).

Ålesund is also the main entrance to **Storfjorden**, where the cruise ships turn in to reach their goal of **Geirangerfjorden ❹**, claimed by many to be Norway's most beautiful fjord. One road (No. 60) to Geiranger goes through Stranda, main town of inner Storfjorden, another (No. 1) via Ørsta, both ending at **Hellesylt**. From there you can travel to the inner end of Geirangerfjorden by boat or, in summer, there is a path along the fjord's high southern wall.

In this most secret of fjords far from the sea, great waterfalls tumble hundreds of metres in such delicate cascades that they are given names – **De Syv Søstre** (The Seven Sisters) and the **Brudesløret** (Bridal Veil). Lofty mountains reflected in the mirror-still water give the fjord a gentle grandeur and, in some places, farms cling to unlikely pockets of green. A small landing stage or two indicate that people climb up and down to these distant farms.

The spectacle is much too beautiful to miss and everyone stays on deck until the boat reaches **Geiranger ❺** village, which huddles under the half circle of moun-

BELOW: the coastal town of Ålesund seems to float on the water.

tains. Half-way up the winding road behind the village is the appropriately named **Hotel Utsikten Bellevue**, which must have one of the best views in Norway, and further on the road passes by **Dalsnibba**, the highest peak in Sunnmøre.

For keen walkers, instead of taking the road down Trollstigen to Åndalsnes it is now possible to follow the well marked Kløvstien, the old mountain track that was the only way through the mountains before the road.

Along the troll road

Heading north once more (along Road 63) towards Åndalsnes, the first stretch to Eidsdal on the Norddalsfjord is known as the **Ørneveien** ❻ (Eagle's Road), and it is not difficult to see why as it winds ahead to **Ørnesvingen**, another vantage point. Over the fjord is the start of an even more spectacular road across the **Gudbrandsjuvet** gorge. Mountains rise into the distance to the west, until you reach the top of **Trollstigen** ❼ (the Trolls' Ladder or Trolls' Causeway). This is the heart of inner Romsdal. To the east is **Trolltindane**, around 1,800 metres (6,000 ft), and this fascinating mountain range can be admired before or after the journey on Trollstigen. From vast amounts of snow up here (even in July) it is only a short but exciting 15-minute journey down through 11 gigantic bends hewn out of solid rock into the green valley towards Åndalsnes.

Åndalsnes is known as "the village between fjell and fjord". It sits on a promontory in a circle of fjord and mountain, looking up to tops that challenge climbers of every nationality. They arrive by the score to tackle **Trollveggen**, part of craggy **Trolltindane** ❽, which rises almost vertically from Romsdalen in the east, to its summit bowl of permanent snow. Trollveggen itself has more than 1,000 metres (3,300 ft) of vertical and overhanging rock, first climbed in 1965. New routes are still being discovered. By less hazardous paths, the climb up Trolltindane takes around four hours and requires boots and strong clothing.

Åndalsnes is the terminus for the train from Oslo through **Romsdalen** ❾,

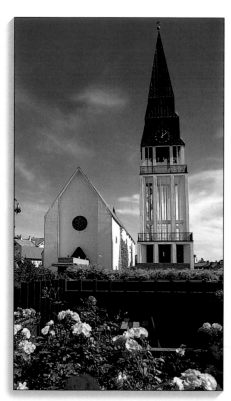

BELOW: Molde, the city of roses.

which brings enough visitors each year to double or treble the population. A 19th-century British traveller, Lady Beauclerk, described Romsdalen as "precipitous, grey rocks ending in points apparently as sharp as needles... emerging into the sunniest, and the most lovely little spot... sheltered from every wind by the snowcapped mountains that surrounded it, while a most tempting river ran through the dale". It is as true today as it was then.

Famous climbers

The pleasant valley was the base camp for early climbers such as William Slingsby and Johannes Vigdal who, in 1881, made the first ascent of **Store Vengetind**. In the same year, another early pioneer, Carl Hall, made the second ascent with two local climbers to the sharp point of **Romdalshornet**. It had first been conquered 50 years before by two local farmers.

To cater for all this early interest, a local police sergeant, Anders Landmark, opened a simple wooden inn at **Aak**, regarded as Norway's first tourist hotel, and many of Europe's mountain addicts stayed there. Some 5 km (3 miles) into the valley from Åndalsnes, it has recently reopened as a mountain sports centre, with summer courses in climbing and scrambling and, in winter, instruction in ice climbing and mountain (or Telemark) skiing. Rafting and canoeing are also good possibilities on the Rauma river, one of Nor-

Map on page 278

way's well-known fishing rivers, which runs through the valley. But it is not necessary to be a rock climber to get high into these mountains. Most have easy alternative routes, and roads reach more than 850 metres (2,800 ft).

Back to the coast

Proceeding back towards the coast and Molde along Road 64, it is worth taking a detour into Langfjorden until you reach **Nesset** ❿ on Eresfjorden, deep into the mountains. Norway's prominent 19th-century writer and patriot Bjørnstjerne Bjørnson, who had a summer home in the area, described the Nesset mountains: "some standing white, others standing blue, with jagged, competing, agitating peaks, some marching along in ranking row."

The view today from the ferry along the **Eikesdalsvatnet** ⓫ shows you what he meant. The mountain peaks rise abruptly out of the fjord sides, and you get a glimpse of **Mardalsfossen**, Northern Europe's highest waterfall at over 650 metres (2,000 ft) high. In the 1970s, hundreds of people chained themselves together near the waterfall, to prevent the building of a hydro-electric power station. It became a hot political issue and, though they did not win the final battle, the protesters ensured that the summer falls still exist. The struggle also brought the unexpected gift of making Nesset famous and encouraging climbers and other visitors.

Molde ⓬ is part of an archipelago sheltered from the Norwegian Sea; its mild climate, green vegetation and rose gardens earn it the title "Town of Roses". The statue of the Little Rose Seller stands in the marketplace. Stalls sell everything from fruit and flowers to clothes and, of course, roses. This modern and easy-going town was almost entirely rebuilt after German bombing in World War II. It is an excellent base for touring the fjords by boat or car. From **Varden**, Molde's best

BELOW: transporting hay the traditional way on a mountain farm in Romsdal.

When rough weather comes in from the west, the coastal Atlanterhavsveien (Atlantic Road) lives up to its name.

vantage point, you look over fjord and island to the snowcaps of the Sunnmøre mountains – townspeople claim you can see 87 peaks – and half an hour away to the north are small fishing villages which brave the worst of the west winds.

Molde has the inevitable outdoor museum, the **Romsdalsmuseet** (open mid-June–mid-Aug, hours vary; entrance fee; tel: 71 20 24 60), which includes the Hjertøya Fishery Museum – in a particularly beautiful spot where the timber houses, national costumes and folk dancing seem to fit in with the landscape. The museum's collection of *bunads* (national costumes), showing the fine details of shawl, head dress, bodice, jewellery and embroidered purse, is one of the most appealing. The Fishery Museum (open mid-June–mid-Aug), 10 minutes by boat from the marketplace, is in the form of a small fishing village from the 1850s.

Yet there is little that is traditional about Molde's entertainment. The modern stadium is well used, with an all-year football ground located, spectacularly, by the sea, and the streets are often full of musicians, particularly during the famous **Molde International Jazz Festival** (mid-July; tel: 71 20 31 50).

Another fine route is to take Roads 64 and 664 from Molde to the 16th-century village of **Bud**, right on the west coast. Here a boat trip goes to the old fishing-station of **Bjørnsund**, now only inhabited in the summer. Before Bud, a walk from Road 64, reveals **Trollkirka ⓭** (Troll Church) – a cave, some 70 metres (230 ft) long, divided into three sections, with a great waterfall tumbling down from the upper opening into a white marble basin in the mountains.

Travelling the Atlantic Road

BELOW: the harbour at Torvik on the island of Averøya.

From Bud a small coastal road leads back to Road 64 and the **Atlanterhavsveien** (Atlantic Road) to Kristiansund, over **Averøya ⓮**, the biggest island

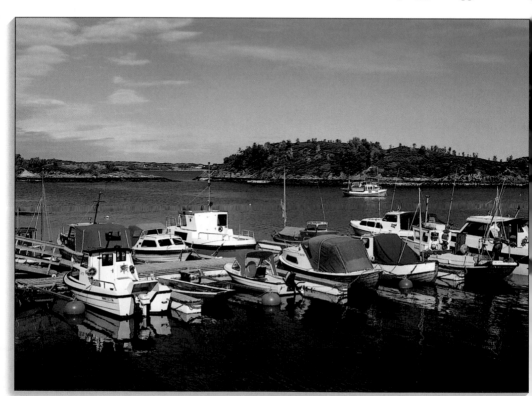

Map on page 278

in the area. As this road heads north across the rim of the ocean, it's a bit like driving on the sea itself. Averøya deserves more than the view from a car window.

Archaeologists believe that this was one of the first places to be settled after the last Ice Age, and their finds in 1909 are remnants of the early **Fosna Culture** that existed around 7000 BC. ("Fosna" was the original name of Kristiansund.) One of the best ways to get around is a 50-km (30-mile) tour which varies from seaward skerries and small islands linked by bridge or causeway, to hills around 500 metres (1,600 ft) high. There is a fine stave church at **Kvernes** (open July–Aug 10am–5pm; entrance fee) with an unusually richly decorated mid-17th century interior.

Near **Bremsnes** ⓯, on the northeastern tip of Averøya, is the Viking **Horgsteinen** (Stone of Horg), where the victor of Hafrsfjord, Harald Hårfagre, had his famous hair cut and washed, having fulfilled his vow not to touch it until Norway was united. It is just 15 minutes by ferry from Bremsnes to Kristiansund.

The *klippfisk* capital

Unlike Ålesund and Molde, **Kristiansund** ⓰ has little protection from the worst the North Atlantic can do. It is right on the coast, with weather-beaten rocks pounded by the sea, yet not far inland are grassy areas and small woods. This is the *klippfisk* town, for long the biggest exporter of Norwegian dried cod. There are only 17,000 inhabitants but, because of the centuries-old links with other countries thanks to its sailors and fishermen, and the foreign merchants who settled here, the atmosphere is quite cosmopolitan.

Like most Norwegian towns with "Kristian" in their title, Kristiansund was named after a Danish King, Christian VI, who gave it town status in 1742. A

BELOW: the Vågen Kystkultur Museum (Coastal Culture Centre) on the waterfront at Vågen, Kristiansund.

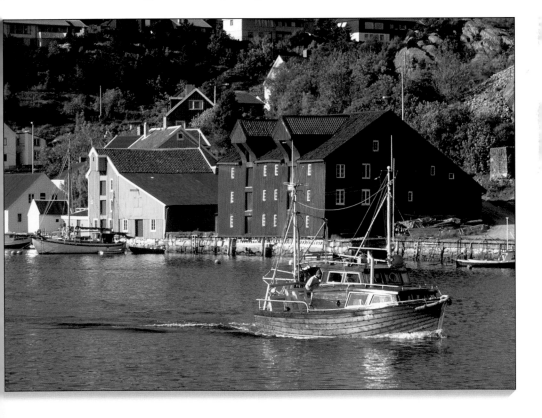

A Country Afloat

To the world, Norway and seafaring are synonymous; the very word Viking means "Men of the Bays". From the age of sail until after World War II, the Norwegian merchant fleet was one of the world's largest, and Norwegian could be heard in ports worldwide.

Among the country's most popular museums by far are the Sjøfartsmuseum (Maritime Museum) on the Bygdøy peninsula in Oslo, along with the Vikingskipshuset (Viking Ship Museum), with magnificently preserved long ships, the Kon-Tiki Museum, with the rafts used by ethnographic explorer Thor Heyerdahl, and the Frammuseet (Fram Museum), built around the sturdy vessel that carried Fridtjof Nansen and Roald Amundsen on their heroic polar explorations.

Norwegians seem happiest when they are in, on or around the sea. Each year, over a third of the population spend their summer holidays partly or completely in craft that range from small dinghies to large motor launches and ocean-going yachts. Even the most conservative estimates place the number of pleasure craft in Norway at 650,000, about one for every seven Norwegians. The sea is a natural part of life.

Geography and topography are the deciding factors. There are thousands upon thousands of islands, and the fjords and coastal archipelagos are a paradise for competitive and recreational sailors, king and commoner alike.

King Olav V, the father of the present King Harald, was, in his day, the country's foremost sailor in more than name only. He won a Gold Medal in sailing in the 1928 Olympics, making him the world's only Olympic medallist monarch. He also won medals in the Sailing World Championships in 1971 and 1976.

In founding its first sailing club in 1868 in Tønsberg, then a major merchant fleet port, Norway triggered a long latent urge. In 1883 the Royal Norwegian Sailing Association was formed in the capital, and in 1900 sailing became an Olympic sport. Norwegians were a major force in Olympic and championship sailing and in regattas worldwide.

By chance, Norway's leading position in international sailing coincides approximately with the country's yacht production. In the days of wooden yachts, Norwegian yards and naval architects were among the world's best, and one in particular stands out: born in the port of Larvik, Colin Archer (1832–1921) grew up with boats and at an early age started building craft to his own design. Among his best known are the stable, sturdy rescue schooners that bear his name and the three-masted Arctic exploration vessel *Fram*, built in 1892. The tradition of boat building continues to this day, albeit somewhat altered: fibre-glass hulls and masts changed the picture completely. Nowadays, Norway exports motor cruisers and imports yachts.

Wherever there's water, there are all manner of motor and sailing craft. Small boat harbours in and near major cities, particularly Oslo, Kristiansand, Ålesund, Stavanger and Bergen, never fail to impress visitors by the numbers and types of crafts lying there. From wind-surfing in fjords to major regattas, Norwegians love being on the water. ❑

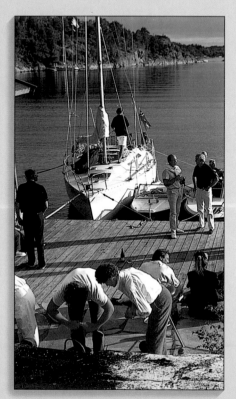

LEFT: relaxing after a day's sailing.

good introduction is by *sundbåtene*, the harbour boats which for more than 100 years have linked the town's islands. **Mellemverftet** (open Mon–Fri 8am–7pm; tel: 71 67 71 95) once one of four shipyards in **Vågen**, is working again as a centre for preserving the craft of ship-building, carefully restoring the beautiful lines of traditional Norwegian boats.

Kristiansund consists of three islands. One of them is **Innlandet**, the oldest preserved part of the town with its first customs house (1660–1748), hospital, school and other buildings which are being restored. Walk to the **Sjursvika** on the east side for a look at the old warehouses. These interesting parts of the harbour are being amalgamated into a coastal culture centre, to tell the history of the maritime people of old, alongside harbour life that continues today.

The **Nordmøre Museum** (open Tues–Fri 10am–2pm, Sun noon–3pm; entrance fee; tel: 71 67 15 78) includes archaeological finds from the Fosna culture and the history of *klippfisk* processing. But the town's oddest monuments are the tall pointed natural stones, tributes to town dignitaries: Bäck-strøm, who built the reservoirs, Brinchman, the provider of the water supply, Bræin, the musical founder of a musical family, which gave birth to an annual Opera Festival, and Hanson, the polar explorer.

"Fishwife", next to the harbour in Kristiansund.

Kristiansund's main church was destroyed by bombing in 1940. The architect responsible for its replacement named his creation "Rock Crystal in Roses", and whether you love it or loathe it, you cannot ignore this stark, white building. Inside **Atlanterhavskatedralen** (Atlantic Ocean's Cathedral; open all year), the choir wall is a 30-metre (100-ft) sweep of 320 stained-glass panels which at the foot symbolise the heavy, dark colours of the earth soaring up to eternal light.

BELOW: fishing for trout or salmon is a popular pastime in the country.

Island excursions

An entirely different church stands on the island of **Grip**, northwest from Kristiansund. The island has a long and eventful history of flood and storm, and the islanders often took refuge in the small church. In 1796, a nor'wester tore down and washed away 100 houses and, when the same thing happened seven years later, the pastor recorded the piteous prayer: "Almighty God, spare us further destruction and misery". Whether it was that plea or not, the ancient little red stave church survived, only 8 metres (25 ft) above the sea. Once 400 souls lived on Grip, scraping a living from fish: today people live there only in summer when it metamorphoses into a holiday island and makes a popular excursion from the town. A wedding in the 15th-century church is a very special occasion.

To the north and northeast of Kristiansund, the last big island is **Smøla ⓱**, at the mouth of the Trond-heimfjord, where the county ends in a gaggle of islands which retain something of the life of the old farmer-fishermen.

Sanden is one of several buildings that form Smøla's scattered museum, with the main 18th-century building, warehouses, barn and a store house on wooden pillars, just as it was when the last owners left a few years ago. A number of these old fishing grounds where cod was split, salted and dried on the rocks are now marinas with simple accommodation,

Map on page 278

seafood menus, and the atmosphere of earlier days. The idyllic island of **Kuli** off Smøla is rich in relics, the most famous being the Kuli stone. On this stone the name Norway is mentioned for the first time in an inscription which dates to the first years after the coming of Christianity.

Land of the trolls

Inland, the northern part of the county ends in a criss-cross of fjords eating into the islands and peninsulas which lead to **Trollheimen**, the "Home of the Trolls", where the mountains reach nearly 1,600 metres (5,000 ft). This haunt of climbers and skiers is bounded by two important valleys, **Surnadalen** and **Sunndalen**, with between them the tiny **Todalfjorden**. Beside the last is the surprise of the **Svinvik Arboret** ⓱ (Arboretum; open May–Sept; entrance fee; tel: 71 66 35 80), beautiful gardens with thousands of plants, including rhododendrons and conifers. Despite the northern latitude, plants from all over the world grow at Svinvik, owned and run today by the University of Trondheim.

On the way to Sunndalen along Road 70 from Kristiansund, you come to **Tingvoll** ⓲, which has Nordmøre's oldest church, popularly known as the **Nordmøresdomen** (Nordmøre Cathedral; open June–Aug; entrance fee), in an area with a large selection of churches from different centuries and styles. The Tingvoll church is believed to date from the 12th century; it's a well preserved granite and brick structure surrounded by a stone wall with an arched entrance way.

Sunndalen is deep in the Nordmøre wilderness, with narrow valleys between the mountain ranges forming sheltered farming country which supplies grain for most of the county. At the end of the fjord lies the industrial town of Sunndalsøra, once a mecca for the British "Salmon Lords": the **Leikvin Kulturminnepark** (Heritage Park; open May–Oct; entrance fee) at Grøa records their privileged position in society up to the end of the 19th century. The river Driva debouches into the fjord and the surrounding mountains are of breathtaking beauty – a magnificent area for walking and skiing as well as fishing.

Road 70 follows the course of the valley to Oppdal on the third side of Trollheimen. On foot, there are more energetic routes over the mountains, with a mountain centre in Innerdalen and ski lifts as well. The **River Driva** is one of the most famous in a country of good salmon and trout rivers. Between the head of Sunndalen and Grødalen, next-door at Åmotan, the spectacular **Jenstadjuvet** ⓴ (gorge) is the place where five valleys and their watercourses meet in two furious waterfalls. Grødalen has an oddity in **Alfheim**, a small hunting lodge from 1876 built in Scottish Highland style by a Scot, Lady Arbuthnott, who became something of the "laird" of the valley. Her old farm at Elverhøy is now the **Sunndal Museum** (open June–Aug; entrance fee; tel: 71 69 61 80).

To the north, Surnadal has another good salmon river, the **Surna**; side valleys lead up to the heart of Trollheimen, and to signposted trails from mountain hut to mountain hut, in what seems like the top of the world. At valley level, the road through Surnadal is the inland route out of West Norway, straight on to the city of Trondheim, the gateway to the north. ❏

BELOW: in autumn, mountains and forests are bright with berries.
RIGHT: De Syv Søstre (Seven Sisters), Geirangerfjorden.

TRONDHEIM

Map on page 292

Although the city has lost its political role, to many Norwegians it remains the country's historical, cultural and religious capital, and is host to the annual celebrations of its patron saint, St Olav

A thousand years ago, Trondheim, then Nidaros, was the capital of Norway, and the resting place of King Olav Haraldson. Founded in 997 by King Olav Tryggvason, a reminder of Trondheim's early days and of the old harbour is provided by the **wharves** and the narrow streets *(veitene)* which run between the wooden buildings. Though they date back only to the 18th century, these coloured warehouses echo the architecture of medieval times, and it is not too difficult to feel what the atmosphere must have been like around that busy harbour when fish and timber dominated the city.

Today, Trondheim is the home of SINTEF, Scandinavia's largest foundation for scientific and industrial research, and is at the forefront of Norwegian education and church affairs. Not far from SINTEF is the Norwegian University of Science and Technology (NTNU), the country's second largest university. The city has been a scientific centre since the 18th century – the **university museum**, from 1760, is Norway's oldest scientific institution – and today both SINTEF and the university attract high-tech businesses to Trondheim, with the advantage of being able to turn to the research establishments for help.

Modern though it may be, Trondheim has retained much of the charm of the past, with the heart of the old city lying on what is virtually an island between the **Nidelva** river and **Trondheimsfjorden**, joined only by a narrow neck of land to the west, once the western fort. One building that unites past and present is the **Nordenfjeldske Kunstindustrimuseum** (National Museum of Applied Art; open all year; entrance fee; tel: 73 80 89 50) on Munkegata.

Saint and martyr

Though King Olav Tryggvason had attempted to introduce Christianity to Norway in the late 10th century, many Norwegians still clung to their pagan gods, and it was only after the death of his successor, Olav Haraldson, at the Battle of Stiklestad some 30 years later *(see page 297)* that Christianity acquired a focal point in Norway. Olav's men buried him in sandy ground near the river but when miracles began to happen he was moved to the town's only church. Then, according to the sagas, a spring began to flow near his first grave and "men were healed of their ills by the waters". The king was declared a saint and martyr in 1164.

His nephew, Olav Kyrre, built the great stone church over the place where the saint's body had lain; which is now **Nidarosdomen** (Cathedral; open all year; to book tours tel: 73 53 91 60; entrance fee includes entrance to Archbishop's Palace), which is Trondheim's finest building. Once again, the saint's body was moved and the cathedral became a place of pilgrimage. For centuries, pilgrims came from the south

PRECEDING PAGES: Trøndelag countryside in autumn.
LEFT: gutting the catch.
BELOW: looking out over the city to Trondheimsfjorden.

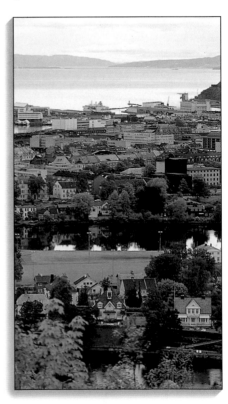

of Norway, from Sweden and Finland, and from Iceland, the Faroe Islands and Greenland to pay homage to St Olav. When the Reformation came to Norway in 1537, the cult of the ancient relic was abolished and pilgrimages ceased. From mid-June to mid-August, a special musical evening Mass is held for visitors.

Trondheim is the site of the world's first bicycle lift, "Trampe", built on Brubakken hill in 1995. It operates like a ski tow. Cyclists pay using keycards at the bottom and are pulled 130 metres (430 ft) to the top.

Royal tradition

Until the Reformation, Nidaros Cathedral was the seat of the archbishop, and the setting for the coronation of Norwegian monarchs, a tradition revived after 1814, when Norway shrugged off its 400 years of Danish rule and united with Sweden. In 1991 King Harald V was crowned in Nidaros Cathedral. The **crown jewels** are on display in a side chapel (open June–Aug Mon–Fri 9am–6pm, Sat 9am–2pm, Sun 1–4pm; Aug–June times vary).

The **great arched nave** is in a Gothic style and, looking back to the west end, the most striking feature is the brilliant stained-glass **rose window** above the main entrance, the work of Gabriel Kjelland in 1930. Both inside and out are many statues of saints and monarchs; but the beautiful interior lines of the cathedral, built in a green-grey soapstone, are its finest feature.

Next door to the Cathedral is Scandinavia's oldest secular building, once the **Erkebispegården Ⓓ** (Archbishop's Palace; open mid-June–mid-Aug Mon–Fri 10am–5pm, Sat 10am–3pm, Sun noon–5pm; mid-Aug–mid-June times vary; entrance fee). In 1222, Archbishop Guttorm was empowered by King Håkon Håkonsson to mint and circulate coins, a privilege which his successors exercised until 1537 and the Reformation. Their mint was uncovered in the 1990s and is one of the highlights of the palace. The building was at one time a military establishment, and the **Rustkammeret** (Army Museum; open June–Aug

Mon–Fri 9am–3pm, Sat–Sun 11am–4pm; entrance fee) includes exhibits on World War II and the resistance movement. Nearby is **Waisenhuset**, a beautiful timber building dating from 1772.

All around the original medieval city are the remains of fortifications, which were reinforced or built in the late 17th century by a military architect from Luxemburg, General Johan Caspar de Cicignon, after the great fire of 1681 devastated most of medieval Trondheim.

From the cathedral area it is just a short walk to **Gamle Bybrua ⓔ** (Old Town Bridge) also erected after 1681 when de Cicignon was constructing **Kristiansten festning ⓕ** (Kristiansten Fort) on a hill to the east, at that time outside the city proper. The first bridge had a sentry box and excise house at either end and the western building still remains, now used as a kindergarten. The present bridge and gates were built in 1861. The local tourist office (tel: 73 80 76 60) organises guided tours to these sites.

View over the city

Kristiansten Fort, now part of the city, provides one of the best views of Trondheim. From here you can see the old stone walls of the 13th-century **Vår Frues Kirke ⓖ** (Church of Our Lady; open Wed 11am–2pm, concerts held Sat 2pm from June–Aug) and **Stiftsgården ⓗ** (open June–Aug Mon–Sat 10am–5pm, Sun noon–5pm; entrance fee), on **Munkegata**, Scandinavia's largest timber mansion. Stiftsgården was built as a private house in the 1770s and today serves as the official residence of the Norwegian Royal Family when visiting the city.

Northeast from the bustling harbour of the **Ravnkloa ⓘ** at the northern end of Munkegata, and past the ornate railway station, is **Fosenkaia**, where sight-

Map on page 292

Gamle Bybrua (Old Town Bridge) offers good views of the warehouses along Kjøpmannsgate.

BELOW: colourful old buildings along Trondheim's waterfront.

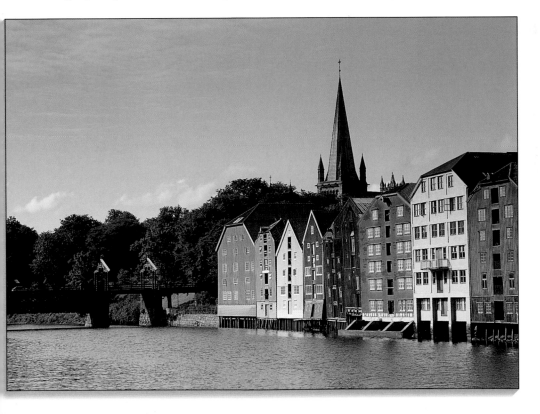

seeing and other boats tie up. At midday, the Hurtigrute coastal express (see page 261) will be lying at one of the two main quays, with a half-day to spend in Trondheim before it heads north. Returning south on a summer evening, the ship is outlined against the light as its passengers make an excursion to see the midnight sun from the summit of **Mount Storsteinen**. The remains of Trondheim's old defences, **Skansen**, lie to the west where the city gate once stood. Skansen is now a park. Also near the harbour is a curious warehouse built out on iron stilts over the sea; its shape is explained by the fact that it was a World War II U-boat bunker when German forces occupied the city.

Well out into the fjord is the islet of **Munkholmen** ❿ (hourly ferry from Ravnkloa; open late May–Aug; entrance fee) where Benedictine monks built a monastery very early in the 11th century, one of the first two monasteries in Norway. Even earlier this had been Trondheim's execution ground and in 1658 it became a prison fort. You can make a tour of the fort and the island offers good sea bathing and a restaurant.

St Olav, who introduced Christianity to the Vikings.

BELOW: a good way to get around the city in the snow is by *sparkstotting* (kick-sledge).

Walking around

Trondheim is an easy walking city where many people still live in the centre. Two places best toured on foot are **Hospitalsløkka** ⓚ, the area around the old Trondheim Hospital, and **Bakklandet** ⓛ, on the eastern side of the Nidelva, not far from the old town bridge and opposite the riverside warehouses.

In the grounds of the hospital, which was founded in 1277 and is Scandinavia's oldest surviving hospital, lies the first **octagonal timber church** (1705) to be built in Norway. The surrounding area (løkka) is full of old timber houses, lovingly restored by their present owners. Bakklandet is another area of old wooden houses, and was originally the working-class section of the town. It and the Mollenberg and Rosenborg districts have been restored to form complete communities of houses and shops.

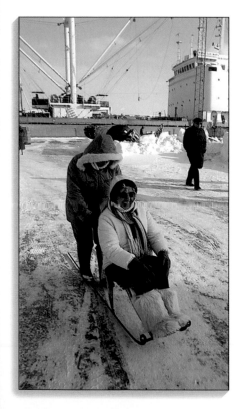

Looking into the past

For an understanding of the past of this ancient area of Trøndelag, two museums are invaluable. At the **Vitenskapsmuseet** ⓜ (Museum of Natural History and Archaeology; open May–Sept Mon–Fri 9am–4pm, Sat–Sun 11am–4pm; Sept–Apr Tues–Fri 9am–2pm, Sat–Sun noon–4pm; entrance fee) the main exhibits trace the history of the area up to the Middle Ages, and the development of church art from the 13th to the 18th century. There is also a display covering Trøndelag flora and fauna. **Sjøfartsmuseet** ⓝ (Maritime Museum; open June–Aug 10am–4pm; entrance fee), situated in an old penitentiary from 1725, covers shipping, fishing and whaling.

Trøndelag Folkemuseet (bus 8 or 9 from Dronningensgate; open June–Aug daily 11am–6pm; Sept–May Mon–Fri 11am–3pm, Sat–Sun noon–4pm; entrance fee) in Sverresborg, on the west side of the city, looks at life in days gone by. Here, more than 60 reconstructed buildings from the Trondheim area are centred round a market square, including a post office and dentist's surgery. There is a stave church dating from 1170 and exhibits of old trades and crafts, such as *passementerie* (the making of trimmings and lace for women's Sunday best). Within the museum are the remains of King Sverre's palace, **Zion**, from around 1180, and the 18th-century tavern has a good restaurant. There is also a Ski Museum.

Trondheim also has Norway's oldest theatre building, **Trøndelag Teater**, in the centre of the old town, as well as **Teater Avant Garden**. Other arts are represented by galleries and institutions such as the **Kunstforeningengallerei Ⓞ** (Academy of Art; open June–Aug Mon–Fri 10am–4pm; entrance fee; tel: 73 52 66 71), showing and selling contemporary paintings.

Of great interest is the **Ringve Museum** (Museum of Musical History, **Ringve Ⓟ**; buses 3 and 4 from Munkegaten; opening hours vary; entrance fee; tel: 73 87 02 80). The museum is in an ancient manor. A permanent exhibition opened in 1999 in the former barn. Here, light and sound guides you through various historic stations, such as "the invention of the piano" or "pop and rock". Since the late 19th century, it belonged to the Bache family. In 1946, the last representative, Christian Anker Bache, died and his widow, Russian-born "Madame Victoria", worked steadily to build up the couple's collection of musical instruments from all over the world. Her persuasiveness in prising relics from many countries is legendary and when the museum opened in 1952 the collection had grown magnificently. Almost all the instruments are played by the music-student guides during the tour. In addition to the more formal, classical instruments, there are examples of music boxes, old folk instruments such as the *langeleik*, a sort of Norwegian zither, and clay flutes shaped like birds and soldiers.

Just before her death in 1962, Madame Victoria opened the museum's concert hall, which seats 270; it was built into the old cow sheds and is used for more

The Ravnkloa clock by the fish market.

BELOW: Trondheim is a major stop for the Hurtigruten coastal steamers.

Map
on page
292

TIP

For a bird's-eye view of the city from the 120-metre (400-ft) telecommunications Tyholttårnet (tower; open all year; entrance fee) take buses 20 or 60. There is also a revolving restaurant.

BELOW: an old view of Stiklestad by Johannes Flintoe for an 1839 edition of the *Norse Sagas*.

formal musical occasions. After the museum, leave time for a stroll around the **Ringve Botaniske Hage** (Botanic Gardens; open every day), just next door, the most northerly botanical garden in the world.

Outdoor life

Trondheim's back garden is **Bymarka** to the west, where Gråkallen (Old Man) at some 520 metres (1,700 ft) is the city's favourite skiing area. In summer, it is a good spot for walking. Its counterpart to the east is **Estenstadmarka**.

Fishing is good in the River Nidelva, which is renowned for the size of its salmon. The Gaula to the south is another fine fishing river, while the fjord itself is ideal for sea-fishing from boat or shore.

As well as the hourly boats to Munksholmen, in summer the tourist office runs 1½-hour tours of Trondheim from the sea, which leave from Ravnkloa at 2pm; there is also a two-hour tour of Trondheim, which takes in a number of sites and museums, departing daily at noon next to the Tourist Information Office. You can also visit the ancient manor of **Austråtborgen** (open May–Aug; entrance fee) at Ørland on Trondheimsfjorden. Another idea is to take a short leg of the Hurtigrute and return by coach or train. Alternatively, you can travel southeast to the **Strikkemuseum** (Knitting Museum; open all year; entrance fee) at Selbu, which shows the history of the famous Selbu knitwear from 1853. Road 705 to Selbu features a particularly scenic route marketed as **Ferieveien** ("holiday road").

For most people Trondheim means history and culture. Like the pilgrims of old, visitors come to see the cathedral, the Archbishop's Palace and de Cicignon's 17th-century city, and for historical events such as the annual 10-day **St Olav festival** at the end of July *(see opposite page)*. ❑

Stiklestad

Stiklestad is a name that is revered by Norwegians. A momentous battle on this site in 1030, at which King Olav - Haraldson died at the hands of King Canute, was a turning point in Norwegian history. For Stiklestad, 100 km (60 miles) north of Trondheim, saw the foundation of Norwegian national unity and the adoption of the Christian faith. A church marks the spot where Olav died.

In the 11th century Norway was a country constantly disrupted by disputes between rival chieftains, and Olav's ambition was a united Norway. He also aimed to create a Christian country with Christian laws and churches and clergy.

He was not the first to attempt this. In the previous century Olav Tryggvason (a descendant of Harald Hårfagre) had been converted to Christianity in England and confirmed by the Bishop of Winchester. He returned to his native land in 995 with the express purpose of crushing the chieftains and imposing his new-found faith. But Olav Tryggvason's conversion had not swept away all his Viking instincts and in his religious zeal he used great cruelty to convert the populace. As a result, he fell in the Battle of Svolder in the year 1000, due to the defection of some disenchanted Norwegian chieftains.

Olav Haraldson was also a descendant of Harald Hårfagre and he ascended the throne in 1015. But, like his predecessor, Olav foolishly made too great a use of the sword to establish Christianity. The result was the same: with his eye on the Norwegian throne, King Canute of Denmark and England gave support to discontented factions within the country and in 1028 invaded Norway, forcing King Olav to flee to Russia.

Undaunted, King Olav returned with a few followers, but whatever loyalty he had once inspired had been lost through his ruthless methods. He died on 29 July 1030 at the Battle of Stiklestad. Olav's corpse was taken to the then capital, Nidaros (Trondheim) and buried on the banks of the river Nidelva.

When the body was disinterred a year later, it showed no signs of corruption: his face was unchanged and his nails and hair had grown, at that time taken as a sign of sanctity.

Following this revelation, Olav was proclaimed a saint and his body placed in a silver shrine in Nidaros Cathedral. Faith in the holiness of King Olav – or St Olav as he now was – spread and, until the Reformation, his shrine became a goal of Christian pilgrims.

Canute's triumph at the Battle of Stiklestad was brief. He ceded the reins of power to his son Svejn but, as the rumours of Olav's sanctity grew, support for Canute evaporated and Svejn was exiled to Denmark in 1035. All the while, St Olav's son, Magnus, had also been in exile, in Russia. Norway now invited Magnus to return and accept the crown.

Stiklestad has been a place of pilgrimage ever since. People still come at the end of July to commemorate the battle. Stiklestad has a beautiful open-air theatre, and on the anniversary of the battle, a cast of more than 300 actors, choristers, dancers and musicians reenact the events of July 1030. ❑

RIGHT: a statue of St Olav in front of the Stiklestad open-air theatre.

NORTH, INTO THE ARCTIC

Map on page 302

North of Trondheim lies a beautiful but often harsh landscape, caught between the warm sea and the mountains inland, and cutting across it an imaginary border into the vast expanse of the Arctic

The city of Trondheim is the gateway to the north. But anyone who looks for an immediate change in scenery will be disappointed. The first county north of Trondheim, Nord Trøndelag, has wide areas of rich agricultural land with prosperous-looking farms. Running right up the middle of the county is Norway's north to south jugular, the E6 highway, which lures drivers ever further north. But this is also rail country, and the Nordland railway follows much the same route. Just north of Trondheim, a branch line (with a companion road) reaches over the border into Sweden. It veers off at the small village of **Hell**, whose station must be one of the most photographed in the country and whose tickets are collectors' items. In September, Hell hosts an annual Blues Festival, which attracts international stars to this otherwise quiet settlement.

From a motorist's point of view, there is not a great deal of interest along this section of the E6 and the inclination is to keep going north; but make time for **Værnes ❶**, which has an interesting church from the Middle Ages with a fine baroque pulpit. Adjoining that is the **Stjørdal open-air museum** (open July–Aug Mon–Wed and Fri 10am–4pm, Sun noon–4pm; entrance fee; tel: 74 82 70 21). The **Frostatinghaugen rock carvings** at Frosta are the site of the first Norwegian legislative assembly (AD 600–1000) with rock carvings going back a further 3,500 years.

Some 6 km (4 miles) east of Stjørdalshalsen on the E14 is the **Falstad Museum** (open June–Aug; entrance fee; tel: 74 02 28 24) at Levanger. Located in the main building of Norway's only SS concentration camp, the museum includes two execution sites and a cenotaph in the Falstad forest. About 4 km (2½ miles) further on lies **Hegra Festning** (Fort; open May–Sept 10am–5pm; entrance fee). Built following independence, it was the site of several battles during World War II as well as a 25-day German siege. The fort has been restored and includes a Resistance museum.

St Olav's battleground

Just north of Verdalsøra is the road to **Stiklestad ❷**, the battleground where King Olav Haraldson was killed in 1030, and revered by Norwegians as the birthplace of Norwegian national unity *(see page 297)*. The **Nasjonale Kultursenter** (National Arts Centre; open all year; entrance fee; tel: 74 04 42 00) in Verdal produces an annual open-air play about St Olav (July), a spectacular dramatisation of the battle and Olav's death. The centre also has exhibitions about local natural and cultural history, and includes a Resistance museum, a folk museum and Stiklestad Church from 1180.

The first town of any size north of Trondheim is **Steinkjer**, which has been a centre of commerce for

PRECEDING PAGES: Arctic reflections. **LEFT:** the turbulent waters of the giant maelstrom south of Bodø. **BELOW:** a favourite subject for English-speaking photographers.

North, into the Arctic

0 20 km
0 20 miles

more than 1,000 years. Like so many northern Norwegian towns, Steinkjer was destroyed in World War II. After the German invasion in 1940, the king and government moved north, eventually to Tromsø, before they left to continue the government in exile from London. This meant that these sparsely populated northern areas suffered dreadful destruction through the bombing which followed the German invasion.

The Nord Trøndelag county museum has two branches near the town, one of which is sited in the former factory of **Dampsaga** (open all year; entrance fee) and features some works by the Norwegian painter Jacob Weidemann (born 1923), who also decorated Steinkjer church with murals and a beautiful stained-glass window.

North of Steinkjer it is worth branching off the E6 onto Road 763, which runs along the eastern side of Snåsavatnet (lake), to take a look at the impressive rock carvings near **Bøla** ❸ (open May–Oct). Of these, the best is the 6,000-year-old Bøla reindeer. The scenery around the lake is remarkably soft and gentle for a latitude between 63 and 64 degrees north, and at its northern end is **Snåsa**, the centre of South Sami (Lapp) culture. It has a Sami school and cultural centre which includes a museum (open June–Aug; entrance fee; tel: 74 15 14 90).

To the east, about 50 km (30 miles) away and close to Sweden, the **Gressåmoen Nasjonalpark** ❹ (National Park) contains an area of typically thick Trøndelag forest and mountain landscape.

Dotted throughout Norway – and particularly in the north – are small towns or villages which are essentially crossroads for many forms of transport. Typical is Grong, where the E6 runs north to south and the road and railway to Namsos, on the coast, goes off to the west, while just south of the town the secondary road No. 74 runs east through wild countryside to the Swedish frontier at Gåddede. It is also the junction of two rivers, the Namsen and the Sanddøla, both popular with anglers. Each river has an impressive waterfall not far from Grong: to the north, **Fiskumfossen ❺** on the Namsen and to the south, **Formofossen** on the Sandøla. You can learn all there is to know about salmon at the **Namsen Laksakvarium** (Aquarium; open June–Aug; entrance fee) at Fiskumfossen.

Map on page 302

Touched by the Gulf Stream

This is the beginning of the long valley of **Namdalen**, while to the northeast is **Røyrvik**, a huge mountainous area which stretches to the Swedish frontier. Half this region is above the tree line and there are three major lakes: Tunnsjøen, Limingen and Store Namsvatnet. The first has an island peak soaring to 820 metres (2,700 ft), and was once a Sami place of sacrifice to their gods.

Here the contrast between the east and west of Nord Trøndelag is very marked. The frontier mountains to the east, which bulge into Sweden, have a harsh beauty but much of the land is desolate and empty. To the west, the coastal scenery is a pleasant surprise, green and fertile. All year round, the Gulf Stream warms the western coast to the very north of Norway, making the climate much gentler at the same latitude than it is further inland and allowing the Hurtigruten (coastal steamers) to continue working even in the depths of winter.

The north end of Namdalen valley marks the border with the county of **Nordland**, the beginning of the real north. This border is straddled by the **Børgefjell Nasjonalpark ❻** (National Park), a district of high mountains, lakes and numerous watercourses, a backpacker's idyll for walking and to see nature.

In these northern territories, distances are long, and Nordland stretches 500 km (300 miles) north to Narvik. The Polarsirkel (Arctic Circle) runs through the middle and the county includes the long, narrow islands of Vesterålen, and

The Bøla reindeer.

BELOW: a picnic on the coast by the light of the midnight sun.

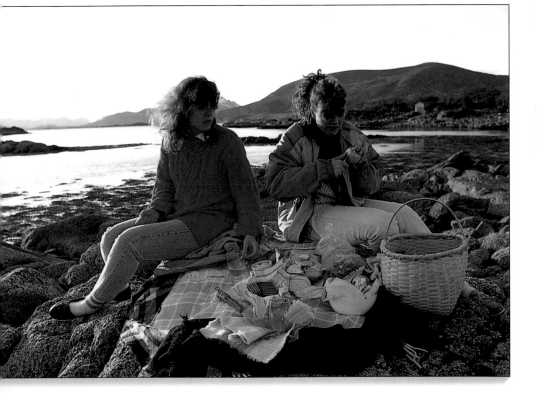

the grey peaks of the Lofoten Islands *(see The Far North, pages 315–18)*. Nordland has immense variety. If you take in all the fjords and islands, it contains a quarter of Norway's coastline, as well as mountains more than 1,900 metres (6,200 ft) high, countless islands and skerries, the second largest glacier in Norway, Svartisen, and the largest inland lake, Røssvatnet.

Near the Helgeland coast is **Bindalen** (valley), green with forests. At one time, the discovery of gold turned it into a mini-Klondike. Today, it has gone back to sleep. Close to Bindal is the mountain massif of **Tosenfjellet**, a favourite haunt of potholers and cavers. The biggest cave is **Etasjegrotten** ❼, which is 1,400 metres (4,600 ft) long, where cavers have discovered an underground lake.

Between Trofors and Mosjøen on the E6, is the wide but shallow **Laksfossen** (waterfall) which has a 16-metre (50-ft) drop. At **Mosjøen** ❽, an industrial town where a splendid location fights for domination with a large aluminium works, there is **Dolstad** church, built in 1734 and the oldest octagonal church in north Norway. Look closely at the traces of the old ornamental decor and at a wooden angel in the ceiling which is lowered for use as a baptismal font. Near the church is the **Vefsn Open-air Museum** (open June–Aug Mon–Fri 8am–3.30pm, Sun 11am–4pm; entrance fee; tel: 75 11 25 30). Founded in 1909, it brings together 12 buildings from the surrounding district and a collection of some 5,000 objects from the old days of farming, fishing, hunting and domestic life.

Last stop before the Arctic

Beyond the town the scenery changes as farmland gives way to bare mountains *(fjells)*. There are camping sites with tents and cabins on both sides of the road north to cater for the outdoor holidaymakers who especially love these northern regions. **Mo i Rana** is also on a fjord and, like Mosjøen, is dominated by industry – in this case, the steelworks of Norsk Jernverk. These industries in small remote towns may displease the casual visitor but they illustrate a Norwegian determination to minimise the pull of the more populated south and to help people to find work locally.

Though Mo i Rana itself may be too modern for a visitor's taste, it is within reasonable distance of several "musts" on the list of many visitors to Norway – caves, a glacier and the Polarsirkel (Arctic Circle). The **Grønnligrotta** ❾ (caves; open June–Aug; entrance fee; tel: 75 13 92 00) lie about 20 km (12 miles) north of the town and guides shepherd parties through a glittering underground world of stalactite-hung caverns. At **Setergrotta** the cave calls for care and is more suitable for enthusiasts, with unexplored caves, crevices and passages, and interiors of marble and limestone.

From Mo i Rana, it is easy to reach Norway's second-largest glacier, **Svartisen** ❿ (The Black Ice), which covers 370 sq km (140 sq miles) and is up to 100 metres (330 ft) thick in places. It is also one of the lowest-lying glaciers on the European mainland, reaching down to within 170 metres (560 ft) of sea level. The route lies off the E6 32 km (20 miles) north of Mo i Rana, which heads northwest to Svartis lake. You then cross the water by boat, and walk about 3 km (2 miles) to the glacier.

TIP

The best time to see Norwegian waterfalls is in late May, or even June this far north, when summer creeps northwards melting the snow and ice to swell the rivers.

BELOW: on the edge of the glacier.

Map on page 302

Crossing the line

Many try but few have managed to explain why it should be so exciting to cross a line you cannot see. But most people experience an inexplicable thrill and sense of achievement as they cross the **Polarsirkel** ⓫ (Arctic Circle). It seems to mark the end of modern comforts and the beginning of the wild north, and nowhere is that sense of entering the unknown stronger than on highway E6 on its long trek north.

From Mo i Rana, the road makes its way through the temperate landscape of Dunderlandsdalen, past Storsforshei iron ore mine. Then, beyond Krokstrand, the scenery begins to change as the road approaches **Saltfjellet**, a wild and majestic mountain valley flanked by bare, brooding mountains. Apart from the road, railway line and river, there is nothing else until you come to the monuments that mark the Arctic Circle. Alongside the official markers are numerous small stone cairns erected by visitors who felt a common need to mark the event. A short visit to the architecturally pleasing **Polarsirkelsenteret** (Arctic Circle Centre; open May–June and Aug 9am–8pm; July 8am–10pm; Sept 10am–6pm; tel: 75 69 02 40) is a good way of celebrating the moment. The centre provides information on the flora and fauna, the climate and Sami culture – and also sells souvenirs. Nature, it would seem, cannot be left to its own devices.

There is a darker and sadder side to this area, which dates back to World War II when thousands of prisoners of war, mainly Yugoslavs, were used to build the railway. Many perished in the bitter winter conditions, and their memorial stands in the wild mountains where they worked and died.

The summit of the Saltfjell road, at **Stødi**, is 700 metres (2,300 ft) high; these mountains mark the limit for most temperate flora and fauna, though a few

BELOW: reindeer have right of way on the roads.

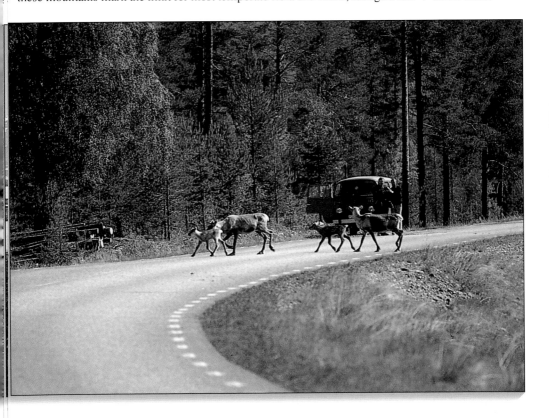

LAND OF THE MIDNIGHT SUN

Some of Norway's most stunning natural wonders lie within the Arctic Circle and are a prime target for tourists visiting the north in summer

The phrase "Land of the Midnight Sun" was originally coined by the French American explorer Paul Belloni Du Chaillu (*c.* 1831–1903), who published a travelogue by the same title in 1881 after travelling extensively in northern Europe. The name caught on: more than 100 years later, tourists still flock to the North Cape every summer to experience this natural spectacle.

The midnight sun is the appearance of the sun above the horizon at midnight. The phenomenon is due to the inclination of the Earth's axis, and to the fact that the axis points in the same direction during the whole period of the Earth's yearly revolution around the sun. It may be witnessed at any point on the Arctic Circle on 21 June or on the Antarctic Circle on 21 December. Within these circles the length of time the sun is in the sky without setting gradually increases, being 65 days at latitude 70° and 134 days at latitude 80°. For six months, the sun never sets at the poles.

WINTER DARKNESS

Of course, the down side to the phenomenon is that during the winter the sun never appears above the horizon and thus all regions within the polar circles are plunged into darkness as they experience a long polar night. In Tromsø this period of darkness lasts from 27 November to 15 January, while the midnight sun can be seen from 20 May to 22 July. For the people of the north, the midnight sun is not so much a phenomenon as a way of life.

▷ **AURLANDSFJORD**
At the head of enchanting Aurlandsfjord is Flåm and the start of the 10-km (6-mile) mountain railway up to Myrdal.

◁ **PREIKESTOLEN**
Preikestolen (the Pulpit Rock) soars 280 metres (920 ft) above Lysefjord. The view stretches towards Stavanger and the fjords.

▽ **GLACIER WANDERING**
The Jostedal glacier is the largest glacier on the European continent. The ice can be up to 230 metres (750 ft) thick in parts.

THE NORTHERN LIGHTS

▷ **BRIKSDAL GLACIER**
One of Jostedal's more famous side-arms is the Briksdal glacier, accessible from April to October. The glacier lies at the end of the beautiful Olden valley.

▽ **FOLGEFONN GLACIER**
Near Sorfjord (below) is the Folgefonno glacier, 500 metres (1,640 ft) above sea level. The glacier is growing at a rate of 1.5 metres (5 ft) per day.

The northern lights, or *aurora borealis*, are a huge natural light-show, filling the winter sky with patterns of light and colour.

In medieval Europe this remarkable phenomenon was thought to be reflections of heavenly wariors; we now know that it originates from electric particles sent out into space by the sun. These are drawn into the Earth's magnetic field where they collide with other particles in our atmosphere. The resulting electric charges give rise to the greenish patterns of light which dance across the night sky.

The sun has a number of holes in its corona from which high energy particles stream out. These particles are ejected into the solar system as solar wind, which meets the Earth's magnetosphere, compressing it on the daylight side, while drawing out the tail at night.

The solar wind particles accelerate to Earth along the open magnetic fields of the polar regions. When the particles collide with air molecules their energy is transferred into light. These processes occurring simultaneously result in the northern lights.

◁ **WATER POWER**
Norway's rapids and waterfalls are very important commercially: Norway is self-sufficient in electricity from hydropower. They also provide recreation opportunities for fishing, kayaking and white-water rafting.

THE FAR NORTH

For many, the aim of travelling this far north is to visit Nordkapp, Norway's northernmost tip; along the way you can go island-hopping in the Lofotens or cross the expanse of the Finnmarksvidda

Viewed from the mainland across the broad expanse of Vestfjorden, the **Lofoten Islands** present an imposing wall of jagged peaks rising up sheer from the sea. On the west these mountains form a mighty breakwater from the onslaught of the Arctic Ocean, a 112-km (70-mile) archipelago which stretches from the tiny island of Røst in the south to the waters of the narrow Raftsundet in the north. In winter the coast is one of the stormiest in Europe, while the unsurpassed summer beauty of the islands makes them one of Norway's major tourist attractions. The midnight sun is visible from 27 May till 17 July.

Between the mountains, which are composed of some of the oldest rocks in the world, are stretches of fertile farmland, fjords and deep ravines while the coastline is sprinkled with fishing villages and one or two small towns.

A phenomenon peculiar to the Lofotens is the annual cod fishing which in the past involved up to 6,000 boats and 30,000 fishermen. Between January and March these migrant fishermen lived in simple waterside wooden cabins called *rorbuer*. By 1947 the number of fishermen was declining and today it is down to 2,000, and this seasonal event has been replaced by a year-round fishing fleet. In the summer, the cod is left to dry on traditional wooden racks by the harbour.

Svolvær ❶, the main town on the island of Austvågøy and has been a trading centre since the 17th century. Virtually surrounded by water, and confusing to the visitor on that account, it is flanked by sharp, pointed rocky peaks. Some of these rise almost straight up from the gardens and the town has its own special mountain, the Svolværgeita ("Svolvær goat").

The town is connected to the mainland by ferry to Skutvik, and by coastal steamer and air to Bodø. It, like the Lofotens as a whole, has attracted many artists and craftsmen and is now the site of the **Nordnorsk Kunstnersentrum** (North Norwegian Artists' Centre; open all year; entrance fee). Scenes like those described above are captured on canvas by local artist Dagfinn Bakke who owns and runs a gallery here (open May–Aug), while at nearby **Kabelvåg ❷** there is an art school and an impressive wooden church which looks old but was in fact built in 1898.

Payment in fish

On the outskirts of Kabelvåg is the **Lofotmuseet** (Lofotens Museum; open times vary; entrance fee; tel: 76 06 97 90) sited where Vågar, the first town north of the Polarsirkel (Arctic Circle), existed in the Middle Ages. In the 14th century, 80 percent of Norway's national export was stockfish, allowing Vågar a broad market and cultural exchange with Europe. The main museum building was originally in the centre of the thriving fishing community and one room is furnished

PRECEDING PAGES: Røst in the Lofoten. **LEFT:** small boats and *rorbuer* (old fishing cottages) in Stamsund. **BELOW:** island fisherman.

Many of the old rorbuer *on the Lofotens have been restored and fitted with modern conveniences and are now rented out to summer visitors.*

as a fish station owner's office from the 1880s. He would own all the *rorbuer* and the fishermen who rented them would pay in fish from their catches. There is a typical *rorbuer* from 1797, with its primitive and crowded living conditions, and a boathouse with three traditional boats of various sizes. Another building is devoted to the development of the Lofoten fishing industry which in its modernised form plays a vital role in the economy of the islands.

Kabelvåg gained a new attraction in 1989 with the opening of the **Lofotakveriet** (Aquarium; open all year; entrance fee), which is designed as a small fishing village, and includes both salt and freshwater fish and a seal tank.

Island hopping, Norwegian style

To journey south on the E10 means going from island to island, all of which, bar one, have gradually been linked by impressive bridges. The one remaining ferry connection was replaced by an undersea road tunnel in 1990. This route must rank as one of the most outstanding in Norway. At every turn the traveller is confronted with another seemingly haphazard series of jagged peaks and possessing a stark beauty which contrasts with the green scenery at sea level.

On the southern tip of Austvågøy is **Henningsvær**, one of numerous Lofoten fishing villages and home to the Karl Erik Harr Gallery. The imposing bridge over Gimsøystraumen, 840 metres (2,760 ft) long, provides access to the small island of Gimsøya. From here a second bridge takes the road across Sundklakkstraumen to Vestvågøy. **Stamsund**, on a secondary road, is a coastal village and a port of call for the coastal steamer.

The **Vestvågøy Museum** (open June–Aug Mon–Fri; entrance fee; tel: 76 08 49 00) is at Fygle, near Leknes, and has exhibits showing how the fisherman-farmer's

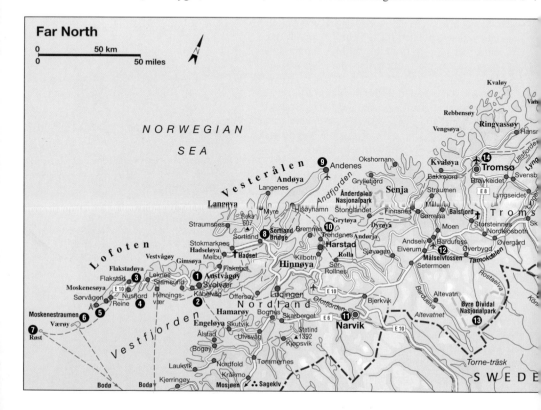

life has changed over the years. **Leknes** is the main centre of population on the island and a typical small Norwegian town with a long straggling main street. A few miles south at Lilleeidet was the ferry to **Flakstadøya**, which was replaced by a tunnel that goes 50 metres (165 ft) below the surface of Nappstraumen.

The west coast of Flakstadøya provides the surprise of wide **sandy beaches**. On a sunny summer's day, the sight of children paddling belies the fact that it is in the Arctic. The hamlet of **Flakstad ❸** has a pretty 18th-century church with an onion dome, while nearby are monuments to those who died in World War II and fishermen whose lives were lost at sea. **Nusfjord ❹** and Sund are two other fishing villages on the island. The former is on UNESCO's list of preservation-worthy environments while Sund has a small fisheries museum (open June–Aug; entrance fee). One section is devoted to early marine engines while the adjoining smithy is used by Hans Gjertsen, who is noted for his stylishly crafted steel cormorants. Also on the island is **Storbåthallaren**, the oldest known Stone Age settlement in northern Norway, populated 6,000 years ago.

The last bridge takes the road across to the island of Moskenesøya. This also has its quota of fishing villages of which the most picturesque is **Reine**. The road clings close to the coast and looks across the Vestfjorden.

Ending at Å

The E10 finally runs out at Å ❺ – aptly named, as "Å" is the last letter of the Norwegian alphabet – which marks the end of the line of peaks that make up the **Lofotenveggen** (Lofoten "wall"). It has one of the few trading posts to be preserved in its original condition. There is the small **Fiskevaersmuseum** (Fishing Village Musuem: open all year, closed weekends Sept–June; entrance fee) in a

Map, below

TIP

Whale safaris are very popular, so it is worth booking in advance. Trips leave from Andenes, Stø and Nyksund and last 3–5 hours. If you don't spot a whale first time around, repeat the journey for free. Details from: Tourist Information Office in Svolvær, tel: 76 06 98 00 or visit: www.whalesafari.no.

BELOW: a statue looks out to sea from Leknes on the Lofoten island of Vestvågøy.

19th-century barn, and a café opposite offers coffee and home-made cakes.

Beyond the tip of Moskenesøya is the **Moskenestraumen** ❻, a maelstrom which may not match the Saltstraumen near Bodø but which was once greatly feared by sailors. Even in calm weather it seethes and boils and was made famous through the works of Jules Verne, in *Journey Beneath the Sea*, and Edgar Allan Poe. The maelstrom separates Moskenesøya from the small island of **Værøy**, beyond which is the even smaller island of **Røst** ❼. These are the "bird islands", which attract thousands of different species including puffin, auk, eider, guillemot, kittiwake and cormorant. Both islands have small airfields with scheduled flights to Bodø, obviating a sea trip which, because of the rapidly changing sea conditions, can be unpleasant. Thanks to the Gulf Stream, it never gets very cold on Røst or Værøy and sheep can graze on the meadows throughout the winter.

Vesterålen: home of the Hurtigruten

North of Svolvær the views may be splendid but they do not quite measure up to those in the south. In truth, this is only a question of degree because the Lofotens have such a richness of views that they almost give you scenic indigestion. Heading north, the road keeps close to the Austnesfjord, beyond which, to the northeast, is Raftsundet and the narrow **Trollfjorden** which is used by the coastal steamer in summer. At Fiskebøl the ferry takes the visitor away from the Lofotens to **Melbu** on the first of the Vesterålen Islands, **Hadseløya**. As if to emphasise that you have left the Lofotens behind, Melbu has the **Vesterålen Museum** (open all year; entrance fee; tel: 76 15 75 56), housed in an Empire-style manor house.

Between Melbu and Stokmarknes on the northern side of the island is **Hadsel Kirke** (church; 1824), distinctive in style and with an altarpiece from 1520.

Stokmarknes is the headquarters of the Vesteraalen Steamship Company, founded by Richard With, sometimes called the father of the coastal steamer. At the **Hurtigruten Museum** (open mid-June–mid-Aug daily 10am–6pm; mid-Aug–mid-June Sat noon–4pm, otherwise 2–4pm; entrance fee), you may buy special Hurtigruten tickets for return trips to Svolvær.

From whaling to whale safaris

The Hadsel bridge carries the main road to the island of **Langøya**. Here the principal town is **Sortland**, a commercial centre with a fishing harbour that has a busy and pleasant atmosphere. The western side of the island has imposing mountains, the most unusual being the sway-backed **Reka** at 620 metres (2,000 ft) which is popular with climbers.

The Sortland Bridge, one of the many stunning bridges between islands in the Lofoten and Vesterålen archipelagos.

The **Sortland Bridge** ❽, 960 metres (3,150 ft) long, is the link to **Hinnøya**, Norway's largest island, which hosts a popular festival every June in Harstad. Away to the northwest is the long island of **Andøya**, which is also connected by bridge and, unlike most other Vesterålen islands, is flat. Much of the land is peat, renowned for its cloudberries. **Andenes** ❾, at the northwestern extremity, is a large fishing village with the **Polarmuseet** (Polar Museum; open June–Aug; entrance fee; tel: 76 14 20 88). It was a fishing village in the Middle Ages and then a Dutch whaling base in the 17th century. Today, it is one of the starting points of the famous **whale safaris** *(see "Tip" opposite)*.

Hinnøya's varied scenery includes farmland along the coastal fringe, green valleys, rugged mountains and fjords. Following the E10 southeast from the Sortland Bridge you come to Lødingen on the eastern coast, with a ferry service to **Bognes** on the mainland and the E6. A little further to the north is **Trondenes** ❿ which

BELOW: morning service at Hadsel Kirke (church), Vesterålen.

has a 13th-century stone church (open all year). In the bay below there are Viking burial mounds. Also here are the **Adolfkanonen** (Cannons; open May–Aug, or call Harstad Tourist Office; tel: 77 01 89 89), massive long-range guns installed by the Germans during World War II to protect the approaches to Narvik.

A final lengthy bridge carries the E10 over **Tjeldsundet** and on to the mainland, although to the confused motorist it may appear to be another island as the road skirts along Ofotfjorden, which provides deep-water access to Narvik. If the Lofoten and Vesterålen islands are ignored the only alternative way north is by the E6. From Fauske it clings to the side of fjords, going through a succession of tunnels, with the **Rago Nasjonalpark** away to the east. This is a vast mountainous area with no roads, judged to be the most magnificent but least accessible of all Norway's National Parks.

A superb section of highway has been built from Sommarset, where formerly there was a ferry, which cuts across exciting mountainous country. There are several tunnels, the longest being below the Sildhopfjell. North of Kråkmo, at **Sagelv**, there are 5,000-year-old rock carvings of reindeer. At Ulvsvåg a road goes off west to **Skutvik** for the ferry to Svolvær. The road continues on to Engeløya island which was a seat of power many centuries ago and there are numerous graves and burial mounds, the biggest being at **Sigarshaugen**.

Back on the E6, a little north of **Bognes**, are more rock carvings depicting 40 different subjects. To the east of Tysfjorden is a mountainous section popular with climbers, especially **Stetind**, 1,392 metres (4,567 ft) high, which is called the "world's greatest obelisk". There are many caves for those who prefer to go down rather than up, the best known being **Råggejavie**, 620 metres (2,000 ft) deep. For the rest of the way to Narvik the road clings to the side of Ofotfjorden.

BELOW: Rus students celebrate their graduation from the gymnasium in Sortland, Vesterålen.

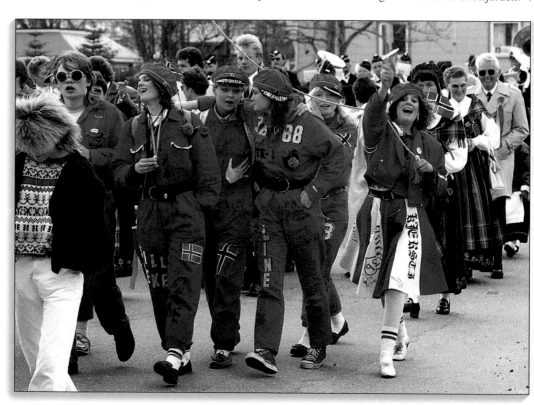

Narvik

The deep, ice-free waters of the Ofotfjord allowed **Narvik** to become a major centre for exporting iron ore mined in northern Sweden. A railway was completed from the mining town of Kiruna to the port in 1883. Narvik is now the end of the Ofotbanen line, the Norwegian railway connecting with the northern Swedish line. In World War II Narvik was the scene of bitter fighting and German forces occupied it for over five years – portrayed in the **Krigsminnemuseum** (War Museum; open Mar–Sept; entrance fee). For an overview of Narvik take the cable car (in summer) 650 metres (2,132 ft), to the top of Fagernes. At ground level Narvik is uninteresting, which is maybe why the local tourist office sells tickets for the "tourist train" (June–Aug), a three-hour guided tour between Narvik and the Swedish border, with photo opportunities and a chance to buy Sami souvenirs.

Troms, a county of contrasts

North of Narvik the E6 crosses Rombakfjorden over another major bridge, passes the junction with the road to Sweden, and joins with E10 at Bjerkvik. Then follows a climb up Gratangseidet county boundary into Troms. Troms has widely contrasting scenery, all typically North Norwegian: rugged mountains, with sharp peaks, countless islands and skerries, a softer landscape at sea level and fast-flowing rivers and numerous lakes. The county is split up by a number of major fjords and is also notable for its extensively forested valleys.

Setermoen, just north of Narvik, lies in the heart of a military area and has a large garrison. The military presence is also apparent further north at Bardufoss, with its major airbase. From Bardufoss the E6 follows the Målselv river until it turns abruptly east past Takvatnet where a major new cut-off provides some stunning views of distant mountains. Near **Balsfjord Kirke** (church) about 10 km (6 miles) from Storsteinnes are rock carvings which are 2,500 to 4,000 years old. The area around Balsfjord has some of the richest farming land in Troms and goat farming is a major activity.

Alternatively, before you get to Bardufoss turn eastwards at Elverum onto Road 857 from which you can reach **Målselvfossen** (waterfall). It may only have a drop of 15 metres (50 ft), but it extends over 600 metres (2,000 ft). There are salmon ladders and the Målselv river, which is renowned for its salmon, was discovered by English anglers in the 1840s. At Rundhaug a secondary road follows the Målselv river to Øverbygd, then continues along **Tamokdalen** until it rejoins the E6 near Øvergård. To the south, adjacent to the border with Sweden, lies the **Øvre Dividal Nasjonalpark** , where all four of Norway's major predators – bear, wolf, lynx and wolverine – have their habitat.

City of the Arctic

Tromsø occupies most of the island of Tromsøya and overflows on to the adjoining island of Kvaløya. With a population of 60,000, it is the largest city in northern Norway and, until the opening of the bridge in 1960, everything had to be ferried across from the mainland. Today, there is a second bridge and an amazing network of road tunnels under the city, including subterranean car parks and roundabouts that appear to be formed around

Map, pages 316–7

TIP

The rock carvings near Balsfjord Kirke (church) are part of the Tennes Heritage Trail, which is one of the many trails included in *Fotfar mot Nord* (Trails to the North) available from tourist offices.

BELOW: *rallar* (railwaymen's) statue in Narvik.

giant stalactites. The tunnel system links the city centre with Tromsø Langnes international airport: if you arrive by air and take a taxi the driver will gladly take you via the tunnel system (at the extra cost of the toll). The town has variously been called the Gateway to the Arctic, the Arctic Ocean City and the Paris of the North.

Archaeological finds indicate settlements dating back 9,000 years. Tromsø became an ecclesiastical centre in 1252 and much of the subsequent development from 1300 to 1700s was influenced by the Hanseatic League. Trade restrictions led to strong dependence on Bergen throughout the Middle Ages. In 1794, the town was granted *kaupang* (market town) privileges and the right to independent trade, and became a focal point for the Pomor trade, with Russian ships bringing timber, rape, flour and other items from the White Sea in exchange for fish and goods brought by the Hanseatic traders.

In the early 19th century Tromsø was the natural starting point for trapping expeditions to the pack ice both to the north and the east to Svalbard (Spitsbergen). It has also been the site of a number of sea battles, including the sinking of the German battleship *Tirpitz*, pride of the German fleet, which was bombed by British bombers while guarding the entrance to Tromsø in 1944.

Tromsø has one of the greatest amounts of Northern Light activity in the world, but in midsummer the skies are too light for this phenomenon.

Heavenly winds

Though fishing (for shrimps, herring and other fishes) is of prime importance, Tromsø University and a new regional teaching hospital are also ranked as major employers here. **Tromsø University Museum** (open all year, hours vary; entrance fee; tel: 77 64 50 00) focuses on the cultural and natural history of the

Tromsø's nickname, Paris of the North, stems from the 18th century when traders brought the latest fashions from the French capital to sell to the wives of rich, local merchants.

BELOW LEFT: racks of drying fish have their own "guards" to deter hungry birds.
BELOW RIGHT: Tromsø Domkirke (cathedral) in winter.

north, and the Sami, and contains a reconstructed Viking longhouse. Polar explorers are the centre of attention at the **Polarmuseet** (Polar Museum; open all year, hours vary; entrance fee; tel: 77 68 43 73) in the historic harbour area.

The **Nordnorsk Kunstmuseum** (Art Museum of Northern Norway; open all year Tues, Wed and Fri 10am–5pm, Thur 10am–7pm, Sat and Sun noon–5pm; entrance fee) has been going from strength to strength since moving in 2001 to its first permanent home facing Roald Amundsens Square. Sami and Northern Norwegian art is well represented in the permanent collection.

In the centre of the town is the **Domkirke** (Cathedral; open June–Aug, closed Mon) completed in 1861, which is one of the country's largest wooden churches. On the mainland is the striking **Ishavskatedralen** (Arctic Ocean Cathedral; open June–Aug daily 10am–8pm; Sept–May times vary; entrance fee), designed by Jan Inge Hovig and completed in 1965. The Cathedral features a huge stained-glass window by Victor Sparre covering the entire east wall, 23 metres (75 ft) high, depicting the Second Coming. Nearby is the cable car to the top of the **Storsteinen**, 420 metres (1,380 ft), from where there are magnificent views over the town and the surrounding area. Tromsø also contains Europe's northernmost brewery, Mack, established in 1845 and famous for its Arctic Ale. The brewery is a short walk from the centre and there is a beer hall on the premises.

Where glacier and sea meet

To the northwest of Tromsø a number of islands stand guard where the lengthy Ullsfjorden and **Lyngenfjorden** reach the sea. Between these is a long wide peninsula. On its eastern side, lie the range of mountains known as the **Lyngsalpene ⑮** (Lyngen Alps). The full majesty of these snow-capped peaks and glaciers is best

Map, pages 316–7

BELOW: The Ishavskatedralen represents the shape of a Sami tent and the iciness of a glacier (Arctic Ocean Cathedral), Tromsø.

seen from the eastern side of Lyngenfjorden. There is a short cut that avoids the main road and affords fine views of the mountains. Take Road 91 just south of Tromsø through the Breivik valley, a ferry across Ullsfjord to Svensby then drive to Lyngseidet and a second ferry across Lyngenfjorden to Olderdalen and the E6.

The more obvious route is south along the E8 to where it joins the E6 at Nord-kjosbotn and then northeast through Skibotn, keeping along the shore of the Lyn-genfjord with its views of the mountains across the water. After continuing east along the side of the Rotsundet, opposite the island of Uløya, the road swings inland before meeting Reisafjorden. There are fine views to the west, which are even better after climbing over the summit of **Kvænangsfjellet**. There is an impressive panorama of islands and mountains before descending to Burfjorden.

Just past Alteidet, a minor road goes north to the Jøkelfjord where the **Øksfjordjøkelen** (glacier) calves into the sea, the only one in Norway to do so. To the east is the boundary into Norway's most remote county, Finnmark.

Finnmark

No-one describes Finnmark without a combination of superlatives and impressive statistics. It is Norway's most northerly county and the largest, covering 48,000 sq km (18,500 sq miles), equal to 15 percent of the entire country, and yet it has only 75,000 inhabitants, 1.7 percent of the population.

Finnmark lies along the same latitude as Alaska and Siberia, but the Gulf Stream ensures that the harbours do not freeze even in the depths of winter. Inland, the temperature can drop to a chilling –50°C (–70°F); while during the short summer it may hit 32°C (90°F). Between mid-May and the end of July the sun never sets – you can read a newspaper outside at midnight – while in winter the sun stays snug below the horizon from the end of November to the end of January.

The scenery is spectacular, with the highest areas in the northwest and a vast mountain plateau, the **Finn-marksvidda**, to the south and southeast. The bare grey rocks of the coast take the full force of the winter storms. It is the vastness of the uninhabited areas that make the greatest impression: ranges of mountains and fjells stretch away to the horizon, seemingly without end, silent and awe-inspiring. The coast has its own gaunt beauty with sudden patches of green which catch the visitor unawares.

Much of this wonderful county is now easily accessible by car or public transport on well-surfaced main roads, while there is an extensive network of air services which land at tiny airports dotted all over the area, and the ubiquitous coastal steamer serves towns and villages along the coast.

Despite the inhospitable nature of the region and the ferocity of the winter, the people of Finnmark are greatly attached to their part of Norway, which has been inhabited for 10,000 years. They include not only Norwegians and Sami (Lapps) but also many Finns. The Norwegians settled the coast in the 14th century, but major changes in the 18th and 19th centuries brought in people from the south of the country. At the same time came a large migration from Finland and Sweden.

BELOW: contrasting styles at the Sami market in Hammerfest.

Scorched earth

World War II was a nightmare for the county when, as Soviet liberators crossed the northern border in the autumn of 1944, the German occupation forces began a "scorched earth" policy as they retreated south, burning towns and villages and even individual farms as they went. Signs of this can be seen in **Alta**, the first town across the county border from Troms and the biggest in the county, where some of the architecture is undistinguished, often the case in north Norwegian towns which had to rebuild rapidly after World War II.

On the southern outskirts is an outstanding collection of prehistoric rock carvings at **Hjemmeluft** ⑰ (signs from Alta; open all year, times vary; entrance fee; tel: 78 45 63 30). Discovered in 1972 and on UNESCO's World Heritage List, there are about 4,000 carvings on four different sites. The biggest concentration is at Hjemmeluft itself. These 'stories in pictures' are about 2,500 to 6,000 years old and depict people, animals (particularly reindeer), boats and weapons. Traces of these early inhabitants, the Komsa people, were discovered in 1925 on Komsafjell, which bulges out into Altafjorden. The dwelling sites go back some 10,000 years – a sobering reminder of how long humans have lived in this inhospitable region.

Sami culture

Finnmark has few roads, so it's easy to find your way. Going south from Alta is Road 93 to **Kautokeino** ⑱ and the Finnish frontier. Kautokeino is the largest Sami community in the country, the centre of Sami education, and possibly the coldest town in Norway. The **Kulturhuset** has the only Sami theatre in Norway, and the **Samisk Museum** (open all year; entrance fee) has exhibits showing life in old Kautokeino. Northwards from Leirbotnvatn (around the fjord from

Map, pages 316–7

One of the prehistoric carvings at Hjemmeluft.

BELOW LEFT: selling skins and other Sami goods.
BELOW RIGHT: an early print of a Sami women and child.

Watch out for elks crossing.

Alta) to the village of **Skaidi** is 45 km (28 miles) of sheer emptiness. The eE6 takes a lonely course through the wild countryside. Almost the only building is the small **Sami chapel**, dwarfed by its surroundings. The only signs of life away from the road are the herds of reindeer. You are constantly aware of how little human activity has impinged on the grandeur of its great empty spaces.

History of disasters

Skaidi is a popular base for anglers, hunters and winter sports enthusiasts. It is also the junction of the E6 and Road 94 to **Hammerfest ⑲**, 56 km (35 miles) away on the island of Kvaløya. Hammerfest, on its bare rocky island, is the world's most northerly town. Founded in 1789, for centuries it was the best ice-free harbour in northern waters, although storms and hurricanes plus many man-made disasters have repeatedly wrought havoc on the town. In 1825, a hurricane destroyed houses and boats, and an even more ferocious storm in 1882 moved the German Kaiser, Queen Victoria and the Tsar of Russia to donate money to repair the damage. In 1890, the town had ambitious plans for a hydro-electric power station but, only a month after work started, fire again destroyed two-thirds of the town. In the following year, nevertheless, Hammerfest became the first European town to have electric lighting when it purchased a generator from Thomas Edison in 1891.

The harbour has always been of importance both commercially and strategically and ships have long called there. For more than 100 years it was also the principal Norwegian base for hunting and fishing. When Norway was invaded in 1940, it was a growing and flourishing community. The retreating Germans burned down the entire town and by 10 February 1945 it had been wiped out except for the **chapel** in the graveyard. Today, it is Norway's main trawler port.

BELOW: boats and warehouses in Hammerfest harbour.

Map, pages 316–7

Measuring the planet

Hammerfest clings to the shore line which is backed by a steep escarpment. Its most notable monument is the **Meridianstøtta** (Meridian Column), which was erected by King Oskar II in the late 19th century to mark the first international measurement of the Earth (1816–1852), a joint enterprise by Russia, Norway and Sweden.

On the highest point of a walk from the town up the escarpment is the Midday Pole, topped by a cannonball. When the shadow from the pole points directly to the Meridian Column, the time is 12 noon precisely.

In 1809, after Norway entered the Napoleonic wars, two British warships attacked Hammerfest. The town fell and the British stayed for a week of plunder and destruction. The cannonball on top of the Midday Pole is the permanent reminder of this unhappy event. To prevent further attack the military built a redoubt or **Skansen** in 1810 with eight guns, which Hammerfest folk are happy to report never fired in anger. This walk also passes a beacon built by the town's young people in 1882–83 "as they had no other amusements".

More noticeable today is the circular **Isbjørnhallen** (Polar Bear Hall) used for sporting events and exhibitions. At the other end of town is the equally striking **church** (open June–Aug), its form inspired by traditional fish-drying racks. Its altar piece, which dates from 1632, comes from the town's first church. In a shrewd move in 1963, Hammerfest created the **Isbjørnklubben** (Royal and Ancient Polar Bear Society), which offers one of the more attractive souvenirs of its kind. To get a certificate of membership, you must apply in person to the society's **museum** (open June–Aug daily 9am–5pm; Sept–June Mon–Fri 11am–1pm, Sat–Sun 11am–2pm; entrance fee; tel: 78 41 31 00) in the Town Hall.

BELOW: Nordkapp (North Cape) in winter.

En route to China

From Skaidi the E6 goes northeast across the wild, uninhabited territory before the road descends to the sea at Olderfjorden. Here most visitors turn north for **Nordkapp ❷⓪** (North Cape). This is for many the Holy Grail, the end of their pilgrimage by car, motor-home, motorbike, bus or even bicycle. The alternative is to fly to Honningsvåg or sail there by coastal steamer or cruise liner.

The road hugs the edge of Porsangenfjorden, with rugged country to the landward side, and ends at Kåfjord, where a ferry and tunnel connects to **Honningsvåg** on the island of Magerøya. Between Honningsvåg and Nordkapp lie 35 km (21 miles) of the only genuine Arctic scenery in Europe. It may be bare and treeless but there is an unusual beauty about the island which, on a sunny day, is emphasised by the clarity of the atmosphere; too often, alas, it is misty.

The name North Cape was given to this imposing headland by an Englishman, Captain Richard Chancellor. In 1553, as master of the *Edward Bonaventure*, he was seeking a new route to China when he rounded Europe's most dramatic northern point; but it was not until the 19th century that Nordkapp began to attract visitors. In 1845, passengers from the *Prinds Gustav* were rowed ashore and then had to struggle up 300 metres (1,000 ft) to the plateau at the top. After a visit by the intrepid King Oskar II in 1873, Thomas Cook arranged the first organised tour for 24 Englishmen in 1875. By 1880, a path with primitive railings from Horn Bay to the top had appeared and you can still see the remains of the quay by taking the 11-km (7-mile) walk from the plateau. The coastal steamers have provided the biggest impetus to tourist traffic and by 1920, the wild grandeur of the headland had learned to live with the incongruity of its first building. The road from Honningsvåg opened in 1956, as did a centre with the usual souvenir shop, cafeteria

Following Richard Chancellor's attempt in 1553 to find the Northwest Passage to China, it was to be more than 300 years before Nils Nordenskjøld finally succeeded in travelling from the Atlantic to the Pacific via the north in 1879.

BELOW: the children's statues at Nordkapp (North Cape).

and post office. In 1989, this earlier building gave way to the **Nordkapphallen** (North Cape Hall; open all year, times vary; entrance fee; tel: 78 47 68 60), with its circular Compass Restaurant and, below, the Supervideograph, where a 225-degree screen and wrap-around sound bring the four seasons of Finnmark to the visitor, whatever the time of year. Nordkapp illustrates the seasonal extremes in this area. Twenty-four-hour darkness occurs from November to the end of January, while the midnight sun lasts from mid-May to the end of July.

An underground tunnel leads from the new hall and champagne bar, which is like an amphitheatre cut out of the rock and overlooks the Arctic Ocean. Even if you suffer from vertigo, look briefly from the balcony which provides a spectacular view straight down to the sea far below. Along the tunnel are tableaux depicting historical events at Nordkapp. On what is in danger of becoming a crowded plateau are seven circular, wheel-like sculptures. They are monuments to the children of the world, sculpted in 1988 by seven children from seven lands as monuments to "joy, friendship, and working together".

Map, pages 316–7

The comical puffin can be found all along the northern coasts.

"Haddock" English

Apart from the main road to Nordkapp itself, there is only one other road on the island, which leads to the village of **Gjesvær** on the west coast. On the eastern side of Magerøya is the little fishing community of Skarsvåg. Honningsvåg, where the ferry arrives, has been a fishing harbour for many years and an important pilot station. In the old days, the trawlers were the most frequent visitors, and up to 4,000 called each year. Most were British and, through their visits, Honningsvåg developed "haddock English", a mixture of sign language and occasional English words. Like other centres in the north, Honningsvåg was burned down during World War II, and by the end of the war, the 1884 church was the only building left standing. Honningsvåg today also has a small local museum, the **Nordkappmuseet** (North Cape Museum; open June–mid-Sept Mon–Sat 10am–7pm, Sun noon–7pm; mid-Sept–June Mon–Fri noon–4pm; entrance fee).

BELOW: the Midday Pole in Nordkapp (North Cape).

Most villages and towns in Finnmark sit along the coast but the two main Sami communities are the exception: Kautokeino and **Karasjok** ㉑ are deep inland. Returning from Nordkapp, continue south through Lakselv at the end of Porsangenfjorden to get to Karasjok. The town's 1807 **Gamle Kirke** is the oldest church in Finnmark, having survived the war, and **De Samiske Samlinger** (the Sami Museum and Library; open June–Aug daily 9am–7pm; Sept–May times vary; entrance fee) has a notable collection of Sami literature. Karasjok is the seat of the Sami Parliament and Samiland's capital. Since 2002, **Sápmi** (Sami theme park; open Sept–May 9am–4pm; June–Aug 9am–7pm; entrance fee) depicts Sami culture and history through dwellings, food and handicrafts.

At Karasjok the E6 makes a massive U-turn and heads north again, keeping company with the **River Tana** through its every twist and turn, all the way to **Tana Bru** ㉒, which is at the first bridge across the river and is the meeting place of four roads. One is the alternative route east from Lakselv (Road 888), which veers away from the E6 at the head of the Porsanger

Mending fishing nets on the quayside.

BELOW: a good catch: Atlantic salmon at Honningsvåg.

fjord. This long road has few communities but an abundance of beautiful scenery and it rolls ahead across two magnificent inland stretches – from **Børselv** to **Laksefjorden** and across the **Ifjordfjellet**. At Ifjord the road pushes further north to the Nordkyn peninsula and **Kjøllefjord** ㉓, Mehamn and Gamvik, across the very top of the country. About 15 km (9 miles) from Kjøllefjord, including a 30-minute ramble along a well-prepared trail, is the remains of the **Oksevåg whaling station**, which was used during the Finnmark whaling season from 1864–1905. Further walks are marked through the **Slettnes Nature and Heritage Reserve** at Gamvik (open all year).

Over the bridge at Tana Bru, the road divides; the E6 winds a long route east towards **Kirkenes**, only 5 km (3 miles) from the Russian border, while Road 890 heads north to **Berlevåg** and **Båtsfjord**, crossing the highest pass in Finnmark, the **Oarddojokke** at 400 metres (1,300 ft) above sea level. Berlevåg and Båtsfjord are fishing villages, both on the far coast of the Varanger peninsula. Places of interest include the **Løkvika Fiskehytte og Partisanhule** (Fishing Cabin and Partisan Cave; open all year).

Continuing east on the E6, you come to **Varangerbotn** ㉔. In this part of Norway, where the fjords bite deep into the land, you are rarely far from water. Varangerbotn has a small but interesting Sami museum, the **Samiske Museum** (open June–Aug; entrance fee), and it is worth making a detour along the north coast of the Varangerfjord on Road 98 to **Vadsø** ㉕, the administrative centre of Finnmark. At **Nesseby**, you will find a wooden church (1858) and Varanger's oldest log cabin (1700). This remote area is rich in archaeological finds, with graves and places of sacrifice to indicate human occupation as early as 9000 BC.

Finnish migration

A monument in Vadsø explains why many inhabitants are of Finnish origin and Finnish-speaking (Kvens), and the local **Ruija Kven Museum** (open June–Aug times vary; entrance fee; tel: 78 94 28 90) is housed in two buildings, one a Finnish-style dwelling, Tuoainengården, and the other, Espengården, a patrician house from 1840. Vadsø's **church**, built in 1958, is of striking appearance. In front, the King Stone bears the signatures of King Olav V of Norway, President Kekkonen of Finland and King Carl Gustav of Sweden, who all visited the town in 1977 to unveil the **Innvandrermonumentet** (Immigrant Monument) to the Finns who came to find food and work in Finnmark in the 1800s. Another landmark is the **Luftskipsmasta** (mooring mast) used by Amundsen's airship, *Norge*, in 1926 and Nobile's airship *Italia*, two years later.

Beyond Vadsø there is only the town of **Vardø** , Norway's easternmost town and the only one situated in the Arctic climate zone. There have been fortifications at Vardø since around 1300, but the present octagonal star-shaped redoubt was built in 1734. The only remnant of the original fortress is a beam which bears the signature of King Christian IV and is dated 1599, while later monarchs have added their names: King Oskar II (in 1873), King Håkon VII (in 1907) and King Olav V (in 1959); the beam is in the **Vardøhus Museum** and **Festning** (Fortress; open June–Aug Mon–Fri 8am–6pm, Sat–Sun noon–6pm; Sept–May Mon–Fri 8am–3.30pm; entrance fee).

Along the coast west of Vardø is the abandoned fishing village of **Hamningberg** with its old architecture and church – one of the few not destroyed in World War II. As you return south again, you come to **Ekkerøya**, Finnmark's only bird rock accessible by car. Here bird-watchers gather to see breeding kittiwake, black guille-

After two months of winter darkness, Vardø celebrates the return of the sun, usually around 20 January, with a gun salute on the first day that the entire disk is visible above the horizon.

BELOW: the harbour at Vadsø.

Map, pages 316–7

mot, Steller's eider and grey phalarope. Beyond Varangerbotn, the E6 follows the coast through another huge, uninhabited area to the southeast and some beautiful views across the waters of the Varanger fjord. **Bugøynes** is an old fishing village on the coast which, like Hamingborg, escaped destruction in the war. Further east, **Bugøyfjord** is an old trading centre and birthplace of the Sami artist John Savio.

Only 8 km (5 miles) from the Finnish border to the southwest, the little town of **Neiden** has the only Greek Orthodox Church in Norway, where the Skollé Lapps worship. Each year since 1965, the church has held a service to bless the waters of the River Neiden to ensure that their reputed healing powers continue, a service which attracts believers from many areas. The restored Labahå farm at Neiden, built by Finnish immigrants, is part of the **Sør-Varanger Museum** (open all year; entrance fee) at Svanvik.

This easternmost wedge of Norwegian territory became important with the discovery of iron ore at Bjørnevatn and, since 1906, it has been mined and shipped from the port of **Kirkenes ㉗**. The region is also a centre for fishing, farming, forestry and reindeer husbandry. Kirkenes is dominated by the installations of the Sydvaranger Iron Ore Company. Although it has acquired a luxury hotel, the Rica Arctic, the town's somewhat rough and ready appearance is explained and easily forgiven when you learn that the 20th century brought no less than four wars fought in or near it. Apart from Malta, Kirkenes acquired the unsolicited honour of being the most bombed centre in Europe in World War II. It was liberated by the Russians in 1944, which engendered a rare lack of nervousness of, and sympathy for, the "Russian Bear". Subterranean tunnels used to shelter residents during the war can be visited. Kirkenes is the final point of call for the Hurtigruten coastal steamer before it returns south to Bergen.

BELOW: post boxes brighten up the winter landscape.
RIGHT: winter in Kautokeino.

Unusual border post

The extreme eastern tip of Norway, at **Grense Jakobselv**, has a chapel built on the order of King Oskar II in 1869 as an unusual means of protecting Norwegian interests. The idea of a chapel rather than a fort at this strategic location came about when the Norwegians noticed that the Russians attended their own Orthodox church not far over the border. Faced with a Protestant church, the argument ran, the Russians would realise they had strayed into Norwegian territory – this somewhat unusual approach to maintaining the frontier was highly successful.

In the extreme north of Finnmark, Norway is sometimes only a kilometre or two wide between the border and the sea, and a long pocket of the country hangs south between Russia and Finland. Here the **Øvre Pasvik Nasjonalpark ㉘** includes the largest virgin forest in the country. This comparatively flat area has pine forests, bare rock, swamps and two watercourses which are tributaries of the Pasvik river (the official boundary between Norway and Russia). Wildlife in the park includes moose, reindeer, bear and wolverine; there are whooper swans, great grey owls, bean geese, sea eagles, gyr falcons, spotted redshanks and cranes; the whole area is protected from development and pollution to form a peaceful border, 122km (76 miles) long between East and West. ❑

SVALBARD

Nearly as close to the North Pole as to Norway, the Svalbard archipelago (more widely known as Spitsbergen) teems with bird, mammal and plant life in the short Arctic summer

Map on page 338

NORWAY

rom Tromsø in the north of Norway, the big airliner drones almost due north for an hour and a half. Far below is a seemingly empty sea, hidden here and there by banks of clouds. Suddenly the traveller becomes aware that through the clouds, stark, jagged mountain peaks project like huge fangs, and that the clouds in between are in reality great snow-covered glaciers. This is Svalbard, the land of the pointed mountains.

The Svalbard archipelago lies 640 km (400 miles) north of the mainland of Norway and has two main islands, Spitsbergen and Nordaustlandet, with numerous smaller islands dotted around in the seas nearby. In winter, the pack ice of the Arctic is all around and only some 950 km (600 miles) separate the islands from the North Pole.

The smooth asphalt runway lies on the narrow coastal plain between the mountains of Spitsbergen and the sea of Isfjorden. With a minimum of formality, you are through customs and on to a land where the forces of nature are still in control. On the landward side, the mountain slopes darkly up in to the clouds, traversed by a row of pylons; now disused, they carried coal from the mines down to the loading jetties.

PRECEDING PAGES: rock formations on Spitsbergen.
LEFT: a young polar bear.
BELOW: the Russian mining settlement of Barentsburg.

Why an airport?

The Svalbard coal mines are rare in that the mine shafts do not go down into the ground but are driven horizontally into the mountains. The township of **Longyearbyen ❶** was built solely to accommodate the people who came north, mainly from Norway, to work at the hard and dangerous job of mining coal from the inside of the mountains.

Coal was first discovered in the early 17th century, but for many years it was used only as a source of fuel for trappers. Only since around 1900 have serious attempts been made to exploit this resource, and the first to claim mining rights was a Norwegian skipper from Tromsø, called Zakariasen. He was followed by others including John Longyear, an American after whom the village is named.

Around 1,400 people live in the village, mainly in modern, well insulated houses, served by facilities such as shops, a bank, restaurants and bars, a café, and a new sports centre with a swimming pool. There is even a fine little **museum** which, as well as stuffed examples of typical Spitsbergen birds and mammals, displays many artefacts from the days when the only people to live in these Arctic islands were a few hunters and trappers.

As if to remind you that summer, if sweet, is short, in front of most houses you will see a parked skidoo, a motor scooter with rubber tracks and steer-

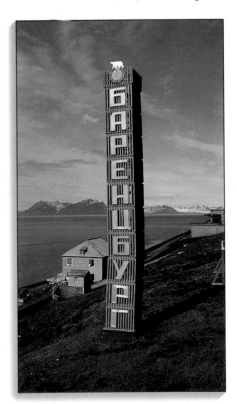

ing "skis", which is the only means of transport in the long winter months when snow lies thick on the ground.

Mineral rights

After World War I, Norway was granted sovereignty over the archipelago, though the various countries who agreed to the treaty reserved the right to exploit minerals. Sweden already operated a coal mining business but sold out to a Norwegian company in 1934.

Today, Russia is the only one of the original signatories to the Svalbard Treaty to retain an interest in coal mining, and has a substantial operation at **Barentsburg ❷**, only a few miles further down the fjord from Longyearbyen. Around 2,000 people, mostly Ukrainians, live in a coal-dusty village on the steep fjordside which, nevertheless, has an indoor farm of dairy cattle and chicken sheds. Kittiwakes scream from their nests on the window ledges and, on an esplanade below, well-dressed fur-hatted groups sell cheap Russian souvenirs and, now and then, a family "treasure" to the occasional summer cruise-ship passenger.

Nature in the raw

Svalbard should not, and is unlikely ever to become, a place for mass tourism: the islands cannot support it and, in any case, the appeal is to people who like to find their own wildlife and explore nature in the raw. However, the cruise ships are beginning to threaten the peace. Longyearbyen has two hotels and hardly a day goes by without a luxury cruise ship depositing its passengers on the shore for a barbecue or a short trip around the area. For safety reasons, visitors are normally accompanied by men with loaded guns and may not leave the

One of the characteristically spiky peaks that gave Spitsbergen its name.

BELOW: cruise ships are an increasingly common sight in summer.

Map on page 338

pre-set routes. Thus, the polar bear takes care that mass tourism never spoils the environment and only a few well equipped campers dare go further afield.

The area around Longyearbyen is a pleasant place during the summer, the stark mountains offset by a valley which has meadows spangled with flowers. Here, you will find the tiny bells of cassiope mixed with purple saxifrage and, perhaps, a patch of boreal Jacob's ladder, *Polemonium boreale*, an Arctic rarity with beautiful flowers. Near the shores where the glaucous gulls congregate, look for the fleshy leaved *Mertensia maritima*, or oyster plant.

The polar winter is a different matter. The sun does not rise above the horizon and everything is locked in darkness, lit only by the moon and the multi-coloured rays of the **aurora borealis** (northern lights; *see page 311*).

When the sun reappears and gathers strength, the ice pack retreats north, speeded by the warming influence of the Gulf Stream. This warm current flows up the west coast of Spitsbergen and ensures that, in summer, ships can have an ice-free passage right to the north shores of the islands. The sun's return is cause for a week-long Sunfestival in March with concerts and outdoor events.

Spitsbergen is mountainous and glaciated with around 60 percent covered in permanent ice. The highest mountain, **Newtontoppen**, is more than 1,700 metres (5,500 ft) high. Farther from the influence of the Gulf Stream, the second largest island, **Nordaustlandet**, is almost completely covered in ice.

Unknown and unexplored

According to the old Icelandic annals, in 1194 land was found to lie "four days sailing from Langanes, at the northern end of the sea". They called it Svalbard, but then the islands were forgotten for several hundred years. The next mention

TIP

Svalbard offers a wide range of activities for the outward bound enthusiast including dogsledging and skiing, camping expeditions, walks with packhorses and boat trips. See www.svalbard.net for details.

BELOW: a coal train in Ny-Ålesund.

The Norwegian botanist Hanna Resvoll-Holmsen took this self-portrait in 1908, while camping at Colbay.

BELOW: taking a really close look at an Arctic skua.

was in the journals of the great Dutch explorer, Willem Barents, in 1596. Barents, with two ships under his command, was trying to find a northern route to China when he sighted an island which, from the shape of its mountains, he named Spitsbergen. The two ships then parted, one to carry news of fjords filled with whales and walrus back to Holland, while the other ship with Barents on board continued eastward, only to become trapped in the pack ice and forced to spend the winter there, during which Barents and many of his crew died.

Story of the whales

By 1610 hunting expeditions had begun to arrive around the coast of Spitsbergen. News of the numbers of whales spread and soon the Dutch **whalers** were joined by English, French, Basques and Danes. Inevitably trouble flared as they disputed rights and fought pitched battles when warships came north to defend the claims of their whalers.

The English and Dutch at last agreed on a division of hunting territories and some peace was restored. The Dutch set up a shore base on **Amsterdam Island**, which grew to be almost a town with a fort, church and whale-oil refinery, and a summer population of a couple of thousand. They called it **Smeerenburg ❸**, the "Blubber town", and you can still find the outlines of stone buildings and the furnaces built to render the whale blubber into oil. The large numbers of bleached whale bones testify to the growing demands for whale oil, and in some places there is further mute testimony in the graves of men who died, either in battles or from more natural causes. Under the pressure of all the killing, it was inevitable that the whale stock would decline and by around 1750 whaling ceased.

This intensive whaling was purely a summer activity. In winter the islands were deserted except by accident. In 1630, an English ship was wrecked and the crew managed to cling to life throughout the winter. In 1633, some Dutchmen wintered at Smeerenberg, but the following year those who attempted to stay on all died of scurvy. The English had intended to colonise the archipelago but even prisoners under sentence of death refused to face the prospect of the Arctic night.

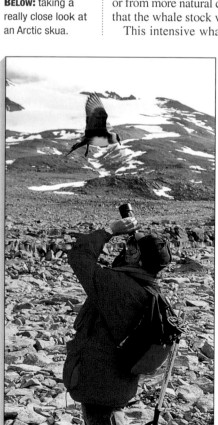

Tough life

The Russians were made of sterner stuff, however, and in the early part of the 18th century a number of hunting parties built houses on Svalbard and continued to hunt bear, fox, walrus and seals throughout the winter darkness. Not until the late 18th century did Norwegian hunters first arrive. They too over-wintered and today their cabins still lie along the shores of many fjords. Though mainly deserted, scientists and explorers often make use of the huts and many are kept in a good state of repair.

A trapper led a tough and rigorous life. He had to set his traps, mainly for Arctic fox whose beautiful pelts were most valuable in winter, in a hunting territory that covered many square kilometres. He also shot or caught polar bears in baited "fell-traps" and hunted seals, not just for food and skins, but for the oil which he then extracted from the blubber.

Ever since its discovery Svalbard has attracted

scientific expeditions. The first on record was in 1773 and included no less a personage than Horatio Nelson, then a midshipman. In 1827, the first Norwegian geological expedition took place under Professor B.M. Keilhau, and this was soon followed by expeditions from many nations. Today, the **Norsk Polarinstitut** is the clearing house for all expeditions to this Arctic outpost.

Map on page 338

Natural laboratory

Svalbard offers a splendid environment for the study of ecology and **natural history** by scientist and amateur alike. Almost every visitor who makes the long journey north has more than a passing interest in wildlife in general and birds in particular, and Svalbard's short Arctic summer offers a rich feast. For though the archipelago can seem desperately inhospitable, in the 24-hour days of summer the tundra slopes between the mountains and near the sea offer enough thin soil to encourage and support a surprising number of plants. These, in turn, support other wildlife such as insects, birds and a few mammals. The surrounding seas, although cold, are rich in fish and invertebrates which attract sea birds and sea mammals who use the shores and cliffs for breeding and resting. Kittiwakes, glaucous and ivory gulls push north as soon as daylight allows and are soon followed by Arctic terns, all the way from the southern hemisphere. The kittiwake is essentially an ocean bird which feeds almost exclusively at sea. At nesting time they set up huge noisy colonies on suitable cliffs, or even on window ledges in some places. Another ocean wanderer is the fulmar. Most of the Svalbard fulmars are in the "dark grey phase" of development and therefore-largely confined to Arctic waters, which at first puzzles some bird-watchers from further south. Four species of auks breed in Svalbard: Brünnich's guille-

The small yellow blooms of the Svalbard mohn.

BELOW: soil patterns in Sassendalen.

Map on page 338

The seal hunters who once flocked to Svalbard in the summer months used to refer to ringed seals as "floe rats".

BELOW: at the edge of the pack ice (with a rifle for protection).
RIGHT: in summer the Arctic ice breaks up under the influence of the warm Gulf Stream.

mot, the little auk, puffin and black guillemot. While Brünnich's guillemot nest on open but inaccessible ledges, the others seek the safety of crevices or burrows, where predators such as Arctic fox and glaucous gulls have less chance of getting at their eggs or young. There are also some waders.

The large expanses of barren mountains do not offer much in the way of food for land birds, but try the slopes and valleys which are often carpeted in dwarf birch and polar willow, and you will find snow buntings foraging for seeds and singing from the rocks. The ptarmigan also uses this habitat and it is the only bird to stay through the winter. Three kinds of geese breed on Svalbard – pink-footed, Brent and barnacle – and the many naturalists who have studied the barnacle geese now realise that the entire Svalbard population travels to Scotland each year, to spend the winter in the Solway area in the southwest, then return in spring to breed. When you spot the plentiful flocks of common eider along the shores, look closely because you may be lucky enough to find a few king eiders, showing off their superior plumage to their less flashy kin.

Arctic monarch

There is only one kind of grazing mammal on the islands and that is the hardy Svalbard reindeer. Smaller than the Samiland reindeer, you come across groups which seem quite tame, living a Spartan life off plants and lichens in the valley bottoms. The only other land mammals are the fox and the bear. The Arctic fox is a very attractive looking little animal, with a coat of varying shades of white and grey in summer and pure white in winter. Though it was hunted heavily in the past, it is still remarkably tolerant and curious about humans and is not too difficult to find on the sea-bird cliffs in summer, where it digs out nests or picks up any young birds that have fallen from the ledges.

The undoubted king of the Arctic is the polar bear. Adult males especially lead a nomadic life on the pack ice for much of the year and live mainly on seals, while young males and females with cubs tend to spend the summer on the island feeding largely on a vegetarian diet. Though they were formerly hunted for their skins, polar bears are now protected and can be killed only if they threaten human life. They are not uncommon, especially on favourite breeding islands, such as **Barentsøya** and **Edgeøya**.

The fjords of Svalbard may no longer be "filled with whales and walrus", as they were said to be in the 15th century, but you will certainly find sea mammals around the islands. Though it is now rare to see any of the great whales, species such as the lesser rorqhual or minke whales come into the fjord quite often. The beluga or white whale is easiest to identify with its white body and lack of a dorsal fin. You might be lucky enough to sight the remarkable narwhale, with its spear-like tusk projecting out in front.

The immense herds of walrus which in days past thronged places like **Moffen Island** have never fully recovered from over-hunting, but sometimes small groups appear at Moffen or on the south of Edgeøya, where they feast on the clam beds or rest on the shore: a hopeful sign in an age when Svalbard is visited for its stark natural beauty and summer wildlife. ❏

INSIGHT GUIDES
Travel Tips

✵® INSIGHT GUIDES Phonecard

One global card to keep travellers in touch. Easy. Convenient. Saves you time and money.

It's a global phonecard

Save up to 70%* on international calls from over 55 countries

Free 24 hour global customer service

Recharge your card at any time via customer service or online

It's a message service

Family and friends can send you voice messages for free.

Listen to these messages using the phone* or online

Free email service - you can even listen to your email over the phone*

It's a travel assistance service

24 hour emergency travel assistance – if and when you need it.

Store important travel documents online in your own secure vault

For more information, call rates, and all Access Numbers in over 55 countries, (check your destination is covered) go to www.insightguides.ekit.com or call Customer Service.

JOIN now and receive US$ 5 bonus when you join for US$ 20 or more.

Join today at

www.insightguides.ekit.com

When requested use ref code: **INSAD0103**

OR SIMPLY FREE CALL
24 HOUR CUSTOMER SERVICE

UK	0800 376 1705
USA	1800 706 1333
Canada	1800 808 5773
Australia	1800 11 44 78
South Africa	0800 997 285

THEN PRESS **0**

For all other countries please go to "Access Numbers" at www.insightguides.ekit.com

* Retrieval rates apply for listening to messages. Savings based on using a hotel or payphone and calling to a landline. Correct at time of printing 01.03

(INS001)

powered by ✦*ekit*

"The easiest way to make calls and receive messages around the world"

CONTENTS

Getting Acquainted

The Place

Area 323,878 sq km (125,000 sq miles).

Location Norway stretches from Pysen Rock, south of Odden (latitude 57°57'33") to Knivskjelodden (71°11'8"). The westernmost point is Steinsøy by Utvær (4°30'12" E) and the easternmost point is Hornøy in Vardø (31°10'10" E).

Topography Norway is mountainous, with elevations reaching around 2,500 metres (8,500 ft).

Capital Oslo, on the southeast coast at the head of Oslofjord.

Population 4.57 million. At about 11 people per sq km (29 per sq mile), Norway has the second-lowest population density in Europe after Iceland. Oslo is home to around 512,000 people – more than 10 percent of the national total. Other major cities' estimated populations: Bergen 230,000, Stavanger 110,000, Trondheim 151,000. The north is very sparsely populated.

Language Norwegian, of which there are two variations: *bokmål* and *nynorsk*. The Sami population (Lapps) in North Norway speak Lappish. English is widely understood in the sizeable towns.

Religion Around 86 percent are Evangelical Lutheran Church (state church) of Norway. The church is supported by the state, and the clergy is nominated by the king, but complete religious freedom is guaranteed. Other churches, mostly Protestant and Roman Catholic, represent about 4 percent of the population.

Time zone Central European Time, 1 hour ahead of Greenwich Mean Time, 6 hours ahead of Eastern Standard Time. The clock is set forward an hour to summer time at the end of March, and back an hour at the end of September.

Currency Norwegian krone (NOK), divided into 100 øre.

Weights and measures Metric. Distances are given in kilometres (km) but Norwegians often refer to a *mil* which is 10 km (thus 10 mil = 100 km). When talking about land area you will often hear the word *mål*. This old measure of 984.34 sq metres has been rounded up to 1,000 sq metres (or 1 decare).

Electricity 220 volts AC, 50 cycles. Plugs have two small round pins, so you may need an adapter for appliances you bring with you.

International dialling code +47. To ring out dial 00 and then the international number.

Topography

Norway is a narrow country 2,600 km (1,600 miles) long, shaped like a tadpole swimming south. At points along the tail it narrows to as little as 6 km (4 miles). Most of the country's 21,925-km (13,623-mile) continental coastline lies along the North Sea. Norway borders Sweden (1,620 km/1,005 miles), Finland (720 km/450 miles) and, in the north, Russia (196 km/ 122 miles). It has sovereignty over a few islands within the Arctic Circle, the largest being Svalbard (or Spitsbergen).

The south is hilly and partially forested. The most fertile food-growing region is the southern quarter of the country. Although the whole coast is indented with fjords, the west coast area from Stavanger to Bergen and Bergen to Trondheim contains the most-visited fjords.

The Glomma is the longest river (600 km, 373 miles) in Norway. With its source in South Trøndelag and outflow into the Oslo fjord, the river and its tributaries drain about one eighth (41,500 sq km/25, 770 sq miles) of the country. Rivers flowing southwest along the steep western slope are generally short and have numerous rapids and falls. Those flowing southeast along the gentle eastern slope are generally longer.

Norway has thousands of glacial lakes, the largest of which is Lake Mjøsa (362 sq km/140 sq miles) in the southeast.

Climate

In Oslo the January average daytime high is -2°C (28°F) and the nighttime low is -7°C (19°F); Bergen is less cold (high 3°C/37°F, low -1°C/30°F). Further north sub-zero temperatures can last for months and a good number of roads shut over winter due to long-term snow, although right on the coast it is usually a little milder. February and March are the best skiing months. March and April and sometimes even early May are the wet spring months when skies are grey, and roads are buckled due to thaws and refreezes; during this time the daily high temperature slowly lifts from about 4°C (39°F) to 16°C (61°F).

Come summertime and the season of the midnight sun, Oslo enjoys daily temperatures averaging 20–25°C (68–77°F), while the

Night Skies

● **Midnight sun** In some parts of Norway the sun does not sink below the horizon for several weeks in the summer. The best time to see the "midnight sun" is mid-May to late July. Longyearbyen on Svalbard has the longest period of midnight suns, from about 20 April to 20 August.

● **Aurora borealis** The northern lights, or aurora borealis, are most likely to occur from November to February. You need to go north of the Arctic Circle, which cuts through Norway just south of Bodø on the Nordland coast. There is, unfortunately, no guarantee they will occur every year.

Glaciers

One of the highlights of Norway is seeing the glaciers, but every year there are fatalities, when tourists are careless. Glaciers are in motion, so crevasses several metres wide and 30–40 metres (33–43 yards) deep occur, often covered with snow. Never climb or venture under a glacier without a guide.

Glacier Information Centres at the following places show films and exhibitions about the glaciers, and offer tours:
Oppstryn (tel: 57 87 72 00)
Fjærland (tel: 57 69 32 88)
and Jostedalen (tel: 57 68 32 50).

sunlight-bathed north has a perfect hiking temperature, hovering around 17°C (63°F). October sees temperatures dip below 10°C (50°F), then continue their slide towards zero. The first snow can be expected any time from mid-October to early December, depending on the location.

May and September are very popular with visitors. Transport, hotels and museums are often crowded in these two months. The Easter ski break is a time of mass exodus from schools and jobs to the slopes and trails. Otherwise, Norwegians mainly holiday from mid-June to early August. The traditional common holiday is all of July *(ferietide)* when factories shut down.

Government

Norway's national assembly, the *Storting*, is the mainstay of its political system. There are 165 members who sit in two chambers *(Odelsting* and *Lagting)*; elections occur every four years. There are 19 major local government sub-divisions (counties or *fylke)*, all of which are divided into smaller municipalities *(kommune)*. The government is headed by a prime minister who leads the majority party or a coalition of parties in the *Storting*. The Norwegian monarch

fulfils a symbolic role as the country's Head of State.

Across the political spectrum from left to right are the Red Electoral Alliance (RV), the Socialist Left Party (SV), the Labour Party (A), the Centre Party (SP), the Liberal Party (V), the Christian Democratic Party (Kr.F), the Conservative Party (H) and the Progress Party (Fr.P). Norway's constitution dates from 17 May 1814; a painting of its signing hangs in the *Storting* chamber.

Norwegians were subject to Danish rule for many centuries, and then entered a union with Sweden which lasted from 1814 until 1905. National Day is celebrated across the nation on the constitution's anniversary, 17 May, with parades, music and dancing.

Economy

Norway has been a member of NATO and the OECD since 1949, and is a founder member of the UN. The nation spends more money per capita on foreign aid than any other country. It is also a member of the Council of Europe and the EEA (the country turned down European Union membership in referenda in 1972 and 1994).

With Denmark, Sweden, Iceland, Finland, the Faroe Islands and Greenland, Norway is also a member of the Nordic Council (founded in 1952). The Council has 87 members, meets once a year in full session and has a permanent secretariat in Copenhagen.

Its most successful agreement is granting freedom for all Nordic citizens to travel without passports within the Nordic region *(Norden)* and work without a work permit. The 1955 social security convention also guarantees them the welfare benefits, from unemployment to health care, of the country in which they are working. Discussions on a customs union have not had similar success. Sweden and Finland's accession to the EU has complicated matters.

As well as funding a mass of technical, educational and arts

initiatives across the Nordic countries, Norway has introduced Nordunet, a communications network for education, with regular educational exchanges; information networks for medical data; facilities for the disabled, public administration; and environmental programmes, including a Nordic convention on world environment. Individual subjects are based in different centres, such as Helsinki's studies on environmental monitoring, and Oslo's Nordic Industrial Council, which co-ordinates industrial collaborations.

Norway's economy has boomed thanks to North Sea oil. Oil and gas account for around 35 percent of exports. Norway has been saving its oil-boosted budget surpluses in a Government Petroleum Fund, which is invested abroad and is valued at more than $43 billion.

Other long-established industries include timber, pulp and paper, hydro-electric power, gas, shipping and some mining. Fish and agricultural products have long been staples of the Norwegian economy.

The Cost of Living

Norway has a name for being expensive, and certainly this is true in some respects: the price of a cup of coffee in a smart city café can be exorbitant and even the smallest of items like toiletries can be double the amount they are elsewhere in Europe. Look out for "Lavpris" shops, which offer lower prices. It is true that the cost of alcohol is enough to make even heavy drinkers think twice about another bottle of wine; beer is a cheaper alternative and can be bought from supermarkets at good prices. Discount cards on accommodation *(page 364 & 365)* and public transport *(page 359 & 360)* are available, plus Norway offers tourists Tax-Free Shopping *(page 374)*. The Oslo Youth Information Centre publishes a budget guide to the capital, *Streetwise*. It is available from tourist offices.

The revenue from ocean fisheries has now been surpassed by fish farming, particularly salmon. Commercial whaling is carried out on a modest scale (roughly 600 minke whales a year) against the wishes of the International Whaling Commission (IWC). Newer industry revolves around computers and business services. Tourism is a continually increasing source of capital, too. Some of Norway's most successful commerical ventures include Statoil, Norsk Hydro, Kværner, Aker RGI and Royal Caribbean Cruise Lines.

The People

Although young people tend to be a lot less formal than their parents, Norwegians do still like to go about life with some surprisingly rigid rules of behaviour. To first time visitors their attitudes can appear off-hand or even rude, but they are not intended that way.

Norwegians are great hand shakers. Whenever strangers meet, there is always a handshake accompanied by an exchange of full names. When meeting casual acquaintances, you usually shake hands as you arrive and leave.

Norwegians are very polite. Whenever you are served something you will hear the phrase *Vær så god*, which basically means "You are welcome" and "It is a pleasure to serve you" rolled into one. The only equivalent to "please" in Norwegian is *vennligst*, which is formal and not frequently used. Nor do they say *takk* (thank you) as frequently as English-speaking people. Fortunately Norwegians of all ages, at least in urban areas, usually have a good grasp of English and don't mind using it.

The only thing remotely unruly in Norwegian manners occurs in the busy streets of Oslo. People jostle each other with impunity: don't be offended if you don't get an apology after someone bumps into you – as long as it's gentle. Of more concern, especially if you are driving, are the mad darts and leaps people make across streets, without regard for traffic lights.

Coffee is the national stimulant and served whenever people meet. But the real difficulty is coping with the mounds of pastry often served with the coffee; if you must refuse, do so politely, especially if you are turning down home-made pastries.

Note: Norwegian society is very closely tied to family and long-term friends from school days. Many do not feel inclined to go much further to extend their relationships to outsiders. Consequently, establishing friendships, even within a neighbourhood, could take time.

Public Holidays

- **1 January** New Year's Day
- Palm Sunday
- Maundy Thursday
- Good Friday
- Easter Sunday
- Easter Monday
  (making a five-day Thursday to Monday holiday block)
- **1 May** Labour Day
- **17 May** National Independence Day
- Ascension Day
- Whitsun
- Whit Monday
- **25 December** Christmas Day
- **26 December** 2nd Christmas Day

Dates vary each year.

Doing Business

Norwegians have all the state-of-the-art props when it comes to doing business. Don't be caught out without possessing a firm

Visiting a Norwegian Home

Norwegians usually eat dinner around 5 or 6pm, but dinner parties generally start later, at around 7.30pm. An invitation for any other time of the day usually means coffee and cake (if in doubt call the host and make certain). Let's say you've been invited to dinner and you want to make a good impression. Norway is not a "drop-in" society so you can expect the food to be well planned and of high quality. You could do far worse than taking note of the following protocol:

1 Norwegians are very punctual and expect others to be. Guests usually arrive exactly on time, jokingly called *Norsk time*,

sometimes even early. Make sure you dress correctly for the occasion (again, if in doubt ask the host in advance).

2 When entering a room, shake hands with everybody present, unless a large function makes that impossible. Introduce yourself to those you have not met before; give a friendly greeting to those you do know, but still shake hands.

3 If it's your first visit to someone's home it is customary to take a small gift along (usually flowers, a plant or chocolates).

4 Dinner parties in Norwegian homes follow a fixed pattern and include short speeches

even on family occasions. After tapping his glass, the host will always give a welcome speech and then propose a *skål*. It would be discourteous to touch the wine *before* this initial toast (but expect a liberal helping of *skåls*!).

5 Second helpings *(annen servering)* are so much the rule in Norwegian homes that the host will specifically point out if the dish is only to be passed round once. The secret is not to take too much the first time.

6 Every meal in Norway is concluded with a *takk for maten* (thank you for the food) and, if it's dinner, a general *skål*.

Business Hours

Office hours are 8 or 9am–4pm; lunch is taken early, usually between about 11.30am–12.30pm, or noon–2pm for a restaurant lunch or lunch meeting, which are business-like affairs. Shopping malls open Mon–Fri 10am–9pm, Sat 9am–6pm and close Sundays.

handshake, mobile phone, snappy-looking business card and, if possible, a laptop.

Like all Scandinavians, Norwegians take their summer holiday very seriously as a time for retreating to a fjord or mountain *hytte* (usually a log cabin). During the common holiday of all of July, offices and factories empty, and it is virtually impossible to arrange an appointment or do any business. May, with its holidays, can also be a difficult time.

Nothing about doing business should take you too much by surprise here. People take work seriously, but also know how to maintain a pleasantly relaxed business atmosphere. Norwegians dress for business much as they do elsewhere; although in summer dress codes are relaxed slightly.

Norwegians are rarely deceitful. They may well mention the bad points of something first, to get them out of the way; then it's on to the sell. In other words, you won't be drowned in a sea of hype, and the honesty can be a little hard to get used to. Ultimately you'll appreciate not having to figure out the pitfalls for yourself.

If you are looking up someone's number in a phone book, you'll find his or her profession listed next to the name; not only is this a matter of professional pride, but a real help in a country with a limited number of surnames.

So much for generalisations; there will always be exceptions. The only really important things to remember are that liquid lunches are unusual, and the work day ends at 3.30 or 4pm.

Most Norwegian consulates and embassies have commercial attachés. Three organisations in Oslo deal with tourism, business and trade:

Innovation Norway (Trade Council) (Innovasjon Norge) Drammensv. 40, 0243 Oslo Tel: 22 00 25 00

The Norwegian Tourist Board P.O. Box 722 Sentrum, Stortorvet 10 NO-0150 Oslo Tel: 24 14 46 00 Fax: 24 14 46 01 E-mail: norway@ntr.no www.visitnorway.com

Oslo Promotion AS Grev Wedels plass 4 0151 Oslo Tel: 23 10 62 00 Fax: 23 10 62 01 E-mail: oslo@oslopro.no www.oslopro.no

ODIN, the central web server for the Norwegian Government, office of the Prime Minister and the ministries, can be found at: www.odin.dep.no

Bergen Convention Bureau – Bergen Tourist Board P.O. Box 4055, Dreggen NO-5023 Bergen Tel: +47 55 31 38 60 Fax: +47 55 31 56 82 E-mail: convention@visitbergen.com

Planning the Trip

Passports and Visas

A valid passport is all that is necessary for citizens of most countries to enter Norway. Visas are not required. Norway is a member of the Schengen agreement, allowing citizens of other Schengen countries to enter without passports. If you enter from another Scandinavian country (Denmark, Finland, Iceland, or Sweden), you won't get a new entry stamp. Tourists are generally limited to a three-month visit; it is possible to stay longer, but you must apply for a visa after the initial three months (Scandinavian passport holders are exempt from this requirement) or if you plan to work in Norway.

Health and Insurance

The are no major health hazards in Norway. No vaccinations are necessary to enter Norway and the tap water is (generally) good. A degree of common sense is required when travelling in remote areas, especially during the winter. When hiking/skiing in the mountains always let someone know of your travel intentions, and use guides wherever possible. **Treatment** Norway has reciprocal treatment agreements with the UK and many other European countries; your own National Insurance should cover you to receive free treatment at public hospitals. You will, however, have to pay towards medicine, so it is advisable to take out medical insurance. EU citizens should obtain the relevant documentation to entitle them to this (for British citizens an E111 form from post offices). People from countries without such agreements, and those without an E111, will have to pay a small fee. If you are concerned whether you need extra cover, check in your own country before you go.

Money Matters

The Norwegian krone (NOK) is divided into 100 øre. Notes come in denominations of NOK 50, 100, 200, 500 and 1,000 and coins are 50 øre and NOK 1, 5, 10 and 20.

You can change currency at post offices, the Oslo S train station, international airports, some hotels and commercial banks. It is always useful to carry a certain amount of cash with you in case of emergency.

Public telephones take either phone cards (purchased from kiosks) or NOK 1, 5, 10, or 20 coins. The cost of a local call is NOK 4. Road toll stations are sometimes unmanned and require coins the driver needs to insert (usually NOK 20) in order to raise the barrier.

Credit Cards/Travellers' Cheques

Use of credit cards is widespread in Norway, with Eurocard, Visa, Access, American Express and Diner's Club the most common. Few petrol stations will take them, however, so make sure you have a fair amount of cash with you if you're driving. Check with your own credit card company about acceptability and other services.

Travellers' cheques are accepted and should be purchased before travelling to Norway. In most banks you can generally get cash on a Visa card, up to a limit of NOK 2,500 a week.

Customs Regulations

The following can be brought into Norway by visitors:
● **Money** Notes and coins (Norwegian and foreign) up to NOK 25,000 or equivalent. If you intend to import more, you must fill in a form (available at all entry and exit points) for the Customs Office.

● **Alcohol** Permitted imports for people aged 20 and over include 1 litre of spirits (up to 60 percent vol.) plus 1 litre of fortified wine (up to 22 percent vol.) or 2 litres of wine (if no spirits), and 2 litres of beer, or 4 litres of beer.
● **Tobacco** European residents over the age of 18 may bring 200 cigarettes or 250 g of other tobacco goods.
● **Sweets** 1 kg duty-free chocolate and sweets.
● **Meat** Up to 3 kg of meat products can be imported from an EEA member country as long as the product is stamped with the country of origin.
● **Sundries** Other goods (excluding articles for personal use) may be brought in duty-free up to a value of NOK 1,200.
● **Prohibited goods** Narcotics, medicines (except for personal use), poisons, firearms, ammunition and explosives. Note: the mild narcotic leaf *khat* is illegal in Norway.
● **Agricultural produce**
This comes under strict surveillance. If it concerns you, get specific details beforehand.

What to Bring/Wear

You're in for a pleasant surprise if travelling to Norway in summer. As it is protected by the Gulf Stream it can get even warmer than some of its southern neighbours. In the south, temperatures above 25°C (77°F) are not unusual. The average temperature for the country as a whole in July, including the far north, is about 16°C (60°F), 22°C (71°F) in Oslo. Bring swimming gear, as the water in most fjords, except northern Norway, is 20°C+ (68°F+) in mid-summer.

Pack the clothes you would normally wear in northern Europe, including jumpers and a raincoat, and take some strong walking shoes.

The mountains can be cold, so bring some warmer garments. You are not usually required to dress formally for dinner at Norwegian resort hotels. Spring and autumn

Animals

Some animals must be quarantined upon arrival in Norway, but if your pet comes from an EU country there is no official quarantine. Nor is there a requirement, as there used to be, to keep pets under "house arrest" for a month. Vets' fees are very high compared to the UK so pet insurance is essential.

are rainy (an umbrella is always useful), and nights can be chilly. It is rainy year-round on the west coast.

In winter bring very warm clothing and dress in layers (cotton against the skin and then wool). Woollen mittens or gloves and hats (covering the ears) are strongly advised (and face cover and goggles, if you are skiing). In the far north, temperatures drop to below -20°C (-4°F). In January, the average daytime temperature in Oslo is -2°C (28°F) and -7°C (19°F) at night. Inland areas are generally colder than the coast.

A first-aid kit is recommended for those who plan to make any trips to remoter parts. And be sure to include medicines for preventing and treating mosquito bites, as from mid-summer into early autumn biting insects are rife, especially in Finnmark.

Tourist Information

There are around 350 local tourist offices around Norway, as well as 18 regional tourist offices.
General information
The Tourist Information Centre
Fridtjof Nansens Plass 5, Oslo
(by the City Hall)
Tel: +47 22 11 78 80
Fax: +47 22 83 81 50
E-mail: info@oslopro.no
www.visitoslo.com
Regional information
Regional tourist offices are experts in the county they cover. They are usually open to personal callers, and will also supply advice and information in writing or over the phone.

Oslo/Oslofjord
The Tourist Information Centre
(details as above)
Akershus Tourist Board
Schweigaardsgt. 4
N-0185 Oslo
Tel: 22 05 58 75
Fax: 22 05 58 99
E-mail: info@akershus.com
www.akershus.com
Destinasjon Vestfold AS
Thor Dahls gate 1–5
N-3210 Sandefjord
Tel: 33 48 60 00
Fax: 33 46 61 01
E-mail: info@vestfold.com
www.visitvestfold.com

East Norway
Buskerud Opplevelser BA
Engene 44
N-3015 Drammen
Tel: 32 89 02 50
Fax: 32 89 17 73
E-mail: info@buskerud.no
www.buskerud.no
Fjell og Fjord Ferie
Gamlevegen 6
N-3550 Gol
Tel: 32 02 99 26
Fax: 32 02 99 28
E-mail: fjellogfjord@online.no
www.eventyrvegen.com
Hedmark Reiseliv BA
Grønnegate 11
N-2317 Hamar
Tel: 62 52 90 06
Fax: 62 52 21 49
E-mail: post@hedmark.com
www.hedmark.com

South Norway
Arendal Turist Kontor
Lanbrygga 5, Pollen
4803 Arendal
Tel: 37 00 55 44
Fax: 37 00 55 40
www.arendal.com
Destinasjon Sørlandet
Vestre Strandgate 32
4612 Kristiansand
Tel: 38 12 13 14
Fax: 38 02 52 55
E-mail: destinasjon@sorlandet.com
www.sorlandet.com
Telemarkreiser
P.O. Box 3133 Handelstortget
N-3707 Skien
Tel: 35 90 00 30

Fax: 35 90 00 21
E-mail: info@telemarkreiser.no
www.visittelemark.com

Fjord Norway
Bergen
Vagsallmenningen 1
N-5014 Bergen
Tel: 55 55 20 00
Fax: 55 55 20 01
E-mail: info@visitbergen.com
www.visitbergen.com
Fjord Norge AS
P.O. Box 4108 Dreggen
N-5835 Bergen
Tel: 55 30 26 50
E-mail: info@fjordnorway.no
www.fjordnorway.com
Møre og Romsdal Reiselivsråd
Fylkeshuset
N-6404 Molde
Tel: 71 24 50 80
Fax: 71 24 50 81
E-mail: mr-reiselivsrad@eunet.no
www.visitmr.com
Rogaland Reiseliv
Arkitekt Eckhoffs gate 1
4001 Stavanger
Tel: 51 51 66 00
Fax: 51 51 67 97
E-mail: firmapost@rfk.rogaland-f.kommune.no
www.rogaland-f.kommune.no
Sognefjord Reiseliv BA
P.O. Box 53

Tourist Info Abroad

Australia
The embassy deals with tourist information.
17 Hunter Street, Yarralumia,
Canberra ACT 2600
Tel: 2 62 702700
UK
Norwegian Tourist Board
Tel: (brochure line, calls cost 50 pence per minute) 0906 302 2003
Fax: 020 7839 6014
E-mail: infouk@ntr.no
www.visitnorway.com
US/Canada
Norwegian Tourist Board
Tel: 212 885 9700
Fax: 212 885 9710
E-mail: usa@ntr.no
www.goscandinavia.com

N-6898 Balestrand
Tel: 57 69 16 17
Fax: 57 69 14 31
E-mail: destination@sognefjord.no
www.sognefjord.no/midtresogn

Central Norway
Midt-Norsk Reiseliv AS
P.O. Box 65
N-7400 Trondheim
Tel: 73 84 24 40
Fax: 73 84 24 50
E-mail: turistinfo@mnr.as
www.visitcentral-norway.com

North Norway
Finnmark Reiseliv AS
Sorenskriverveien 13
N-9511 Alta
Tel: 78 44 00 20
Fax: 78 43 51 84
E-mail: post@finnmark.org
www.visitnorthcape.com
Nordland Reiseliv AS
P.O. Box 434
N-8001 Bodå
Tel: 75 54 52 00
Fax: 75 54 52 10
E-mail: nordland@nordlandreiseliv.no
www.visitnordland.no
Svalbard Reiselivsråd
P.O. Box 323
N-9171 Longyearbyen
Tel: 79 02 55 50
Fax: 79 02 55 51
E-mail: info@svalbard.net
www.svalbard.net

Getting There

BY AIR

Scandinavia's flagship carrier, **SAS** (Scandinavian Airline Services), runs a wide range of flights between Oslo Gardermoen Airport and other world capitals (usually involving a feeder service to and from one of the main European hubs – usually London, Copenhagen or Frankfurt), with some direct services to and from Bergen, Oslo, Stavanger, Tromsø and Trondheim. SAS also operates a direct service from New York (Newark) and Chicago.

SAS and the Norwegian airline **Braathens** are joined by other major international airlines – including

British Airways, Lufthansa, Air France, and **KLM** – in connecting Oslo and other cities with daily flights to Europe.

Approximate flying times to Oslo are: London, 2 hours, Frankfurt, 1 hour 50 minutes, Paris, 2 hours, Budapest, 3 hours 35 minutes, and Warsaw, 3 hours 25 minutes.

SAS offers five daily non-stop flights from Heathrow to Oslo and two to Stavanger. **BA** operates four flights a day from Heathrow to Oslo and one daily from Manchester to Oslo. **Ryanair** offers low-cost flights from London Stansted to Oslo Torp, near Sandefjord, 130 km (80 miles) south of Oslo. They also fly from Glasgow Prestwick to Oslo Torp and from London Stansted to Haugesund.

Braathens operates daily flights to Bergen from London Gatwick and to Stavanger from Aberdeen and Newcastle. It also flies from Dublin to Oslo. **Wideroe** flies to 33

destinations within Norway and has flights from Manchester, Aberdeen, Newcastle, Copenhagen, Gothenburg and Stockholm. It is based at Oslo Torp airport in Sandefjord, 130 km (80 miles) south of Oslo. **Coast Air** has scheduled flights from Aberdeen to Bergen, Monday to Friday. **Norwegian Air Shuttle** operates on a daily basis from eight major airports in Norway, in addition to flights from London and southern Europe to Oslo as well as from Oslo to regional routes in northern Norway. All airports are serviced by buses and taxis. Oslo's Gardermoen Airport has a number of train services *(see Getting Around page 359)*.

SAS

In the UK
World Business Centre
Newall Road
London Heathrow
Hounslow TW6 2RE

Reservations from the UK
Tel: 0845-6072 7727
Fax: 020-8990 7127
www.scandinavian.net
In North America
c/o United Airlines
437 Madison Ave (enter on 50th St)
New York
Tel: 1-800 221 2350
In Norway
Tel (reservations): 81 52 04 00

Braathens
In the UK
Tel: 0845 607 27727
www.braathens.no
In Norway
Tel: 81 52 00 00

British Airways
In the UK
Speedbird House
P.O. Box 10
Heathrow Airport
Hounslow TW6 2JA
Tel: 0845 773 3377
www.ba.com
In Norway
British Airways
Dronning Mauds g 1–3
0250 Oslo
Tel: 800-33142 (freephone)
Fax: 22 82 20 49

Ryanair
In the UK
Enterprise House
Stansted Airport
Stansted
Essex CM24 1QW
Tel: 0871 246 0000
www.ryanair.com

Coast Air
Reservations through British Airways (see above).

Norwegian Air Shuttle
In the UK
Tel: 0191 214 0994
In Norway
P.O. Box 115
N-1330 Fornebu
Tel: 67 59 30 00
www.norwegian.no

Widerøe
In Norway
Elvind Lychesuei vei 10

Specialist Tour Operators

● **Activity holidays**
Inntravel
Nr Castle Howard, York YO60 7JU
Tel: 01653 617788
Scantours
47 Whitcomb Street,
London WC2H 7DH
Tel: 020 7839 2927
● **Arctic voyages/dog-sledging/whale watching**
Arctic Experience & Discover the World
29 Nork Way, Banstead,
Surrey SM7 1PB
Tel; 01737 214214
Arcturus Expeditions
P.O. Box 850, Gartocharn,
Alexandria G83 8RL
Tel: 01389 830204
● **Christmas holidays**
Page & Moy
136–140 London Road,
Leicester LE2 1EN
Tel: 0116 250 7979
● **Norway specialists**
Norsc Holidays
1 The Lawns, Charmouth
DT6 6LR
Tel: 01297 560033

Taber Holidays
30A Bingley Road, Saltaire, Shipley,
West Yorkshire BD18 4RS
Tel: 01274 594 642
● **Skiing/Walking**
Crystal Holidays
King's Place, Wood Street,
Kingston, Surrey KT1 1JY
Tel: 08701 606040
Waymark Holidays
44 Windsor Road, Slough SL1 2EJ
Tel: 01753 516477
Mountain & Wildlife Ventures,
Brow Foot, High Wray, Ambleside
LA22 0JF
Tel: 015394 33285
● **Tours**
Explore Worldwide
1 Frederick Street, Aldershot,
Hampshire GU11 1LQ
Tel: 01252 760000
ScanMeridian
Clareville House 32–34 Panton
Street, London SW1Y 4EA
Tel: 020 7431 5322
Great Rail Journeys
Saviour House, 9 St Saviourgate,
York YO1 8NL
Tel: 01904 521900

N-1338 Sandvika
Tel: 67 11 60 00
Fax: 67 11 61 95
E-mail: sandvika@wideroe.no
www.wideroe.no

BY SEA

Fjord Line and DFDS Seaways operate the only direct services from the UK to Norway, with sailings from Newcastle and Bergen (Fjord Line), and Kristiansand (DFDS).

There are three sailings per week in each direction in the summer (two per week in other seasons). Both companies offer a wide selection of holiday ideas for the winter and summer, ranging from chalets to resorts and motoring breaks in first-class hotels.

Smyril Line operates a weekly sailing from Torshavn in the Faroe Islands to Bergen via Lerwick, with connections to Aberdeen.

Fjord Line
Royal Quays
North Shields
Tyne & Wear
NE29 6EG
Tel: 0191 296 1313
Fax: 0191 296 1540
E-mail: fjordline.uk@fjordline.com
www.fjordline.com

DFDS Seaways
Scandinavia House
Parkeston Quay, Harwich
Essex CO12 4QG
Tel: 0870 5333 000
Fax: 01255 244 475
www.dfdsseaways.co.uk

Smyril Line
Holmsgarth Terminal
Lerwick ZE1 0PR
Tel: 01595 690845
Fax: 01595 692287
www.smyril-line.com

BY RAIL

Numerous rail services link Norway with the rest of Scandinavia and Europe. From the Continent, express trains operate to

Fjord Tours

● **Fjord Line**
International Ferry Terminal, Royal Quays, North Shields NE29 6EG
Tel: 0191 296 1313
● **Norvista**
31–35 Kirby Street London EC1N 8TE
Tel: 0870 7447315
● **Taber Holidays**
30A Bingley Road, Saltaire, Shipley, West Yorkshire BD18 4RS
Tel: 01274 594642
● **Yes**
Broadway, Peterborough PE1 1RS
Tel: 01733 340345

Copenhagen, where inter-Scandinavian trains connect to Oslo. There are train connections in Oslo to other cities in Norway. First- and second-class coaches are available on these express trains, plus sleeper coaches on all of the overnight expresses.

Seat reservations are required on all night and long-distance day trains, as well as on express and high speed 'Signatur' services.

The Norwegian State Railway (NSB) is part of the InterRail, EuroDomino, Eurailpass and Eurail Youthpass system, which offers various discount tickets (including to students). InterRail: www.interrailnet.com, Eurail: www.eurail.com. The new high-speed LINX trains between Oslo and Stockholm and Copenhagen have cut travel times considerably. For more information, visit: www.linx.se

There are frequent connections from Copenhagen, Stockholm and Gothenberg to Oslo.

You can also get to northern Norway from Stockholm, with Trondheim and Narvik the principal destinations, again usually twice daily (the line in Norway terminates at Bodø).

International arrivals and departures are located at Sentral-stasjon (Oslo-S). Gardermobanen, the high-speed rail link to/from Oslo Gardermoen Airport has a terminal

at Oslo S, and trains also run to/from Asker via Nationalteatret station. NSB provides train information and also operates as a travel bureau across Norway:
Norwegian State Railways
NSB Reisesenter
P.O. Box 673,
N-5001 Bergen, Norway
Tel: 81 50 08 88*f*
www.nsb.no

BY ROAD

Most major shipping lines to Norway allow passengers to bring cars. But coming by car increases sea travel costs, and petrol is expensive in Norway.
Norges Automobil Forbund
(NAF or Norwegian Automobile Association)
Østensjøveien 14, 0609 Oslo
Tel: 22 34 14 00
Fax: 22 33 13 72
Emergency tel: 810 00 505
www.naf.no
Kongelig Norsk Automobilklub
(KNA or Royal Norwegian Automobile Club)
Cort Adelersgt. 16 Oslo
Tel: 21 60 49 00
Emergency tel: 22 30 30 50
(members only).

Practical Tips

Security and Crime

The streets of Oslo are relatively safe compared with the bigger cities of Europe and North America, even though the tabloids report an abundance of muggings, stabbings and other crimes of violence, as they do everywhere.

Crime against tourists is rare, however. Take the same precautions here as anywhere: park safely and hide valuables out of sight. The same applies when out on the town. Simply stick with the happy crowds and avoid the sleazy joints.

Norwegian cities late at night are usually full of young people, many of them drunk: this is mainly because of the lengthy opening hours and the Nordic drinking culture (a Norwegian often drinks to get drunk).

Most bars have good bouncers, so alert them if you're having trouble. Police patrols are supplemented and now outnumbered by private-sector security personnel and *Nattravene* (Night Ravens, a Guardian Angel-type patrol).

Another potential threat can be drug abusers. However, they are usually placid and generally gather around Jernbanetorget (central station). Simply give them a wide berth. There is no strict rule here; a no-go area today could be tomorrow's in place.

Medical Services

Doctors and Hospitals
The standard of health provision in Norway is very high, and even in remote areas you should have no problem getting medical help. Just

about all doctors and nurses speak good English, and if they don't they'll soon find someone who does.

In medical emergencies EU members will receive free treatment at state hospitals *(see page 351 for reciprocal arrangements)*, but have to pay towards the non-hospital costs and for prescriptions.

If you are ill, ask your hotel, tourist office or a pharmacy for the address of an English-speaking GP. Private doctors are listed in the directory under *Leger* (doctors). Make sure you keep receipts if you have medical insurance.

Pharmacies
For minor problems, head for a pharmacy, or *Apotek (for opening hours see page 351)*. Most larger cities have all-night pharmacies *(see box)*. In other cities enquire at your hotel, or try the emergency number in the phone book under *Legevakt* (doctor on duty).

Night Pharmacies

● **Oslo**
Jernbanetorvets Apotek, across from Central train station, Jernbanetorget 4B
Tel: 22 41 24 82
Open 24 hours a day.
● **Bergen**
Apotek Nordstjernen, Bus Station
Tel: 55 21 83 84
Open Monday to Saturday 8am–midnight, Sunday 9.30am–midnight.
● **Stavanger**
Loeveapoteket,
Olav V's gt. 11
Tel: 51 91 08 80
Open daily until 11pm, Christmas, New Year, Easter and Whitsun 9am–8pm.
● **Trondheim**
St Olav Vakt-apotek,
Kjøpmannsgate 65
Tel: 73 88 37 37
Open Monday to Saturday 8am–midnight, Sunday 10am–midnight.

Where there is a rota of 24-hour pharmacies in a city, a list will usually be posted on the door of each one.

Dentists
Emergency dental treatment in Oslo, outside regular dentists' office hours, is available from:
Oslo Kommunale Tannlegevakt, Tøyen Senter, Kolstadgata 18, (near Tøyen T-bane station).
Tel: 22 67 30 00.
Open Mon–Sat 7am–10pm, Sun and public holidays 11am–2pm.

Media

Newspapers
Most larger kiosks (like the *Narvesen* chain found at railway stations, airports and so on) and some bookshops sell English-language newspapers.

Deichmanske Bibliotek, the main public library, is at Henrik Ibsen's gate 1 in Oslo; you'll find a selection of international papers and periodicals in its reading rooms, as well as free internet access.

Bookshops
There are several bookshops in Oslo with English-language sections, including; **Erik Qvist** at Drammensveien 16, tel: 22 54 26 00 and **Tanum Karl Johan** at Karl Johansgate 37/41, tel: 22 41 11 00.

Radio
English broadcasts on short wave can be picked up if atmospheric conditions are favourable. Best results can usually be heard on short wave frequency 9410.

During the winter months **BBC radios 1**, **2**, **3** and **4** can sometimes be received on AM but reception is often distorted. **Radio 5** can be picked up on 909 and 693 medium wave (best reception in the evening). On Sundays **Radio Norway** (93 FM) broadcasts the news from Norway in English in *Norway This Week*, a 30-minute programme at 5pm.

Internet Cafés

Free internet access is available at most public libraries in Norway. Screen time is limited and you may need to reserve your slot in advance. The Oslo Tourist Information Service, Oslo Promotion, publishes a list of internet cafés in the capital. These include: **Arctic Internet**, Oslo Central Station. Open daily 8am–midnight. Tel: 22 17 19 40; **Coffee and Juice Netcafé**, Nedre Slottsgate 12. Open 10am–1am, Sun noon–midnight. Tel: 22 41 21 90; **Qba**, Olaf Ryes Plass 4. Open weekdays 8am–1am, Sat 11am–1am. Closed Sun. Tel: 90 55 34 34.

For local frequencies of the **BBC World Service** enquire at the nearest tourist office.

Television

Norway has three main television stations: **NRK** (Norsk Rikskringkasting), **TV2** and **TV Norge** (TVN). Cable TV is common here and allows you to pick up a variety of channels including **BBC Prime**, **BBC World**, **CNN**, **Swedish TV1** and **TV2**, **Discovery**, **MTV**, **French TV5**, **Eurosport**, **TV3** and so on, depending on the distributor. Most hotels have pay channels in addition to the above. English films on Norwegian television are subtitled, not dubbed.

Postal Services

The central post office in Oslo, at Dronningensgate 15 (the entrance is on the corner of Prinsensgate), is open Monday–Friday 8am–6pm and Saturday 9am–3pm. Other post offices are open weekdays 8am–5pm, Saturday 9am–1pm, though there may be half-hour or hour variations.

Letters and postcards cost the same price for the UK and Europe, slightly more for North America. Post takes 2–3 days to Europe and 7–10 days to the US.

Telecommunications

Calls abroad can be made from hotels – with a surcharge – or from phone booths or the main telegraph office at Kongensgate 21 (entrance Prinsensgate), Oslo. You can also send faxes and telegrams from this office.

Norwegian pay-phones take 1, 5, 10 and 20 kroner pieces. Phonecards, which can be used in the green phone booths, can be bought in *Narvesen* kiosks and at post offices. Credit cards (Visa, American Express, Diners, Eurocard and Mastercard) are accepted in card phones.

When calling from Norway to foreign countries always dial 00 first. Cheapest calling times are outside business hours: 5pm–8am. Extra cheap international calling cards, such as Eurocity, can be purchased from a variety of kiosks (corner shops) in most major towns.

Telephone directories have a page of instructions in English in the index. When looking up names, remember the vowels æ, ø, and å come at the end of the alphabet, in that order.

Opening Hours

● **Shops** Monday to Friday 9am–5pm, Thursdays until 8pm, Saturday from 9am until 1, 2 or even 3pm.
● **Shopping centres** Until 8 or 9pm on weekdays, 6pm on Saturday.
● **Banks** 8.30am–3.30pm, weekdays only.
● **Pharmacies** Monday to Friday 9am–5pm, Saturday mornings and on a rota basis in larger cities.

Religious Services

The Lutheran church is Norway's state church, with around 86 percent of the population registered as Lutherans. Oslo has many Lutheran places of worship, including one American Lutheran church (Fritzners g. 15, tel: 22 44 35 84, fax: 22 44 30 15)

Services are held in English at the **American Lutheran church** and the **Anglican/Episcopalian church** (St Edmund's, Møllergate 30, tel: 22 69 22 14).

Minority religious groups are Pentecostalists, Baptists, Seventh Day Adventists, Evangelical Lutherans, Methodists, Catholics, Jews (the **synagogue** is at Bergstein 13, near St. Hanshaugen, tel: 22 69 65 70) and Moslems. The **Oslo Cathedral** (Protestant), Domkirke at Storgate, tel: 23 31 46 00, puts on concerts for tourists at 8pm every Wednesday). For up-to-date information, consult the daily press or latest *Oslo Guide*, or visit the Tourist Office.

Tipping

Tipping is easy. Hotels include a service charge and tipping is generally not expected. Restaurants usually have the service charge included, in which case it's your choice to add anything (5–10 percent is customary). The same applies to taxis. Table service in bars (particularly outdoor tables) requires tipping. With hairdressers a tip isn't quite as customary, but again 5–10 percent would be appropriate – and appreciated. Cloakrooms usually have a

Useful Numbers

● **Fire** 110
● **Police** 112
● **Ambulance** 113
● **Medical problems**
For emergency medical treatment in Oslo *(legevakt)* ring 22 11 80 80.
● **Internal directory enquiries** 1881/1880
● **International directory enquiries** 1882

Some US phone companies have their own international access numbers, to allow US citizens cheaper calls, as follows:
● **Sprint** 800-19 877
● **AT&T** 800-19 011
● **WorldPhone** 800-19 912

fixed fee of about NOK 5–10; if not, leave a few krone for the attendant.

Gay and Lesbian Travellers

In common with the rest of Scandinavia, Norway has a very relaxed attitude to homosexuality. There is very little hostility to gays and lesbians in general society and, partly as a result, the commercial gay scene is relatively small. Tourist offices carry details of the main places and events, including the Gay Pride celebrations in Oslo and Bergen and the annual Oslo Gay Film Festival.

The main bars and clubs include:
London Pub, Hambros Plass 5, Oslo. Tel: 22 70 87 00.
Soho Club, Kirkegate 34, Oslo. Tel: 22 42 91 00.
Finken Café and Bar, Nygardsgate 2a, Bergen. Tel: 55 32 13 16.

Disabled Travellers

Visitors in need of assistance should contact **Norges handikapforbund**, Schweigaardsgt. 12, 0185 Oslo, tel: 24 10 24 00, fax: 24 10 24 99, www.nhf.no

Hotel listings in accommodation guides have symbols designating disabled access and toilets. In the *Oslo Guide* under Outdoor Activities you'll find some listings that specially mention capacity for disabled visitors, such as the Bogstad ski area in Nordmarka.

It is becoming more usual for hotels to adapt their furnishings to the needs of people with physical disabilities. These hotels are indicated in *Accommodation in Norway* (available from the Norwegian Tourist Board). The Norwegian State Railways (NSB) have carriages specially furnished for the disabled, and the new Coastal Express ships have lifts and cabins for disabled people. The **Euro Terra Nova AS**, at Møllergata 4, 0179 Oslo, offers brochures on coach tours around Norway especially for wheelchair users. They also provide hotel

Embassies in Oslo

Canada
Wergelandsvn 7
Tel: 22 99 53 00
www.canada.no
UK
Thomas Heftyesgate 8
Tel: 23 13 27 00
www.britain.no
United States
Drammensveien 18
Tel: 22 44 85 50
www.usa.no
Australia
Australian Consulate,
Jernbanetorget 2
Tel: 22 47 91 70
Fax: 22 42 26 83
New Zealand
General Consulate of New Zealand
Løvenskiold-Vaekerø AS, Drammensvn 230, (P.O. Box 38, Skoien), 0212 Oslo 2.

bookings and hire cars, tel: 22 94 13 50, fax: 22 94 13 61 www.euroterranova.no. Guidebooks for Nordland county (North Norway) can be ordered free of charge from Nordland Reiseliv.

The Society for Accessible Travel and Hospitality (SATH) provide information and advice for travellers with disabilities. Their website is: www.sath.org.

Travelling with Kids

Norway is a welcoming and safe place for children; this is one reason why you will see them out on their own here at a young age. Children can usually travel and stay in hotels for less than the adult tariffs.

Family attractions include:

IN AND AROUND OSLO

International Children's Art Museum (exhibits and workshops), Lille Frøens vei 4, tel: 22 46 85 73 (open all year, entrance fee).
Horseriding, minigolf and Minizoo Ekeberg near Ekeberghallen, tel: 22 68 26 69.

Puppet Theatre Frognerveien 67, tel: 22 34 86 80 (open May–Sept).
Tusenfryd Amusement Park Ås, Østfold. Open June–Aug (May–Sept times vary). Transport by bus 541 from Oslo-S or Rådhuset, tel: 64 97 66 99; www.tusenfryd.no. Main attractions include: roller-coaster with loop and corkscrew, Spaceshot, flume ride, carousel, magic carpet, climbing wall and so on. Height restrictions apply on some of the rides here.
VikingLandet (adjacent to Tusenfryd, open May–Sept, times vary),tel: 64 97 66 99. Live a Viking for a day. VikingLandet gives you an authentic picture of the Viking Age. Experience the buildings, the market place, smithy, farm animals and fields. Not to be missed is **Plus Toktet**, a Viking Voyage deep in a mountain cave. Combination tickets with Tusenfryd are available, but you need two days to do the lot.

AROUND NORWAY

The Troll Family Park near Lillehammer, tel: 61 27 72 22; www.hunderfossen.no. Main attractions are: River Rafting, the Fairy Tale Castle, the World's Largest Troll, Fairy Tale Cave, Supervideograph, The Photo Adventure, Energy Centre (exhibition centre for oil and gas), Wax Museum and Experience Centre for Ice Cream. Outdoor entertainment twice daily throughout the summer season.
Kongeparken near Stavanger, tel: 51 61 71 11; www.kongeparken.no. Over 40 attractions, including life-sized model of The Giant Gulliver (85 x 7.5 metres), riding tracks, bob track, farm, car track, Wild West City, birds and fun fair.
Telemark Sommarland Bø in Telemark, tel: 35 06 16 00; www. sommarland.no. Norway's biggest water park with various wet and dry attractions, including many waterslides and Stuka, a 26-metre/80-ft high water chute; Flow Rider, said to be the world's biggest surf

wave, and a floating river. Plus live entertainment, pony rides, Wild West City and children's playground.

Kristiansand Dyrepark
tel: 38 04 97 00; www. dyreparken.com (open June–Aug). Norway's largest wildlife park and most-visited tourist attraction. The park has a wide range of other attractions: amusement park, water park, show and entertainment park, leisure park and Cardamomaby – a tiny village from a well-known children's book by the Norwegian author Thorbjørn Egner.

Youth Information in Oslo provides information on all subjects for young people:
Møllergata 3, Oslo
Tel: 22 41 51 32
www.unginfo.oslo.no
Open Mon–Fri 11am–5pm.

It's a Dog's Life

All dogs in Norway are required by law to wear a name tag clearly showing the telephone number of the owner (these are available from pet shops). Dogs must be kept on a leash between 15 April and 15 August while walking in forests and fields, to protect the environment and the local wildlife.

During the winter months, special notices are posted in public places, to inform you of whether or not dogs have to be placed on leads.

Note that it is illegal for a dog to foul a public place – you are expected to pick up the mess using a plastic bag and to deposit this in a litter bin. Failure to do so may result in a fine. Dogs are not allowed in restaurants; shops and other public buildings usually show a sign if dogs are not·welcome. Guide dogs are an exception to this rule.

Getting Around

Public Transport

There is an excellent network of domestic transport services – a necessity in a country so large and often impassable by land. You may have to use more than one means (for example, train and bus or plane and bus) but if you're determined to travel beyond Oslo you'll find these services indispensable.

Although covering great distances can be expensive, Norway offers transport bargains through special tourist cards like the Fjord Pass, the Bonus Pass (all Scandinavia), plus some of the pan-European programmes like InterRail and Eurail. Within larger cities, tourist passes cover urban transport and many museums.

FROM THE AIRPORT

Gardermoen Airport is 50 km (30 miles) north of Oslo. It is served by The Airport Express Train/Flytoget to Oslo S (the Central Station) every 10–20 minutes and takes 20 minutes. Details at www.flytoget.no. For about half the price, regional and local trains also connect Oslo and the airport and take about 45 minutes; there is normally a train at least every hour. Note that rail passes are not valid on The Airport Express. For train schedules and prices visit www.nsb.no.

The airport bus departs six times an hour to and from the Radisson SAS Scandinavia Hotel via Oslo Busterminal, Clarion Royal Christina Hotel, Helsfyr and Furuset. It takes 40 minutes.

The regular Bus 344 from the Radisson SAS Scandinavia Hotel via

Oslo S departs three times an hour and takes 50 minutes. Buses 332 and 355 also make the journey. For further information, tel: 177 or 23 00 24 00.

If you arrive from London Stansted at **Torp Airport**, Oslo's second airport, at Sandefjord on the southwest side of the fjord, buses and trains will take up to 2½ hours to reach the capital, depending on traffic conditions.

Bergen Airport is at Flesland, 19 km (12 miles) south of the city. The airport bus goes to the Radisson SAS Royal Hotel at Bryggen, via Radisson SAS Hotel Norge and the bus station. For details, tel: 177.

All other major city airports are serviced by buses and taxis.

BY AIR

Considering its size, Norway is exceptionally well served by domestic airlines, with about 50 airports and airfields scattered throughout the country.

The four domestic airlines are SAS, Braathens, Widerøe and Norwegian Air Shuttle. Each offers discount travel passes.

SAS Scandinavian Airlines
at Oslo and Bergen airports.
Bookings tel: 815 20 400
Info tel: 67 59 67 19
Main office tel: 67 59 60 50

Braathens
Flytogterminalen, Jernbanetorget 1, Oslo, and at Bergen Airport.
Tel: 815 20 000

Widerøe's Flyveselskap ASA
Vollsvien. 6, P.O. Box 131, N-1324 Lysaker, and Bergen Airport.
Tel: 67 11 60 00
Fax: 67 11 61 95
Bookings tel: 810 01 200.

Norwegian Air Shuttle
P.O. Box 115, N-1330 Fornebu
Tel: 67 59 30 00.

BY RAIL

Rail services are far more comprehensive in the south than in the north, and tend to fan out from Oslo, so you will have to supplement your trip with ferries and buses, unless you are travelling strictly in the south or to the major towns.

Oslo S (Oslo Sentralstasjon) is Norway's busiest railway station, located in central Oslo at the eastern end of Karl Johansgate on Jernbanetorget. Long-distance, express and local suburban trains arrive and depart here. It is also the terminal for the Oslo Gardermoen Airport high-speed rail link (some trains continue under the city to Asker via Nationalteatret station). The end of the line in Norway is at Bodø, but the most northerly railway station is at Narvik, which is reached through Sweden by train or by bus from Fauske. Most of Norwegian State Railways (NSB's) lines run through tourist country, presenting continuous panoramas of unspoiled scenic beauty. The Oslo–Bergen line is hailed as one of the world's most spectacular for its scenery.

Most trains are modern and efficient, but the older rolling stock has a touch of nostalgic luxury. New inter-city express (ICE) trains offer one class only. There is a wide range of special offers that can make your holiday reasonable.

National rail passes from NSB are valid for 3–8 travel days in any month. The rail pass is sold under the name of Norway Rail Pass in the US, while in Europe the offer is

called EuroDomino Norway (see www.nsb.no). The ScanRail Pass offers unlimited travel all over Scandinavia, as well as discounts on certain ferries, buses and at hotel chains. Note that ScanRail passes bought outside Scandinavia are more flexible and better value than those bought in Scandinavia. Visit www.scanrail.com for more information.

If you plan to take special fast trains, you must book ahead. Ticket sales are from the main hall of the train station (tickets for ordinary trains may also be bought on board).

For information about timetables, ticket prices and bookings contact Trafikanten, Jernbanetorvet 1, by Oslo S, tel: 81 50 01 76 or 177.

BY BUS/COACH

Where the rail network stops, the bus goes further: you can get to practically anywhere you want by bus. Usually it is not necessary to book in advance, just pay the driver on boarding. NOR-WAY Bussekspress (bus pass) guarantees a seat for all passengers. On sale only outside Norway through the company's agents, the pass is valid all year round and offers two categories for travel on the national network: (i) unlimited travel within seven consecutive days or

Tickets and Info

For tickets, routes, times and all other queries about public transport, **Trafikanten** in Oslo offers an information and booking service. Its office is at Jernbanetorvet 1, by Oslo Sentralstasjon (at the bottom of the glass tower at the front of the station). Tel: 81 50 01 76 (lines open Mon–Fri 7am–11pm, Sat–Sun 8am–11pm). Info line: 177. Office open Mon–Fri 7am–8pm, Sat–Sun 8am–6pm.

(ii) unlimited travel within a 14-day period.

Children up to 4 years travel free, 4 to 16 years pay 75 percent of the adult price.

NOR-WAY **Bussekspress AS**, Karl Johans gt. 2, NO-0154 Oslo, tel: 81 54 44 44; www.nor-way.no

---

WATER TRANSPORT

Ferries

You are never very far from the sea in Norway. Ferries are an invaluable means of transport that allow short cuts across fjords to eliminate long road journeys. In Oslo, ferries to the fjord islands leave from the quay near Aker Brygge.

Ferries (such as the Horten-Moss ferry across Oslofjord between Vestfold and Østfoldare) are crucial to commuters in busy areas. Almost all town marinas have places for guest boats. A mooring fee is required.

Long-distance Boats

Hurtigrute, the Norwegian Coastal Express service, is a vital means of water transport for Norwegians, but also a superb way for visitors to see Norway's dramatic coast. In summer, boats leave daily, travelling between Bergen and Kirkenes in 11 days and putting in at 35 ports.

Travel agents can give details, and sell special coastal passes to 16–26-year-olds. The steamers take cars, and should be booked well in

Norway in a Nutshell

One of the most pleasurable ways of seeing Norway is to take a **Norway in a Nutshell** journey *(see page 241)*. The trip uses various forms of public transport and takes you from Myrdal to Flåm, Gudvangen and Voss through some of the country's most beautiful scenery. A selection of packages is on offer. Tel: 81 56 82 22. www.fjord-tours.no

The railway line from Myrdal to Flåm is a masterpiece of engineering. When you have made the 850-metre (2,800-ft) descent you are at the head of one of the longest fjords in the

world, Sognefjorden, and on the brink of another scenic high.

The trips can be made in either direction and from any of the stations between Oslo and Bergen. **Norway in a Nutshell round trip:** train from Oslo to Myrdal/Flåm, boat to Gudvangen, bus to Voss, train to Oslo. **Norway in a Nutshell one way:** train from Oslo to Myrdal/Flåm, boat to Gudvangen, bus to Voss, train to Bergen.

Tickets are sold at the railway stations in Oslo and Bergen or from travel agencies. Discounts for children and senior citizens.

advance. Either contact your local travel agent or:

Troms Fylkes Dampskibsselskap ASA
Bookings tel: 77 64 82 00
Fax: 77 64 82 40
E-mail: booking@tfds.no
Ofotens og Vesteraalens
Dampskibsselskab ASA
Bookings tel: 76 96 76 93
Fax: 76 96 76 11
E-mail: booking@ovds.no
Hutigruten
Bookings tel: 810 30 000
www.hurtigruten.com

Travel Passes

The Oslo Pass, issued for one, two and three days, with half price for children, is your ticket to unlimited public transport (including city ferries) and free entry to many museums. If you want a card for travel only, there are all kinds of passes including a Minikort (four rides at a discount) and Flexikort (8 rides at a discount), plus passes appropriate for longer stays.

The Oslo Pass may be purchased at the Central Railway Station (Oslo S), Trafikanten *(see box: Tickets and Info)*, as well as all *Narvesen* kiosks and hotels, camp sites and tourist offices.

Other cities offer similar tourist travel cards: for example, the Bergen Card, a 24-hour or 48-hour pass available from tourist information offices, the railway station, hotels, camp sites and the Hurtigrute terminal.

BUSES AND TRAMS

Oslo's bus and tram system is comprehensive and punctual; there are detailed timetables at every stop. Trafikanten *(see box: Tickets and Info)* can suggest bus or tram routes to get you where you wish to go. There are night buses on some routes and very early morning buses (starting at 4am) so that public transport is available virtually around the clock. Bergen and Trondheim also have tram systems.

UNDERGROUND

Oslo's underground is called the T-bane *(see map on page 392)* and is very simple to use. There are five lines that converge under the centre of Oslo. A new circle line linking the existing lines is due for completion during 2006. You can catch any train to any of the far-flung suburbs from any of the stations between Tøyen and Majorstuen. Station entrances are marked with "T". Trafikanten *(see box: Tickets and Info)* has route maps. The most scenic route must be T-bane 1 up to Frognerseteren. From there enjoy panoramic views back down Oslo.

TAXIS

Taxis are widely available, even in many suburban and rural areas, so you need never risk drink driving (for which penalties are severe).

No matter where you are in Oslo, telephone 023 23 and you will be transferred to the nearest taxi rank. Mini-buses and taxis (for up to four people) can also be booked on 22 38 80 70. Otherwise, you can take a taxi from one of the many taxi ranks scattered around the city. In Oslo, pirate taxis gather at Stortorget, opposite GlassMagasin.

In Oslo taxis are more expensive at night or if ordered by phone. At night there are two things to watch out for: when everyone leaves the bars and restaurants late, long queues build up at taxi ranks. This can be extremely uncomfortable in the winter if you are not dressed

Road Information

Vegmeldingssentralen (The Road User Information Centre) is an office of the *Statens Vegvesen* (Public Roads Administration). Its main function is to monitor and provide information about roads and road conditions. You may also get information about distances and ferry timetables. Open 24 hours all year, tel: 175 or 81 54 89 91.

correctly. The problem has given rise to a second difficulty: "pirate" taxis. These either cruise up out of the blue or a "dummy" comes and asks you if you want a taxi without queuing. Pirate taxis are a risk, but if do use one, make sure you agree a price beforehand.

Private Transport

BY CAR

Norway's roads are extremely good, particularly in view of the treacherous weather conditions encountered in winter. Be prepared for tunnels, though, as some routes have long lengths of road underground.

EU driving licences are valid in Norway, but drivers from other countries must carry an International Driving Licence. Drive on the right.

Traffic regulations are strictly enforced *(see Rules of the Road, below)*.

Winter Driving
With Norway's winters, you should never assume all roads are passable. Small roads in the north are often closed so the authorities can put all manpower into keeping main roads safe, and even the E6 highway from Oslo to Trondheim has been known to close occasionally. If you intend to travel on minor roads, seek a local's advice and go prepared for anything.

Snow Tyre Hire
If you're driving in Norway in winter you can hire the appropriate tyres and snow chains by the week. Ask in any petrol station.

In the UK contact:
Snowchains Europroducts
Tel: 01732 884408
Fax: 01732 884564
www.snowchains.co.uk

Breakdown and Accidents
The AA and RAC are affiliated to the AIT (Alliance Internationale de Tourisme), so members receive free assistance (with journey planning as well as backup in case of breakdown or accident) from

Norway's NAF (Norges Automobil-forbund). More comprehensive repairs can be carried out at NAF-contracted garages (for which you will have to pay). NAF also patrol Norway's main roads and mountain passes from mid-June to mid-August. They have emergency phones along the mountain passes. **NAF**, Storgaten 2, N-0155 Oslo
Tel: 22 34 14 00
Fax: 22 33 13 72
24-hour emergency service (for members of AIT clubs), tel: 22 34 16 00/81 00 05 05.

If you are involved in an accident where there are no injuries, tele-phone **Falken Redningskorps AS** on 02468 or **Viking Redningstjeneste AS** on 22 08 60 20/80 03 29 00. Their offices cover all of Norway and provide a 24-hour service.

In an emergency you can contact **Alarmsentralen** (Air Ambulance), tel: 67 92 74 00.

It is not necessary to call the police for minor accidents, but drivers must exchange names and addresses; leaving the scene without doing so is a crime.

Only call the **police** (on **112**) or an **ambulance** (on **113**) if it's a real emergency.

Rules of the Road

It is essential for visitors to Norway to be aware of Norwegian driving regulations, some of which vary significantly from those in the UK and on the Continent. Here are a few tips to help you drive safely, but for further guidance it's worth getting a copy of *Velkommen på norske veier* (Welcome to Norwegian Roads) which includes an English section and is available at tourist offices.
• **Speed Limits** The maximum speed limit is usually 80 kph (50 mph), though 90 kph (56 mph) is permitted on some roads (mainly motorways). The limit is reduced to 50 kph (30 mph) in built-up areas, and even 30 kph (18 mph) on certain residential roads. On-the-spot fines are given for drivers found speeding (this may be as much as NOK 3,500). Some roads have automatic cameras, others radar traps.

• **Giving Way** This can be very confusing to the visitor. Roads marked at intervals by yellow diamond signs indicate that you have priority. On all other roads you are required to give way to traffic entering from the right. This is further confused by the fact that some roads have a series of white triangles painted across them at junctions, which mean stop and give way, though as you can imagine these easily become obliterated by snow and ice in the winter.

On roundabouts, priority is from the left. Always give way to trams, buses and taxis. Many roads have a right-hand lane exclusively for buses and taxis.
• **Drinking and driving** You are strongly advised not to drink at all if you anticipate driving within at least 8 hours. The current permissible limit is 0.02 per ml, and penalties are severe (imprisonment, a high fine and loss of licence are automatic).
• **Documentation and equipment** You must always have the following with you in your car: driving licence, car registration documents, European accident statement form, insurance policy and a reflective warning triangle. A snow shovel and tow rope are also useful in winter. For regularly updated information in the UK, the AA runs a very good fact line for just a small charge on tel: 0870 600 0371; www.theaa.com.
• **Lights** It is obligatory to drive with dipped headlights on during the daytime, even on the brightest summer day. This rule applies to all vehicles, including motorcycles and mopeds. We recommend you carry spare bulbs. Do not forget that right-hand drive cars require black adhesive triangles (often supplied by ferry companies), or clip-on beam deflectors, so you don't dazzle oncoming drivers.
• **Seat belts** must be worn, both front and back (again, there are on-the-spot fines for failing to comply).
• **Tyres** It is obligatory to use winter tyres from October to April. These are either tyres with studs *(piggdekk)* or specially designed tyres for use

in ice and snow. Studded tyres are preferred but these may soon be prohibited in urban areas for environmental reasons. Every car brought into Norway has to have two sets of tyres.

Caravanning
For information contact:
P.O. Box 104
1921 Sørumsand
Tel: 63 82 99 90
Fax: 63 82 99 99
www.caravanklubben.no

Car Hire
Hiring a car in Norway can be expensive, but may be worthwhile if shared between several people. Otherwise, watch for special weekend and summer prices.
Avis Bilutleie-Liva Bil AS
P.O. Box 154, N-1361 Billingstad (near Oslo)
Tel: 66 77 11 11
Fax: 66 77 11 30
Booking tel: 81 53 30 44
www.avis.no
Europcar
Grini Næringspark 10, P.O. Box 173, 1332 Østerås
Tel: 67 16 58 00
Booking tel: 67 16 58 20/ 800 41 400
www.europcar.no
Hertz Bilutleie
P.O. Box 331, N-1324 Lysaker/Oslo
tel: 67 16 80 80
Booking tel: 67 16 80 00
www.hertz.no

CYCLING

Cycling in Norway is safe, as there is so little traffic on many minor roads. But you must ride with caution as, though there are a few cycle routes, it is not an integrated system. Cyclists are not allowed to go through the larger tunnels, for example (because of car fumes). Out in the countryside you'll find surfaced cycle paths. Cycling is a good way of exploring outside Oslo: bicycles are allowed on most trains and buses for a small charge.

Special cycle trains are laid on during the summer. Pick up a copy of *Oslo Guide*, and under Outdoor Activities you'll find suggestions for a *Nordmarka* (Oslo's forest land) route; tourist offices have details of mountain cycle tours.

Information

The Syklistens Landsforening (Cycling Association) can help planning tours and cycling holidays. Cycling Association, Storg. 23C Pb. 8883 Youngstorget, 0028 Oslo. Tel: 22 47 30 30; fax: 22 47 30 31; e-mail: slf-bike@online.no.

For the preparation of cycle routes and transport for bicycles, contact Skiforeningen, Kongeveien 5, 0787 Oslo. Tel: 22 92 32 00; fax: 22 92 32 50; e-mail: ski@skiforeningen.no

Cycle Rental

In Oslo, Bergen bikes can be hired from hotels, camp sites, local tourist offices or sports shops, as well as small cycle-hire shops. **A/S Skiservice**, dept. bike, Voksenkollen Stasjon, Tryvannsvcicn 2, 0394 Oslo. Tel: 22 13 95 00 **Glåmdal Cycledepot**, B. Bulls plads 2 (Vestbanen), Oslo. Tel: 22 83 52 08 Off-road and mountain bikes are for hire from **White Water AS**, which deals in extreme sports gear. White Water AS, Cort Adelers g 27, Oslo. Tel: 22 01 20 00.

ON FOOT

There is almost nowhere in Norway you can't go happily on foot; it is a nation of devout walkers, and walking is one of the most popular outdoor activities at weekends.

The law of access to the natural environment, known as "everyman's right", allows you to walk wherever you want in the wilderness such as seashore, forests, mountains and in other non-cultivated regions. This should be done with consideration. Use paths and roads when walking in agricultural and populated areas.

It is preferable to make use of campsites if you are staying

overnight outdoors. If you pitch a tent in the wilderness, it should be situated at least 150 metres (160 yards) from the nearest house or hut. Open fires are prohibited from 15 April to 15 September.

Detailed maps are available from the Norwegian Mountain Touring Association. To join the association, write to the address below (family membership is available). Membership gives you rights to use the association's huts. If you subscribe at a slightly higher rate, you'll get the magazine and yearbook. The map and guidebook selection is excellent; survey maps of Norway are sold; sketch maps are free.

The Norwegian Tourist Board publishes a handbook, *Mountain Hiking in Norway,* which gives

suggested itineraries for mountain walks and details of chalets and where to stay. Contact Scandinavia Connection, 26 Woodsford Square, London W14 8DP; tel: 020 7602 0657; www.scandinavia-connection.co.uk.

Den Norske Turistforening, (Norwegian Mountain Touring Association) Storgate 3, P.O. Box 7 Sentrum, 0101 Oslo, tel: 22 82 28 00; fax: 22 82 28 01; www.turistforening.no Closed weekends.

Hitchhiking

Hitching is not as common here as elsewhere in Europe; but it is not impossible. You'll have the best chance on busier coastal roads. Using a sign is recommended.

Toll Roads

Road	Toll area	Price (in NOK)
E6	Trondheim–Stjørdal	45
E6	Østfold	20
E10	Nappstraumen Tunnel (Nordland)	65
E18	Vestfold	20
E18	Eidangerhalvøya (Telemark)	15
E18	Aust-Agder	20
E18	Kristiansand (Vest-Agder)	10
E39	Rennesøy (Rogaland)	90
E39	Trekantsambandet (Hordaland)	75
E39	Nordhordaland Bridge (Hordaland)	45
E39	Øysand-Thamshamn (Sør-Trøndelag)	15
E39/ Str.70	Kristiansund Mainlandconnection (Møre og Romsdal)	63
E134	Åkrafjord (Hordaland)	40
E69	Kåfjord-Honningsvåg (Finnmark)	135
Str.4	Oppland (Gjøvik-Raufoss)	15
Str.5	Sogndal-Fjæland (Sogn og Fjordane)	150
Str.5	Naustdalstunnel (Sogn og Fjordane)	40
17	Helgeland Bridge (Nordland)	82
Str.23	Oslofjordtunnel (Akershus)	50
Str.64	Skålavegen (Møre og Romsdal)	55
108	Hvalertunnel (Østfold)	50
Str.207	Bjorøy (Hordaland)	120
562	Askøy Bridge (Hordaland)	100
Str.566	Osterøy Bridge (Hordaland)	40
Str.658	Ålesund-Ellingsøy-Giske/Vigra (Møre og Romsdal)	55
Str.714	Hitra-Frøya, Dolmøy (Sør-Trøndelag)	70
Str.714	Hitra-Festland, Sandstad (Sør-Trøndelag)	70
Str.714	Hitra-Fjellværøy, Ansnes (Sør-Trøndelag)	60
755	Skarnsund Bridge	62
Str.769	Namdalsprojeckt (Nord-Trøndelag)	13
Oslo Toll Road		20
Stavenger Toll Road Workdays 6am–6pm		5
Bergen Toll Road		15
Trondheim Toll Road		15

Toll prices are for a private car (with trailer of maximum weight 3,500 kg/7,700 lb). They are subject to change without notice and credit cards are not accepted, so Norwegians tend to keep a stash of change handy in the car.

Walking in the National Parks

The Ministry of Environment has set up 21 National Parks to ensure the protection of the country's distinctive characteristics.

Børgefjell 1,447sq km/559 sq miles, on the border between Nord Trøndelag and Nordland. Fishing and hunting (licences required) for hare and grouse is available.

Dovrefjell 256 sq km/100 sq miles, central Norway, comprising a chain of valleys. The western part of the park is dominated by precipitous slopes, with the mountain Snøhetta rising to 2,286 metres (7,500 feet).

Femundsmarka 390 sq km/150 sq miles, between Hedmark and Sør-Trøndelag. Lakes and streams make Femundsmarka a dream for anglers.

Gressåmoen 182 sq km/70 sq miles, in Nord-Trøndelag. Gressåmoen National Park was established to protect ancient and almost undisturbed spruce forest.

Gutulia 19 sq km/7 sq miles directly south of Femundsmarka, bordering with Sweden. The undisturbed forest supports numerous species of birds.

Hardangervidda 3,422 sq km/ 1,320 sq miles, covering parts of the Hordaland, **Telemark** and **Buskerud** regions in southern central Norway. The park is the home of the largest herd of wild reindeer in Europe, and also the southern limit of many arctic plants and animals, such as the Arctic fox and snowy owl.

Jostedalsbreen 1,230 sq km/ 475 sq miles, situated between the Sognefjord and the Nordfjord, is the largest glacier in mainland Europe, being 80 km/50 miles long.

Jotunheimen 1,145 sq km/442 sq miles, extends over parts of Oppland and Sogn and Fjordane. Jotunheimen features Norway's highest mountains. It also has cabins.

Ormtjernkampen 9 sq km/3 sq miles, just northwest of Lillehammer, in the county of Oppland.

Rago, 167 sq km/65 sq miles, approximately 25 km/15 miles north of Fauske in Nordland. Rago is dominated by a wild mountain landscape with deep ravines.

Reisa 803 sq km/310 sq miles, in Nordreisa in Troms, about 60 km/ 37 miles from Finnmark. Consists of narrow valleys and ravines, mighty waterfalls, river gorges and potholes.

Rondane 580 sq km/225 sq miles, just south of Dovrefjell Park, in Oppland. Known as the last outpost of the vulnerable wild reindeer.

Saltfjellet – Svartisen 2,105 sq km/ 813 sq miles in the county of Nordland. Svartisen glacier (370 sq km/140 sq miles) is the largest ice-sheet in northern Scandinavia.

Stabbursdalen 98 sq km/38 sq miles, south of Porsanger peninsula in Finnmark. The world's northernmost pine forest.

Øvre Anarjåkka 1,399 sq km/540 sq miles, in the south of Finnmark. This remote area is characterised by an ancient rolling landscape of birch forest, sparse pine, bogs and lakes.

Øvre Dividal 743 sq km/287 sq miles, in the region of Troms, bordering Sweden. The park has a rich mountain flora, with square-stemmed heather and Arctic rhododendron growing abundantly.

Øvre Pasvik 119 sq km/46 sq miles, the easternmost corner of Norway in Finnmark, bordering Finland and Russia. The largest area of primeval forest in the north.

Ånderdalen 69 sq km/27 sq miles, on the island of Senja in Troms.

On Svalbard

Nord-vest Spitsbergen 3,560 sq km/ 1,375 sq miles, covers the northwestern corner of Spitsbergen. Large colonies of sea birds, reindeer and walrus; plus areas of cultural and historical interest.

Forlandet 640 sq km/247 sq miles; a long, thin island with flat beaches, high mountain peaks and small glaciers. The warming effect of the Gulf Stream makes this the nesting place of many bird species.

Sør Spitsbergen National Park 5,300 sq km/2,046 sq miles, covers the southern parts of Spitsbergen. Over half the park consists of glaciers or permanent snow and ice.

For more information

Contact regional tourist boards or the Directorate for Nature Management, N-7485 Trondheim. Tel: 73 58 05 00; e-mail: direktoratet@dirnat.no www.naturforvaltning.no

Where to Stay

Norwegian hotels are notoriously expensive, but, in common with the rest of Scandinavia, they reduce their rates during the outdoor summer holiday period when business decreases. This makes May to September attractive when compared with standard rates. Weekends are also usually cheaper. Normal weekday rates outside summer are geared towards business occupants, which partially explains why they're so high.

When it comes to places to stay, Norway has something to suit every requirement. The range covers hotels from the luxurious to the simple, to more modest guesthouses, camp sites, cosy self-catering chalets, and youth and family hostels. Facilities and service are of international standard. A lot of hotels provide luxury attractions like fitness centres and secretarial services, and newer Norwegian hotels are very business conference-oriented.

The British-style bed and breakfast is developing in Norway, and country or farm holidays offer an opportunity to experience day-to-day farm life at close quarters.

Full board terms are available to guests staying at the same establishment for at least 3–5 days. Reductions for children are 75 percent for under 3s and 50 percent for 3–12-year-olds, providing the child stays in the parents' room. Guesthouses *(pensjonat)* offer lower rates and are generally good.

There is no central Norwegian hotel booking service, so you have to go through travel agents and tour operators to find rooms, or book directly (as practically everyone speaks English this is very easy).

Hotel Chains

The major hotel chains are all well represented in the five main congress towns of Oslo, Stavanger, Bergen, Trondheim and Tromsø. Some chains offer passes, discount schemes and cheque systems to help reduce the cost of accommodation.

Best Western Hotels Norway Best Western Euro Guestcheque
P.O. Box 2773 Solli
N-0204 Oslo
Tel: 800 11 624 (toll-free)
www.bestwestern.no

Choice Hotels ASA
Sommerogt 13-15
P.O. Box 2454, 0201 Oslo
Tel: 22 40 13 00
Booking tel: 22 33 42 00
www.choice.no

Fjord Tours AS
Norway Fjord Pass
Strømgt 4, 5015 Bergen
Tel: 55 55 76 60
Fax: 55 31 20 60
E-mail: fjordtours@fjordpass.no
www.fjordpass.no

The Fjord Pass

If you are travelling around Norway in summer, the Fjord Pass is well worth buying because it gives you a 20 percent discount on all categories of accommodation.

Valid at around 200 hotels, guest houses, apartments and holiday cottages throughout Norway in summer, it is the only Norwegian discount card to be accepted by members of several hotel chains.

The Fjord Pass is available from travel agents or tourist information offices, as well as from hotels.
For details contact:
Fjord Tours AS
Norway Fjord Pass
P.O. Box 1752 Nordnes,
N-5816 Bergen.
Tel: 55 55 76 60
Fax: 55 55 16 40
E-mail: fjordtours@fjordpass.no
www.fjordpass.no

Norlandia Hotellene
Scan + Hotel Pass
P.O. Box 6615 St Olav plads,
N-0129 Oslo
Tel: 22 98 97 00
Booking tel: 23 08 02 80
Fax: 22 98 97 10
E-mail: service@norlandia.no

Raddison SAS International Hotels
P.O. Box 185, N-1324 Lysaker
Tel: 800 160 91 (toll-free in Norway)/67 12 02 20
www.radissonsas.com

Rica Hotels
Rica Hotellferie Pass
P.O. Box 3, N-1375 Billingstad
Tel: 66 85 45 60
E-mail: rica@rica.no
www.rica.no

Scandic Booking Services
Scandic Club Card
P.O. Box 173 Skøyen, N-0212 Oslo
Tel: 23 15 50 00
E-mail: info@scandic-hotels.com

Hotels

The hotels are listed geographically starting with the most expensive. There is also a separate box on page 368 for budget hotel accommodation.

OSLO

Bristol
Kristian VII's gate 7, N-0164
Tel: 22 82 60 00
Fax: 22 82 06 01
E-mail: booking@bristol.no
Superb Moorish-style lobby; close to the city's main shopping street. Rooms are decorated with antiques. Patronised by the wealthy. **$$$**

Clarion Royal Christiania Hotel
Biskop Gunnerusgaten 3, N-0106
Tel: 23 10 80 00
Fax: 23 10 80 80
Recently restored luxuriantly; magnificent atrium, spacious rooms, wonderful service and breakfasts; convenient location near Oslo S station. **$$$**

Continental
Stortingsgaten 24–26, N-0161
Tel: 22 82 40 40
Fax: 22 82 40 65

Price Categories

Price categories are indicated by dollar signs and are per night for two people in a double room with breakfast in high season
$$$ More than NOK 1,700
$$ NOK 1,100–1,700
$ Less than NOK 1,100

Established in 1909 and run by Elisabeth Brochmann, fourth generation owner of the hotel. This is where Norwegian guests of state are accommodated. **$$$**

First Hotel Millennium
Tollbugaten 25, P.O. Box 289
N-0106
Tel: 21 02 28 00
Fax: 21 02 28 30
One of two new hotels built in Oslo by the Swedish First Hotel group. This was built in an existing city centre building with the help of leading Norwegian architects, Platou. **$$**

Frogner House Hotel
Skovveien 8, N-0265
Tel: 22 44 79 90
Fax: 22 56 05 00
E-mail: mail@frognerhouse.com
Beautiful old building just west of the centre; quiet, with cosy rooms. **$$**

Gabelshus Hotel
Gabelsgt 16, N-0272
Tel: 23 27 65 00
Fax: 23 27 65 60
E-mail: resepsjonen@gabelshus.no
A pleasant ivy-clad hotel with excellent service and a good traditional kitchen. The hotel was first opened in 1912. **$$**

Golden Tulip Rainbow Hotel Stefan
Rosenkrantzgt 1, N-0159
Tel: 23 31 55 00
Fax: 23 31 55 55
E-mail: stefan@rainbow-hotels.no
One of a chain of hotels scattered throughout Norway; its location couldn't be more central and the buffet lunches are great. **$**

Grand
Karl Johansgate 31, N-0159
Tel: 23 21 20 00
Fax: 23 21 21 00/01
E-mail: grand@rica.no

Opposite the Stortinget, one suite is reserved for the winner of the Nobel Peace Prize in December, and official government receptions are held in the rococo banqueting hall. Spacious contemporary-style decor in the bedrooms. **$$$**

Holmenkollen Park Hotel Rica
Kongveien 26, N-0390
Tel: 22 92 20 00
Fax: 22 14 61 92
E-mail: holmenkollen.park.hotel.rica@rica.no
Set high in the leafy Holmenkollen district, this grand old-style, wooden building looks right out over Norway's most famous ski jump. A modern annexe was added in the 1980s. Excellent facilities. **$$**

Noble House Hotel & Suites
Kongensgt 5, N-0153
Tel: 23 10 72 00
Fax: 23 10 72 10
noble.house@firsthotel.no
This modern hotel in the heart of old "Christiania" won the "Prix Européen de la Reconstruction" for its design. **$$**

Radisson SAS Plaza Hotel
Sonja Henies pl 3, N-0134
Tel: 22 17 10 00
Fax: 22 17 73 00
This is the tall glass structure between the Central Station and Oslo Spektrum, with external panoramic lift and roof-top pool. Popular among rock stars playing at the Oslo Spektrum, to which it is connected by a covered walkway. **$$$**

Radisson SAS Scandinavia Hotel
Holbergsgate 30, N-0166
Tel: 23 29 30 00
Fax: 23 29 30 01
Luxurious, like all SAS hotels, this one also has very fine restaurants

Booking in Oslo

In Oslo, the Tourist Information centres at Fridtjof Nansens Plass 5 (Mon–Sat 9am–5pm), and at the Central Station (daily 8am–11pm) will book accommodation in the capital for those requesting it in person. This service covers private rooms, pensions and hotels.

City Packages

The Oslo and Bergen Packages offer great value for money. They are available at weekends and during the holiday seasons. The price includes accommodation with breakfast (there are 40 hotels to choose from in Oslo alone) plus the Oslo or Bergen card which includes free entrance to many museums and attractions, free inner city transport and numerous discounts. The package can be booked through tourist information offices in Oslo or Bergen or through a travel agency, but not directly with the hotel.

and a rooftop bar. Buses to and from airport. **$$$**

Tulip Inn Rainbow Norrøna
Grensen 19, N-0159
Tel: 23 31 80 00
Fax: 23 31 80 01
E-mail: norrona@rainbow-hotels.no
Completely renovated 3-star hotel but with century-old atmosphere intact. Central. **$**

OSLO AREA

Clarion Oslo Airport Hotel
N-2060 Gardermoen
Tel: 63 94 94 94
Fax: 63 94 94 95
E-mail: oslo.airport@clarion.choice hotels.no
One of many chain hotels being built around the airport. **$$**

Golden Tulip Rainbow Hotel Oslofjord
Sandviksvn 184, 1330 Sandvika
Tel: 67 55 66 00
Fax: 67 55 66 88
E-mail: oslofjord@rainbow-hotels.no
Set in a handsome fjord town 15 km (9 miles) from central Oslo (shuttle buses and public transport available). Great views over fjord and islands. **$**

Quality Airport Hotel
N-2050 Jessheim
Tel: 63 92 61 00
Fax: 63 92 61 01
E-mail: resepsjonen@quality.choice hotels.no

Another established hotel perfectly situated for Oslo Gardermoen Airport in the small nearby suburb of Jessheim. **$$**

Scandic Hotel Høvik/Oslo
Drammensvn 507,
N-1322 Høvik
Tel: 23 15 53 00
Fax: 23 15 53 11
E-mail: hovik@scandic-hotels.com
Attractive hotel with good dining and bar facilities; 6 km (4 miles) from Oslo centre. **$$**

Scandic Hotel St. Olav
St. Olavs Plass 1, 0165 Oslo
Tel: 23 15 56 00
Fax: 23 15 56 11
E-mail: stolav@scandic-hotels.com
Smart new hotel with good tapas bar. Close to theatres with rooms named after Norweigan actors. **$$**

KRISTIANSAND

Rica Hotel
Dronningeensgt. 5,
4610 Kristiansand
Tel: 38 17 40 00
Fax: 38 17 40 01
E-mail: firmapost@hotel-norge.no
Large hotel containing a reasonably priced café that includes freshly baked bread and cakes on its menu. **$$**

Fell & Fjord Hamresanden
Hamresandv. 3
Tel: 38 04 72 22
Fax: 38 04 71 44
E-mail: ha-ap@online.no
Good value with rooms, apartments and camping. Many sporting facilities nearby including fishing, golf and hiking **$**

BERGEN

Best Western Victoria Hotel
Kong Oscarsgate 29, 5017
Tel: 55 21 23 00
Fax: 55 21 23 50
E-mail: mail@victoriahotel.no
Once a staging-post inn, this now has 43 comfortable, modern rooms with own facilities. Full of character and an admirable art collection. Family-run hotel in the Best Western group. Fully licensed

lobby bar and Greek restaurant.
Central. **$$**

Clarion Admiral
C. Sundtsgate 9–13, 5004
Tel: 55 23 64 00
Fax: 55 23 64 64
E-mail: booking@admiral.no
Part of the Choice chain and one of
Bergen's finest. The hotel has a
superb view over the harbour to
Bryggen, while the restaurant has
excellent cuisine. **$$**

**Golden Tulip Rainbow Hotel
Rosenkrantz**
Rosenkrantz 7, 5003
Tel: 55 30 14 00
Fax: 55 31 14 76
E-mail: rosenkrantz@rainbow-hotels.no
Comfortable, early 20th-century
hotel located in the street behind
Bryggen (the wharf) in the heart of
the old town; well modernised in
light, airy colours. Restaurant and
piano bar. Hotel nightclub entrance
is next door. **$$**

Hotel Pension
Harald Hårfagresgt 35, 5007
Tel: 55 54 44 00
Fax: 55 54 44 44
E-mail: booking@parkhotel.no
This family-operated hotel has 40
specially decorated rooms and is
located in the University quarter. **$**

Radisson SAS Hotel Norge
Ole Bulls Plass, 5012
Tel: 55 57 30 00
Fax: 55 57 30 01
E-mail: bergen@radissonsas.com
One of Bergen's best-loved hotels
and meeting places, right in the
centre, with 350 rooms and suites
of highest standard. Four
restaurants including gourmet
Grillen. Winter garden, swimming
pool. **$$$**

Radisson SAS Royal Hotel
Bryggen, 5003
Tel: 55 54 30 00
Fax: 55 32 48 08
E-mail: bergen@radissonsas.com
The classic Norwegian architectural
style makes this an unusually
handsome hotel as it is actually
several old warehouses. High-grade
facilities. **$$$**

Scandic Hotel Bergen
Håkonsgaten 2, 5015
Tel: 55 30 90 90
Fax: 55 30 90 91

E-mail: bergencity@scandic-hotels.com
Newly extended and now the biggest
Scandic hotel in Norway. Wireless
internet access available. **$$$**

Strand Hotel
Strandkaien 2B, 5013
Tel: 55 59 33 00
Fax: 55 59 33 33
E-mail: post@strandhotel.no
Superb harbour views make for a
pleasant stay. Family-run hotel with a
cosy breakfast room, bar and dinner
served in the Lido restaurant. **$$**

STAVANGER

Best Western Havly Hotel
Valberggt 1, N-4006
Tel: 51 89 67 00
Fax: 51 89 50 25
E-mail: post@havly-hotell.no
Modest with well-appointed rooms.
Pets allowed. **$**

Commandør Hotell
Valberggt 9, N-4006
Tel: 51 89 53 00
Fax: 51 89 53 01
E-mail: comhot@online.no
Home comforts in a cosy milieu.
Licensed for wine and beer only. **$**

"The Little House"
Vaisenhusgt 40, N-4012
Tel: 51 89 40 89
The Little House was built in 1869
and retains an old-world charm, with
its home-from-home rooms (each
with bath and access to kitchen).
Central location. **$**

Radisson SAS Royal Hotel
Løkkeveien 26
Tel: 51 76 60 00
Fax: 51 76 60 01
E-mail: reservations.stavanger@
radissonsas.com
The hotel has SAS's usual excellent
services. **$$**

Scandic Hotel
Eiganesvn 181, P.O. Box 570 Madla
N-4040 Hafrsfjord
Tel: 21 61 43 00
Fax: 23 15 50 01
E-mail: stavanger@scandic-hotels.
com
One of the quality Scandic hotels
ideal for conferences. The Scandic
chain has a "green" policy and
includes "environmental rooms"
that are constructed from 97
percent recyclable material. **$$**

Skagen Hotel and Guesthouse
Skansegt 7
Tel: 51 93 85 00
Fax: 51 93 85 01
E-mail: Lbjorgum@world-online.no
Great harbourside location. Very
friendly. **$**

BALESTRAND

Kvikne's Hotel
N-6899
Tel: 57 69 42 00
Fax: 57 69 42 01
E-mail: booking@kviknes.no
Swiss-style hotel on the edge of
Sognefjord. A good centre for
walking, mountain hiking and glacier
trips. **$$**

Midtnes Pensjonat
N-6898
Tel: 57 69 11 33
Fax: 57 69 15 84
E-mail: booking@midtnes.no
Centrally situated guest house.
Many of the rooms have views of
Sognefjord. Boat and bike hire can
be arranged. **$**

TRONDHEIM

Elgeseter "Bed & Breakfast"
Tormodsgate 3
Tel: 73 94 25 40
Fax: 73 82 03 31
Convenient location 10 minutes'
walk from the centre. **$**

Grand Olav Clarion Hotel
Kjøpmannsgaten 48
Tel: 73 80 80 80
Fax: 73 80 80 81
E-mail:
booking.trondheim@clarion.choice
hotels.no

Top-class hotel situated in the heart of historic Trondheim. Close to shops, bars and restaurants. Runs an airport bus. **$$$**
Prinsen Scandic
Kongensgate 30
Tel: 73 80 70 00
Fax: 73 80 70 10
E-mail: prinsen@scandic-hotels.com
A wealth of facilities here including

81 rooms, the fine Pinocchio restaurant, a bistro, bar, grill room, wine tavern and beer garden. **$$**
Radisson SAS Royal Garden Hotel
Kjøpmannsgt 73
Tel: 73 80 30 00
Fax: 73 80 30 50
E-mail: sales@trdzh.rdsas.com
With 298 well-appointed rooms plus solarium, indoor pool,

gymnasium, sauna and several good restaurants. Runs an airport bus every 15 minutes. **$$**
Quality Hotel Augustin
Kongensgate 26
Tel: 73 54 70 00
Fax: 73 54 70 01
E-mail: hotel-augustin@hotel-augustin.no
Close to main city square. This huge old brick hotel has comfortable rooms and covered parking. **$$**

Budget Hotel Accommodation ($)

Ålesund
Atlantica Hotel
R. Rønnesbergsgt. 4
Tel: 70 12 91 00

Bergen
Steens Hotel
Parkview 22, 5007
Tel: 55 30 88 88
Fax: 55 30 88 89

Bodø
Bodø Hotel
Prof Schyttesgt 5, P.O. Box 1055
N-8001. Tel: 75 54 77 00

Drangedal
Gautefall Hotel & App
Gautefallheia, N-3750
Tel: 35 99 97 77

Geilo
Solli Sportell
Skurdalsvegen 25, N-3580
Tel: 32 09 11 11
Ustedalen Høyfjellshotel
N-3581. Tel: 32 09 01 11

Geiranger
Villa Utsikten
P.O. Box 19, N-6216
Tel: 70 26 30 03

Haugesund
Røvaer Sjøhus
5549 Røvaer. Tel: 52 71 80 35

Honningsvåg
Hotel Havly
Storgt 12, N-9751
Tel: 78 47 29 66

Lillehammer
Bjørns Kro og Motell
Vinges 2600. Tel: 61 25 83 00

Molde
Comfort Hotel
Amtm Kroghsgt. 5, N-6400
Tel: 71 25 15 55

Mosjøen
Sandvik Gjestegård
Mjåvatn. N-8650
Tel: 75 11 50 00

Moss
Mitt Hotel
Rådhusgt. 3, N-1500
Tel: 69 25 77 77

Oslo
Hotel MIM
Staffeldtsgate 4, N-0166
Tel: 72 98 62 00
WestSide Hotel
Eilert Sundts gt. 43, N-0355
Tel: 22 56 87 70
Albertine Hostel
Storgata 55, 0182.
Tel: 22 99 72 10

Sognefjord
Sognefjord Hotel
P.O. Box 144, N0-5840
Hermansverk.
Tel: 57 65 34 44

Stord
Grand Hotel
N-5401 Stord
Tel: 53 41 02 33

Svolvær
Hotel Havly
N-8301. Tel: 76 06 90 00

Trondheim
Inger Stock Bed and Breakfast
Porsmyra 18
Tel: 72 88 83 19

TROMSØ

Grand Nordic
Storgt 44
Tel: 77 75 37 77
Fax: 77 75 37 78
E-mail: Resepsjon.gnt@nordic.no
Close to the centre, 4 km (2½ miles) from the airport. Full conference facilities and well-appointed rooms. **$$**
Ishavshotel Tromsø
Fr. Langesgt. 2
Tel: 77 66 64 00
Fax: 77 66 64 44
E-mail: rica.ishavshotel@rica.no
First-rate luxury hotel close to the centre, specialising in conferences and comfort. **$$$**
Saga Tromsø
Richard Withs plass 2
Tel: 77 60 70 00
Fax: 77 60 70 10
E-mail: hotelhelp@choicehotels.com
Small conference hotel with relaxing atmosphere. **$$**
Scandic Tromsø
Heiloveien 23
Tel: 77 75 50 00
Fax: 77 76 50 11
E-mail: tromso@scandic-hotels.com
Modest conference hotel located in Tromsø suburb close to the airport. Outside pool. **$$**
With Home Hotel
Sjøgata 35–37, N-9000
Tel: 77 68 70 00
Fax: 77 68 96 16
E-mail: booking@with.no
A first-class hotel with a difference. Situated by the waterfront in Tromsø's dock district, it offers a beautiful view to the Tromsø bridge and the famous Arctic Cathedral, and a maritime atmosphere. **$$**

Price Categories

Price categories are indicated by dollar signs and are
per night for two people in a double room with breakfast in high season

$$$ More than NOK 1,700
$$ NOK 1,100–1,700
$ Less than NOK 1,100

SVALBARD

Radisson SAS Polar Hotel
P.O. Box 554, 9171 Longyearbyen
Tel: 79 02 34 50
Fax: 79 02 34 51
E-mail: reception.longyearbyen
@radissonsas.com
Hotel with views over Isfjorden and Hiorthfjellet mountain. **$$**

Spitsbergen Funken Hotell
P.O. Box 500, 9171 Lonyearbyen
Tel: 79 02 62 00
Fax: 79 02 62 01
E-mail: spitra@spitzbergentravel.no
Once the meeting hall for the local mining company, it is now a modern hotel. Restaurant with views over Lonyeardalen and Isfjorden. **$$**

Spitsbergen Nybyen Gjestehus
P.O. Box 500, 9171 Longyearbyen
Tel: 79 02 63 00
Fax: 79 02 63 01
E-mail: guesthouse@spitzgbergen
travel.no
A simple guesthouse with a living room and a kitchen for tea-making.
Open Mar–Sept. **$**

Chalets (Hytter)

There are abundant holiday *hytter* (cabins or chalets) available for rent. These usually house four to six people. If you want to spend just one night in a chalet and then move on, you can stay in one on a campsite without booking ahead. You can obtain a brochure with details about holiday chalets (including a price list) from:
Den Norske Hytteformidling,
Kierschowsgate 7,
P.O. Box 3404 Bjølsen,
N-0406 Oslo
Tel: 22 35 67 10
Fax: 22 71 94 13

Fishermen's Cabins (Rorbuer)

In the Lofoten islands in northern Norway, you can rent a traditional former fisherman's cabin, called a *rorbu*. The fishermen used to come to Lofoten from other parts of the coast for the winter cod fishing season from January to April, and would make these cabins their temporary homes. Most of them have been modernised, and some have their own shower and toilet.
Contact: Lofoten Tourist Office;
tel: 76 09 15 99, fax: 76 09 24 25;
www.lofoten-info.no

Camping

Norway has more than 1,000 camp sites, classified by 1–5 stars, depending on the standard and facilities available. The fixed charge per plot is usually NOK 80–150, with additional charges per person.

With the Norwegian camping card *(Norsk Campingkort)* you receive a faster checking-in service along with special discount deals. The card is available from participating campsites. Many campsites have cabins that may be booked in advance. Some are small and basic, but others are large and well equipped with a sitting room, 1–2 bedrooms, kitchen, shower and toilet. Ekeberg Camping (tel: 22 19 85 68) and Bogstad Camping–the largest campsite in Norway–also have cabins (tel:22 51 08 00).

For further information, write to:
Norwegian Camping Guide, Essendropsgt. 6, N-0305 Oslo.
www.camping.no

B&Bs

British-style bed and breakfasts are catching on in Norway, and they are all of a high standard. You can book at local tourist offices or at Oslo's central railway station. Or look out for signs for *Rom* or *Husrom* outside houses as you drive.

A guidebook, *Bed & Breakfast in Norway*, with listings throughout the country, is available from bookshops in Norway or from:
Scandinavia Connection
26 Woodsford Square,
London W14 8DP
Tel: 020 7602 0657
www.scandinavia-connection.co.uk
B&B Norway AS
Østerdalsgt. 1J, N-0658 Oslo
Tel: 22 67 30 80
Fax: 22 19 83 17
E-mail: bbnorway@online.no
www.bbnorway.com

Youth and Family Hostels

There are approximately 100 youth hostels in Norway, all of a relatively high standard. They are divided into three categories, indicated by a corresponding number of stars.

A night's accommodation costs between NOK 75 and NOK 175, breakfast NOK 60–70 for members of the YHA. Further information can be obtained by contacting *Hostelling International Norway*, or your local YHA office.

Reserving space during the high season is essential, as hostel accommodation is the cheapest way to travel and everyone knows it.
Norske Vandrerhjem (Hostelling International Norway),
Torggata 1, 0181 Oslo
Tel: 23 13 93 00
Fax: 23 13 93 50
E-mail: hostels@vandrerhjem.no
www.vandrerhjem.no

Where to Eat

What to Eat

Norwegians eat hearty breakfasts, but light lunches; the size of the evening meal *(middag)* depends on the day of the week and the occasion.

With the abundant supply of seafood and what can be gleaned from forest and field, the Norwegian diet has traditionally been healthy and appetising. For example, white bread is rarely purchased as most Norwegians prefer brown bread or dry Ryvita crackers for breakfast. However, the younger generation has a tendency to eat frozen pizzas and easily prepared meals.

The hunting season (early autumn) offers some irresistible temptations: pheasant, grouse, fresh elk and reindeer steaks served with peppercorns and rich wild mushroom sauces. It is also a good time of year to make the most of seafood (usually available in months with an R in them).

Outside main meals, there are many coffee breaks. Inevitably pastries will be served if you are in someone's home or having an informal meeting. The platter may be laden with *bolle* (raisin buns) and *wienerbrød* (lighter pastries laced with fruit or nuts) and anything else the baker can conjure up.

Frokost (breakfast) is more or less a variation of the lunch *Kaldtbord*, a spread including breads (try *grovbrød* and knekkebrød), sausage, cheese (try the piquant *Gudbrandalsost*, a delicious burnt goats' milk cheese with a dark golden colour), eggs, herrings, cereal, *gravlax* (marinated salmon), and coffee and tea.

The lunch version has hot dishes, such as sliced roast meats, meatballs or fish. *Øllebrød* (beef marinated in beer and served inside pitta bread with salad) makes a hearty, inexpensive lunch; an open-faced shrimp or ham sandwich is another staple.

Dinner in a city restaurant can be anything you wish. In someone's home you might eat mutton stew or a fish ragout. Boiled potatoes with dill or parsley usually accompany a hot main course. When dining in more remote places, the menus will invariably be limited by availability. *Smørbrød* is a snack (called *aftens* when eaten late at night), usually of bread or crackers with butter, cheese and salami or ham.

For dessert, ice cream is a favourite, as is apple pie. In summer there are all kinds of puddings based on the fresh berries that grow profusely in the Norwegian woods.

Where to Eat

There has been a significant increase in what's on offer when you choose to eat out in Norway. Pizza is very popular and the cynic may even describe it as the Norwegian national dish. Asian food has also become a local favourite, although Indian restaurants tend to tone down the

Drinking Notes

No one talks about a trip to Norway without complaining of the high cost of alcohol.

For those who can afford the prices, serving hours are long; in Oslo you can drink spirits until midnight and wine or beer until 3am. Outside Oslo times are less predictable; the Christian Democratic Party is anti-alcohol and holds sway in many west-coast areas, rendering some counties virtually dry. But there are exceptions to this: in Oslo, for example, there are some no-alcohol hotel/restaurants and in the "dry" counties it is always

spices to suit the more delicate Norwegian palate, so you may wish to tell the waiter to beef it up a bit. Continental European cuisine has always played a role in Norwegian cuisine (such as Viennese and French style dishes), but pride in native foods and an interest in "new Scandinavian" cuisine has emerged in Europe.

At lunchtime many restaurants offer special fixed-price menus. More casual meals can be had from informal establishments, which come under a range of names such as *stovas, kros, bistros, kafés, kafeterias,* and *gjæstgiveris* and may sell alcohol as well as coffee and soft drinks. For an even more casual meal buy a hot dog *(pølser)* or a waffle from a kiosk; these stay open late to catch pubcrawlers. And yes, there is McDonald's.

Evening dining yields up some wonderful surprises in terms of choice, some unpleasant ones in terms of cost. Any large city should give the best cross-section of what is available throughout the country. The following is a small selection of what is on offer.

Restaurants

Restaurants are grouped by area starting with Oslo. They are listed alphabetically in price order, with the most expensive first.

possible to find a hotel/restaurant that serves some form of alcohol.

The *Vinmonopolet* (state off licences/liquor stores) in cities are open Mon–Fri 9am–5pm and Saturday 9am–2pm; but closed on election days, holidays and the preceding day.

Most Norwegians drink beer and/or wine. Traditional *Akevitt*, similar in taste to Schnapps, is derived from potato and caraway seeds, and is also a favourite. It can be sipped neat in small glasses at room temperature, or served cold with beer to accompany salty, spicy or pungent dishes.

OSLO

International
Dinner
Stortingsg 22
Tel: 23 10 04 66
No punches-spared Szechuan cuisine. **$$**
Fuji
Munkedamsveien 100
Skillebekk
Tel: 22 43 11 80
If you like sushi, this is the place for you. **$$$**
Mother India
Pilestredet 63B
Tel: 22 60 81 04
A good Indian atmosphere, serving fabulous food in the nearby suburb of Bislett. **$**
Spaghetteria Santinos
Tordenskioldsg 8–10
Tel: 22 41 16 22
Popular downtown pizzeria. **$$**
Zorbas
Torggaten 32
Tel: 22 20 78 56
Great Greek food. **$$**

Norwegian
Annen Etage
Hotel Continental
Stortingsgaten 24/6
Tel: 22 82 40 70
Grand style, setting and food. **$$$**
Bagatelle
Bygdøy Allé 3
Tel: 22 12 14 40
The best restaurant in Scandinavia with two Michelin stars. **$$$**
Feinschmekker
Balchensgate 5
Tel: 22 12 93 80
Has one Michelin star. Expensive but good value. **$$$**
Gamle Raadhus
Nedre Slottsgate 1
Tel: 22 42 01 07
Old-style restaurant with hearty Norwegian specialities. In a 17th-century building that was Oslo's first town hall. **$$**
Grand Café
Karl Johansgate 31
Tel: 22 42 93 90
A virtual shrine to Ibsen, who spent many hours here. Wide choice from pastry and coffee to elk stew. **$$**

Kastanjen
Bygdøy Alle 18
Tel: 22 43 44 67
A bistro serving Norwegian-style food. **$$**
Stortorvets Gjæstgiveri
Grensen 1
Tel: 23 35 63 60
Authentic Christiania inn with warm atmosphere. Live jazz. **$$**
Sult
Thorvald Meyers Gt 26
Tel: 22 87 04 67
Seafood is the speciality. Sult is one of the leading lights of "new Scandinavian cuisine" in Norway. **$$$**
Theatercafeen (Hotel Continental)
Stortingsgate 24
Tel: 22 82 40 00
Well-known Viennese-style café. **$$**

Pizza
Peppes Pizza
Holmens gate 5, Aker Brygge, Drammensveien 40, Konghellegt. 3, Frognerveien 54, Stortingsgt 4, Karl Johansgt 1, Hegdehaugsveien 36.
Tel: 22 22 55 55
Specialises in pan-fried pizzas. Cheaper on Monday. **$–$$**

Vegetarian
Vegeta Vertshus
Munkedamsveien 3B
Tel: 22 83 42 32
Vegetarian heaven; this place even got a write-up in the *New York Times*. No drinks licence. **$**

BERGEN

Bryggen Tracteursted
Bryggen 6
Tel: 55 32 18 75
Traditional Norwegian fare and great fish dishes. **$$**
Dickens
King Olavvs Plass
Tel: 55 36 31 30
This informal setting is popular and relaxed, serving good meals, light snacks and just drinks. **$$**
Fiskekrogen
Fish Market
Tel: 55 31 75 66
The very best of Norwegian cuisine. Superb fish dishes served by friendly and knowledgeable waiters. **$$$**

Price Guide
The symbols at the end of each entry give an indication of prices, based on a typical three-course evening meal per head, excluding wine.
$ Less than NOK 150
$$ NOK 150–400
$$$ More than NOK 400

Fløien Folkerestaurant
Top of Fløien funicular
Tel: 55 32 18 75
Good, reasonably priced food with intoxicating view. Work up an appetite by walking there! **$$**
Holbergstuen
Torvalmenning 6
Tel: 55 31 80 15
In the heart of the town. Good traditional dishes. **$$**
Mago Café
Neumanns GT.5
Tel: 55 96 29 80
Ecological restaurant that claims to be good for your digestion as well as tasty. Organic vegetables and free-range meat and fish. **$**
To Kokker (Two chefs)
Bryggen, Bergen
Tel: 55 32 28 16
Located on the famous Bryggen in Bergen, this well-known restaurant's specialities include game, fish and seafood. **$$$**
Wesselstuen
Ole Bulls plass 6
Tel: 55 55 49 49
Fish and stews are served here to a loyal local crowd. **$$**

TRONDHEIM

Bryggen
Øvre Bakklandet 66
Tel: 73 87 42 42
One of the best and most elegant restaurants in Trondheim right by the River Nidelva. Serves an international menu using the finest ingredients. **$$$**
Big Horn Steakhouse
Munkegt. 14, Ravnkloa
Tel: 73 50 94 90
Specialises in tasty spare ribs and juicy steaks. **$$**

Grenaderen
Kongsgårdsgt. 1e
Tel: 73 51 66 80
In a 16th-century forge with a large
terrace. Offers a traditional menu
including fish and reindeer. **$$**

Havfruen
Kjøpmannsgt. 7
Tel: 73 87 40 70
Some of the finest Norwegian fish
and seafood, plus meat. Trendy bar.
$$

Zia Teresa Pizzeria Trattoria
Vår Frue Strete
Tel: 73 52 64 22
Pizza with a Norwegian twist. **$$**

TROMSØ

Compagniet
Sjøgata 12
Tel: 77 66 42 22
Gourmet fare. **$$$**

Peppermøllen Mat-og Vinhus
Storgata 42
Tel: 77 68 62 60
Menu features about 160 dishes,
using Norwegian ingredients. Fish is
obviously a speciality. **$$**

Vertshuset Skarven
Strandtorget 1
Tel: 77 60 07 20
This popular restaurant serves
several varieties of steak. **$$**

STAVANGER

Cartellet
Øvre Holmegate 8
Tel: 51 89 60 22
Fascinating architecture worth a
visit itself. International food. **$$$**

Sørensens Dampskibsekspedisjon
Skagen 26
Tel: 51 84 38 20
Popular and friendly restaurant
serving Norwegian cuisine. **$$**

Storyteller
Skagen 27
Tel: 51 59 99 70
Extensive à la carte menu, featuring
tasty American and Cajun dishes. **$$**

Straen Fiskrestaurant
N. Strandgt 13–15
Tel: 51 84 37 00
The best fish and seafood
restaurant in town. **$$**

Culture & Nightlife

Music and Opera

In summer the arts take to the
outdoors in Norway, and classical
music and opera are no exception.
For Oslo dates, pick up the *What's
On in Oslo* guide. The very active
Oslo Philharmonic, founded by
Edvard Grieg, is conducted by
Mariss Jansons, with frequent visits
by acclaimed guest conductors and
soloists. Den Norsk Opera (National
Opera) stages big productions such
as *La Boheme* and *Don Giovanni*
during the year. At Holmenkollen in
summer, orchestral and operatic
performances are given from a
floating stage on the lake.

Each September, a "drive-in"
opera performance is held at
Youngstorvet (Young's Market
Square), outside the Opera House
in the open air.

Akershus Fortress and the Henie
Onstad Art Centre (Høvikodden)
are two other fine settings for
summer concerts.

Whether the performers are
Norwegian or foreign, the season
winter or summer, Norway has a
rich and varied musical and operatic
life (consult area guide for festivals
schedule; some English and
American newspapers give a pan-
European list of festivals at the
start of each summer). This may be
your chance to listen to some of the
conductors and performers you'd
previously only heard on Deutsche
Gramophone CDs, or a first
opportunity to see Grieg performed
by Norwegian musicians.

Theatre and Dance

Theatre is booming in Norway, with
small, contemporary theatres

springing up everywhere; but
performances are in Norwegian.
The exception is September's
Gløgerne Kommer festival of
performing arts, when international
dramatists take to the stage.

Dance has also come into its
own here and is now a significant
part of the Gløgerne Kommer.
Classical ballet is performed at the
Oslo Opera House. Traditional folk
dances can be seen in many towns
on National Day (17 May), or at
Oslo's Konserthus every Monday
and Thursday at 9pm in July and
August, when the Bondeungdoms-
laget folk dance group performs.

Cinema

The Norwegians love films, a fact
attested to by the vast number of
cinemas; Oslo has around 40
screens including the impressive
wide-screen cinema at Coloseum in
Frogner. First-run and repertory
films are always shown in the
original language, with Norwegian
subtitles. Kiosks, newspapers, and
local city guides have listings.
Booking by telephone is possible
and recommended for Sundays, the
traditional movie night.

Nightlife

Oslo, once considered a big yawn at
night, is now vying with Stockholm
and Copenhagen to be
Scandinavia's nightlife capital.
Loads of new bars, pubs and clubs
have come on to the scene, but
many can't recoup their
investments quickly enough and go
out of business (some also close
down once they have made a quick
killing). So check locally for up-to-
date venue listings, or see the
official *Oslo Guide* provided by Oslo
Promotion on the website
www.visitoslo.com. All the major
cities have both official and
unofficial nightlife guides.

In Bergen, Stavanger, Trondheim
and Tromsø nightlife exists to a much
lesser extent. But you can guarantee
that most large hotels have
nightclubs and bars. In small towns,
you may be out of luck altogether.

International rock, folk, and jazz musicians often include Oslo on European tours; some even start their tours here.

There are only two things you need to be warned about before a night out: the high cost of drinking, and age restrictions: some clubs have minimum ages as high as 26 (although 21 and 23 are more common).

Festivals and Cultural Events

January
● Stavanger: Traditional Jazz Festival. International and Norwegian artists perform more than 30 concerts. Tel: 51 84 66 67.
● Tromsø: Northern Lights Festival. Music ranging from baroque to contemporary and from jazz to classical. Tel: 77 68 90 70.
● Longyearbyen: Polar Jazz. The world's nothernmost jazz festival, 645 km (400 miles) from the North Pole. Tel: 79 02 23 29.

February
● Kristiansund: Opera Festival. Two or three opera productions plus church music, ballet and other concerts. Tel: 71 58 99 60.
● Lillehammer: Winter Arts Festival featuring international performers of music, theatre and figurative art. Tel: 61 05 05 00, fax: 61 05 07 81.

March
● Alta: Northern Lights Winter Festival with music, theatre, markets, ski and snowmobile competitions and more. Tel: 97 00 33 79.

Bergen Festival

Bergen's International Festival in late May offers music, drama, ballet, opera, jazz and folk arts.

For a festival brochure and further details contact: Bergen International Festival, P.O. Box 183, 5804 Bergen. Tel: 55 21 06 30 Fax: 55 21 06 40 www.festpillene.no

● Narvik: Winter Festival. Church music, jazz, classical music, markets, carnival and sports events. Tel: 76 94 87 00.
● Lillehammer: Blues Festival. International and Norwegian musicians. Tel: 61 28 60 55.
● Oslo: Church Music Festival. Concerts in Oslo Cathedral and other churches in the city. Tel: 22 41 81 13.

April
● Bergen: Music Festival including blues, country & western, cajun and rock. Norwegian and international performers. Tel: 55 21 50 60.

May
Constitution Day (May 17). Celebrations and parades all over Norway.
● Stavanger: International Jazz Festival. Tel: 51 84 66 67.
● Bergen: International Festival. One of Norway's artistic highlights. World-class music, dance, theatre. Also Nattjazz – an international jazz festival. Tel: 55 21 06 31.
● Al: Norwegian Folk Music Week with concerts, song and dance. Competition between the best fiddlers and dancers in the region. Tel: 32 08 56 45.
● Bergen: Dragon Boat Festival in the harbour. Tel: 55 56 05 10.
● Bomlo: Mostra spelet. Outdoor historical play. Tel: 53 42 07 90.

June
● Sarpsborg: Gleng Music Festival. Folk, rock, blues, jazz and classical music. Indoor and outdoor concerts. Tel: 69 15 68 00.
● Hardanger Music Festival. Music and culture from the Hardanger fjord area, with chamber, church and folk music. Tel: 53 67 15 15.
● Oslo: Norwegian Wood. Rock music festival with Norwegian and international artists. Tel: 81 53 31 33.
● Harstad: North Norway Festival. The region's largest cultural event, with music, theatre, dance and art exhibitions. Tel: 77 04 12 30.
● Vinstra: Country and Western Festival. Non-stop country music

with international and Norwegian artists. Tel: 61 21 69 39.

June/July
● Grimstad. Norwegian Short Film Festival. With around 80 short and documentary films. Tel: 37 04 40 41.
● Vestfold Arts Festival. Norwegian and international artists perform all in locations all over the county. Tel: 33 37 10 00.

July
● Kristiansand. Quart International rock music festival. Performers from the US, Britain and Europe. Tel: 38 14 69 69.
● Forde: Norway's largest folk music festival with more than 250 performers from all over the world. Tel: 57 72 19 40.
● Molde: International Jazz Festival. Norway's largest jazz festival, with more than 400 performers, many are world famous. Tel: 71 20 31 50.
● Bo: Telemark Festival with traditional folk, blues and jazz music. Tel: 35 95 19 19.

July/August
● Vinstra: Peer Gynt Festival. Art exhibits, music, processions with national costumes, open-air theatre. Performance of Henrik Ibsen's Peer Gynt and Edvard Grieg's music, by Gala Lake. Tel: 61 29 47 70.

August
● Oslo Jazz Festival: More than 60 concerts during six days. Tel: 22 42 91 20.
● Stordal Opera Festival in the ruins of the medieval Steinvikholm Castle. Norway's best opera singers perform. Tel: 74 82 18 66.
● Stavenger International Chamber Music Festival. Renowned soloists and new talents perform chamber music in various ensembles. Tel: 51 84 66 70.

September
● Stavenger: International literature festival. Symposiums, readings, poetry, concerts and plays with Norwegian and international writers. Tel: 51 50 79 40.

October
● Oslo: Ultima Contemporary Music Festival. Norway's largest.
Tel: 22 42 99 99.
● Lillehammer Jazz Festival. Mainly Norwegian performers.
Tel: 61 05 08 00.

November
● Fagernes. Salt Cured Trout in the Valdres Manner. You can sample many versions of this local favourite on the first weekend of the month.
● Hammerfest: Music and Theatre Festival focusing on culture in Northern Norway
Tel: 78 41 21 85.

December
● Oslo: Parade past the Grand Hotel to honour the winner of the Nobel Peace Prize plus a Nobel concert in the Spektrum Theatre.
Tel: 22 12 93 00.

Shopping

What to Buy

Popular souvenirs from Norway include knitted jumpers, cardigans, gloves and mittens, pewter, silver jewellery and cutlery, hand-painted wooden objects (like bowls with rose designs), trolls and fjord horses carved out of wood, goat and reindeer skin, enamel jewellery, woven wall-designs, furs, handicrafts, glassware and pottery – to name just a few (see *Tax-free Shopping, below*, on how to reclaim VAT).

The major department stores are *Glassmagasinet* and *Steen & Strøm*, both of which have a good selection of most of these items. However, if you want speciality stores in Oslo, there is a *Where to Shop* guide, as well as a detailed "Shopping" section in the *Oslo Guide* (see www.visitoslo.com). Karl Johansgate, Grensen, and Bogstadveien are all major shopping streets. With the exception of Oslo, most Norwegian towns are so compact that your best bet is to window shop and go into the places that look most appealing.

Anyone interested in buying Norwegian art will have ample prospects – from south to north, Norway abounds in galleries. Get a local recommendation.

If you are food shopping, fruit and vegetable prices vary considerably throughout the year. Look out for *Lavpris* (low-price) shops offering discounts. The first Saturday of each month is "Super Saturday" when shops in Oslo open longer and offer special discounts. Bear in mind that most bottles (whether plastic or glass) have a returnable deposit of NOK 1.

Tax-free Shopping

If you are a resident of a country other than Norway, Sweden, Denmark or Finland, you are entitled to tax-free shopping on purchases in excess of NOK 308 at any of the 3,000 stores connected to the scheme.

The store issues you with a tax-free voucher for the amount of VAT paid. When you leave Norway, a refund of 11–18 percent (depending on the sale price) will be refunded on presentation of the goods, the tax-free voucher and your passport, on condition that the item has not been used while in Norway.

Global Refund has its own representatives at a total of 100 refund places, including airports, international ferry terminals and at the main border crossings. Check opening times, as they are not open 24 hours, and make sure there is a refund desk if you are using a small border crossing. Customs officials cannot refund VAT. For details, contact Global Refund Norge, P.O. Box 48 N-1332 Østerås, tel: 67 15 60 10; fax: 67 15 60 29.

Shopping Hours

● **Weekdays**
Generally 9am–5pm, with late Thursday opening for many stores until 7 or 8pm.
Stores may close earlier in summer, especially on Fridays.
● **Saturday**
Usually 9am–1, 2 or 3pm.
● **Shopping centres** such as Aker Brygge, Palléet and Oslo City in Oslo, Galleriet in Bergen and City Syd in Trondheim are open later, until 8 or 9pm week nights.
● **Kiosks** tend not to close until 10pm or even 11pm and are usually open all weekend.
● **Supermarkets** Most stay open until 8pm.
● **Petrol stations** are usually open until 11pm.

Sport

Participant Sports

If Norwegians can contrive a sport as an excuse to be outdoors, they'll do it. That's why there are such great facilities here; all Norwegians love sport. (For a full listing of the range of sports and sports facilities in the Oslo region, see the Outdoor Activities pages of the *Oslo Guide*.) There is a Forest Safari programme, where for a half or whole day you can partake in a range of activities in the Marka (Oslo's forest) in between which you are carted around by Land Rover. Visit the main tourist information office for details.

Boating

Foreign visitors are always welcome in boating circles, and there are hundreds of sailing and boating clubs and associations throughout Norway. The national organisation for recreational and competitive motor-boating is: Kongelig Norsk Båt Forbund, Vågebyveien 23, 0569 Oslo, tel: 22 35 68 00, fax: 22 35 68 11.

The most popular volumes of the six-volume *Den Norske Los* (Norwegian Pilot), the meticulously detailed manual of all navigable waters, is available with Norwegian and English texts. Volume 3 covers the southwest coast from south of Stavanger to north of Bergen; Volume 2 the Oslo Fjord and the south coast. If you are planning a sailing holiday, obtain a copy of *Guest Harbours in Norway* (available from Scandinavia Connection, *see page 378*), which provides valuable information, including place descriptions, sketch maps and details of the coast guard escort service.

Canoeing

Numerous rivers and lakes in Norway offer canoeing and kayaking. Some of the best include the Femund area, Østfold, Aust and Vest Agder, Telemark and suburban Oslo. Contact the local tourist office for details, or **Norges Padleforbund** (Norwegian Canoe Association), Service Boks 1, Ullevaal Stadion, 0840 Oslo
Tel: 21 02 98 35
Fax: 21 02 98 36
www.padling.no.

Cycling

As a particularly popular method of transport in Norway, cycling is considered relatively safe. Special routes exist during summer and special cycle paths can be found in rural areas. For further details on planning a cycling holiday and renting bicycles, see *Getting Around*, page 362–3.

Fishing

With a coastline of 21,465 km (13,330 miles), as well as countless fjords, lakes and rivers, Norway is a fisherman's paradise. In summer there are many boat cruises, and in some fjord towns groups can charter boats for fishing or pleasure.

The fishing is excellent in Norway, whether you're at sea or on a fjord, lake or river; enquire locally about short-term permits. To fish sea char, salmon, sea trout or inland fish, you must be over 16. A fee is payable. See *Angling in Norway* (available from Scandinavia Connection, *see page 378)* for full details.

Golf

This popular sport has caught on in Norway and many landowners, be they farmers or municipal authorities, have turned over land to developing golf links. Norwegian golf courses are by and large difficult and challenging. Ninety-nine percent of them require either a Green Card or a handicap under 20. Green fees are more expensive than at other European golf courses.

In the Oslo region professional competitions are held at Bogstad,
Larvik, Borre and Vestfold golf clubs, but by far the most beautifully situated is the Tyrifjord golf links. For further information and club details, contact:
Norges Golfforbund, P.O. Box 163, Lilleaker, 0216 Oslo
Tel: 22 73 66 20
Fax: 22 73 66 21
E-mail: ngf@golf.no
www.ngf@golf.no

Hiking

One of the country's favourite pastimes, hiking can be done anywhere and combines well with other activities such as berry-gathering or swimming in a lake. The country's mountain ranges and high plains make ideal walking terrain. The most popular areas include the Jotunheim mountain range; the Rondane and Dovrefjell mountains; the Hardangervidda plateau in the Trollheimen district; and the Finnmarksvidda plain. Mountain cabins are open from the end of June until mid-September, and at Easter.

Glacier Hiking

Not for the lily-livered, glacier hiking is an exhilarating and exciting experience – which should only be attempted with an experienced local guide.

Several Norwegian tour companies offer guided glacier walks *(breer)*, most particularly in the following areas:

Fjord Norway: Hardangerjøkulen, Folgefonna, Buarbre, Bondhusbre, Smørstabbe, Fannaråkbre and Nigardsbre.
Oppland: Styggebre.
Norland: Svartisen and Engenbreen.

Alternatively, you could contact one of the **Glacier Information Centres** in western Norway at Oppstryn (tel: 57 87 72 00), Fjærland (tel: 57 69 32 88) and Josterdalen (tel: 57 68 32 50).

The Norwegian Mountain Touring Association (DNT) runs about 300 guided hikes of varying difficulty during the summer, and glacier walks in winter. It also has a wealth of information on hiking and maps for all Norway and can recommend cabin-to-cabin hiking holidays. Foreigners can write requesting membership, which gives you certain free publications and hut access.
Den Norske Turistforening (The Norwegian Mountain Touring Association)
P.O. Box 7 Sentrum, 0101 Oslo
Tel: 22 82 28 00
Fax: 22 82 28 01

Horse-riding

Norway offers a wide range of opportunities for the rider, whether you wish to hire a pony for trekking or take lessons. Enquire at the local tourist office or at your hotel or camp site for further information or visit www.elveli.no.

Winter Norway

Norway is often dubbed the "Cradle of Skiing". What we today know as a sport is the way Norwegians used to get around, and Norway is said to be responsible for the invention of ski waxing and the laminated ski.

But skiing is just one of Norway's winter attractions. There are snowmobile trips to the North Cape, reindeer safaris and dog-sled races over the plane of Finnmarksvidda.

You can go on horse-drawn sleigh rides, or try your hand at sledding, ice fishing, snow boarding or ice skating. Several companies offer winter train journeys along the spectacular coast

For details of tour operators who specialise in winter holidays in Norway, see Specialist Tour Operators on page 354. Or contact the Norwegian tourist board, which has a list of holiday agents offering packages.

Skiing

Along with hiking, this is the primary participant sport in Norway. Even in the summer Norwegians take to the slopes (as a rule from June to September), and the sight of people swooping down the slopes in bikinis and trunks is something to behold.

There is both downhill and cross-country skiing available. The main ski resorts are at Lillehammer, Trysil, Geilo, Hemsedal, Norefjell (the nearest to Oslo) and Voss, but there are many more; all tourist offices can advise on local ski facilities for cross country and slalom.

Ask the Norwegian Tourist Board for a copy of the Winter Travel Planner for details of ski operators and resorts, or log on to www.skiinfo.no.

Swimming

Temperatures at beaches along the coast and inland reach 24°C (68°F,) and even in the north it can be warm enough to swim. Nude sunbathing beaches are to be found in Oslo, Moss, Halden, Drammen, Tønsberg, Larvik and Molde.

Most larger hotels have pools and there are numerous leisure centres throughout Norway.

Watersports

There are several possibilities for waterskiing and windsurfing along the coast, as well as on Norway's numerous lakes.

White-water rafting is available on the following rivers: Sjoaelva in Oppland, Trysilelva in Hedmark and Driva in Sør-Trøndelag

The Norwegian coast offers very good conditions for diving. There are several diving centres along the west coast, particularly in the counties of Møre and Romsdal.

Spectator Sports

Annual skiing competitions, such as the Holmenkollen Ski Festival (see page 105) and Bislet Games, are the primary spectator sport in Norway. Check local guides.

There are several horse trotting and race tracks in Norway.

Other popular spectator sports include marathon running, football, ice hockey and boat races. Again, check the Oslo Guide (www.visitoslo. com) or a local area guide or tourist office for further details.

Sporting Events

January
● Geilo: World Kicksledding Championships.

February
● Oslo: Holmenkollen Ski Marathon. Cross country 42 km (26 miles) through Nordmarka, Oslo's vast outdoor park. Also Biathlon World Cup.

March
● Oslo: Holmenkollen: Ski Festival with world cups in cross-country skiing, Nordic Combined and ski jumping.
● Lillehammer: World Cup Alpine Skiing Finals. Downhill, Slalom, Giant Slalom and Super G at the Kvitfjell and Hafjell.
● Hemsedal: Winter Golf Tournament. Norway's only winter golf tournament on snow ("whites" instead of "greens").
● Oslo: Holmenkollen: world's largest ski competition for children 4 to 12 years old. Including cross-country races and family games. Tel: 22 92 32 00.
● Svolvaer: World Cod Fishing Championships. Up to 300 competitors from near and far.

May
● Oslo: Holmenkollstafetten Street relay race.

June
● Oslo: Esso/Mobil Bislett Games. International track and field competition with some of the best athletes in the world.
● Trondheim: Midnight Golf Tournament over 18 holes. Every night until 2am.
● Telemark: Bicycle race from Skien to Rjukan and back to Skien.
● Spitsbergen Marathon. The world's northernmost marathon. Also half marathon and 10K's.

- Tromsø: Midnight Sun Marathon. Marathon and other competitions at midnight. Concerts and other entertainment.
- Trondheim: The Great Challenge. Bicycle race from Trondheim to Oslo. Also shorter distances: Lillehammer-Oslo and Eidsvoll-Oslo.

July
- Ekebergsletta: Norway Cup: World's largest international football tournament for children
- Lofthus. Fédération Aéronautique Internationale Paragliding Competition.

August
- Rena/Lillehammer: International bicycling race from Rena to Lillehammer.

September
- Oslo Half Marathon.
- Suldalslagen. International Salmon Fishing Competition.

October
- Oslo Horse Show. Competitions, Grand Prix.

December
- Lillehammer Ski Festival. Opening of the World Cup season.

Language

There are two variations of the Norwegian language: *bokmål* and *nynorsk*. Both belong to the western group of the Scandinavian branch of the Germanic languages, one of the subfamilies of the Indo-European languages. The Sami population (Lapps) in North Norway speak Lappish. English is widely understood in the sizeable towns.

Useful Words and Phrases

Yes *Ja*
No *Nei*
Good morning *God morgen*
Good afternoon *God eftermiddag*
Good evening *God kveld*
Today *I dag*
Tomorrow *I morgen*
Yesterday *I går*
Hello *Hei*
How do you do? *Goddag?*
Goodbye *Adjø/Ha det bra*
Thank you *Takk*
How much is this? *Hvor mye koster det?*
It costs *Det koster...*
How do I get to...? *Hvordan kommer jeg til...?*
Where is...? *Hvor er...?*
Right *Høyre*
To the right *Til høyre*
Left *Venstre*
To the left *Til venstre*
Straight on *Rett frem*
Phrase book *Parlør*
Dictionary *Ordbok*
Money *Penger*
Can I order please? *Kan jeg få bestille?*
Could I have the bill please? *Kan jeg få regningen?*
Could I have the key please? *Kan jeg få nøkkelen?*
What time is it? *Hvor mye er klokken?*

It is (the time is...) *Den er (Klokken er...)*
When? *Når*
Where? *Hvor?*
Could I have your name please? *Hva er navnet?*
My name is *Mitt navn er...*
Do you have English newspapers? *Har du engelske aviser?*
Do you speak English? *Snakker du engelsk?*
I only speak English *Jeg snakker bare engelsk*
May I help you? *Kan jeg hjelpe deg?*
I do not understand *Jeg forstår ikke*
I do not know *Jeg vet ikke*
It has disappeared *Den har forsvunnet*
Chemist *Apotek*
Hospital *Sykehus*
Doctor *Lege*
Police station *Politistasjion*
Parking *Parkering*
Department store *Hus/Stormagasin*
Toilet *Toalett/WC*
Gentlemen *Herrer*
Ladies *Damer*
Vacant *Ledig*

Days and Months

Note that days and months in the Norwegian language do not take capital letters.

Sunday *søndag*
Monday *mondag*
Tuesday *tirsdag*
Wednesday *onsdag*
Thursday *torsdag*
Friday *fredag*
Saturday *lørdag*

January *januar*
February *februar*
March *mars*
April *april*
May *mai*
June *juni*
July *juli*
August *august*
Septembe *september*
October *oktober*
November *november*
December *desember*

Numbers

0	null
1	en
2	to
3	tre
4	fire
5	fem
6	seks
7	syv or sju
8	åtte
9	ni
10	ti
11	elleve
12	tolv
13	tretten
14	fjorten
15	femten
16	seksten
17	sytten
18	atten
19	nitten
20	tjue
21	tjue-en
22	tjue-to
30	tretti
40	førti
50	femti
60	seksti
70	sytti
80	åtti
90	nitti
100	hundre
200	to hundre
1,000	tusen

Engaged *Opptatt*
Entrance *Inngang*
Exit *Utgang*
No entry *Ingen adgang*
Open *Åpent*
Closed *Stengt*
Push *Skyv*
Pull *Trekk*
No smoking *Røyking forbudt*
Breakfast *Frokost*
Lunch *Lunsj*
Dinner *Middag*
Eat *Spise*
Drink *Drikke*
Cheers! *Skål!*
Hot *Varm*
Cold *Kald*
Aircraft *Flymaskin*
Bus/coach *Buss*
Car *Bil*
Train *Tog*
Ticket *Billet*

Single/return *En vei/tur-retur*
To rent *Leie*
Free *Ledig*
Room to rent *Rom til leie*
Chalet *Hytte*
Can we camp here? *Kan vi campe her?*
No camping *Camping forbudt*
Grocery store (in countryside) *Landhandel*
Shop *Butikk*
Food *Mat/kost*
To buy *Kjøpe*
Sauna *Badstue*
Liquor store/off-licence *Vinmonopol*
Clothes *Klær*
Overcoat *Frakk*
Jacket *Jakke*
Suit *Dress*
Shoes *Sko*
Skirt *Skjørt*
Blouse *Bluse*
Jersey *Genser*
Wash *Vaske*
Launderette *Vaskeriautomat*
Dry cleaning *Renseri*
Stain *Flekk*

Further Reading

Tourist Publications

Listed below are some useful publications available from Scandinavia Connection, 26 Woodsford Square, London W14 8DP
Tel: 020 7602 0657
www.scandinavia-connection.co.uk

Adventure Roads in Norway by E. Welle-Strand. A selection of fascinating routes chosen by some of Norway's foremost travel experts shows you where to find the best scenery. The routes and places of interest are marked on maps and the book is illustrated with beautiful colour photographs.

Angling in Norway by John Berge. An illustrated soft-cover guide covering salmon, sea trout and freshwater fishing, as well as updated information on the latest fishing regulations and conservation measures.

Bed and Breakfast in Norway by A.M. Bjørgen. Details of guest houses and rooms in private homes, farms and mountain dairies.

A Cultural Odyssey: Focus on Norwegian Art edited by G. Jerman. An illustrated overview of Norwegian painting, literature, theatre, film, music, architecture, crafts and design.

Fjord Norway by Olave Grinde and Per Eide. An introduction to Norway's fjords, covering towns and museums, flora and fauna and Norwegian cuisine.

Guide to 366 Guest and Natural Harbours along the Norwegian Coast edited by G.S. Iversen. An indispensable book for sailors, packed with information and containing sketch maps and place descriptions.

Hurtigruten: The World's Most Beautiful Sea Voyage by Erling Storrusten. A day-by-day account of the voyage by coastal express from Bergen to Kirkenes and back, plus information on what to see and do when ashore.

Living In Norway: a Practical Guide by Michael Brady and Belinda Drabble. With more than 850 topics in 49 chapters, provides a wealth of information for new residents and anybody who might want to know more about Norway.

Lofoten and Vesterålen by L. Ryvarden. An illustrated book describing these magical northerly islands, their towns and fishing stations, museums, nature and culture, as well as the northern lights and the midnight sun.

Møre and Romsdal by P.A. Westavik. A colourful journey through one of Norway's most diverse regions in terms of scenery and culture.

Motoring in Norway by E. Welle-Strand. With colour illustrations and sketch maps, describing the most attractive routes in Norway, road conditions, sights and scenery. Symbols indicate catering, accommodation, and service stations.

Naughty in Norway by Barbara Godfrey. A very funny account of two British girls with a sense of adventure which led them in 1953 to embark on short-term careers as housemaids in a sympathetic Norwegian household near Oslo. Interesting glimpses of Nordic customs and everyday life in a nation then still recovering from the ravages of a savage Nazi Occupation.

Norway in Pictures by Eric Braun. Newly revised, this book portrays the history and government, economy, people, geography and culture of Norway with some wonderful photography.

Norway's Stave Churches by E. Valebrokk and T. Thiis-Evenson. The authors provide detailed descriptions and photographs of Norway's remarkable *stave* churches.

Road Map of Norway A 1:1 million map covering the country on one sheet. This is particularly suitable for tourists because of its easy-to-follow legend. It shows all trunk roads, as well as secondary roads of special interest to travellers. The reverse side suggests motoring tours, and there are town maps of Oslo, Bergen, Trondheim, Stavanger, Kristiansand and Tromsø.

Walking in Norway by Constance Roos. Describes some twenty walking routes in the main mountain areas of Norway, ranging from the far south to the Arctic regions. All the trips are accessible by public transport. With trail maps for all the routes.

Other Insight Guides

Europe is comprehensively covered by over 200 books in Apa Publications' three series of guidebooks.

Insight Guides provide the reader with a full cultural background and top-quality photography. Titles in this part of Europe include: *Denmark, Finland, Iceland, Sweden* and *Scandinavia.*

Insight Pocket Guides are written by local hosts and contain tailor-made itineraries to help users to get the most out of a short stay. Each title comes complete with a pull-out map that can be used independently from the guide. Scandinavian destinations in the series include *Oslo & Bergen, Stockholm* and *Denmark.*

Apa also publishes **Insight Compact Guides**, mini encyclopedias which give you the facts about a destination in a very digestible form, supported by maps and colour photographs. Titles in the series include *Iceland, Finland, Denmark* and *Copenhagen.*

Feedback

We do our best to ensure the information in our books is as accurate and up-to-date as possible. The books are updated on a regular basis, using local contacts, who painstakingly add, amend and correct as required. However, some mistakes and omissions are inevitable and we are ultimately reliant on our readers to put us in the picture.

We would welcome your feedback on any details related to your experiences using the book "on the road". Maybe we recommended a hotel that you liked (or another that you didn't), as well as interesting new attractions, or facts and figures you have found out about the country itself. The more details you can give us (particularly with regard to addresses, e-mails and telephone numbers), the better.

We will acknowledge all contributions, and we'll offer an Insight Guide to the best letters received.

Please write to us at:
**Insight Guides
P.O. Box 7910
London SE1 1WE
United Kingdom**
Or send e-mail to:
insight@apaguide.co.uk

ART & PHOTO CREDITS

Picture Spreads

Map Production Lovell Johns Ltd.
© 2004 Apa Publications GmbH & Co.
Verlag KG (Singapore branch)

INSIGHT GUIDE
NORWAY

Cartographic Editor Zoë Goodwin
Design Consultants
Carlotta Junger, Graham Mitchener
Picture Research Hilary Genin,
Victoria Peel

Index

Numbers in italics refer to photographs

Oslo T-bane